A History of Psychology in Autobiography

VOLUME VII

A Series of Books in Psychology

A History of Psychology in Autobiography

VOLUME VII

EDITED BY

Gardner Lindzey

CENTER FOR ADVANCED STUDY IN THE BEHAVIORAL SCIENCES

W. H. FREEMAN AND COMPANY
San Francisco

Sponsoring Editor: W. Hayward Rogers
Project Editor: Pearl C. Vapnek
Designer: Marie Carluccio
Production Coordinator: Fran Mitchell
Compositor: Typesetting Services of California
Printer and Binder: The Maple-Vail Book Manufacturing Group

Library of Congress Cataloging in Publication Data

Main entry under title:

A History of psychology in autobiography

(The International university series in psychology)
Vols. 1–3 edited by Carl Murchison; v. 4 edited by
E. G. Boring and others; v. 5 edited by E. G. Boring
and G. Lindzey; v. 6–7 edited by G. Lindzey.
Vol. VI, published in The Century psychology series,
has imprint: Englewood Cliffs, N.J., Prentice-Hall.
Vol. VII, published in The Freeman psychology series,
has imprint: San Francisco, W. H. Freeman and Company.
1. Psychology—History—Collected works.
2. Psychologists—Biography—Collected works.
I. Murchison, Carl Allanmore, 1887–   ed.
II. Boring, Edwin Garrigues, 1886–   ed.
[DNLM: 1. Psychology—Biography—Periodicals.
2. Psychology—History—Periodicals. W1 H186]
BF105.H5   150'.92'2 [B]   30-20129
ISBN 0-7167-1119-2
ISBN 0-7167-1120-6 pbk.

Printed in the United States of America

9 8 7 6 5 4 3 2 1

To Henry A. Murray,
erudite and elegant exemplar

Contents

Preface

No doubt every chronic author–editor has some labor of love he finds gratifying for reasons unrelated to personal prestige, great scientific or scholarly contribution, or even financial reward. Perhaps most such addictions are associated with significant experiences early in the individual's academic life. This is certainly true for me and the series *A History of Psychology in Autobiography*.

While still a beginning graduate student, I stumbled on the early volumes in this series and found myself fascinated by the varied accounts, some quite revealing of the person and others little more than a dull chronicle of past scholarly publications. Many of the autobiographies, in this and previous volumes, provide evidence for an intimate interaction between the professional and scientific and the personal and idiosyncratic. Of particular interest to me are the contrasts between equally distinguished psychologists whose origins, values, motivations, and aspirations were so varied that there could be little surprise at manifest theoretical differences and research orientations.

All would agree that Clark Hull, Jerzy Konorski, and Edward Tolman made fundamental contributions to learning theory; yet it is hard to detect much commonality in the backgrounds of these scholars as revealed by their autobiographies. One was an impoverished Midwesterner, a product of small schools and public universities; another a Polish medical student with little background in psychology; and the third an elegant New England Puritan with an M.I.T.–Harvard background. Despite the startling differences in the details of their lives and the manner in which they describe themselves and their scientific careers, there is a refreshing similarity in the humble beginnings from which their influential research sprang.

Konorski describes how he and his close friend and collaborator Stefan Miller encountered the writings of Pavlov and in their immediate excitement conceived of important new studies that remain even today major contributions to the field of learning. Searching for a place to conduct these studies, they managed to borrow a small room and then proceed to equip their laboratory:

The first thing we had to do was to buy a dog. For this purpose we went to the marketplace, found the area where people sold dogs, and after long deliberations, chose a young and nice bulldog, which cost ten zlotys (about one dollar). We called him Bobek. He immediately became friendly with us and we brought him to our "laboratory." The housekeeper agreed to let him stay in her apartment.

Our next task was to organize a conditioned reflex laboratory in the room which was assigned to us. Putting together two square stools we made a "Pavlovian stand" and used cardboards for a screen. The bowl was made of tin and was fixed to the front part of the stand. Pieces of food were thrown from the small aperture in the screen by the experimenter. I do not remember how the horizontal bar above the stand was fixed in order to keep the animal in the harness during the experimental sessions. Since in the department of psychology there was a kimograph with a long tape, we utilized this for recording the dog's movements. For a long time we used a strip of toilet paper, which was both cheap and convenient, provided that it was relatively smooth and did not have transversal perforations. You can imagine the comical picture presented by two serious young men going to a paper store and asking to be shown all the possible varieties of toilet paper, scrutinizing them thoroughly, and choosing the one which fulfilled both conditions. Recording of movements was accomplished by a very primitive and crude arrangement made mainly out of pieces of wire.*

Hull describes the origins of his experimental research in terms that differ in detail but are markedly similar in their general flavor:

The vacation before I began my regular work in the Wisconsin laboratory I spent at my old home in Michigan. Pursuing my plan to investigate the evolution of concepts by an adaptation of the Ebbinghaus methodology, I designed and constructed with the few hand tools there available an automatic memory machine which I used throughout most of my dissertation experiment. The drum was made from a tomato can fitted with wooden heads. The automatic stepwise movement of the drum was controlled by a long pendulum; the coarse-toothed escapement wheel controlled by the pendulum was filed from a discarded bucksaw blade. To substitute for a needed gear, a thread was reeled around a large, flanged wooden wheel and then around a spool pinned to the escapement shaft, and the shaft of the large wheel was turned by a heavy lead weight. At that time a person with a little initiative could construct a useful behavior laboratory in a wilderness, given a few simple tools and materials; this is true to a considerable extent even now for a wide range of important experiments. Men trained in laboratories where everything is provided, including a skillful mechanician, often are helpless when they go to serve a small college which usually has little laboratory equipment.†

Only a few years earlier, on the edge of the Pacific, Edward Tolman was taking the first steps that would lead to the many influential studies conducted by him and his students:

When, however, I joined the department at Berkeley as instructor in 1918, I found it was up to me to suggest a new course. Re-

---

*J. Konorski, Autobiography in G. Lindzey (Ed.), *A History of Psychology in Autobiography*, Vol. VI (Englewood Cliffs, N.J.: Prentice-Hall, 1974), pp. 187–188.

†Hull, C., Autobiography in E. G. Boring, H. S. Langfeld, H. Werner, and R. M. Yerkes (Eds.), *A History of Psychology in Autobiography*, Vol. IV (Worcester, Mass.: Clark University Press, 1954), pp. 148–149.

membering Yerkes' course and Watson's textbook I proposed "comparative psychology." And it was this that finally launched me down the behavioristic slope. Only a few students enrolled and at first a lot of time was spent in arguing against anthropomorphism and the Clever Hans error. But, before too long, I actually acquired some rats from the Long–Evans strain which had been developed in the Anatomy Department. And I and a few graduate, or advanced undergraduate, students began trying out minor experiments in learning. (Even though I had been clumsy in the physical and chemical laboratories at M.I.T., I *could* build mazes.)*

Should not every beginning graduate student in psychology be exposed to these accounts as an antidote for the antiseptic courses in experimental design and data analysis to which all are exposed? More important for all of us is the reminder, clear in these autobiographies, that important contributions to psychology can be derived from the most improbable settings and may take enormously varied forms. It seems a safe assertion that in every volume of this series there have been contributors who were totally unfamiliar with the work of other contributors. No need to dwell on those authors who were familiar with the work of other authors and held it in low regard! Psychologists—even academic psychologists—are a diverse lot.

Arrangements for this volume were carried out with the guidance of a committee: Richard C. Atkinson, Frank A. Beach, Kenneth E. Clark, Richard J. Herrnstein, Ernest R. Hilgard, Kenneth MacCorquodale, Roger W. Russell, Seymour Wapner, and Gardner Lindzey. The committee included two members who have contributed to previous volumes in the series (Beach and Hilgard). Wapner provides connection with Clark University where the series began. Clark, Lindzey, and MacCorquodale provide continuity with the last two volumes, which appeared in the Century Psychology Series.

We are delighted to have our admired friend D. O. Hebb as a contributor to this volume. Twice before we invited him to

---

*E. C. Tolman, Autobiography in E. C. Boring, H. S. Langfeld, H. Werner, and R. M. Yerkes (Eds.), *A History of Psychology in Autobiography,* Vol. IV (Worcester, Mass.: Clark University Press, 1954), p. 329.

participate and received polite but firm declinations. When he agreed to undertake the task, he predictably completed the assignment elegantly and promptly. We are also pleased that this volume has a higher proportion of foreign contributors than any recent volume in the series. If we consider the contributions of Hebb and Bruner as foreign (both were written outside the United States), there are five chapters written by non-American contributors, the largest number in more than forty years.

In all recent volumes some expected contributors (in this case, four) have found it impossible to meet the deadline for publication. We take solace in the fact that all four have agreed to continue preparing their manuscripts with the knowledge that they will be represented in the next volume of the series.

Once again the royalties for this volume will be contributed to the American Psychological Foundation to be used in a manner that is beneficial to the field of psychology. There is a special appropriateness to this assignment of royalties. One of the major functions of the American Psychological Foundation is to select annually the recipient of the Gold Medal Award, for a lifetime of contribution to the field of psychology. It is a tribute to both selection processes that of the nineteen psychologists who have received this award, thirteen have contributed to this series.

I am indebted to the Center for Advanced Study in the Behavioral Sciences for having facilitated the preparation of this volume, and particularly to Mrs. Genevieve Carter for her patience and skill in taking care of the many details associated with assembling this book.

Stanford, California
October 1979   G. L.

Preface to Volume VI

History can be packaged in many forms. One of the most intimate and authentic of these is the autobiography. While events transcribed in this manner may suffer from the astigmatism imposed by personal needs and too little perspective, they are enormously enriched by the background factors and events in the writer's life that could only be known directly by him. Thus, if the autobiographer is willing, he can provide the student of history with information that is otherwise virtually unattainable. The articles in this volume, as in the other volumes in the series, vary substantially in terms of how much they reveal of the subjective determinants and personal experiences surrounding the development of individual careers and psychology itself. At their best, however, they document much that could not have been recovered from the objective record.

These autobiographies have a relatively long tradition— more than four decades—within the short-term field of psychology. Psychologists, as befits their position midway between the natural sciences and the humanities, typically have been ambivalent about examining their own past. Thus, it is not surprising that the series twice has had to be rescued from oblivion (first by Edwin G. Boring and subsequently by Boring and Gardner Lindzey jointly). For the moment the future of the series seems assured, and one might even speculate that the formation of a Division of the History of Psychology of the American Psychological Association suggests some amelioration in the characteristic reluctance of psychologists to be concerned with their origins.

Initial plans for this volume began in 1966, and the following year, upon publication of Volume V, the new editorial committee was formed. It was comprised of Edwin G. Boring, Gardner Lindzey, Gardner Murphy, Kenneth MacCorquodale, Roger Russell, and Seymour Wapner. Thus, its membership included several persons from the previous committee, including one member (Boring) who had served on the editorial committee of all five previous volumes, and two members who had previously contributed their autobiographies to the series (Boring and Murphy). Invitations began to be sent out in 1968, and most of the manuscripts were in hand by 1970. At the final stage we had fifteen firm acceptances and four somewhat ambiguous commitments. As it turned out, none of the ambiguities materialized, and two of our contributors who had made firm commitments found it necessary to withdraw very late in our arrangements. Thus, the final volume contains only thirteen autobiographies rather than the fifteen we had intended.

The members of the editorial committee based their judgments concerning who should be invited to contribute on the impact or influence of the individual on American psychology. In spite of this somewhat chauvinistic criterion, several European psychologists and several nonpsychologists were extended invitations. We are happy that one of our autobiographies is by the distinguished social anthropologist Margaret Mead, who turns out to have had more than glancing contact with psychology and psychologists.

We are very pleased that once again the series includes contributions from psychologists outside of North America, and we only regret that they are not more numerous. Based on our limited experience with this volume, it appears that

Europeans and psychoanalysts are less likely to agree to prepare an autobiography than are American, academic psychologists.

We deeply regret that Professor Edwin G. Boring died while this volume was being prepared. Not only had he been an active participant in the preparation of every volume in the series, but also it was his initial letter to Carl Murchison that led to establishing the series. In view of these circumstances it seems only proper that this volume be dedicated to Professor Boring.

One unusual feature of this book is that it includes the first "autonecrology," to use Boring's term, in the form of Professor Luria's autobiography. Professor Luria found himself unable to contribute to the previous volume but at Boring's invitation began at once to prepare an autobiography for the next volume to assure that he would be represented there even if he was no longer living. Happily, Professor Luria is still very much alive. Unfortunately three of our contributors, Clarence H. Graham, Jerzy Konorski and S. S. Stevens, died during the period following preparation of their autobiographies but prior to their publication. We have followed Professor Boring's precedent and invited a small number of persons who were unable to contribute to this volume to prepare, at their early convenience, autobiographies to be included in Volume VII.

The process of selecting contributors was essentially the same as that described in the preface to the previous volume, which is reprinted on the following pages. We also provided the contributors with the same guidelines for the preparation of their bibliographies. Once again the contributors have agreed that the modest royalties earned by this volume will go to the American Psychological Foundation.

Gardner Lindzey

Preface to *Volume V*

Autobiography improves with age as it ripens into history. When the first volume of *A History of Psychology in Autobiography* appeared in 1930 psychologists found it interesting. Its readers for the most part were familiar with the writings of the men and women who spoke through its pages; often they knew the biographers personally or had at least listened to them, and they profited from seeing how the owner of an important name regarded his own work and what importance he assigned to events that appeared to have shaped his life. When first written, these stories lay, nevertheless, almost in the present, for—except in the speculation about how childhood forms a man—an intellectual autobiography that covers forty years does not consider that it is speaking of the past until much later. Now, however, thirty years have gone by since those first three volumes of 1930-1936 were published, and the lives described in them are now history—recent history, to be sure, but long enough ago for psychologists to send their students to sense in these accounts the attitudes of an earlier generation and the atmosphere in which it thrived, the spirit of a time when psychology was smaller, less complex, and more intimate.

How the value of present effort increases with time becomes evident when one examines the table at the end of this preface. Of the fifty-eight psychologists who contributed to the first four volumes, only five are still living. Of the forty-three who wrote for the first three volumes, only one is left—Sir Frederic Bartlett. It is necessary to get these personal records before mortality intervenes, yet not before the lives described are approaching completion. The present committee has lost Heinz Werner, who died after accepting our invitation to contribute, but we are fortunate in being able to include Kurt Goldstein, who completed his biography before he died. Three other psychologists (Heymans, Höffding, de Sanctis) died before the volume containing their contributions could be published, and three others (Calkins, Zwaardemaker, Hull) died in the year of publication.

Yet all in all the great men and women of psychology have been a hardy lot. Of the fifty-four contributors who have passed on at the date of this writing, only one, Woodworth, reached the 90's. The youngest to die was Klemm at 54, and the next youngest was Franz at 59. The median age of these autobiographers at death is at present between 77 and 79, in between Drever and Terman. Two were in their 50's, eleven in their 60's, fifteen in their 70's, twenty-five in their 80's, and one in his 90's.

At the end of the 1920's, when the new historians of the still new psychology were complaining that insufficient information was available about the lives, and thus the motivations, of the eponyms whom it was their task to describe, the present series was begun by Carl Murchison and the Clark University Press. At the time, the committee asked that the contributors tell of the motivations that guided them in their professional careers, not fully realizing in the then unformed state of motivational psychology how little a man knows correctly of his own motivations. When, after a lapse caused first by the exhaustion of the pool of sufficiently mature prominent psychologists and then by the distraction of World War II, the project was revived twenty years later, the invitation was changed to stress conscious motivation less and the events of the life more. Here follows an excerpt from the Preface of Volume IV, published in 1952:

The reader of this volume will see how much our autobiographers differ from one another in the nature of their efforts. Perhaps they differ most in the degree with which they find unity in their lives. Presumably every one of them would like to see his intellectual history as the evolution of a single purpose, for integrity is good and simplicity is elegant. No one, of course, fully succeeds in this undertaking, for the story of every life is constrained by the exigencies of its owner's environment.

Some of these accounts are more intellectualistic than others, and it may be that they show the greater unity, either because some irrelevancies are omitted from the life history or because irrelevancies are actually, at least to a certain degree, omitted from the actual living. Other accounts are more environmentalistic, because social and institutional events and accidents have figured so largely in them. The environmentalistic autobiographer may have had a chief long-term goal, have pursued it, have achieved it with some fair degree of success, yet he may feel that the unforeseeable accidents of living have determined much of his life and have perhaps even altered his goal. The intellectualist, if such we may call him, may, on the other hand, have suffered disruption of plans less than his colleague, but it is probable that he has also been less interested in the effect of external forces upon himself.

No one, not even the members of this group of distinguished psychologists, can hope to deal adequately with the springs of his motivation. What he tells about himself and what he shows about his values can, however, go far toward instructing the reader as to how human motive moves to make science progress. The accidents of living do not always seem irrelevant to progress when they operate in the manner shown in the pages of this book. Psychology in autobiography cannot be complete, but it can make a contribution to the history of psychology which is unique.

Here follows an excerpt from the invitation to contributors to the present volume. It is an extension and modification of the instruction for 1952.

The important decisions in regard to the contents of your autobiography are yours. We hope, however, that the document will devote some attention to the historical details of your life. In connection with the *facts of life,* we hope you will identify yourself with regard to such matters as place and date of birth, significant educational and professional experiences, and family. We are, of course, particularly interested in the *intellectual and professional* aspects of your life as they have influenced and been influenced by events, ideas, and persons in and out of the field of psychology. Your perception of major developments and issues within psychology during your lifetime and your relation to these events will be of special importance. We should appreciate any discussion of your *feelings, motives, and aspirations* or of significant events that would increase the reader's understanding of you and your contributions to psychology. In brief, we are interested in your intellectual life history, but at the same time we feel that it should be illuminated by as much information about your personal background and inner motives as you are ready and able to divulge.

Considerable pressure has been put upon the committee to include a complete bibliography of the contributors. Complete bibliographies for such men as these would run from 100 to more than 500 citations apiece. Psychologists look wistfully at Murchison's *Psychological Register* of 1932 and hope for its updating, but neither that nor the inclusion of bibliographies here is practicable. The committee has space for only fifteen biographies of 12,000 words each, and it would have to decrease this number to add the bibliographies. Also, there would be duplication, for complete bibliographies are often published elsewhere for distinguished psychologists. The memoirs of academies sometimes include them. There are, moreover, already available some fairly complete bibliographies of psychologists whose publications have been listed in the *Psychological Index* and in *Psychological Abstracts* from 1894 to 1958; they are in the *Author Index* to those two serials published in four volumes in 1960 by G. K. Hall and Company of Boston.

Why are only Americans included as contributors in the present volume? The early volumes were divided approximately in the proportion of eight Americans to seven Europeans. Of course psychology was then and is even more now predominantly American; the language of this book is English and its character American. Nevertheless the present committee began with the expectation that its American character would be assured by our choosing those foreigners who had made an impression upon American thought in psychology, the Europeans or others who appeared as most important in the United States even if not in their own countries. We did indeed correspond with some Europeans and quite early met with two declinations, but the crucial desideratum that fixed our decision was the great scarcity of psychologists in Europe and elsewhere who had notably influenced the thinking of American psychologists, who had not already contributed to a previous volume, and who were over 60 years old. Let the critic who suspects us of xenophobia try naming a few psychologists, foreign to America, who meet these three specifications.

On the other hand, this committee, whose authority ceases with the publication of this volume, looks forward hopefully to a Volume VI that will again be truly international. With the multiplication of psychologists on six continents it becomes more difficult to choose the outstanding names than it was when psychology seemed limited to Western Europe, Great Britain, and America, but the discrimination should not be impossible.

In the first four volumes sixty-one psychologists were invited to contribute and only three declined (Cattell, Lashley, and Köhler). For the present volume eventually we asked twenty-two psychologists. Werner died. Three would have liked to participate but had too many commitments for even our deferred deadline. They thought that if they could be asked early for a Volume VI, they could accept. Three others declined for personal reasons.

The present committee was formed by accretion. The idea of reviving the series began with Lindzey, who secured the agreement of Appleton-Century-Crofts to undertake the publication. Boring, who has been on all five of the committees and had conducted the negotiation with President Jefferson of Clark University for the transfer of the rights from Clark University to Appleton-Century-Crofts, agreed to act as chairman if Lindzey would be Executive Officer. The Committee is grateful to President Jefferson and Clark University for relinquishing these rights in the interests of this historical and scientific enterprise. MacCorquodale was included because of his long association with Lindzey and Appleton-Century-Crofts in the editing of the Century Psychology Series. Wapner was a natural continuation of the Clark ancestry for the series. Werner at Clark had been a member of the previous committee. Newbrough and Sharp had on their own initiative been conducting a poll of psychologists to assess the desirability of reviving the series. Clearly it was best to fuse the two enterprises. The American Psychological Association was asked to sponsor the undertaking, as it had Volume IV, appointing a new committee if it deemed wise, but it declined, believing that the present committee did not need its help. Nevertheless we felt that our committee could profit from more intelligence, so we added Beach and Hobbs to our membership. This committee has prepared the present volume, but it is not self-perpetuating. We believe, however, that Lindzey will be an adequate care-taker for the interests of the series between volumes. Especially must we mention the indispensable assistance of Miss Leslie Segner in the final preparation of the manuscript for publication.

We thank the contributors. They will receive no royalties but we hope they find satisfaction in this bit of immortality that it is possible for us to give them. They have now gained posterity for an audience, and long years after they are gone they can still be speaking to the strange new psychologists who will be their intellectual descendants. The small royalties that accrue from the sales of this volume quite properly go to the American Psychological Foundation.

Frank A. Beach
UNIVERSITY OF CALIFORNIA
Edwin G. Boring, *Chairman*
HARVARD UNIVERSITY
Nicholas Hobbs
GEORGE PEABODY COLLEGE
FOR TEACHERS
Gardner Lindzey, *Executive Officer*
UNIVERSITY OF TEXAS

Kenneth MacCorquodale
UNIVERSITY OF MINNESOTA
J. R. Newbrough
NATIONAL INSTITUTE OF
MENTAL HEALTH
Joseph C. Sharp
WALTER REED ARMY INSTITUTE
OF RESEARCH
Seymour Wapner
CLARK UNIVERSITY

January 1967

Contributors to Volumes I-VII

VOLUME IV	VOLUME V	VOLUME VI
1952	*1966*	*1973*
W. V. D. Bingham	G. W. Allport	F. H. Allport
E. G. Boring	L. Carmichael	F. A. Beach
C. L. Burt	K. M. Dallenbach	R. B. Cattell
R. M. Elliott	J. F. Dashiell	C. H. Graham
A. Gemelli	J. J. Gibson	E. R. Hilgard
A. Gesell	K. Goldstein	O. Klineberg
C. L. Hull	J. P. Guilford	J. Konorski
W. S. Hunter	H. Helson	D. Krech
D. Katz	W. R. Miles	A. R. Luria
A. Michotte	G. Murphy	M. Mead
J. Piaget	H. A. Murray	O. H. Mowrer
H. Piéron	S. L. Pressey	T. M. Newcomb
C. Thomson	C. R. Rogers	S. S. Stevens
L. L. Thurstone	B. F. Skinner	
E. C. Tolman	M. S. Viteles	

VOLUME VII

1980

A. Anastasi	D. O. Hebb
D. E. Broadbent	Q. McNemar
J. S. Bruner	C. E. Osgood
H. J. Eysenck	R. R. Sears
F. A. Geldard	H. A. Simon
E. J. Gibson	

A History of Psychology in Autobiography

VOLUME VII

Anne Anastasi

Anne Anastasi

Being neither historian nor literary biographer, I must tell this story within the framework of what I am—a psychologist. As such, I consider this account to be a case history, albeit one based largely on introspection and subject to all the biases and distortions of memory for events long past. But to make a virtue of necessity, I decided to focus on those incidents that I recalled most vividly. I have recorded those happenings that came up spontaneously as I let the vague past unfold before my eyes. It seemed to me that there may be some significance in the fact that these particular incidents survived the dimming effects of time and now come to mind so readily. Perhaps it's nothing more than their being consistent with my self-concept. But what *is* an autobiography, if not an elaborated self-concept?

This, then, is the story of the perceived environment that shaped my life.

Early Childhood

Although I do not recall the event, the record shows that I was born in New York City on December 19, 1908. My earliest recollection of my family includes three characters: my grandmother, her son, and her daughter. My grandmother was a grande dame; my uncle was a dilettante; and my mother was a realist—someone had to be to keep the family alive. My father had died of a stomach ailment when I was a year old. He had been an attendance officer for the New York City Board of Education. He had a sister who was high school teacher; and his mother and father were both living at the time. Shortly after my father's death, the two families had a disagreement—about what, I never learned. However, my grandmother refused to have any further contact with my father's relatives and I never met any of them.

We all addressed my grandmother as "Maman," with the accent on the second syllable. I called my mother "Mimi," which I was told signified "little mother." No one in the family had been trained to earn a living. My mother's education seems to have been overloaded with languages and the humanities. My uncle, I was repeatedly told, had had eight years of Latin and six years of Greek—and he still had some of his old notebooks to prove it. Through varied and repeated recourse to Operation Bootstrap, my mother broke into the business world. She taught herself bookkeeping with books borrowed from the public library. The rest she picked up on the job. First, she was in the piano business, including an interlude when she started her own piano factory, the Ebe Piano Company, of which she was president and my uncle vice-president. My uncle chose the company name. He had wanted to call it Euterpe, after the Muse of music; but on finding that this name had been previously registered by another company, he had to settle for a more indirect allusion. Ebe (commonly spelled Hebe in the English transliteration) was the goddess of youth, cupbearer of the gods, and hence associated with joy, feasting, and gladness. She is the sort of goddess who would especially appeal to my uncle. As for the piano company, it shut down within a few years when radios drove pianos out of the market.

After diverse, intervening jobs, my mother became office manager of one of New York's largest foreign newspapers, *Il Progresso Italo-Americano*, where she remained until her retirement. She succeeded, but it was a struggle. And from this struggle came her indomitable drive to make sure that I received a good professional education so that I would always be able to earn my way comfortably if I had to. This goal, constantly recurring in family discussions, is among my earliest childhood recollections; and it was reinforced by the spectre of poverty hovering in the background. I repeatedly heard that if my mother were to be run over by a car on her way home from work, we would all starve. Therefore, any time she was late, I would stand by the window, watching eagerly until I saw her coming.

My grandmother took charge of my early education which, according to her accounts, began very early indeed. She claimed that, when I was six months old, she had taught me to identify the digits one to six on a large calendar and that I could point to the correct number when it was named in any order. I suspect I was responding to secondary cues, like Clever Hans, the well-known performing horse (Pfungst, 1911; Rosenthal, 1976). I do not know when I started to read because being read to and reading myself seemed to merge imperceptibly. One of my earliest childhood memories is a vivid visual image of Maman seated on a large, thronelike chair while I was seated on a footstool, both literally and figuratively at her feet, for Lessons. The reading included some children's stories with a moral at the end, which I was always asked to explain. But it also ranged widely over many subjects—arithmetic, history, geography, natural science. Whether I myself read or was read to, there were always frequent pauses for questions, explanations, exercises. Maman had a way of imbuing everything with glamor and drama; and I looked forward to my Lessons. She also told exciting stories about her own childhood experiences, such as her visits to her physicist uncle who had been director of the seismographic observatory on Mt. Vesuvius. In a lighter mood, there were accounts of the costume balls and royal receptions she had attended as a popular young woman.

I had no playmates of my own age—not even an imaginary playmate—although I did have an imaginary staircase which I greatly enjoyed. Our visitors were generally adults; and I was usually expected to recite poetry for them, after dropping a proper curtsy. On the rare occasions when the adult visitors brought along a young child, I was expected to treat her/him as a guest and it wasn't much fun. I really preferred the poetry recitations. There were a couple of humorous poems Maman had taught me which were always good for a laugh from the audience. But the repertoire also included *Le Petit Savoyard*, which I found very sad because it dealt with poverty, and the beautiful opening lines of Dante's *Divine Comedy*, which I can still clearly recall. We owned a huge volume of Dante, with terrifying illustrations by Gustave Doré. My mother allayed my fears, however, by explaining that they were just make-believe, like figures of speech. Throughout my early childhood, there was constant harping on this theme: the contrast between reality, on the one hand, and fiction, myths, figures of speech, and the like, on the other.

A child psychologist would undoubtedly find much to criticize in my early upbringing. There was, for example, the conspicuous lack of opportunities for development in the areas of peer relations and physical skills, such as roller skating, bicycling, or even skipping rope. The one overriding positive feature, however, was the presence of adults who regarded child rearing as a serious responsibility. Despite conflicting demands on their time, the needs of their young charge received high priority. When my mother came home from work, she was often very, very tired. But she could always muster the energy to play fascinating games with me before bedtime. There were delightful word games that we made up, and there were role-playing games. My favorite was a continuing game we called the Theresa Game, in which my mother played the part of a mentally retarded adolescent girl and I that of her trusted friend to whom she would come for advice. In each episode, Theresa would describe her latest problem and I would suggest a solution. Often my mother would have to step out of character and, in her natural voice, offer hints as to why some approach would not work, after which the game would resume with renewed vigor. In retrospect, it sounds to me like coping-skills training in a behavior modification program. But at the time, it was like having my very own movie serial or soap opera that went on for months on end.

In the late summer of 1914, when I was five years old, I visited Naples with my grandmother and my uncle. The reason for the trip was to explore the possibilities of a commercial venture they had dreamed up—probably an unrealistic one. My mother remained behind, reluctant to abandon her job until the business venture was put on a more secure foundation. My presence on the trip represented a protracted baby-sitting project: since my mother could not look after me while she was at work, I had to go along with my grandmother. As a baby-sitting experience, however, the journey had its unique features including, as it did, two ocean crossings within less than a month, a near shipwreck, and the outbreak of World War I. My mother lived through several anxious days when our ship was incorrectly reported as sunk in mid-ocean. When we finally arrived, many, many days late, we made a triumphal entry into the port of New York. There was much band-playing, flag-waving, and rejoicing, because those waiting on the dock had not expected to see us again.

My early education also included some unplanned but useful learning experiences. My grandmother's weaknesses, as well as her strengths, taught me some lasting lessons. When she was wrong, she was very, very wrong. Hence her errors often carried the mechanism for their own correction. For instance, she classified all people as either aristocrats or peasants. Although recognizing that there were a few persons in between who performed useful functions—doctors, teachers, and the like—she did not seem especially interested in them. I suspect that early exposure to such a caricature of a stereotype contributed to my distrust of all group stereotypes wherever I encountered them later on. Maman would sometimes resort to outrageous statements as a convenient means of controlling her young charge. One day I was exploring the intriguing contents of my mother's manicure set, which included a tiny jar of white cream. My grandmother put an immediate stop to that with the admonition, "You must *never* touch that—it contains *nitrate of silver!*" The last three words were pronounced in such ominous tones as to leave no doubt that they represented

5

a deadly poison. That evening, when I told my mother about it, she simply replied quietly, "How does she know?" Incidents such as this, over the years, taught me that statements by authority figures, even when uttered with great confidence, are not necessarily correct. Finally, I feel impelled to add that the conspicuous personality differences among the three significant characters in my early family environment may well have contributed to my lifelong interest in individual differences and their causes.

Formal Education

THE ELEMENTARY SCHOOL PERIOD

My regular school attendance did not begin until I was nearly ten, except for a two-month interlude that will be described below. My grandmother resisted my entering school because she believed I would acquire bad manners from the other children. Although we lived in a respectable, middle-class neighborhood, when school was let out at 3:00, there was a quite normal flurry of spirited shouting and boisterous play past our windows. To Maman, this looked like peasant behavior and she wanted no part of it.

To meet the legal requirements when I came of school age, the family hired a regular public school teacher, a Miss Dora Ireland, to give me lessons at home every afternoon. In the mornings and on weekends, I did homework. In fact, my grandmother became quite adept at drilling me with flash cards. But now I no longer sat on a footstool—I had been promoted to a regular seat at the dining-room table for both lessons and homework. Maman sometimes sat in during the afternoon lessons, and on some of these occasions, Miss Ireland tried to tell her that I was not having a proper childhood and that my life was that of a prisoner. Maman always listened politely but remained unconvinced.

Finally, when I was nine, it was agreed I could enter the school where Miss Ireland herself taught, provided that she would escort me to and from school and that I would eat my lunch in the teachers' room. One difficulty was that, while Miss

Ireland lived within a block of us, her school was a long subway ride away. But the arrangement was worked out and Miss Ireland assumed this appalling responsibility.

I was admitted to 3B. After two months, however, the classroom teacher decided that the work was too easy for me and I was transferred to a 4A class. This move proved to be a disaster. The 4A class was very crowded and the only vacant seat was in the last row. Although no one—including myself—suspected it, I was significantly myopic and therefore could not read the blackboard. I complained to both my mother and Miss Ireland that I felt lost and did not know what was going on in class. No one realized that I might need glasses, although I made specific references to the blackboard. In fact, it was not until my freshman year at college that I acquired my first pair of glasses. In all my subsequent schooling, either because I was smaller than most of my classmates or because my name began with an A, I always managed to sit in the front row. But as far as the 4A class was concerned, I dropped out after a few days and resumed my lessons at home.

By the fall of 1918, my family had become convinced that I should enroll in our neighborhood school, P.S. 33, within two blocks of home. I entered 4B and my school career was launched. The work was still very easy, but fortunately I was never again transferred in the middle of the term. I did, however, skip 5A and 6A, so that it was not until 6B that I remained with the same cohort. Consequently, it was not until then that I was able to establish close and lasting ties with any of my classmates.

Throughout my schooling, I retained a deep-rooted notion that any grade short of 100 percent was unsatisfactory. At one time I actually believed that a single error meant a failing score. I recall a spelling test in 4B, in which we wrote ten words from dictation. I was unable to hear one of the words properly, because the subway had just roared past the window (it was elevated in that area). The word was "friend," but I heard it as "brand." As a result, the item was marked wrong and my grade was only 90 percent. That evening when I told my mother about it, she consoled me and advised me to raise my hand at the time and tell the teacher, if anything like that should happen again. But she did not disabuse me of the notion that anything short of a perfect score was a failure. I eventually discovered for myself that one *could* pass despite a few errors; but I always felt personally uncomfortable with the idea. There seemed to be some logical fallacy in calling a performance satisfactory when it contained errors. I was apparently following a content-referenced rather than a norm-referenced approach to performance evaluation.

When I entered P.S. 33, America was undergoing a vigorous melting-pot phase—and I found it thrilling. I learned the oath to the flag, and all the patriotic songs, and what was meant by "a democratic society." I basked in my newly discovered American culture and soaked it all up like sunshine on the beach. It was an exciting period of unprecedented patriotic fervor. But of course, it was 1918 and the United States had recently joined in the war to end all wars that was to make the world safe for democracy. We children zealously collected peach seeds and tinfoil to help the war effort. We memorized the names of famous battlefields, like Chateau Thierry and Verdun. And we sang the sentimental songs of the time: "Just a baby's prayer at twilight for her daddy over there . . . ," "Keep the home fires burning till the boys come home . . . ."

THE NON-HIGH-SCHOOL PERIOD

After graduating from elementary school at the top of my class, having been awarded the gold medal for general excellence, I entered Evander Childs High School. Because the school had outgrown its regular building, the entire entering class that term was assigned to temporary quarters in an ancient elementary school building which probably had been— and certainly should have been—condemned as unfit for human use. In order to accommodate more students, classes were on a double shift. My routine on three out of five school days was to leave home at 10:30, ride a trolley car to the school, engage in a physical education period at 11:00, eat a box lunch in the school yard, and then attend classes from 1:00 to 5:00. There were no lockers, no showers, and meager washing facilities of any sort. Classes were overcrowded, teachers were overworked, and the whole environment was most unattractive. I stood all this for just two months.

Following my high school dropout, there were many family conferences about what to do next. An important person in my life during this period was a Miss Ida M. Stadie. Miss Stadie was a brilliant and dedicated teacher, who at one time in her professional career taught at the Hunter College Elementary School. She was an old and staunch family friend. In fact, she had been secretary–treasurer of our ill-fated Ebe Piano Company. And she remained a family friend long enough to meet my husband and to give us, as a wedding present, a statue of the Winged Victory that she herself had sculpted after a summer visit to the Louvre. It was a typical white elephant but a beloved memento of a fine person.

When she heard about my high school experience, Miss Stadie attacked the problem with her customary directness and exuberance. Pointing a finger at me, she exclaimed, "You don't want to go to high school. What you really want to do is go to college—and there are alternative routes." Then she called for pen and ink and stationery and proceeded to write, in my name, for catalogues to some thirty leading colleges throughout the country. The next few weeks were spent poring over college requirements. We finally settled on Barnard, right in New York City. The crucial point was that several colleges did not specify high school graduation as a requirement. One acceptable route to admission was to submit fifteen units of College Entrance Examination Board tests, which covered most of the courses in a four-year high school curriculum. In 1922, the CEEB had no Scholastic Aptitude Test, no broad achievement tests, no multiple-choice items, and no standard score scale. There were only traditional essay examinations on specific high school courses, such as third-year French; second-year Latin; elementary, intermediate, and advanced algebra; plane and solid geometry. The scores sent to the colleges and to the candidates were reported on a percentage basis, with 60 percent as a passing grade.

With Miss Stadie's help, we located a school in New York City, impressively named the Rhodes Preparatory School, which catered chiefly to adults who wanted to resume their education and prepare for college. There were few teenagers

9

in my classes and none as young as I. This school "guaranteed" college entrance only in the sense that if after two years you had not been admitted to a college, you could continue to take courses at Rhodes indefinitely, tuition-free. I doubt whether a significant number of students took advantage of that privilege. The main point was that the school covered one year of high school courses each semester, offering only the essential courses—no physical education, no extracurricular activities, no tangential electives. I took the appropriate CEEB examinations each June over a two-year period and was admitted to Barnard at the age of fifteen. As a result, I received an A.B. from Barnard at nineteen and a Ph.D. from Columbia at twenty-one. This chronology led to my being included in two studies of educational acceleration. The first, conducted by H. A. Gray (1930) under the direction of Leta S. Hollingworth, dealt with students who had entered Barnard or Columbia College prior to the age of sixteen. The other was one of the surveys by Sidney L. Pressey (1962), in which he contacted a small sample of APA members who had received the Ph.D. degree at or before the age of twenty-three.

While preparing for college, I took every mathematics examination offered by the CEEB, including plane and spherical trigonometry which I taught myself one summer for my own amusement. The text I used was one by George Wentworth and David Eugene Smith (1915). Years later, I was interested to find, in an earlier volume of this series of autobiographies, B. F. Skinner's statement that he had had "four strong years of high school mathematics using no-nonsense texts by Wentworth" (Boring and Lindzey, 1967, p. 389). Parenthetically, my self-taught spherical trigonometry stood me in good stead when, several years after receiving my Ph.D., I worked through Thurstone's *Vectors of Mind* (1935) and, still later, his *Multiple Factor Analysis* (1947). In view of the highly significant role played by the CEEB in my early life, it is gratifying to me that I eventually had the opportunity to serve that organization in a small way. From 1954 to 1956, I was research consultant for the CEEB; from 1953 to 1959, I was a member of its Research and Development Committee, which I chaired during the last year of my term; from 1954 to 1957, I served on the Committee of Examiners in Aptitude Testing and as its acting chairman for one year; and in 1977, I was appointed to the newly constituted Committee on the Scholastic Aptitude Test.

THE COLLEGE PERIOD

To enter Barnard, I needed only fifteen units' worth of CEEB examinations. Since I had actually accumulated sixteen and a half units, I was informed on admission that I would receive three points of college credit in mathematics. This did not really make any difference, since I ended up in the honors program, which did not operate on a point-credit system. But I was secretly amused that a high school dropout was entering college with advanced credit. What did matter, though, was that I could skip "baby" math (the Barnard designation for all elementary courses) and go directly to differential and integral calculus. At that time, I was sure I was going to major in mathematics. In fact, I filled out some special forms in my freshman year for a major in mathematics and a double minor in physics and chemistry. Mathematics had been my first love since elementary school days. Not only was it my favorite school subject, but during vacations I also entertained myself by devising numerical games and working out shortcuts for the operations we had learned in class.

On the basis of my CEEB scores and some local placement tests, I was also admitted to advanced courses in French literature and Latin poetry. I was quite fluent in French by the time I entered Barnard. I had learned some French as a child and had read a good deal in it through elementary school. For my eleventh birthday, for example, I remember receiving a copy of Maeterlinck's *La Vie des Abeilles* from the wife of our family doctor. Then, during my Rhodes School period, a friend and I used to go to a French branch of the YWCA every Wednesday afternoon to sew garments for the French orphans and to engage in conversation. We were told we were not eligible to join the Y because we were underage and not French. But we convinced the director to let us at least participate in the sewing group and borrow books from their library, which she always carefully screened for "les petites." For the same reason, she insisted on telling people I was eleven, when I was actually thirteen, because she claimed that was the only way she could keep the conversation under control during the sewing sessions. At the Y, we also saw regular announcements of French plays and lectures, many of which we attended.

At Barnard, I met two classmates who became my lifelong friends and who were largely responsible for my social life at that stage. We went on many double dates, and through them, I met my escorts for both the junior prom and the senior ball. Our academic interests were quite different. One was an English major. The other went into social work and eventually became director of a women's prison. As for other extracurricular activities, a group of us started a psychology club in, I believe, my junior year and I was elected its first president. In class functions and in athletics, I participated only to the minimum extent required. I elected such sports as archery, which looked as though they would demand relatively little exertion.

Barnard had an excellent faculty at that time. Many professors had international reputations; several taught also in the Columbia Graduate School. I thoroughly enjoyed all my courses and, with two or three minor exceptions, all my grades were A. Not surprisingly, I was elected to Phi Beta Kappa. I also won the Caroline Duror Graduate Memorial Fellowship, "awarded to that member of the graduating class who shows most promise of distinction in her chosen line of work." When the award was announced in the *New York Times,* I received warm congratulatory notes from a couple of my P.S. 33 teachers, who did not know what had become of me in the intervening years.

On Becoming a Psychologist

UNDERGRADUATE LEVEL

During my freshman year at Barnard, I took a required philosophy course in the fall and a required psychology course in the spring. Both were taught by the same instructor, Isabel Leavenworth, whose faculty appointment was in the Department of Philosophy. Despite this "handicap," the psychology course provided solid scientific fare, with Pillsbury (1921) as the text. I greatly enjoyed the course and felt more at home in it than I had in philosophy. Nevertheless, I had no suspicion at the time that I would make psychology my lifework.

My decision to major in psychology was influenced by two events in my sophomore year. One was a course in Developmental Psychology taught by Harry L. Hollingworth, for many years Chairman of the Barnard Psychology Department. Hollingworth was a stimulating teacher, whose lectures were punctuated with keen and witty criticisms of any slipshod reasoning he could spot in the psychological literature. I recall especially his devastating criticisms of psychoanalysis, which he renamed "psychoanalogy." One of the last generalists in psychology, he had a lively curiosity about all natural phenomena. He was also a strong individualist, who vigorously pursued the application of his redintegration theory to all behavior domains (Hollingworth, 1926, 1928, 1930). My initial contacts with him came at a period when his theoretical orientation was taking shape and his major books on the theory of redintegration were yet to be published. The freshness and ferment of his views were reflected in his courses. Several years later, a Barnard classmate reminded me that, after one of "Holly's" classes, I had remarked wistfully, "Once I have my Ph.D. in math, I'm going back to take some more psych courses."

The other significant event was my reading an article by Charles Spearman (1904). In it I learned not only about correlation coefficients, but also about some intriguing relationships among correlation coefficients that later led Spearman (1927) to develop the tetrad equation. Itself an early step toward modern factor analysis, the tetrad equation was the principal statistical technique I was to use in my own doctoral dissertation. The Spearman article clinched matters for me. I could now enjoy the best of two possible worlds: I could remain faithful to my first love, mathematics, while pursuing psychology, too. I changed my major to psychology and embarked upon my chosen career.

At the time, Barnard had an honors program that emphasized independent study in the junior and senior years. Departments differed in their attitudes toward this program and in the extent to which they made use of it. I was offered honors in both chemistry and history. Since I felt attracted to this type of program, I brought the matter up in a conversation with Hollingworth. He explained that his department did not offer honors because of an unfortunate experience with an earlier graduate who, although academically successful, had become lonely and depressed under that system. I was unconvinced and intimated that I might major in chemistry instead. His reaction was that, as long as I wanted to do it at my own risk, he was quite willing to admit me to honors work. The program did not require attendance at any courses, but included a comprehensive examination in the senior year and the completion of an original piece of research.

I plunged into the honors program with zest. I took courses (without credit, but doing all the work) in psychology and anthropology at Barnard and then registered in graduate courses at Columbia, including Carl Warden's course in Comparative Psychology. I enrolled in a course in the Psychology of Advertising given by H. K. Nixon at the Columbia School of Business Administration. I studied German in summer school and then prepared myself for the Barnard foreign language requirement in this language, even though I had already met the requirement in French. Both of these were more rigorous than the corresponding language requirements for the Ph.D. in psychology. I purchased a copy of Garrett's (1926) statistics book and solved all the problems in it. And in my junior year, I completed an experimental study under the direction of Frederick H. Lund, then an instructor at Barnard. Suggested by the work of Bingham (1910) and Moore (1914) on the development of musical preferences, this experiment was concerned with the role of experiential factors in the esthetic judgment of visual forms. It was reported in a joint article in the *American Journal of Psychology* and represents my first publication (Lund and Anastasi, 1928).

The senior-year comprehensive examination lasted about a week and covered a variety of testing techniques: written, oral, and performance. One morning I was asked to administer the Pintner–Paterson Scale of Performance Tests to a child. The subject I obtained for this purpose was the younger sister of one of my old friends from P.S. 33 who had turned up at

Barnard several years after I had entered. The child was very verbal and an irrepressible talker. My unexpected instructions, however, were to administer the tests as though the subject were a deaf mute. My subject role-played admirably, never uttering a word during the whole period. Moreover, she was so bright that all I had to do was spread the test materials before her and wave my hands vaguely over them—and she would proceed to carry out each task. As for the written part of the examination, administered in several sessions, I was later told by Hollingworth that he had used a copy of the Ph.D. qualifying examination from the preceding year—he didn't see why he should prepare a whole new examination for a single student. I recall commenting longingly that I wished it had been the current year's.

GRADUATE SCHOOL LEVEL

After admission to the Columbia graduate school, one of my first objectives was to integrate my undergraduate preparation in psychology with the Ph.D. requirements. In an initial conference with A. T. Poffenberger, then Chairman of the Psychology Department, I raised two questions. First, could I skip the M.A. degree? Second, was it possible to obtain a Ph.D. in two years? My first request was quite out of line with the current departmental policy. But after some consideration and by accepting my published honors research in lieu of an M.A. thesis, the department granted the request. In answer to the second question, I was told it was unlikely but not impossible, especially if I continued right through the summers.

I had already begun to take courses during the 1928 summer session, one of these being Poffenberger's Applied Psychology. Among the other courses taken during my first graduate year were Woodworth's Contemporary Schools of Psychology and his Advanced Experimental Psychology, which was an intensive, doctoral-level course. My laboratory partner in the latter course was G. Richard Wendt, later Chairman of the Psychology Department at the University of Rochester, and the lab assistant was Winthrop N. Kellogg. Other courses included Gardner Murphy's History of Psychology and two courses with H. E. Garrett, Psychological Testing and Advanced Problems in Test Construction.

My first meeting with Garrett occurred just prior to fall registration, when I requested that I be exempt from his required statistics course. He gave me a final examination in the course, which I completed with a perfect score. On this basis, I was also admitted to his test-construction course, which was an advanced statistics course conducted partly as a seminar. Toward the end of the year, this course delved into the literature on individual and group differences in test results. For this portion, I prepared a class report and paper on sex differences. This was the first concrete expression of my interest in differential psychology. It might be added that, in my contacts with Garrett, I soon became skeptical regarding his predominantly hereditarian interpretations of individual and group differences. Although we used to argue about the relative contributions of heredity and environment, his manner in such discussions with his students was typically relaxed and mild. He would not pursue an argument vigorously, but would usually break it off with a lighthearted remark.

At the end of my first year, I took the Ph.D. comprehensive examination, which at that time extended over nine hours in one day. I was later told that I had passed with the highest score in the group.

The summer of 1929 stands out as a peak period in my entire psychological training. It provided three unrelated but equally memorable experiences. First, on Woodworth's recommendation, I was appointed as a research assistant to Charles B. Davenport at the Carnegie Institution of Washington in Cold Spring Harbor, Long Island. Davenport, who had been Woodworth's college biology teacher, had for some years been interested in human heredity, eugenics, and comparative racial research (e.g., Davenport, 1928, 1929; Davenport and Craytor, 1923). The decades of the 1920s and 1930s were a period when psychologists, anthropologists, and geneticists were still looking hopefully toward the development of "culture-free" tests; and it was on a project to devise this type of test that I was engaged as one of three summer research assistants. Actually, our work schedule had to be adapted to the fact that two of us were involved with summer session. I was planning to take courses at Columbia, and another assistant was planning to teach a course at Teachers College. Consequently, the research job for two of us covered all of June and the last two weeks in August.

The "tests" we devised (or "test ideas," there being no standardization or validation) are included in a comprehensive report of the entire, much broader project. In the foreword to this report, there is a hint that the project *may* have helped to shake loose the faith in culture-free tests and innate abilities. The opening sentence read: "This volume is the outcome of a search for 'tests of innate ability.' It has developed into a revelation of the difficulties to be encountered when mental tests are used to measure mental endowment" (Schieffelin and Schwesinger, 1930, p. iv). Our own, rather primitive, operating procedures may be of some intrinsic interest. From 9:00 to 5:00, the three of us sat at a long table in an office we shared with a German interpreter who was busy abstracting literature for another division of the institution. Here we worked assiduously at dreaming up new tests (or adaptations of existing tests) that would require no language, no numbers, and no paper and pencil. One of the tests I devised was an adaptation of the Woodworth–Wells Symbol–Digit Substitution Test (Schieffelin and Schwesinger, 1930, pp. 199-201). Instead of pairing the five simple figures with numbers, I decided to pair them with five colors. On a large sheet of bristol board, I pasted small squares of five colors, in random order; another set of five was used for the key at the top. What I needed next was a supply of circular wooden chips, on which the five forms could be drawn in India ink. Just as we were wondering where to get 59 wooden chips, Davenport arrived for his daily visit. When he learned of our problem, he rushed out mumbling that he had an idea. Soon he was back, triumphantly flourishing an old broomstick and a saw. In two days we had the test materials ready for pilot testing.

I should point out that our project was a small and atypical segment of the research that was in progress at Cold Spring Harbor that summer. I met many of the summer researchers—students, postdoctorals, and senior scientists—as well as members of the permanent staff. Various fields, such as genetics, physiology, neurology, and chemistry were represented, and much excellent work was going on. It was at Cold Spring Harbor, for example, that I first heard about PTC taste deficiency, which was then just beginning to intrigue geneticists.

In August, an international genetics group was apparently meeting in this country, and at Cold Spring Harbor there were elaborate preparations to receive visitors. Those of us who could speak any language besides English were pressed into service as interpreters and wore tags listing the appropriate languages. I recall an amusing incident in which a French geneticist was visiting the laboratory of a staff member who had been breeding rats for deafness. Since the local scientist seemed able to communicate in French, I stayed in the background. But pretty soon I perceived a mounting animation in the discussion, the French geneticist responding incredulously that the findings were completely out of line with other published research, including his own. At that point, I realized that, in his scientific zeal, the American geneticist had been saying *lourd* when he meant *sourd*. Of course, the rats had not been bred for obesity. When I timidly suggested, "Pas lourd, sourd," the difficulty was quickly cleared up. The substitution of one consonant restored scientific discourse and international amity.

In the 1929 summer session, I took two courses with Clark Hull and one with R. M. Elliott. At that time, Columbia had one of the most active psychology departments in the country, with visiting professors and postdoctorals to enrich the local fare not only during the regular academic year, but also—and especially—during the summer session. For several years, Elliott would come from Minnesota to teach two courses, one dealing with the nature of the introductory course in psychology and the other with theoretical issues in psychology. I took the latter and found it intensely stimulating. Hull's two courses dealt with aptitude testing and with psychological research on hypnosis. He was on his way from Wisconsin to Yale, where he was soon to begin his monumental research on learning. His book on aptitude testing (Hull, 1928) had recently been published and was the class text. The hypnosis book (Hull, 1933), which summarized the pioneer experimental research by him and his students, was in preparation. The course he gave in this area was unusually lively, controversial, and widely attended. My personal contacts with Hull continued long after the completion of this summer session. With the establishment of the Institute of Human Relations at Yale, there was much commuting between New York and New Haven by faculty, students, and postdoctorals. In addition, Hull continued over the years to send me materials—published and unpublished—and I followed the development of his learning theory closely.

My remarkable summer of 1929 ended with attendance at the International Congress of Psychology at Yale. This congress was the first to be held in the United States, and it would be over three decades before another met in this country. The 1929 congress met jointly with the American Psychological Association. Karl S. Lashley was president of the APA and James McKeen Cattell was president of the congress. For us graduate students, it was a rare opportunity to hear and meet psychologists whose work we had been studying, including not only most of the leading American psychologists but also the live persons attached to such familiar names as Spearman, McDougal, Pieron, and Pavlov.

By the time I began my second year of graduate work, I had covered most of the basic courses in the department and could pursue more specialized areas. I took a course entitled Clinical Psychology, which today would undoubtedly be called Individual Intelligence Testing. It covered chiefly the Stanford–Binet, also including some practice with a few other instruments such as the Pintner–Paterson and Porteus Mazes. The course was given by Louise Poull at the Randall's Island Children's Hospital, where she was the only psychologist. This was a municipal institution for the mentally retarded of all ages and all degrees of intellectual disability. Dr. Poull explained that it had originally been named a "children's hospital" because the residents were all children in terms of mental age. Housed in dilapidated wooden buildings, the institution has long since disappeared. Randall's Island is now accessible by the Triboro Bridge; at that time, it could be reached only by a diminutive ferry operated by the city.

I also took a course on race differences with Otto Klineberg, given for the first time in 1929. Klineberg had just returned from Europe, where he had gathered the data for his comparative study of racial and national samples in test performance (Klineberg, 1931). Once a week, several students in our department rode the subway up to the Columbia Medical Center to take courses at the College of Physicians and Surgeons. One term the course I took was a survey of neuroanatomy given by Adolph Elwyn, with occasional lectures by Frederick Tilney. Another term, it was an intensive course on the physiology of the nervous system conducted by F. H. Pike.

A major undertaking during my second year was the completion of a doctoral dissertation. My research dealt with the identification of a group factor in tests of immediate memory for rote material (Anastasi, 1930). Mine was one of several dissertations done under the direction of H. E. Garrett on the application of the tetrad technique to the identification of group factors, which had been suggested by the publication of T. L. Kelley's *Crossroads in the Mind of Man* (1928). I recall insisting that the factor I had identified should be called *a* memory factor, rather than *the* memory factor, since I was convinced that there were several memory factors, a finding demonstrated in one of my own later studies (Anastasi, 1932), as well as in factor analytic research by other investigators (e.g., Christal, 1958). One of the eight memory tests I prepared for use in my dissertation, the Picture–Number Paired Associates test, was later utilized in the ETS kit of factor-referenced tests (French, 1954; French, Ekstrom, and Price, 1963; Ekstrom, French, Harman, and Dermen, 1976, p. 94).

Finally, I must mention a notable postdoctoral training experience that occurred in 1931. The Department of Mathematics of the University of Minnesota circulated an announcement of "Special Lectures in Mathematics" for the 1931 summer quarter. This special program was organized to precede the annual joint meetings of the American Mathematical Society and the Mathematical Association of America, which were to be held at the University of Minnesota in September of that year. One of the offerings was a course by R. A. Fisher entitled Statistical Theory of Experimental Design and described as "especially suited to research workers in biology, agronomy, and other experimental sciences." The announcement added that "the privilege of visiting these courses without credit and without cost will be extended as a courtesy to scholars who hold the Ph.D. degree from this or any other graduate school." The Depression of the 1930s being well under way, anything that was offered free had a special appeal. Analysis of variance was largely unknown to psychologists at that time. To be sure, the first edition of Fisher's book had been published as early as 1925. But most of the applications cited in the 1930s seemed to deal with fields of corn and litters of pigs, and some of the psychologists who heard about this new statistical approach were skeptical about its value for psychological research! It was an easy decision for me. I booked a round-trip passage on the Great Lakes steamer (Buffalo to Duluth, with stopovers for sightseeing) and set off on a very full summer, combining my formal introduction to ANOVA with a delightful vacation.

MARRIAGE TO A PSYCHOLOGIST

On July 26, 1933, I married John Porter Foley, Jr., of Bloomington, Indiana. After receiving the A.B. degree in psychology from Indiana University, John obtained the Ph.D. degree at Columbia, where we met. In several ways, John's experiential background complemented and thereby enriched mine. His Indiana upbringing certainly provided the much-needed broadening of my limited and atypical New York City environment. There were also certain avocational interests that we developed together and that influenced some of our joint psychological research. Chief among these was an interest in art, which had been minimal for both of us before our marriage. Together we began to explore what New York had to offer, first in its various museums and, as we grew in sophistication, in the art galleries. For several years, we spent many a Saturday afternoon doing the rounds of the 57th Street galleries. Gradually, this interest led us into collecting in a variety of areas, from Renaissance paintings to early American cup plates and African masks. Our burgeoning interest in African art was significantly advanced by our contacts with Franz Olbrechts, the Belgian anthropologist and eminent authority on

African art who spent a year as Visiting Professor at Columbia. Our association with Franz and Margrete Olbrechts continued for many years by correspondence.

Within psychology itself, my marriage also encouraged me to delve further into areas in which I had limited preparation. For instance, during his graduate work and for several years in his own subsequent teaching and research, John worked largely in animal psychology, a specialty I had touched upon lightly in my own training. Similarly, his studies in anthropology and his research with Franz Boas strengthened my own interest in a field that is most relevant to differential psychology. One of the major influences that shaped my own psychological thinking was the work of J. R. Kantor of Indiana University, who played the same role in John's undergraduate education that Hollingworth played in mine. It was through John that I met Kantor and became interested in studying his published works (e.g., Kantor, 1924, 1926, 1929, 1936, 1958, 1977). In several ways, Kantor resembles Hollingworth. He, too, is a generalist, with a remarkable breadth of knowledge extending over psychology and related fields. He, too, formulated a comprehensive theoretical system, successively named organismic and interbehavioral psychology. And he, too, pursued his interests with vigor and independence. It is, however, in his emphasis on the role of environment and his explication of the specific operation of environment in individual development that I recognize his predominant influence on my own thinking. In summary, my marriage has meant that I enjoyed the benefits of not one but two Ph.D.'s in psychology.

During the early years of our marriage, our biggest problem was geographical. Several of our friends tried to find us two jobs in the same department, but the so-called anti-nepotism rule was then explicit policy in most universities. Of course, with the Depression in full swing, jobs were scarce to begin with. From 1937 to 1944, John taught at George Washington University, while I taught at Barnard; and we commuted on alternate weekends on the Pennsylvania Railroad. I followed up a few job leads, but they proved unsatisfactory for diverse reasons. For instance, I was offered a Washington job that involved the formation and direction of a test-construction unit in a newly established government agency. It sounded attractive enough, but at the end of the interview with the lawyer who was heading up the agency, I was handed a thick, hardcover procedures manual to look over at home. As I turned the pages and examined the varicolored forms, I began to realize how much of my time would be absorbed by sheer bureaucratic details. After struggling with the difficult decision for several days, I took a trip to New Haven to talk it over with Clark Hull. John and I both had a high regard for Hull, not only as a psychologist, but also as a friend. We talked about an hour, during which time we became increasingly depressed by the apparently insolvable dilemma. Hull finally summed it up for me in a colorful phrase that I long remembered: "Trying to get anything done in the government is like swimming in glue." The next day I mailed back the manual and declined the offer.

It was John who finally resolved our geographical problem. While he was at George Washington University, both his teaching and research had been expanding in the direction of industrial psychology. With this background, he accepted an invitation to join the industrial division of the Psychological Corporation in New York City and eventually established his own consulting organization. We bought an old house in midtown Manhattan and settled down in one place at last.

Professional Career

For several reasons, I have dwelt at some length on the influences that helped to shape my preprofessional development. First, as a differential psychologist, I consider such influences of intrinsic etiological interest. Second, my professional contributions are reflected largely in my publications, which are directly accessible. Third, another autobiographical account (Anastasi, 1972) focused principally on an analysis of my professional activities, with little coverage of formative experiences. The same account contains a complete list of my publications from 1928 to 1971. Thus I feel that a relatively brief summary of major professional activities should suffice for the present purpose.

TEACHING AND ADMINISTRATION

My first teaching experience occurred at the age of thirteen, while I was at the Rhodes School preparing for the CEEB examinations. One of my classmates, who had observed me explaining math problems to others, said she knew several high school students who would like some coaching for their Regents exams in math. I was myself ineligible for the Regents because I was not a registered high school student. Nevertheless, within a short time I had a small clientele of pupils who came to my home for private lessons in algebra or geometry at 50 cents an hour.

During my two years of graduate work, I had an assortment of assistantships: grading examinations and term papers for two of Hollingworth's large lecture courses, serving as Lab Assistant in Garrett's course on psychological testing, and conducting the lab sessions in the Barnard course on experimental psychology (with the title of Lecturer). In the fall of 1930, I was appointed Instructor in Psychology at Barnard, a post I held until 1939. At that time, the Ph.D. was required for appointment as a full-time instructor at Barnard. My initial salary was $2,400 a year; after seven years, it was finally raised to $2,700. This was considered an enviable salary for a Ph.D. during those Depression years—in fact, merely having an academic job was a noteworthy achievement. I taught courses in general, experimental, applied, and differential psychology—the last being introduced to fit my own developing interests.

In 1939, I was appointed Assistant Professor, sole member, and "Chairman" of the newly established Psychology Department at Queens College of the City University of New York. The college itself had opened in 1938. The first year, of course, only introductory psychology was taught. Gradually, my own offerings were expanded to include courses in statistics, testing, differential, and applied psychology. The faculty also grew until, by the time that World War II broke out, we had six full-time members. I remained as Chairman during this period.

Although many of us had joined the newly established college in those early years with great expectations about what could be accomplished, our hopes went unfulfilled. By 1946, the administrative climate at Queens College had become such as to make it well-nigh impossible for anyone seriously interested in teaching and research to function effectively. Too many hours were spent in futile committee meetings that led to little or no action. And too much time was absorbed in coping with the crises precipitated by a few unscrupulous persons who tried to pervert the system to their own ends. Within that year, four of the six department members left. I was one of the four. The others (together with their eventual academic positions) were: S. D. S. Spragg, Chairman of the Psychology Department and Dean of the Graduate School, University of Rochester; Benjamin McKeever, Professor of Psychology, University of Washington; and John I. Lacey, Chief, Section of Behavioral Physiology, Fels Research Institute, and 1976 recipient (jointly with Beatrice C. Lacey) of an APA Award for Distinguished Scientific Contribution. It was, apparently, a wise move for all of us to leave Queens College when we did.

In 1947, I was appointed Associate Professor of Psychology in the graduate school of Fordham University, where I remained until my retirement in 1979, having been advanced to the rank of Professor in 1951. All my previous teaching, at Barnard and Queens, had been at the undergraduate level. At the time of my appointment, the only liberal arts college at Fordham University was exclusively male in both its student population and its faculty. Hence I taught only in the graduate school, an arrangement that certainly had its advantages and was, in fact, one of the features that made the offer attractive to me. I was quite grateful for this bit of ancient "sex discrimination." Eventually, when the college was sexually desegregated, I did teach one undergraduate course for a few years. The areas in which I taught at Fordham included statistics, psychological testing, applied psychology, test construction, factor analysis, differential psychology, and intellectual deviates (covering both the retarded and the gifted).

Although my experience at Queens College had turned me against administrative work, I gradually came to realize that, like so many occupational activities, administration covers a wide spectrum of functions and varies greatly in different contexts. Thus, when Fordham University, in accordance with its policy of rotating department chairmanships, invited me to assume this office in 1968, I was psychologically ready to consider it. I accepted the offer, served for the maximum six-year period, and have no regrets. Not that there were no problems! My term as Chairman coincided with a period of maximal student unrest in American colleges, drastic cuts in university budgets, and sharp reductions in government funds for training and research. But the problems were solvable, without excessive wasted effort or needless paperwork and with good faculty and student morale. Over the years, I have found my relations with students, faculty, and administrators at Fordham personally gratifying.

I cannot leave the account of my teaching experiences without mentioning two delightful summers when I taught at the University of Wisconsin (1951) and the University of Minnesota (1958). I have always felt especially close to the psychology departments of those two universities because of the many persons on their faculties whom I esteem as psychologists and value as personal friends. In 1968, I spent another busy and most enjoyable summer at the Fundação Getulio Vargas in Rio de Janeiro. Although my title in this project was Overseas Consultant for the Ford Foundation, more than half of my time was devoted to teaching a survey course in psychological testing and a more advanced course in test construction.

RESEARCH AND PUBLICATIONS

An interest that was manifested early and has persisted throughout my career centers on the nature and identification of psychological traits. My research in this area began with my Ph.D. dissertation (Anastasi, 1930) and was followed shortly by a broader investigation of memory factors (Anastasi, 1932). Then came a methodological study with chance data, conducted in collaboration with Garrett (Garrett and Anastasi, 1932), and an experimental study designed to demonstrate the role of experiential influences in trait formation (Anastasi, 1936b). The results of the latter study led to a minor skirmish with Thurstone, which was typical of the controversies on trait organization and factor analysis that enlivened the journals of the period (Anastasi, 1935, 1938; Thurstone, 1938). Two later publications represent critical surveys and analyses of published research bearing on the influence of experience on trait formation (Anastasi, 1948b, 1970b). The former was my presidential address at the Eastern Psychological Association; the latter was the First Robert C. Tryon Memorial Lecture, which I was privileged to give at the University of California in Berkeley. By this time, a considerable body of research had accumulated, from both comparative and experimental studies, which supported the hypothesis that had stimulated my 1938 study. The results indicate that experiential factors affect not only the level of an individual's intellectual development, but also the trait categories into which his abilities become organized.

A major theme underlying much of my research and writing pertains to the operation of environmental and experiential factors in psychological development. This theme can be recognized in some of the factor analytic research and articles already cited. It is also a thread that runs though several of my collaborative research projects and theoretical papers. Examples include studies of test performance and language development of various samples of Puerto Rican and black children in New York City (Anastasi and D'Angelo, 1952; Anastasi and Cordova, 1953; Anastasi and deJesús, 1953) and a long-term project on the role of experiential factors in the development of creative achievement in children and adolescents (Anastasi, 1970a; Anastasi and Schaefer, 1969; Schaefer and Anastasi, 1968). Also in this category are papers on intelligence and family size (Anastasi, 1956) and on the fallacies of "culture-free" testing and of attempts to assess "innate potential" (Anastasi, 1950, 1961, 1964a). A more direct approach to the heredity–environment problem is presented in a joint paper (Anastasi and Foley, 1948) and, more fully, in my presidential address to the APA Division of General Psychology (Anastasi, 1958).

Another of my major research categories pertains to test construction and evaluation, as well as the interpretation of test results. A few projects in this area, sponsored by the U.S.

Air Force and by the College Entrance Examination Board, involved the development and validation of instruments for specific purposes (Anastasi and Foley, 1952; Anastasi, Foley, and Sackman, 1954; Anastasi, Meade, and Schneiders, 1960). More broadly oriented studies were concerned with procedural and statistical problems of item analysis (Anastasi, 1953) and test reliability (Anastasi, 1934; Anastasi and Drake, 1954). Among several theoretical papers is my presidential address to the APA Division of Evaluation and Measurement, which dealt with common misuses and misinterpretations of tests in relation to the increasing dissociation of test development from the mainstream of psychological research (Anastasi, 1967). Another project belonging in this general category is my editorship of *Testing Problems in Perspective* (Anastasi, 1966), comprising a selection of significant papers presented over a 25-year period at the ETS Invitational Conference on Testing Problems. I also edited a book of readings, entitled *Individual Differences* (Anastasi, 1965), as part of a series on historical antecedents of modern psychology, whose general editors were William Kessen and George Mandler. The publications included in my book illustrated major steps in the rise of the testing movement and in the use of tests in research on the nature and sources of individual and group differences in behavior.

As a final example of my involvement with psychological tests, I must mention the test evaluations I contributed to each volume of the *Mental Measurements Yearbook* since the inception of the series in 1938. I consider it a privilege to have been among the many psychologists participating in this monumental project, which has done so much to raise standards of test publishing. When Oscar Buros, the yearbook editor, published the accessory volume, *Tests in Print II* (Buros, 1974), he graciously dedicated it to five persons who had contributed reviews to all the prior yearbooks. I was gratified to be in that group, and I subsequently learned that, with the publication of the eighth yearbook in 1978, I became the only survivor with reviews in all volumes to date.

The avocational interest in art that my husband and I had developed together led us into various projects which fell on the borderline between art and psychology. These were concerned with children's art, with the artistic productions of self-taught "Sunday painters," and with cultural differences in artistic expression (Anastasi and Foley, 1936, 1938, 1940a). Our visits to art galleries also contributed to our decision to embark on a long-term project concerning the relation of art and abnormality (Anastasi and Foley, 1940b, 1941a, 1941b, 1941c, 1943, 1944). The fact that "psychotic art" was featured in several art shows of the period augmented our own mounting dissatisfaction with the many unsupported claims about the interpretation of "pathological" signs in art products. These claims ranged from far-fetched psychologizing about paintings by professional artists to the use of various projective drawing tests for clinical assessment. Our own research on these alleged indices of abnormality, tested under more nearly controlled conditions, demonstrated that many tended to be related not to pathology but to educational, occupational, and sociocultural backgrounds.

As is often the case, my textbooks grew out of courses I began to teach early in my career and continued to teach over the years. They include *Differential Psychology* (Anastasi, 1937, 1949, 1958), *Psychological Testing* (Anastasi, 1954, 1961, 1968, 1976), and *Fields of Applied Psychology* (Anastasi, 1964b, 1979). All these books have been used widely in foreign countries, both in the original English-language editions and in translations. Various editions of one or another of the three books have been translated into Chinese, Dutch, German, Italian, Japanese, Portuguese, Spanish, and Thai. Partly for this reason, I have enjoyed lasting and productive associations with colleagues in several countries through exchange of publications, correspondence, and personal contacts. Several of these associations have been strengthened through my own travels in various countries in connection with international congresses, conferences, lectures, and other professional activities.

A word about my use of the term "differential psychology" may be in order. Prior to 1937, when my book by this title was first published, this area was commonly designated as "individual differences." Because I felt that a broader term was needed to cover both individual and group differences, I chose a literal translation of the German term introduced by

William Stern (1900) in the first edition of his book and retained in subsequent German editions. I was interested to see that the German translation of my own book, published in 1976, was titled *Differentielle Psychologie*. We had now come full circle!

Another category of my publications, spanning several decades, includes chapters in edited books and survey articles in various encyclopedias on topics related to my three textbooks. I might also mention a number of scattered studies that do not fall into any broadly conceived program. These were undertaken to satisfy my curiosity about specific questions and may reflect, in part, a reaction against undue specialization arising from my generalist orientation. Examples range from an investigation of the effect of shape on the perceived area of two-dimensional figures (Anastasi, 1936a) and a survey of fear and anger among college women by the diary method (Anastasi, 1948a; Anastasi, Cohen, and Spatz, 1948) to a factor analysis of learning behavior in several breeds of dogs (Anastasi, Fuller, Scott, and Schmitt, 1955) and a case study of a musically gifted "idiot savant" (Anastasi and Levee, 1959).

MISCELLANEOUS PROFESSIONAL ACTIVITIES

One of the attractions of the academic life is the diversity of activities it permits and encourages. Over the years, I have served as an individual consultant or as a member of advisory committees for various government agencies at the federal, state, and municipal levels; for educational, industrial, and other types of private organizations; and in association with lawyers in the preparation of cases involving the use of tests or other assessment procedures. In my service on a succession of panels, boards, commissions, and committees, I have had an opportunity to work closely with members of other disciplines, ranging from mathematics and engineering to the humanities, educational administration, and military leadership. With only a few exceptions, communication across disciplines did not prove to be a significant difficulty in these contexts, and I found such interdisciplinary contacts personally gratifying.

Another favorite activity of those in academic life is the invited lecture delivered to groups of diverse sizes and degrees of heterogeneity, from small specialized seminars, institutes, or workshops to association-wide and university-wide audiences. I have had my share of these experiences, which have taken me to some well-traveled, cosmopolitan sites and prestigious university centers, as well as to some intriguing out-of-the-way places.

Participation in association activities has also represented a continuing interest throughout my professional life. The first APA meeting I attended was held at Columbia University in 1928, the year I graduated from Barnard. It was at this meeting that I first encountered the two women who preceded me as presidents of the APA and who were to remain, for fifty years, the sole representatives of their sex to have held this office. One of the sessions at the convention was chaired by Mary W. Calkins (president, 1905) and included a paper presented by Margaret Floy Washburn (president, 1921). In introducing Dr. Washburn, Dr. Calkins said, "I shall now call upon our past president to deliver the next paper." As a first-year graduate student, I found all this quite impressive.

The first office I held in any scientific society was the secretaryship of the Psychology Section of the New York Academy of Sciences in the mid-1930s, followed a couple of years later by the chairmanship of the section. Over the years, I have been a member of and served in various capacities in several other associations, including the American Psychological Association, the Eastern Psychological Association, the New York State Psychological Association, the Psychometric Society, the Psychonomic Society, the Psychology Section of the National Research Council, the Board of Trustees of the American Psychological Foundation, and local university chapters of Phi Beta Kappa and Sigma Xi. Among the many offices I have held are the presidencies of the EPA (1946–1947), the APA Division of General Psychology (1956–1957), the APA Division of Evaluation and Measurement (1965–1966), the American Psychological Foundation (1965–1967), and the APA (1972).

Since I certainly consider it an honor to have been elected by my colleagues to these various offices, it may be appropriate at this point to mention some other items in the general category of "honors and awards." I have received honorary degrees from the University of Windsor in Canada (Litt.D., 1967), Villanova University (Paed.D., 1971), Cedar Crest College (Sc.D., 1971), and Fordham University (Sc.D., 1979). At the 1977 ETS Invitational Conference, I was the recipient of the Educational Testing Service Award for Distinguished Service to Measurement, "presented annually to an individual whose work and career have had a major impact on developments in educational and psychological measurement."

"Honors and awards" provide a pleasant note on which to end one's autobiography. But it is an intrinsic limitation of autobiographies that they can never be complete. To be sure, from my personal standpoint I would not want it to be otherwise! In the interests of fuller coverage, however, I must add that I am currently engaged in a wide diversity and staggering number of professional projects, and I see many more lining up for the future.

1979

Selected Publications by Anne Anastasi

A group factor in immediate memory. *Archives of Psychology*, 1930, No. 120.

Further studies on the memory factory. *Archives of Psychology*, 1932, No. 142.

The influence of practice upon test reliability. *Journal of Educational Psychology*, 1934, *25*, 321–335.

Some ambiguous concepts in the field of mental organization. *American Journal of Psychology*, 1935, *47*, 508–511.

The estimation of area. *Journal of General Psychology*, 1936, *14*, 201–225. (a)

The influence of specific experience upon mental organization. *Genetic Psychology Monographs*, 1936, *18*(4), 245–355. (b)

Differential psychology. New York: Macmillan, 1937. (2nd ed., 1949, with J. P. Foley, Jr.; 3rd ed., 1958. Translations: German, Italian, Portuguese, Spanish.)

Faculties *versus* factors: A reply to Professor Thurstone. *Psychological Bulletin*, 1938, *35*, 391–395.

A methodological note on the controlled diary technique. *Journal of Genetic Psychology*, 1948, *73*, 237–241. (a)

The nature of psychological "traits." *Psychological Review*, 1948, *55*, 127–138. (b)

Some implications of cultural factors for test construction. *Proceedings of the 1949 Invitational Conference on Testing Problems, Educational Testing Service*, 1950, 13–17.

An empirical study of the applicability of sequential analysis to item selection. *Educational and Psychological Measurement*, 1953, *13*, 3–13.

Psychological testing. New York: Macmillan, 1954. (2nd ed., 1961; 3rd ed., 1968; 4th ed., 1976. Translations: Italian, Portuguese, Spanish, Thai.)

Intelligence and family size. *Psychological Bulletin*, 1956, *53*, 187–209.

Heredity, environment, and the question "How?" *Psychological Review*, 1958, *65*, 197–208.

Psychological tests: Uses and abuses. *Teachers College Record*, 1961, *62*, 389–393.

Culture-fair testing. *Educational Horizons*, 1964, *43*(1), 26–30. (a)

Fields of applied psychology. New York: McGraw-Hill, 1964. (2nd ed., 1979. Translations: Chinese, Dutch, German, Italian, Japanese, Portuguese, Spanish.) (b)

(Ed.) *Individual differences.* New York: Wiley, 1965.

(Ed.) *Testing problems in perspective.* Washington, D.C.: American Council on Education, 1966.

Psychology, psychologists, and psychological testing. *American Psychologist*, 1967, *22*, 297–306.

Correlates of creativity in children from two socioeconomic levels. Final Report, Center for Urban Education Subcontract No. 2 (Contract No. OEC-1-7-062868-3060), 1970. (a)

On the formation of psychological traits. *American Psychologist*, 1970, *25*, 899–910. (b)

Reminiscences of a differential psychologist. In T. S. Krawiec (Ed.), *The psychologists.* New York: Oxford University Press, 1972. Pp. 3–37.

With N. Cohen and D. Spatz. A study of fear and anger in college students through the controlled diary method. *Journal of Genetic Psychology*, 1948, *73*, 243–249.

With F. A. Cordova. Some effects of bilingualism upon the intelligence test performance of Puerto Rican children in New York City. *Journal of Educational Psychology*, 1953, *44*, 1–19.

With R. Y. D'Angelo. A comparison of Negro and white preschool children in language development and Goodenough Draw-a-Man IQ. *Journal of Genetic Psychology*, 1952, *81*, 147–165.

With C. deJesús. Language development and nonverbal IQ of Puerto Rican preschool children in New York City. *Journal of Abnormal and Social Psychology*, 1953, *48*, 357–366.

With J. D. Drake. An empirical comparison of certain techniques for estimating the reliability of speeded tests. *Educational and Psychological Measurement*, 1954, *14*, 529–540.

With J. P. Foley, Jr. An analysis of spontaneous drawings by children in different cultures. *Journal of Applied Psychology*, 1936, *20*, 689–726.

With J. P. Foley, Jr. A study of animal drawings by Indian children of the North Pacific Coast. *Journal of Social Psychology*, 1938, *9*, 363–374.

With J. P. Foley, Jr. The study of "populistic" painters as an approach to the psychology of art. *Journal of Social Psychology*, 1940, *11*, 353–368. (a)

With J. P. Foley, Jr. A survey of the literature on artistic behavior in the abnormal: III. Spontaneous productions. *Psychological Monographs*, 1940, *52*(6, Whole No. 237). (b)

With J. P. Foley, Jr. A survey of the literature on artistic behavior in the abnormal: I. Historical and theoretical background. *Journal of General Psychology*, 1941, *25*, 111–142. (a)

With J. P. Foley, Jr. A survey of the literature on artistic behavior in the abnormal: II. Approaches and interrelationships. *Annals of the New York Academy of Sciences*, 1941, *42*, 1–112. (b)

With J. P. Foley, Jr. A survey of the literature on artistic behavior of the abnormal: IV. Experimental investigations. *Journal of General Psychology*, 1941, *25*, 187–237. (c)

With J. P. Foley, Jr. An analysis of spontaneous artistic productions by the abnormal. *Journal of General Psychology*, 1943, *28*, 297–313.

With J. P. Foley, Jr. An experimental study of the drawing behavior of adult psychotics in comparison with that of a normal control group. *Journal of Experimental Psychology*, 1944, *34*, 169–194.

With J. P. Foley, Jr. A proposed reorientation to the heredity–environment controversy. *Psychological Review*, 1948, *55*, 239–249.

With J. P. Foley, Jr. *The Human-Figure Drawing Test as an objective psychiatric screening aid for student pilots.* USAF School of Aviation Medicine, Project No. 21-37-002, Report No. 5, 1952.

With J. P. Foley, Jr., and H. Sackman. *Psychiatric selection of flying personnel: An empirical evaluation of the SAM Personality-Sketch Test.* USAF School of Aviation Medicine, Project No. 21-0202-0007, Report No. 6, 1954.

With J. L. Fuller, J. P. Scott, and J. R. Schmitt. A factor analysis of the performance of dogs on certain learning tests. *Zoologica*, 1955, *40*(3), 33–46.

With R. F. Levee. Intellectual defect and musical talent. *American Journal of Mental Deficiency*, 1959, *64*, 695–703.

With M. J. Meade and A. A. Schneiders. The validation of a biographical inventory as a predictor of college success. *College Entrance Examination Board Research Monographs*, No. 1, 1960.

With C. E. Schaefer. Biographical correlates of artistic and literary creativity in adolescent girls. *Journal of Applied Psychology,* 1969, *53,* 267–273.

Garrett, H. E., and Anastasi, A. The tetrad-difference criterion and the measurement of mental traits. *Annals of the New York Academy of Sciences,* 1932, *33,* 233–282.

Lund, F. H., and Anastasi, A. An interpretation of aesthetic experience. *American Journal of Psychology,* 1928, *40,* 434–448.

Schaefer, C. S., and Anastasi, A. A biographical inventory for identifying creativity in adolescent boys. *Journal of Applied Psychology,* 1968, *52,* 42–48.

Other Publications Cited

Bingham, W. V. Studies in melody. *Psychological Monographs,* 1910, *12*(3, Whole No. 50).

Boring, E. G., and Lindzey, G. (Eds.). *A history of psychology in autobiography.* Vol. V. New York: Appleton-Century-Crofts, 1967.

Buros, O. K. (Ed.). *Tests in Print II.* Highland Park, N.J.: Gryphon Press, 1974.

Christal, R. E. *Factor analytic study of visual memory. Psychological Monographs,* 1958, *72*(13, Whole No. 466).

Davenport, C. B. Race crossing in Jamaica. *Scientific Monthly,* 1928, *27,* 225–238.

Davenport, C. B. Do races differ in mental capacity? *Human Biology,* 1929, *1,* 70–89.

Davenport, C. B., and Craytor, L. C. Comparative social traits of various races. Second study. *Journal of Applied Psychology,* 1923, *7,* 127–132.

Ekstrom, R. B., French, J. W., Harman, H. H., and Dermen, D. *Manual for kit of factor-referenced cognitive tests* (3rd ed.). Princeton, N.J.: Educational Testing Service, 1976.

Fisher, R. A. *Statistical methods for research workers.* Edinburgh: Oliver and Boys. 1925.

French, J. W. *Kit of selected tests for reference aptitude and achievement factors.* Princeton, N.J.: Educational Testing Service, 1954.

French, J. W., Ekstrom, R. B., and Price, L. A. *Kit of reference tests for cognitive factors* (rev. ed.). Princeton, N.J.: Educational Testing Service, 1963.

Garrett, H. E. *Statistics in psychology and education.* New York: Longmans, Green, 1926. (Later editions: 1937, 1947, 1958.)

Gray, H. A. *Some factors in the undergraduate careers of young college students* (Teachers College Contributions to Education, No. 437). New York: Teachers College, Columbia University, 1930.

Hollingworth, H. L. *The psychology of thought.* New York: Appleton, 1926.

Hollingworth, H. L. *Psychology: Its facts and principles.* New York: Appleton, 1928.

Hollingworth, H. L. *Abnormal psychology: Its concepts and theories.* New York: Ronald, 1930.

Hull, C. L. *Aptitude testing.* Yonkers, N.Y.: World Book Co., 1928.

Hull, C. L. *Hypnosis and suggestibility: An experimental approach.* New York: Appleton-Century, 1933.

Kantor, J. R. *Principles of psychology.* New York: Knopf. Vol. I, 1924; Vol. II, 1926.

Kantor, J. R. *An outline of social psychology.* Chicago: Follett, 1929.

Kantor, J. R. *An objective psychology of grammar.* Bloomington: Indiana University Publications (Science Series, No. 1), 1936.

Kantor, J. R. *Interbehavioral psychology: A sample of scientific system construction.* Chicago: Principia Press, 1958.

Kantor, J. R. *Psychological linguistics.* Chicago: Principia Press, 1977.

Kelley, T. L. *Crossroads in the mind of man: A study of differentiable mental abilities.* Stanford, Calif.: Stanford University Press, 1928.

Klineberg, O. A study of psychological differences between "racial" and national groups in Europe. *Archives of Psychology,* 1931, No. 132.

Moore, H. T. The genetic aspect of consonance and dissonance. *Psychological Monographs,* 1914, *17*(2, Whole No. 73).

Pfungst, O. *Clever Hans (the horse of Mr. von Osten): A contribution to experimental, animal, and human psychology* (trans. by C. L. Rahn). New York: Holt, 1911.

Pillsbury, W. B. *Essentials of psychology* (rev. ed.). New York: Macmillan, 1921.

Pressey, S. L. Age and the doctorate—then and now, with some possibly radical suggestions. *Journal of Higher Education,* 1962, *33*, 153–160.

Rosenthal, R. *Experimenter effects in behavioral research* (enlarged edition). New York: Wiley, 1976.

Schieffelin, B., and Schwesinger, G. C. Mental tests and heredity, including a survey of non-verbal tests. *Eugenics Research Association Monograph Series,* 1930, No. III.

Spearman, C. "General intelligence" objectively determined and measured. *American Journal of Psychology,* 1904, *15*, 201–293.

Spearman, C. *The abilities of man.* New York: Macmillan, 1927.

Stern, W. *Über Psychologie der individuellen Differenzen: Ideen Zur einer "Differentielle Psychologie."* Leipzig: Barth, 1900. (Later editions: 1911, 1921.)

Thurstone, L. L. *Vectors of mind: Multiple-factor analysis for the isolation of primary traits.* Chicago: University of Chicago Press, 1935.

Thurstone, L. L. Shifty and mathematical components: A critique of Anastasi's monograph on the influence of specific experience upon mental organization. *Psychological Bulletin,* 1938, 35, 223–236.

Thurstone, L. L. *Multiple factor analysis.* Chicago: University of Chicago Press, 1947.

Wentworth, G., and Smith, D. E. *Plane and spherical trigonometry.* Boston: Ginn, 1915.

Donald E. Broadbent

A Moment to Look Around

It is a shade disconcerting to be asked for an autobiography just as one is starting a new job. It is even more disconcerting if the job is an opportunity one has sought for many years. Perhaps the sensation is nearest to that of arriving eagerly at a party and being seized immediately to give somebody a ride home. Still, if the hour is getting a little late, perhaps it is a good idea to think about the errors of map-reading that made it so and the helpful assistance of those encountered on the road. With these thoughts in mind, granting the request makes it a little more likely that the end of the party will be worthwhile.

To return from the metaphor to the real world, psychological research is subject to fashion, as are other fields of science. If we think about past enthusiasms, we can realize how short-lived our present convictions will likely be. What follows, therefore, is not yet the final summing up of a completed life; it is merely an attempt to plot the trajectory of a life and to see where all of us are going.

The Thrust of Human Problems

I was born on May 6, 1926, in Birmingham, England. My father was, for most of the time the family stayed together, an executive in a British-based, multinational company. He must have been a good one. Class boundaries were stiffer in those days than Americans or the modern British can imagine, and our background was relatively poor. But he rose meteorically, and in the 1930s, we lived briefly at a level of affluence I shall never see again. It did not last, however. At the start of World War II, he parted from the company and from the family, and I never saw him again. My mother's theory was that the rapid shift of role and class had been too great a strain. Whether this is true or not, it colored her attitude toward my own schooling. Hence I became part of an extraordinary paradox: In those days before Social Security, my mother kept herself and me by clerical work in small local offices of the civil service, and for most of the war, we lived in a four-roomed cottage that had no bathroom and required us to make essential periodic trips outside to the end of the yard. Yet, at the same time, she was determined that never, under any circumstances, would I later be handicapped in dealing with people who had a heavier ballast of educational advantage. So instead of getting me the best schooling she could afford, she made up her mind with sublime arrogance as to which she thought was the best school in the country, and that was where I went: Winchester.

How on earth did she do it? Partly by luck, since our family's brief period of affluence had meant that she had been able to get me trained for a scholarship. And although I only got an "exhibition," which does not cover all the fees, the school heard of the circumstances and made up the difference. My father's company coughed up enough from his pension fund to pay for my keep, so that I might as well have been at Winchester as at the local grammar school. Lastly, it was wartime; clothes were rationed, expensive side trips and facilities were impossible, and all of us lived in a world where the unthinkable was being thought every day.

I dwell on this because it has probably made my attitude toward psychology dour and puritan, in a way that has sometimes offended younger colleagues. It is perhaps an attitude that is particularly irritating when expressed in the accent and style of the upper-class British. Nevertheless, I decided then, and still believe, that self-realization and the development of personal experience are neither dignified nor respectable goals in life, that most of the world lives within extremely tight economic margins, and that positions of privilege (such as the conduct of scientific research) demand obligations in return. Hence, for example, the fact that I never held a university job.

This form of puritanism was, of course, very much reinforced by other features of the time and of my surroundings. Affluent or poor, we all slept underground night after night while the bombers came over. As a schoolboy, I had clips on my bicycle for carrying a rifle, and we diligently practiced for our role in the case of a parachute attack on that region of England. We were to locate parachutists, to shadow their movements using our bicycle mobility and knowledge of the terrain, and to call up elder and more lethal assistance by radio. The scheme was not as mad as it sounds; we were at least ordered to avoid engaging the enemy ourselves if at all possible. Furthermore, the actual discomfort and danger was minimal compared with, say, the things that were happening at that time to Boris Lomov, now of the University of Moscow. (Twenty-five years later, he told me about his own life at the time in Leningrad during the siege.) Nevertheless, we all listened diligently in intense, adolescent male groups to Churchill's speeches, and when that inspired breaker of all normal rules of English dropped triumphantly into cliché to declaim "You can always take one with you," we rippled with sympathetic enthusiasm.

To be fair, we listened also to the broadcasts of J. B. Priestley. Nowadays, he has perhaps become associated too much with grumbles about the injustice of taxation in the upper-income brackets; but at that time, he put forward tellingly and clearly the case for one kind of society rather than another, for the merits of pluralism and debate rather than monolithic organizations, and for socialism in its non-Marxist form as compared with the doctrines of the corporate state. (Socialism in its Marxist form, incidentally, was neither emotionally nor intellectually respectable, because it led its supporters, with apparently rigorous logic, into alliance with the Nazis.) The general inspiration of these broadcasts was very much reinforced by the intellectual influence of Winchester, which was one of the first schools to teach economics to boys of that age range.

Above these various subordinate values there was, of course, a more general one; only in retrospect do I realize how unusual it was. The school was closely linked to the Church of England, the headmaster in my time later became Bishop of Peterborough, and all the most intelligent people I knew in those formative years were Christians. To me, therefore, my immediate associations with Christianity are rational debate, cool dissection of tendentious philosophical slogans, the use of deliberate symbolic rituals after careful explanations of their meaning, and so on. It took me some time in later life to realize that many other people find this picture hard to recognize; after inquiring into their own experiences, I find this very understandable. Nevertheless, I can only testify to what I myself knew.

British secondary education specializes children at an early age, but in those days Winchester was anxious to push classical learning, and they pointed out to me that I could go quite a long way as a specialist in classics and still have time to come back and do the science course before the end of my time. I did so and began in Roman history to get, for the first time, a feeling that alternative forms of society had actually been tried in the past—much as I could see them in conflict all around me every day. Neither in history, classics, nor later in the physical sciences did I really feel at home, however. The physical sciences were the best, but there were a number of snags in them. First, so much seemed to be known already; would I spend my life merely taking out of a book and using facts that somebody else had found? Second, although scientific progress was essential to solve most of the real-world problems that worried me, would it be enough by itself? Third, somehow I did not really enjoy it; the prospect of doing it all my life repelled me. It was therefore quite a relief, as I got to the age of seventeen, to realize that I was not so brilliant in the physical sciences that I would be exempt from military service; a break doing something else was bound to come.

There was no doubt about the something else. All my life I have been fascinated by flying; one of my earliest memories is an accidental sight of the airship *Graf Zeppelin,* and I spent all my spare time as a boy brooding over the exploits of the early pilots. Everybody had always told me that it could not be a career which as we shall see is ironic. Nevertheless, early interest, politics, and the pressures of the time all made it obvious that I had to get into the RAF as a pilot. In 1943, therefore, I volunteered. The procedure for medical examination and so on was fairly slow; I read the whole of *War and Peace* during the periods I spent waiting. In 1944, I went into the service, by a route that took me to Cambridge, where I took a specially organized, short course in engineering while simultaneously attending ground school. Four days a week, I behaved like a traditional undergraduate, holding long arguments in which I asserted that, after the war, road traffic would get so intense that there would be roads on which pedestrians would not be allowed and which could only be crossed by subways; it was generally felt that these were the sentiments of a fascist beast and not to be taken seriously. The remaining two days I spent in uniform, learning Morse code in a large house a couple of miles from the center of Cambridge—number 15 Chaucer Road, an address that will reappear later.

In the autumn of 1944, I went into the RAF proper and, early in 1945, sailed on the *Acquitania* for New York to learn to fly in the United States. (As has sometimes been noticed, the weather is often bad in Britain, and German fighter sweeps would have been delighted to encounter pupil pilots.) I trained at Clewiston in Florida, and it was at this time that I began to become aware of the possibility of psychology as a real career. Several factors converged to do this. First, I began to realize the importance of psychological problems in practice. I am not thinking solely of the lady in the RAF club in New York, who read my hand (while I was in uniform) and after long thought informed me that I had come a long way from over the sea. There were more insistent and visible problems. For example, the AT6, which I was flying, carried two identical levers close together under the seat, one of which pulled up the flaps and was to be used at the end of the landing run. The other lever pulled up the wheels. With monotonous regularity, one or another of my colleagues would pull the wrong lever, drop an expensive airplane onto its belly in the middle of the field, and after a harrowing interview with our superior officer, disappear to England. Furthermore, some of the airplane's instruments might be accurate, but were uncommonly hard to read; on another aircraft I once went through a landing pattern thinking I was at 2,000 feet when actually I was flying at 2,000 rpm. The technology was fine, but it seemed to be badly matched to human beings.

Next, I had been greatly impressed by the selection battery the RAF applied to me on entry. The notion of actually counting human behavior, and correlating it with a criterion, resonated with all the separate interests I'd been building up. The process had the concrete quality that I'd admired in science, but it could shed light on the human problems that had concerned me. Also, it had clear and direct economic value. This was a new world to me; neither traditional classics nor traditional science had touched on anything of this kind. In Britain, no schoolboy would have heard of psychology at that time. University departments teaching it were extremely scarce; in England proper, there were perhaps five or six such departments, although Scotland was better served. Once again, one needed to think the unthinkable even to contemplate such a subject.

Third, however, this situation was not true in the United States. And here I was. I began to ask questions and found that, in this country, the subject of psychology was much more respectable and widely known. I can even pinpoint one conversation I had with a girl from Greenwich, Connecticut, who was then called Pat Ely and who told me about the psychology course she was taking. I never saw her again, although she did me one favor by mail I shall mention later. Nevertheless, that conversation was probably the crucial point at which I began to explore seriously the possibility of being a psychologist rather than an engineer.

After VJ-Day, Lend-Lease was ended, and with it ended any possibility of British pilots learning to fly in the United States. (You may think we have economic problems now, but it was worse then.) We were shipped home hastily and offered a choice: to sign on as career pilots with the RAF or to accept transfers to ground jobs. I took the latter choice, still probably influenced by my family's view that piloting was no kind of career. In fact, of course, had I taken the other branch, transferred like many of my generation to civil aviation, and remained as fit as I have, I could now possibly be flying a 747 and receiving a much higher salary than I get as a psychologist. However, there were some vacancies in the personnel-selection branch open to me if I decided to do a ground job, so I chose that and went through the training course under, in particular, J. B. Parry. Again, what I heard seemed to me sensible, down-to-earth, and the bridge between technology and human problems that I had been seeking. Day-to-day experience confirmed my impression. To take one dramatic instance, on one RAF station we were asked for advice about five airmen who were unable to read or write. Should they simply be discharged or was their disability due to the disruption of their schooling by war and poverty? A quick application of the Progressive Matrices showed that their scores were perfectly normal—indeed, one man got a higher score than any I had met previously. I heard later that he learned to read in three weeks flat.

By the standards of modern psychologists, this kind of thing is simplistic and unsubtle. Nevertheless, at a certain level it obviously worked better than traditional methods, and the area was undoubtedly the one I wanted. I was sure now that I wanted to be a psychologist; so as my demobilization approached in 1947, I wrote to my old Cambridge College, to which I could go while receiving financial assistance as an ex-serviceman. (Again, luck favored my mother's plans; nowadays, anyone obtaining admission to a British university gets money from the government to attend it, but before the war my chances of financial assistance would have been slim.) In my letter, I said that I would like to read psychology; the Fellows of my College said we would discuss that when I was home. When I returned to England, I went to see them and they pointed out that careers were much better in chemistry. On my part, I declared that I had read no natural science more complicated than *Penguin Science News* for three years, but that I had been reading some psychology. They capitulated and, in the autumn of 1947, I started two years of fulltime study in the subject for my undergraduate degree.

Cambridge: The Mythic Era

I had been unbelievably lucky again. There was a psychology department at Cambridge; had I gone elsewhere, I should probably have found that the subject was impossible to study. Not only that, but the Department happened to teach exactly the kind of psychology I would have chosen, if I had known enough about the subject to do so. The Department was run by Sir Frederic Bartlett, and throughout the war, he had made his laboratory a center for tackling some of the human problems of technology met by the armed forces. As radar was invented, as gunnery control systems became more complex, as operation rooms displayed more and more information, engineers needed increasing guidance on the correct brightness of the display, the gain of the control system, and the minimum size of letter visible on a plotting table. Cambridge could answer these questions, either from textbooks or through experiments that took a reasonably short time, gave sound, useful answers, and generally endeared psychologists to skeptical military men. At the same time, a lot of theoretical ideas were sprouting in this applied environment. Bartlett himself had always had a highly original and sophisticated approach to psychology; his great book, *Remembering*, which we all read diligently and carefully, was years ahead of its time in the description of phenomena (Bartlett, 1932). He was unusual in the 1930s in emphasizing the constructive character of perception and, above all, the reconstructive character of recall; the processes he inferred from his experiments were neither the simple S-R links of behaviorism nor the unified fields of Gestaltists nor the mentalistic concepts of philosophers. Rather, they were active processes, separated into different levels and roles, intercommunicating with each other and yet directed to goals. There was, of course, no language in the 1930s to state such notions at all precisely; but throughout the war, Bartlett had had at his right hand K. J. W. Craik, a young Scot who had made himself thoroughly familiar with contemporary engineering techniques. Craik saw that many of the formal descriptions of control systems could be applied to processes going on inside human beings; the whole nature of the applied problems that he and Bartlett were tackling encouraged such a view, and in the very middle of the war, he produced a book (Craik, 1943) that was one of the first statements of the cybernetic point of view of human beings. These notions had been discussed and spread among the people of the laboratory, and though Craik himself was killed in an accident in 1945, his spirit had communicated itself throughout the building. Therefore, we undergraduates who arrived two years later met for the first time a startling new approach to human beings, one that was not available in any textbook or journal article and one that had potentially revolutionary implications.

Looking back, it is probably as well that the morale was high, because there were certain other difficulties. The balance-of-payments problem, which had brought me back from the United States, was still so serious that textbooks could only be imported in extremely rare cases. There was one copy of Woodworth (1938) in the library, and each student was allowed to borrow it for two weeks; in that time, I took detailed notes from the entire book, which I used for some years afterwards. A much-coveted item was Hilgard and Marquis (1940); I was so desperate to get it that I wrote a blatant, begging letter to Pay Ely, and she sent me a copy, thus enormously increasing my social status among my fellows. I never made any return; but I still remember with great gratitude.

Given that we had no textbooks, what about the lectures? The backbone was carried by Alan Welford, who later went to Adelaide, Australia, and is only now retiring. He gave us an eclectic, clearly presented sweep through human experimental psychology. He made sure that we knew the classic work on constancy, on positive and negative transfer, on Hullian concept learning, as well as the exciting new work on skill. Animal psychology came from C. G. Grindley, who on one interpretation of priorities was the discoverer of operant conditioning; at a very early date, he had noted that one could train a

47

guinea pig to turn its head by food reinforcement (Grindley, 1932). By the time I knew him, personal problems had made him less productive on the research side, but his lectures were fun. I still recall with affection his story of the two talking birds at the London Zoo, one of which had been trained to reel off a very long patter whenever approached by visitors. Inevitably, when this stream of speech ceased, the visitor would turn to the other bird and say, "Don't you say anything?" To this the other bird would reply, "No." Lesson: Remember that the obvious interpretation is not necessarily the right one!

Animal psychology, however, was a theoretical subject; experimental animals were an unwarrantable luxury in wartime Britain. They ate food and needed care. Consequently, there were no animals whatever in the laboratory. Equally, there was no developmental psychology, only the sketchiest psychometrics, and very occasional brushes with social psychology. The Department was a wing of the physiology laboratory, and indeed it might not have been too inappropriate to call it "higher nervous function" or something of that sort. From a formal point of view, the degree was still regarded as one in "moral science," indicating its traditional links with philosophy, but the actual teaching had been organized for some time as part of biology, and it was moved over to that faculty a little later. By the standards of modern, comprehensive, British honors degrees in psychology, the treatment was appallingly patchy. On the other hand, it had a constant thread of excitement that came from being at a frontier where things were really happening. Such a feeling seemed almost an essential part of being in Cambridge in any subject during that five years or so. The spirit in the Cavendish Laboratory has been described at greater length by James Watson (1968); although molecular biologists and psychologists might never meet, their attitudes were highly similar. People like Cockcroft, Thomson, Bertrand Russell, and Bragg passed me in the street; Gold (of the theory of continuous creation) was still in Cambridge, and I visited him once to talk about his views on hearing.

For psychologists, however, the center of the excitement was Bartlett. He would give one lecture a week, not of course following any particular syllabus, but pouring out a steady stream of ideas, odd references to things he had recently read, general concepts that seemed to him widely applicable, and so on. On those occasions, everybody was too enthralled and too occupied with taking notes to interrupt or discuss the lectures; but he was almost incredibly approachable. I doubt if most heads of department nowadays are as easily seen by graduate students as Bartlett was by undergraduates. He had a very endearing quality of never finding fault with someone's work unless he had a substantial respect and admiration for that person; so the first faltering steps of the young student were encouraged rather than stamped into the earth. Another characteristic was his rather uncanny ability to predict the results of almost any experiment performed on human beings; he might not be able to tell you how he arrived at the prediction, but he seemed always to know what somebody would do in a certain situation. These perhaps were merely graces and ornaments; the core of his approach, which he communicated to everybody who knew him, lay in certain principles of research. One of these principles was that problems should be taken from real life whenever possible; another principle, related to the first, was that experimental situations should be left complex rather than be simplified. (The argument for this was that the complex situation controls behavior better; people use many different strategies in simple situations.) A third was that the data should be allowed to determine the theory rather than the theory be used to search for particular data. These principles lay at the core of Bartlett's approach; they still seem to me sound and vital. Recovering from his influence after thirty years, I can certainly agree that he had weak spots; his dislike of nonsense syllables, statistics, and physiology were all overdone. But these were small gaps in a generally inspiring mind.

Looking back again, I can see that the full explosive quality of the Bartlett–Craik approach began to be watered down almost at once. I have recently expanded on this elsewhere (Broadbent, 1977b), but briefly the Bartlett–Craik view was one of different levels of process, with upper levels controlling and modifying lower ones. There were also very substantial feedback components. To create managable research out of this approach, it was necessary to carve individual problems

49

out of it; hence, the restrictions on the upper level of the process were examined separately, giving rise to "single-channel theory." The limits on decisionmaking also gave rise to the "information-theory approach," where the startling contribution of W. E. Hick (1952), in showing that reaction time varied with amount of information conveyed by the stimulus, started a whole research industry. Gradually, each of these problems was tackled more and more by methods that might quite well have arisen from S-R theory or other traditional approaches, so that even now, thirty years later, we are only just regaining the full complexity of the Bartlett–Craik view.

I personally was no exception to this simplification. The key problem to me, at the start, was to relate these apparently mechanical notions about human beings to the more basic values and interests that had caused me to take up psychology in the first place. Within the two-year undergraduate period, however, I had got the message that the kinds of process being discussed were in no sense as simple and subhuman as clockwork or telephone exchanges. Rather, they were merely a method of making precise the valuable statements of human complexity that the most sensitive observers of our species might wish to entertain. In this respect, it was certainly a more suitable language than that of Clark Hull; Cambridge was, and is, a university that teaches by tutorials, and one of my first tutors was Dan Berlyne (now, alas, very recently deceased), who at that time was convinced of the value of Hull and made sure that I understood the system perfectly. Nevertheless, it was, as a language, obviously inferior; as I formulated the point a decade or so later, Roman numerals and Arabic numerals may describe the same phenomenon, but one is very much more convenient for arithmetic.

More personally, I had two successive problems at this time. The first was the level of performance I was going to achieve. With the tutorial system and no quizzes or anything of that sort, it is easy to have no idea of one's own level of performance. I was, therefore, in a good deal of agony throughout the undergraduate period, fearing I would get so bad a degree that I'd be unable to get a job at all. In fact, I got a first-class honors degree, but I had no confidence at all in that possibility until the results were announced. The second problem was getting a job. My aim had been to work in industry, but where were the jobs which would actually pay one to do all the useful things I was sure psychologists could do? It was important to get a job quickly, too, because I wanted to get married, and in those days, it was still the normal presumption that even a fresh graduate husband would have to support his wife financially.

No jobs showed up in industry; but the word began to get around the lab, shortly before the exams, that the navy wanted someone to work on effects of noise. As it happened, I had been very impressed by some notions of Carolus Oldfield (later Professor at Oxford), relating effects of noise to Pavlovian internal inhibition (Oldfield, 1937); and it was clearly a practical problem. I leaped at the job, and a nice period touch was that Sir Frederic asked in puzzlement whether it would not be better for me simply to do research on whatever pleased me without actually seeking employment, but he recovered rapidly when I pointed out that an income was truly necessary for me. I got the job, it was administered through the Medical Research Council, and the intention was that I would receive a little informal postgraduate instruction at Cambridge before I left for a naval laboratory and the main study. As it turned out, however, the naval laboratory disliked the idea of "noisy" research on their premises, and therefore I stayed at Cambridge, as a member of the Applied Psychology Unit, for the next twenty-five years.

Staff Member, APU

The Medical Research Council has, for over fifty years, administered a vote that Parliament makes for the support of general research in medicine. (Nowadays, in particular, the Department of Health and Social Security has a number of mission-oriented contracts and also commissions some research by the MRC itself; but the MRC still funds most of the basic work.) Unlike, say, the National Institutes of Health in the United States, the MRC maintains a number of units all over the country and commonly supplies assistance and equipment to promising university scientists. A unit goes on until its scientist retires. The MRC was also charged with giving medical advice to other government departments, a duty that might sometimes mean doing special research needed for that purpose. Lastly, it was remarkably sympathetic both to occupational medicine and to applied psychology. (There were historical reasons for this, one of which was the fact that the MRC was started about the time of World War I, when the health of munitions workers was a problem.) For all these reasons, it made a great deal of sense to form the Applied Psychology Unit in 1944, to tidy up the various informal arrangements by which Sir Frederic had brought people together to solve wartime problems. Kenneth Craik made an ideal first Director. When he was killed, Bartlett himself took over the directorship; but he had as an assistant director Norman Mackworth, who did most of the day-to-day running of the unit. Mackworth was, by training, a doctor, but he had diverted into psychological research when manpower was needed during the war for some of the problems Bartlett was handling. (There were no trained psychologists being produced, so some doctors were diverted. Other doctors in the unit were W. E. Hick himself, Derek Russell Davis [Davis, 1948], and Alan Carpenter.) Mackworth had set up, for example, a simple mechanical simulation of a radar set and had discovered that the detection of targets dropped steeply after half an hour—the so-called problem of "vigilance" (Mackworth, 1950). This finding was typical of his approach, which might be called "task-centered." He would find an interesting situation, construct a practicable laboratory simulaion, and, by changing the numerous variables, come out with some rather counterintuitive relationships. On the whole, he did not go in for flights of psychological theory; he preferred to produce a sound basis of fact on matters such as effects of heat, cold, number of sources of information being handled, and so on. He was also rather successful at getting quite large facilities from users; for the noise project, he persuaded the navy to build a complete noise chamber miles out in the countryside away from Cambridge, which I could use for my research. This was an undoubted attraction; in addition, I found his direct empirical approach congenial and attractive.

When Bartlett retired in 1952, there was a problem about the future of the unit. If it had been one of those set up to support some particular distinguished scientist, it would have been closed. However, it was also, and perhaps chiefly, meant to take on the research that the MRC was doing for other bodies, such as the navy and the agencies that were attempting to improve industrial productivity. Consequently, when Bartlett retired, the decision was made to continue the unit with another director, rather than close it, and Mackworth was the choice. Furthermore, there was a problem of accommodation, because with Bartlett's great enthusiasm, APU was taking up a very substantial part of the space in the university laboratory. If any of the other fields of psychology were ever to get a voice, some space was needed. Oliver Zangwill, the incoming professor, was understandably perturbed at having such a high proportion of the Department devoted to applied experimental psychology. In the end, the MRC decided to move the unit away from the university to separate premises at 15 Chaucer Road, the same house in which I had attended my Morse code sessions eight years previously. We kept some rooms in the university, in particular the hot room that the navy had built there. However, most of us moved out, and the APU is still in Chaucer Road at the time of this writing. The house was not designed for the purpose, but it was a substantial place with back stairs as well as front stairs, with nurseries and servants' quarters behind partitioned doors, and a reasonably large group could operate there without difficulty. In these quarters, Mackworth continued to carry out research of the mission-oriented type that had characterized the APU since its earliest days. The move provided a solution that met the needs of both the MRC and the university, and though the geographical separation created a slight separation of attitudes, the situation was workable.

I personally was not concerned with the higher flights of strategy, but merely with my own research. Building the noise room in the country took quite a long time. The intention was to use a vigilance task, following Mackworth's wartime success, to study the effects of noise. But the original equipment produced by the navy made loud clicks that were easily audible in the quiet control conditions. It all needed, therefore, to be stripped to pieces, redesigned, and assembled in a fashion that satisfied us that it was giving no such clues. Vigilance tasks are lengthy; each subject required a week of testing. Consequently, progress was frustratingly slow. Mackworth, however, had simultaneously asked me to handle another and quite different set of problems—those arising in communication centers, where many different streams of speech reached a person at the same time. This problem also came originally from the navy, although an RAF interest blossomed before very long. These experiments were much quicker. Instead of delivering fifteen signals to a subject in an hour and a half, one could fire messages at him every five or ten seconds, and accumulate lots of data within a quarter of an hour. Mackworth's tactic started me, therefore, on a strategy I have always used since, to run several projects in parallel, so that the moments of gloom and despondency in one will usually be relieved by moments of achievements and success in another. Furthermore, long and laborious studies, which have never been done because of their length, will usually contribute something of value to the literature but make it very hard to sustain the motivation of the experimenter. Studies using fast techniques help to keep him or her cheerful.

Such studies were perhaps particularly necessary because various personal difficulties made my private life highly stressful throughout that and the next decade. There were compensations, however. I was still flying with the reserve, until it was disbanded in the mid-1950s as being unlikely to react fast enough to the most probable form of attack. (It was entertaining to note the observation of my colleague Ron Lewis that we could not turn off the fuel cock for an emergency landing without undoing our straps and risking a broken skull!) And in this period also, I took to riding motorcycles, perhaps the main pleasure of my youth. But, otherwise, life did not look very bright, and I simply spent most of my time working.

Work itself was not merely a matter of books and experiments. I watched air-traffic controllers juggling with the problems of bringing jet aircraft into a landing. I conducted an experiment actually in the air, on the effects of bad communications on the skill of the pilot. I went to sea with the Royal Navy and watched the startlingly beautiful ballet of men and machines as a carrier recovers its aircraft—beauty sharpened by the tensions of bringing the aircraft of the 1950s onto a ship designed for the lower landing speeds of World War II. In each of these situations, I could see human feats of perception, decision, and control that were clearly highly admirable, in which error might mean death, and yet that lay outside the view of human beings normally put forward by academics.

Not all academics, of course. In Britain outside Cambridge, there was perhaps little interest in such aspects of human nature, and travel was so difficult that international contact was extremely rare. A new phenomenon appeared on the scene, however, when the U. S. navy started to keep a psychologist in London to pass on information about American developments and, also, to find out what we were doing. Henry Imus started these contacts off with enormous success, and the slightly hothouse atmosphere of Cambridge was enlivened by visits from Americans doing similar work in the States. The laboratories that loomed largest in our eyes were the Psychoacoustic Laboratory at Harvard, the group at Johns Hopkins, and the Aviation Psychology Laboratory of Paul Fitts at Ohio State. When the great men from these laboratories occasionally appeared, we could feel the same belief in the practical importance of making technology fit human beings rather than the reverse and the same belief in the intellectual importance of thinking about information processing in the nervous system.

Such an intellectual approach was clearly necessary for the problems Mackworth had given me. In the case of people listening to multiple speech messages, the Harvard work had provided the clue that spatial separation of loud speakers was very important. When one analyzed the pattern of mistakes in detail, however, it was clear that something more than peripheral masking was going on. Rather, there seemed to be something comparable to the outmoded concept of "attention," which had hardly appeared in respectable academic circles for forty years. The reason for its disappearance had been the lack of suitable terminology; common-sense language has great difficulty in discussing the problems of the air-traffic controller, because, in one sense, he does more than one thing at the same time, and in another sense, his capacities are limited. But the new notions of information theory provided a suitable vocabulary. Instead of thinking of a "stimulus" in the outside world, which did or did not produce a response, one could speak of an event that produced some representation within a person, and the representation might correspond in some ways, but not in all, to the various features of the outside event. Thus, there might be transmission of information about a very complex happening through the detection merely of one sensory change that was always associated with the other features of the event. Conversely, there might be loss of information about an event even though the senses were working perfectly. By adopting this kind of vocabulary, one could discuss different theoretical mechanisms for the working of attention, and one could see why such a function might be necessary, because of possible limits on the amount of information that might be dealt with by certain parts of the brain.

These ideas suggested a whole series of experiments, and each one in turn showed phenomena very difficult to describe in other theoretical languages. It is trite now, but at the time it was surprising to realize that the reaction to a stimulus depends on the other stimuli that may be present, although on a particular occasion they do not occur. I can remember hearing, with astonishment, of experiments that resulted in the present series of words for spelling out letters over a radio or telephone: Alpha, Bravo, Coca, Delta, and so on. These experiments were necessary to replace the World War II series (Able, Baker, Charlie, Dog, etc.) because the latter was an Anglo-Saxon series of words unsuitable for people whose native language was not English. When attempts were being made to revise the alphabet, however, it was found that the intelligibility of, for example, Victor for V depended upon the word one used to represent N. If one used Nectar, then Victor was less intelligible than it would otherwise be. It is a measure of our advance that hardly anyone would now be surprised at this.

In the same way, traditional concepts were proving inadequate to deal with the effects of noise on behavior. Oldfield's idea had been that exposure to noise would produce a general inhibition rather similar to that which Pavlov produced. This would suggest that one would get effects of noise only on certain kinds of tasks; the Harvard laboratories had shown very clearly that a number of tests could be performed as well in a noisy environment as in a quiet one, but that would be quite consistent with the inhibition type of theory. One might expect inhibition to be removed by novel and irrelevant stimuli, much as Pavlov showed disinhibition of extinguished responses. Mackworth had shown such disinhibition in his vigilance tasks; perhaps only long and unmotivating tasks would show effects of noise. Indeed, we found that we could get impairments in such conditions. However, all kinds of difficulties appear in the inhibitory theory. For example, continuous measurement of performance showed that the noise produced occasional momentary failures, with perfectly normal or even better reaction in between these failures. Some different conceptual structure was necessary. Perhaps, for instance, it might be more useful to think of the effects of noise as a change in the processing of information by the human and even to apply such changes to the understanding of extinction of conditioned responses, rather than the reverse.

Such a change in ways of thinking was encouraged by the whole atmosphere in which I continued to work. The APU under Mackworth continued to bubble with the kind of cybernetic approach to human problems that Bartlett and Craik had put forward. The unit had over thirty psychologists when I joined it, and I was learning something from every one of them. A complete list is impossible, and a partial one would be unfair, so perhaps I should mention only two who are now dead: Bernard Gibbs and Alfred Leonard. Gibbs had taken up psychological research from the navy, with an interest primarily in control systems such as those used for guns. He was fond of pointing out that models of learning based on the acquisition of stimulus–response links must be inadequate, because if the transfer from one task to another was due to the links they had in common, then the transfer should be equal in both directions. It is easy to show that learning skill A first and then skill B may be much harder than learning skill B first and then skill A. Gibbs suggested that the process of learning was much more likely to be the acquisition of particular feedback loops.

These feedback loops were designed to cope automatically with certain changes in conditions and would therefore transfer easily, while other changes in conditions would go outside the range for which such loops were devised and would therefore give very little transfer. Despite these telling theoretical points, I suspect that Gibbs liked to present the image of the plain, straightforward sailor. At all events he remained rather detached from theoretical psychology.

Leonard was closer to the mainstream, but he brought with him a substantial amount of technical knowledge in the sphere of apparatus. He was one of those who had been forced to leave Germany as a child, and as in other cases, Britain gained enormously from its willingness to receive him. He was an ex-member of the Special Air Service, a radical, and a man of driving enthusiasm. Perhaps occasionally, he was still a little Germanic and did not understand the British sense of humor; I can still remember Mackworth and I being reduced to helpless giggles by his announcing solemnly that he had made a considerable theoretical advance: "I am pretty sure I can tie up Alan Welford and Margaret Vince together." He had taken as a starting point some of Bartlett's ideas about anticipation in skilled performance, and he used his technical knowledge to construct an apparatus that would wait for a subject to make a response and then present a fresh stimulus immediately or after some prescribed delay. Again, this task now seems unbelievably easy; it was not in those days. A task of this kind could go on indefinitely—the experimental subject always having a fresh decision to make—and Mackworth therefore suggested to me that it would be interesting to take up some of the satiation experiments of Lewin by asking people to go on until they could bear the task no longer. Perhaps, for example, they might satiate more rapidly in noise. I did indeed try this, but discovered, to my embarrassment, that sailors in the Royal Navy differ from German students in the opposite direction from that which I had always expected. The classic Gestaltist experiment found that people gave up monotonous tasks after a period; a British sailor, asked to help with psychological research, will go on doing a task until the experimenter asks him to stop! The serious lesson is that the findings of apparently objective experiments depend very much on the relationship and degree of cooperation between the experimenter and the so-called subject.

In addition to these and the many other similar members of APU, I had increasingly useful contacts with people outside psychology altogether. Colin Cherry, Professor of Telecommunications at Imperial College, was one such. He was a leading activist in the early days of information theory, and his students were often doing work that might just as well have been done in a psychological laboratory. I was quite often the external examiner for their Ph.D. theses. Indeed, for a number of years I examined more doctorates in electrical engineering than in psychology. Another and highly formative influence was Peter Ladefoged, a phonetician at the University of Edinburgh. His views on speech came, of course, from a very different background, but we resonated to each other so well that, across a distance of several hundred miles, we produced a whole series of joint experiments and papers. The profitable point to us was that Peter was primarily concerned with speech as such, whereas I was more generally concerned with human information processing. I found his detailed knowledge of speech vital in giving me a particular area to which I could apply my general ideas, while conversely I hope that he found the psychological approach helpful in letting him lay bare a number of the details of the perception of speech. I still regret bitterly his departure to the University of California at Los Angeles and wish we could have gone on collaborating for more than a few years.

Let me sum up these influences. First, we dealt with concrete human situations that psychologists appeared not to have studied. Second, we produced experimental results that were not easy to handle in traditional terms. Third, each of us was part of a close body of colleagues and friends who were generating such concepts, putting them to use, and getting along well with them. Fourth, we had a perspective of psychology that came from other scientific disciplines and from applied problems, so that we did not feel stuck to the forms of approach traditionally used. As the decade wore on, I found more and more that each experiment I published seemed to

59

make sense only in the light of the others I had done and in the light of the approaches all around me, from which I had learned so much. Yet, in most psychological journals, it was necessary to relate the paper to the older concepts and bodies of experiment, which seemed to have so little to do with the problems I met each day. Increasingly, I felt that I could only write about the particular work I had done on attention in the context of the whole sweep of the APU studies. So, in odd moments, I began to write a book rather than generate separate papers. I say odd moments, because I was still employed on short-term appointments, and technically, it was not at all clear that I could properly spend time during working hours doing something other than the research for which I was employed. I therefore did it in evenings and during weekends, on airplanes and trains, and at other times when it would have been impossible for me to do the direct naval work required by each of my short-term appointments. There was also the problem of getting a publisher. A long series of distinguished and well-advised firms turned down the manuscript, and only in the end did I find a new enterprise with a good deal of willingness to take a risk—Pergamon Press, which published *Perception and Communication* simultaneously on both sides of the Atlantic (Broadbent, 1958).

By the time the book appeared, I was really not much interested in its success, because Mackworth had, to my horror, announced his intention of emigrating to North America. The question was not whether anybody would read my book, but whether I would have a job. University posts in psychology were still extremely rare in Britain. One or two isolated lectureships had been established at smaller universities since my own undergraduate days, and Oxford was now going strong, perhaps particularly so in work on physiological psychology and learning theory. But there were only a few such posts, and in any case I did not particularly want to teach; yet there were still no sign of the jobs in directly applied psychology, for which I had originally come into the subject. Enviously, I looked across the Atlantic where the U.S. air force had adopted a contractual requirement that new aircraft should be examined by human-factors specialists. As a result, laboratories of the civil service, of private companies, and non-profit-making institutes had expanded enormously. The contrast with Britain was appalling. A few years later, I gave a radio broadcast that was reported in the press as saying that one American aircraft firm employed more psychologists than the whole of the British aviation industry. The report was in error; what I actually had said was that one American aircraft firm employed more psychologists than all British industry of all kinds and not merely of aviation!

At another conference, this one dedicated to examining the importance of human factors, the contribution from a well-known British automobile firm was to claim that human factors were unimportant. According to this firm, raw-material costs were far more important in the production process than costs of labor, and so, as far as the nature of the product was concerned, there was no difficulty in selling British cars; it was merely a problem of increasing productivity by engineering techniques. A continental firm, which at that time sold scarcely any cars in Britain, simply reported papers on the design of seats and controls; nowadays, their financial state is considerably superior to that of their British competitor.

It was clear, therefore, that my haven of like-minded colleagues and enjoyable work was highly fragile. I preferred to stay in Britain if I could. And, remember, this was the era of McCarthy, when one of my dearest and most anti-Communist friends, with decorations for wartime gallantry, had difficulty entering the United States because of his political allegiances. (When later admitted, he was nevertheless asked to take an oath of loyalty, which he very properly refused on the grounds that it was incompatible with his duty to Her Majesty the Queen.)

If I wanted to stay in Britain, however, the congenial environment of APU would need to be preserved. The MRC, almost unique among British institutions, was keen on applied psychology; it seemed likely that they would want to appoint a new director rather than abolish the unit. For most of a winter, there was anxiety and uncertainty. Then, while giving a colloquium in Ulster, I got a telegram saying that they wanted to appoint me as director. If I accepted, I would get tenure and a raise. I still do not know whether I was right to accept, but at the time it seemed impossible to do otherwise. I held the job for the next sixteen years.

Directing APU: The Initial Phase, 1958–1968

The problems of the job, at that point in time, turned out to be primarily political and administrative—fields in which I had no experience whatever. The unit had a good deal of technical equipment, probably more than any other laboratory in Europe at that time. Most of this came from the Royal Navy, for which the largest part of the work of the unit was performed. Perhaps most important, the supply of experimental subjects came from the navy, and in the days before payment of subjects and in a country where large introductory classes cannot be required to act as subjects to fulfill part of their course duties, the supply of subjects was completely vital. Bluntly, this meant that any failure to deliver the work the navy wanted would be very serious. In general terms, that was very agreeable to me; it meant that the work would have to have a practical orientation rather than an academic one, and that was great. Still, an operation with only one major customer was seriously at risk. The military ought to develop their own teams, and might well do so; British defense budgets were, in the long run, likely to get tighter, since the country was already embarked on the incredible operation of liquidating the largest empire in history in the shortest time on record. It was obvious that the MRC was worried about the dependence on outside customers; conversely, its continued support would depend on the unit's success in meeting the MRC obligation to advise other government departments. In those days, a unit director did not have very clear terms of reference; he had a lot of rope, but could quite well hang himself if he made the wrong decisions.

My guess was that the first essential was to make sure the navy got what it wanted. Next, we ought to look out for other customers, to diversify our sources of practical problems. Both these strategies meant that we would need an array of psychologists capable of tackling whatever problem the customers produced, rather than specializing (for example) in my own field of attention. This was perfectly practical, because we already had a wide range of people in the unit who covered most fields of human experimental psychology. Some of them, admittedly, left for the greener pastures of the United States, but in each case we could replace them with other people of similar scientific interests and thus keep going the projects that we had for the navy. It was relatively easy to find new projects of interest to the army that would fit the skills of the existing staff. And, by expanding the previous interests of Leonard and, especially, of Conrad, we were able to develop a profitable connection with the post office. The mechanization of the mails and the rapid developments of the telephone system were raising a number of problems in such areas as short-term memory and keyboard operation where we possessed the appropriate skills to make a contribution. Conrad, and Christopher Poulton, had been made assistant directors as fast as possible after my own appointment. We had all graduated at about the same time, and they possessed enormous treasures of scientific expertise as well as practical wisdom, which have been of great value to the unit.

A number of other, smaller customers soon came along, including British Rail and the commission on decimalization of the currency. The key problem in handling these various changes was that of limited resources—primarily, laboratory space. When I was appointed, the psychologists of the unit were housed not only in the main building, but also in rooms in the university, at a naval establishment in the town, and in trailers in the garden belonging to customer organizations. Over the next few years, our tenure on each of these overflows fell in; yet if we reduced our numbers, we could not keep up the breadth of scientific area that we needed for the general policy.

The MRC was sympathetic in each of these crises, purchasing the trailers themselves and putting up a hut in the garden. Yet our total space got smaller, and the research that seemed to please the navy most took up an increasing amount of it. We were beset by "sophistication factor" also: To stay in the international league meant many more technicians who needed housing. By 1966, the number of psychologists at APU had dropped to sixteen, only just over half its peak under Bartlett. Nor was applied psychology in better shape elsewhere. In 1949, there had been two other large MRC units in London and a psychological group within an anatomical unit in Oxford. All these had gone or were going by 1966. A civil-service group had been set up, but did not flourish as much as we had hoped. The universities were still relatively uninterested. The national output of psychologists of all kinds was only of the order of 100 per year in the early 1960s.

The aim for my own research was to pursue the topic of attention and, more generally, the cognitive aspects of applied psychology. This aim was not merely theoretical. I believed, with increasing urgency, that data in these areas would be badly needed in the coming era of the computer (Broadbent, 1961b). How could such systems be introduced with full efficiency if human thought processes were ignored? But, equally, the most advanced computer might have a bad keyboard, might be operated on the night shift, might produce an illegible printout. My own pet area could not be developed without solutions to these parallel and neighboring problems; nor were there other British groups, in the chilly atmosphere of the early 1960s, who could cover all these fields. APU had to maintain its general expertise, and expansion of my own interests could only come in step with a general expansion of applied psychology. Hence, every spare moment was used for general publicity for the subject. I appeared regularly on radio and television programs designed for the serious lay public, and I wrote a book (Broadbent, 1961a) that was intended to give the same audience a brief introduction to objective psychology and to learning theory. The name of Skinner was still almost unknown to the British public; I got him to speak to the British Association for the Advancement of Science, interviewed him on the radio, and did the same with Harry Harlow and other trans-Atlantic leaders. (Of course, I disagreed with what they said; but I wanted them to say it.) The meetings of the BA, incidentally, are some of my happiest memories; each year I watched Harry Maule and Denis McMahon combine genial personal warmth, sound scientific judgment, and a steady pressure to put psychology before the eyes of the world. I hope I learned half the skills they possess.

The period was not as grim and embattled as it may sound. It was impossible to live close to my colleagues at APU without becoming convinced that their work was outstanding and that it was bound to be recognized. Many were new—replacements for the emigrants—but they continued the sparkling excitement traditional in the Bartlett era.

Nor had my personal research been hindered. As director, I had for the first time a graduate assistant, Margaret Gregory, a lady with a medical degree incorporating the Cambridge psychology course. She rapidly proved that she was capable, not merely of turning out more experimental studies than I used to do alone, but also of spotting every shade of ambiguity in procedures, of unexpected strategies on the part of subjects, of looseness of thinking in theory. Her only vice was a reluctance to speak in public, so that always she did the work and I talked about it. Twenty years later, the process still continues, except that now we are married. Whatever is good in me, or in my children, we owe to her.

The experiments themselves were provoked by another lady, Anne Treisman, who took her first degree in Cambridge but then did her doctorate in Oxford and became a lecturer there. Anne produced a series of studies showing that unattended speech messages might nevertheless be correctly perceived, particularly if they were probable. These studies are often quoted in support of the view that a complete representation of the outside event is found inside the listener and that selective attention only operates later. But her detailed results are inconsistent with that view. She herself argued that partial and fragmentary information from the unattended channel was provoking a percept that was reconstructive and not the result of a perfect transmission of information.

In my other area of prolonged vigilance, particularly in noise, Anne did no studies herself, but pointed out, in a memorable conversation, that some of my results might be due to changes in the confidence attached to a percept, rather than the actual intake of information. Margaret and I began to look at confidence ratings and, thus, to think about the theory of signal detection put forward by Spike Tanner and John Swets (1954). This theory, like Anne's, made a distinction between the unreliable evidence entering the perceptual mechanism and the decision criterion that produced an output from that evidence. By analysis of the error patterns, Tanner and Swets could distinguish the two. I had thought of their work as a rarefied piece of psychophysics important for precise measurement with highly trained observers, but I had not seen its application to real-world situations. However, when we tried similar studies with sailors, the effects were gross and highly counterintuitive. Tiny changes in error rate controlled enormous changes in correct detections; much of the change in signal detection after prolonged work, or in noise, was due to changes of the decision criterion and not of the intake of information.

In experiments on division of attention, the same techniques showed up Anne's double mechanisms of selection. Dividing attention between the two ears changes one of the parameters in the Tanner and Swets model; hearing probable rather than improbable words changes the other. Looking about me at the work of my colleagues and of human-factors people elsewhere, I could see the same antithesis; many effects on decision latency go with changes of error rate, revealing that they are criterion changes. Others do not and appear therefore to be changes in the analysis of the input information. In the field of memory, my old master Bartlett had used false recall to show the reconstructive character of the process. Modern studies could be analyzed in the same way. The simple determinate model of 1958 needed to be modified, to take account of randomness inside the system and of the strategies a person uses to secure efficient response despite that randomness.

In 1967–1968, I took a year's leave of absence to write down these thoughts and also simply to recover from the stress of the "front-office side" of my job. The book drafted at that time appeared three years later (Broadbent, 1971) and provoked horror at its complexity. To sustain the general thesis fairly, I found that each area of application had to be reviewed in detail, and that made it easy for the reader to lose the forest in the trees. It was good that the grand design of Anne's ideas would stand confrontation with the nuts and bolts of each set of experiments, but the amount of literature had increased so much since 1958 that a detailed review was scarcely readable. Perhaps the main merit of the book was to provide a background and point of departure for clearer summaries such as that of Danny Kahneman (1973).

At all events this was a year for taking stock. Suddenly, the logjam had broken. The universities of Britain were expanding enormously, and their students were clamoring for psychology. By 1973, the annual output of psychology students was in thousands rather than the single hundred of ten years previously. Many of them were to be taught by ex-APU staff whose talents were now indeed getting their just reward. (About half the 1963 staff are now of professor or similar level, which means more in Britain than it does in the United States.) An MRC committee had decided in 1967 that the council itself needed more work of this kind, and steps were in hand to increase APU space. Another unit was to open in Sheffield, at first directed by Harry Kay and later by Peter Warr. I personally was granted a D.Sc. by Cambridge in 1965 (never having gotten a Ph.D.) and, in 1968, was elected to the Royal Society. Now, in a warmer atmosphere for psychology, the time might be ripe for my dream of more studies of judgment, decision, and cognition in applied situations.

The Impasse

It was not to be. The great expansion of psychology was good, but from my point of view, there were definite snags. The expansion was of university departments, not of applied groups. About fifty well-equipped, and sometimes splendidly housed, university schools shifted the main center of the subject firmly toward conceptual and theoretical problems, rather than practical and empirical ones. There were exceptional university groups at Aston, Loughborough, and the University of Wales who were specifically applied, but they were outnumbered by conventional academics. There was still no equivalent of Bell Labs, of Bolt Beranek and Newman, Inc., or of institutes such as those at Michigan or Stanford.

This is the point at which to state my own ambivalence about the academic "cognitive psychology" that has flourished for the last decade. It took its name from the brilliant, short, and lucid synthesis of Dick Neisser (1966). It made respectable, I hope forever, the discussion of internal representations, structures, and processes in human function. It was reinforced powerfully by formulations of genius in linguistics (Chomsky, 1957) and in artificial intelligence (Newell and Simon, 1972). But it was certainly academic rather than applied and, *for that reason,* contained serious intellectual weaknesses. It could slip over into excessive rationalism, where theories were devised for behavior that human beings do not in fact show, or into a mandarinlike concern with small, experimental paradigms. And, in many hands, it suggested that all human cognition had a similar general structure. Yet experiment showed increasingly that individuals used different cognitive strategies and sometimes changed between them, even in apparently simple perceptual situations. Even Skinner at his most provocative and simplistic had not denied human diversity as much as some cognitive theorists did.

Some of the generous-hearted young, for good motives, reacted to this denial by rejecting academic psychology in favor of experiential approaches. Others were bemused by the siren song of elegant syntactic rules into neglecting the empirical question of whether Mrs. Jones, a welfare claimant, really does understand the equivalence of active and passive sentences in her application form. There were also, as always, political overtones; discussions of empirical fact could be criticized as ignoring questions of value or class advantage. To some extent, they do. Not as much, however, as abstract statements that fail to say concretely how resources are to be allocated, which persons should receive which benefits, and what accounting will be made for funds used on behalf of the community. The experiences of my generation had taught us to suspect value statements that ignored such empirical questions; a new generation had not yet learned the lesson.

I developed these themes in a series of lectures at Harvard, and these were later published with some others of a similar type (Broadbent, 1973). From a psychological point of view, the key emphasis was on "strategy." The same computer can behave in different ways, depending on its software; cognitive processes are flexible and a search for *the* model of sentence comprehension is doomed to failure. In the long run, psychology will, like computer science, become an ever-expanding exploration of the merits and disadvantages of alternative cognitive strategies. It will not, like anatomy, describe a mechanism completely and then call a halt to further advance.

In the meantime, APU was still needed to cope with problems of display, control, and abnormal environment. The stationary years left us with a backlog of senior people with international reputations, but without graduate assistance or graduate students. In the universities, more junior academics were better off, so urgent action was necessary to redress the balance. We opened outstations in Oxford, in Sussex, and in another house in Cambridge. The number of scientific staff came back up to the twenty we had had in 1958. Still, adding up the space and the people left no room for more researches in my personal area.

At the same time, the "front-office job" got worse. Luckily, I could talk to Margaret outside working hours. But in three years there were only two days in which I managed an afternoon spent on my own research. The problem was partly the various technicalities of increasing the staff members, but much more the need to democratize our decisionmaking. By 1969, scientists were less inclined to accept a single representative presenting their case to the outside world than they had been in 1960. Besides, APU now had many more senior people, and it was clearly appropriate for them to deal with their own customers and put forward their own proposals to MRC. To devise a structure that would be fair to each of the various staff levels and scientific interests was, however, difficult and time-consuming. I think we succeeded, thanks again to the general wisdom and goodwill of the whole APU staff. But it was an essentially political, not a scientific, activity.

There was a more subtle problem that one observation can illustrate. Personally courteous and considerate as always, my colleagues often apologized if they took up my time by wanting an interview. But I noticed, after a while, that they did so only if they wanted to discuss a scientific point; never did anyone apologize for asking me to query their salary with MRC, to approach the navy to secure facilities for their experiment, or to solve their difficulty in getting equipment they wanted from the workshop. They saw administration as my job now, on which I *ought* to spend time.

The day I was sure of that, I knew I had to go. To meet the formal position that MRC units are supposed to be personal support of a director (though APU, of course, never had been), I gave three years' warning that I would depart in 1974. The council could then make sure they still wanted the unit, of which I had no doubt whatever, and pick another director. Wisely, they chose Alan Baddeley, one of the staff members of the 1958–1968 decade, who had gone on to Sussex and then to Stirling. Remember that I had solved the problem of choosing names to mention at APU by picking *none* of them, because all were creative, energetic, and likable. But if I had chosen a few, Alan would have been among them. His return as director has already been a stimulus, a refreshment, and a source of strength. Those who want to know more should look at the annual list of reports that the unit circulates each year: It goes from strength to strength.

A Moment to Look Forward

A happy ending? Rather, a beginning. I got the facilities I had long wanted to expand my personal research. And, as well as Margaret and myself, the MRC supports at present another assistant for my basic program and two for an applied project. Two SSRC postdoctorals work with me, and there are a number of graduate students. The MRC rents space for us from the University of Oxford, so that I am surrounded by the very best physiological, social, and developmental psychologists, as well as by cognitive people and a sympathetic psychiatry department. I need no more! The time has come, with a third of my career to go, to put up or shut up. What are we going to do?

The theory of attention is reaching one of its periodic leaps forward. Laboratory experiments throughout the world are separating out several kinds of process, related to Anne Treisman's distinctions, but at a new level (Broadbent, 1977a). The selection of particular inputs and of particular items in memory must, according to any analysis by the methods of artifical intelligence, play a crucial part in the control of long sequences of behavior (Newell and Simon, 1972; Broadbent, 1977b). Conceptually and empirically, therefore, psychology is beginning to touch the problems of autonomy and self-control. The possible patterns of organization are revealed in the alternative strategies that subjects show in our experiments. The key problem for research is to find external and observable variables that correlate with these strategies.

Most people spend eight hours a day at their work. The patterns of information processing that they repeat, time and time again, may well be reflected in the strategies they use outside their jobs. Already there is evidence that mental health differs from one occupation to another and that the type of healthy personality does likewise. Therefore, besides the laboratory analysis of attentional and memory strategies, we are also looking at assembly-line workers, press operators, and executives.

Looking back, my main sadness is that the fields of human factors and occupational psychology never fulfilled their early promise. And the process has gotten worse in recent years. The National Institute for Industrial Psychology has collapsed financially, and more civil-service groups have gone. As I have said, I believe that situation is responsible for certain intellectual weaknesses among the strengths of theoretical psychology. But there were two main reasons: First, we engineering psychologists took too limited a scope and did not think about jobs rather than individual displays and controls. Second, social needs have changed; it is the impact of the job on life that is now the big problem, not the efficiency of the worker. If we remember these lessons, occupational psychology may still take the place in general psychology that I believe the subject needs.

At all events, I leave you now with the same ending Kenneth Craik put in his 1943 book: *Tentari!*

1977

Selected Publications by Donald E. Broadbent

Perception and communication. London: Pergamon Press, 1958.

Behaviour. London: Eyre and Spottiswoode, 1961a.

The future of ergonomics. *Proc. DSIR Conf. Ergonomics in Industry.* London: H.M.S.O., 1961b.

Decision and stress. London: Academic Press, 1971.

In defence of empirical psychology. London: Methuen, 1973.

The hidden preattentive processes. *Amer. Psychologist,* 1977a, *32,* 109–118.

Levels, hierarchies and the locus of control. *Quart. J. exp. Psychol.,* 1977b, *29,* 181–201.

Other Publications Cited

Bartlett, F. C. *Remembering.* Cambridge: Cambridge University Press, 1932.

Chomsky, N. *Syntactic structures.* The Hague: Mouton & Co., 1957.

Craik, K. J. W. *The nature of explanation.* Cambridge: Cambridge University Press, 1943.

Davis, D. R. *Pilot error.* Air Publication 3139a. London: H.M.S.O., 1948.

Grindley, G. C. The formation of a simple habit in guinea-pigs. *British J. Psychol.,* 1932, *23,* 127–147.

Hick, W. E. On the rate of gain of information. *Quart. J. exp. Psychol.,* 1952, *4,* 11–26.

Hilgard, E. R., and D. G. Marquis. *Conditioning and learning.* New York: Appleton-Century, 1940.

Kahneman, D. *Attention and effort*. Englewood Cliffs, N.J.: Prentice-Hall, 1973.

Mackworth, N. H. *Researches in the measurement of human performance*. MRC Special Report Series 268. London: H.M.S.O., 1950.

Neisser, U. *Cognitive psychology*. New York: Appleton-Century-Crofts, 1966.

Newell, A., and H. A. Simon, *Human problem solving*. Englewood Cliffs, N.J.: Prentice Hall, 1972.

Oldfield, R. C. Some experiments bearing on internal inhibition. *British J. Psychol.*, 1937, *28*, 28–42.

Tanner, W. P., and J. A. Swets, A decision-making theory of visual detection. *Psychol. Rev.*, 1954, *61*, 401–409.

Watson, J. D. *The double helix*. London: Weidenfeld and Nicholson, 1968.

Woodworth, R. S. *Experimental psychology*. New York: Holt, 1938.

Jerome S. Bruner

I had started this adventure in autobiography in the hope that I might somehow manage to weave together the personal, the early, the "primitive" in my life with the less personal, more intellectual, more directional. But such a process of weaving is so much like the constructing of myths! One inevitably renders everything not so much explicable as, at least, "reasonable" or "compatible." It is very "reasonable" that somebody who had been born blind, with sight restored at age two, should initially have been interested in the part of psychology about perception, should have maintained that interest throughout his life. Why, then, did I never study the blind themselves (displacement?) or why did I, in effect, use the study of perception as an entry port into the investigation of motivation and cognition? A good myth can be made about that, too, this time based on cultural background. Perhaps it was the skepticism of the Judeo-Christian tradition that led me to opt for the study of the relation between appearance and reality and man's capacity for self-deception, rather than the Hellenic assumption that man is the measure. Did the skeptical seed grow in the soil of a secular, unreligious Jewish background? Perhaps. In the end, I find myself in a posture not unlike that of the New Criticism in literature: One had better understand the poem as an entity, a product in itself, rather than as a growth from the thicket of the poet's psychic life. It is not that I do not believe in "psychohistory" or the psychological side of intellectual autobiography. Rather, the effort to understand ideas in their web—whether in my own psychoanalysis over several years, or retrospectively now—is not much helped by tracing their personal roots. The ideas, once sprung, have a reality of their own. Perhaps this was what Yeats meant when, late in life, he wrote:

> *Players and painted stage took all my love*
> *And not those things that they were emblems of.*

Let me give a specific example. I recall reading Stout as an undergraduate—at the urging of the already quite aged William McDougall—and coming upon his famous discussion of anoetic sentience: Is perception autonomous, unwilled, independent of the rest of the operation of mind, or is it the instrument of a will to perceive or to know particular things with some end in mind? I was twenty-one at the time, just beginning to read in that cumulative way that provides a quieter excitement. I recall the high drama I found in this dilemma—whether knowing was selective and relative or whether it fell indifferently like rain. Why did I find this so compelling a matter? Was I a child of my time, sensitized by the then-current issues of relativism? Perhaps. Indeed, I had been to a lecture by Margaret Mead, had met and talked with her, and been enchanted. Or that blindness? Or the force and grace with which Stout argued his point against anoetic sentience? Or was it the Jew in me looking for a way of rejecting all received wisdoms as reflecting the prejudices of bigots? Or was it that I had turned to radical politics in that period of the Spanish Civil War and, as part of it, was ready to adopt the view that knowledge was something cooked up by the powerful and fobbed off as self-evident on the oppressed? I recall a friend of mine who believed that—Sheldon Harte, a gentle soul who, of all unlikely things, became Trotsky's bodyguard and was murdered in Mexico City when that dissenter was done down. I have no idea whether any of these or even deeper things predisposed me to take the positions that I took, or why I found such supporting resonance in Plato's image of the prisoner in the cave. All I know is that once a few initial premises were laid down, the play of the ideas and their logic took over just as surely as Yeats' "players and painted stage."

So I shall keep psychological explanation of my psychology to a minimum. Perhaps it is that I do not understand myself as well as I might, but that is not for lack of trying! I know I went more easily one way than another. But I don't know why. Kenneth Spence once told me that, had I come to him for graduate work, he would have made me into a first-class "behavior theorist." I know he was wrong!

Isaiah Berlin wrote a lovely little book that began with the parable from Aristarchus: "The fox knows many things. The hedgehog knows one big thing." Temperamentally, I am a fox where psychology is concerned. Of that much I am *sure*.

I was born on October 1, 1915, in New York. My father was a prosperous manufacturer of watches, a business at which he did well so that I never had a financial worry even after his death, in my twelfth year, for he left me a trust fund that took care of my education quite independently of family fortunes. He was a witty man, a man nonetheless of strong convictions. He had come to America from a part of Poland that had been alternately Russian and Austrian, arriving in his early manhood with neither friends nor fortune, a draft dodger from the Imperial Czarist Army. He was an antireligious Jew who believed, indeed, that religion was not only an opiate but a breeder of hypocrisy. He saw in America the source of a fresh start not only for himself, but for the world. He believed in energy and intention and high ideals—as in the Ethical Culture Society which he admired but did not join. We lived in a prosperous exurb of New York, Far Rockaway (which has since been virtually engulfed by suburbia). I recall going to the village, at the age of eight, at his request for the *New York Sun* (it was one of those rare days when he had not gone into "the city" on the 8:12) and returning instead with the *New York Journal*, a Hearst paper. He brought me into his library and told me with gravity that I must never bring that paper into the house again, that William Randolph Hearst, in order to sell his papers, had tricked Americans into the Spanish–American War and that guilt for the war dead rested on Hearst's head. My mother, Rose, whom my father had married only a year before fleeing Europe, had been married previously, a union that had sadly ended when her husband died on a business trip to Berlin, leaving her six-months pregnant. They had a daughter of their own shortly after, fourteen years my senior and, in a working sense, my foster mother, Min.

My half-brother and my sister were their "family," when quite by surprise my sister Alice was born twelve years after the family was supposed to have been "complete." My mother believed firmly that children should be raised in pairs. I was planned, born two years later, the issue of a hypothesis!

My childhood was carefree, full of friends and reading and wandering around the salt marshes on the South Shore of Long Island. My mother was interested in my sister's and my health but was, I realized years later, rather bored with raising another brace of young children. She ran a biggish house, with generous help, and it was rather a sanctuary, not only for family cats and dogs but for the odd strays they attracted. Europe was never far away. My father had entered into partnership with his brother, who manufactured watch cases, while he made the movements. This he did in a factory in Switzerland to which he traveled often; I have strong memories of the excitement of seeing him off and, to this day names like *Leviathan, Aquitania, Homeric,* and *Berengaria* conjure up winter departures from the great piers on New York's North River. And there were distant cousins who came from Poland, Germany, France, and England either as immigrants (often to work for my father) or as visitors.

When my father died, in the cold February of 1927, after a year of cancer during which I had come to know him better than when he had been well and busy, I was bereaved and crushed. He had treated me flatteringly as an equal. He would report on what he was reading and would solicit and respect my views—indeed, restate them in a way that always made me prouder of my points than I had proper reason to be. My mother, freed by my father's death of the duties of the house, children, and entertaining, found her own way. We moved often, went off to Florida winters, at first luxuriously and, after the Stock Market crash, much less so. In my high school years, I attended six different schools, took more and more to the water—"messing about in boats"—and by the time, at sixteen, I went off to Duke University as an undergraduate, I was quite prepared to be on my own. About water, I do not know how I became a "water rat," but in good time the taste became functionally autonomous. Aside from brief holiday visits, my "family life" ended then. Because my father and his brother had had a bitter business quarrel just before his illness, I did not see my cousins until many years later, though we had been close. When I came home, it was to "catch up" with my sisters and brother and to help my mother keep her practical affairs in smooth running order. My family attachment became emotionally loosened for a decade, save with my elder sister, my "working mother" to whom I have always felt an attachment that is full of warmth and mutual respect, though we share few interests. For most of her life, she has done a man's job of running a lighting-fixture factory jointly with her husband, while being very much a mother to her two children and a foster mother to her younger brother—though my projects and politics must have seemed most improbable to her!

Going off to college, then, was a critical point in my life— the shedding of an old skin for a new. It also brought to an end a long period of mourning for my father. I recall that, in my seventeenth or eighteenth year, I went to a performance of Handel's *Messiah* in Duke chapel. The classic lines from Matthew rang out, "The trumpets shall sound and the dead shall be raised, be raised incorruptible." I did not weep: the tears simply flowed, as if unstopped. I walked the twilit, winter-chilled, alien North Carolina town for two hours afterwards. I cannot remember anything except loneliness and relief. Before my years there at Duke were done, it had become my place, full of well-known corners, full of shared ideas and gossip, timid love affairs, voracious politics. My war with my mother's detachment was over, my yearning for my father and his commitment was transferred into a world of ideas and music and books and people. It was quite by accident that I became a psychologist. There might have been other doors standing open at that moment. The academic life (in the sense that it took during the 1930s) beckoned. It provided a new identity.

That this identity happened to be psychology was partly the place, partly the people, partly the times. I had gone to Duke, vaguely expecting I would go into the law (with the image of our much respected family lawyer in mind, who administered my trust fund) and vaguely thinking I would shop around. Mostly, I saw college as an opportunity to be independent, on my own. My introduction to psychology was through William McDougall—worldly, rather plodding in lecture style, with bursts of wit, an impeccable and alien figure one could see walking the college paths in heavy tweeds even as winter turned into spring. It did not "grab" me, his introduction to psychology: rather too patly argued and not enough questions left. It was the second stage that was to get me engaged: a course a year later in comparative psychology with Donald Keith Adams, one in neuropsychology with Karl Zener, and another in animal behavior with the zoologist A. S. Pearse, as well as laboratory courses in comparative anatomy and embryology. Adams and Zener were fresh returned from Berlin where they had worked with Köhler, Wertheimer, and the budding young Kurt Lewin. Zener had just translated Lewin's *Dynamic Theory of Personality,* and the next year he lectured on it. The first dispute within psychology of which I became aware was between Thorndike's interpretation of his cats' behavior in puzzle boxes as trial-and-error-*cum*-reinforcement and Adams' monograph on adaptive behavior in cats which stressed the importance of structurable experimental situations into which the animal might, in effect, gain "insights" relevant to solution. As Adams put it, it is possible to design environments that can make their inhabitants "look stupid." The difference between Thorndike's cats (or, years later, Guthrie and Horton's) and Adams' was that, in the first situation, there was a detached, isolated string hanging down from the middle of the ceiling (which, if pulled, miraculously caused a gate to open or a bit of food to enter), whereas with

Adams' cats there was a patent, visible connection between the end of the dangling string and the rest of its environment, including the latch. Thorndike's animals were sampling the situation for loose ends, stimuli that evoked some prepared response. Adams' were scanning as well, but in a perceptually connected environment. In the Thorndike case, there was little to do *but* move about in seeming random trial and error. It is a curious thing about these early "paradigms" or "metaphors" in one's thoughts that one never knows, literally, where they will lead one. Shades of the Thorndike–Adams controversy led me to a "hypothesis theory" of perceptual recognition two decades later, which in turn led Noam Chomsky (as he once reported) to the notion of a Language Acquisition Device that generated hypotheses about well-formed utterance strings.

I finished my undergraduate course work on the double and started graduate school a year early. The Krechevsky–Spence debate on continuity–discontinuity in learning was on the scene. Tolman gave a paper at Duke on "vicarious trial and error," and Kenneth Spence gave one at Knoxville (to the Southern Society for Psychology and Philosophy) on the transposition effect and its base in summed generalization gradients. I also started helping Karl Zener in his work on Pavlovian conditioning in dogs, measuring salivation as the dogs worked around a barrier to get to the food delivery. I had, a couple of years before, got into a row with the college administration about compulsory chapel, which I refused to attend, and was suspended from college; McDougall had saved my skin by "vouching" for me, and for the rest of that year, I helped him in his Lamarckian experiments. It was that trying experience over chapel that, I think, had quite inadvertently "personalized" the Department for me. No undergraduate (or, indeed, no first-year graduate student) could have been luckier in his choice of a Department.

My entry into the life of that lively university was, in fact, a conversion experience. I had found my identity as an adult. I became a "university man." I became a psychologist, too. These things were vague in my mind then; they became clearer. I remained a university man—and when there were moments of temptation to go off into other, related lines of endeavor, I have either refused or gone with a "leave of absence," permission having been granted.

Goodrich and Knapp have written about the conditions that lure students into a career in psychology, and I suspect that I fit one of their conditions well—recruitment by having gotten involved directly in research with a respected teacher. In that last year at Duke, my imprinting on "teacher birds" was fulsome! With the zoologist Bert Cunningham, I began an undergraduate project on hormonal control of sexual behavior in the female rat. It was to be my first published paper—in the *Journal of Comparative Psychology* in 1939. It was an unsophisticated piece of work from the biochemical point of view, but it hooked me on the way of life of research. Hooking, I think, is greatly aided by the mastering of techniques. I learned to reduce whole thymus glands sent frozen from Armour's in Chicago into an aqueous solution of thymocrescin according to a method devised by Rowntree, learned to do vaginal smears and track the oestrous cycle, learned to care for and medicate my animals, devised a behavior inventory for assessing the response of the females to test males, learned to rummage around in the literature. And, en route, I learned the joys of spending the hours before midnight in Cunningham's lab, testing my animals, getting to know the band of young zoologists working on *their* research during those same "unsocial" hours. Riding my bike back to my room over the midnight-empty, two-mile road, my head was full of half-worked-out speculations. Does the thymus, in fact, secrete a substance that *enforces* immaturity, blocks the emergence of adult sexual behavior? And how does a block work? I recall one thought by analogy that particularly excited me: Apparent visual movement obeying Korte's laws depends upon a nervous system tuned in a particular way to translate a display as moving. Might it be the case that a change in biochemical tuning of the nervous system of my female rats led them to "see" the adult male rat in a particular way? Adams had suggested that Köhler's chimpanzees came to *see* a bush not as a bush but as a "treasury" of sticks to be used for raking in a bit of fruit. I asked Adams what he thought, and he, provocative teacher that he was, gave me Mach's *Analysis of Sensation* to read.

I turned next to matters closer to home. I had the good fortune to do a research project with T. L. McCulloch, fresh from Yale, and Clark Hull, the resident behaviorist in the Duke lab. We devised a "quarrelsome" little experiment. Martin Seligman says that it was the earliest study he was able to find on conditioned helplessness. It came to pass in a curious way. Working in McDougall's lab, I had become acquainted with his water maze. It was a two-choice apparatus—the animal being put into a tank of cold water, having then to swim to the right or to the left, to choose between a lighted ramp or a dark ramp by which to escape from the water onto a dry platform. If he chose the wrong ramp, he received a walloping shock. I had noticed that some animals did the task with a fair amount of swimming back and forth to "con" the two ramps before choosing, whereas others simply turned one way and charged the ramp, whether it happened to be lighted or not. Anthropomorphically, it looked as if rats differed in their "confidence" about being able to solve the problem. Could one affect this "confidence" directly? This was seen by me, somehow, as an attack on "simple reinforcement." Now, suppose rat litters were divided into groups that received controlled prior experience outside the water maze—one group under conditions in which they could do nothing about a shock except "freeze," the other control group receiving the same handling but with no shock. And as it turned out, the "shocked-helpless" animals not only took much longer to learn the simple light–dark discrimination, but also showed far less swimming back and forth to inspect the alternatives. It was not a world-shattering experiment, nor did I understand its implications as fully as I might have later, but what it got me started on was important for me. I came to think of motivation not as an impelling drive state, but as something that affected how one picked up information about the environment. Years later, the ideas that were born then cropped up in studies on breadth of learning as a function of drive state and, of course, in the work on perceptual vigilance and defense.

My time at Duke, my postconversion seminary, was coming to an end. My friends there were either moving on or, if staying, urging me to greener pastures elsewhere. Tom McCulloch and Donald Adams urged me to try Yale and, particularly, to work with Robert Yerkes (for though I had dabbled a bit with studies of people, I seemed to be a confirmed animal psychologist). Karl Zener strongly urged Harvard. It had never occurred to me that *either* place would have me! In fact, I was influenced by the odd confluence of two books I read that spring—Kurt Koffka's *Principles of Gestalt Psychology* and Gordon Allport's *Personality*. Both of them, in quite different ways, lured me away from research on animals and that favored Harvard. But I applied to both places and was accepted by both. Irrational choice processes began to work. Harvard was associated in my mind not only with William but with Henry James and with the kind of intellectual purity that was symbolized by Peirce and Santayana (I read his *The Last Puritan* that same spring). And at Harvard, too, were Cannon, Lashley, and a variety of other prima ballerinas of the spirit. Yale, I shamefully confess, was associated in my unconscious with adolescent figures like the Merriwell brothers. (Did Tom Swift go there?) When I went to see Yerkes, I felt little intellectual resonance; charming and likable, he was more a naturalist than a tester of hypotheses. Finally, I asked McDougall for his advice, and he graciously had me to tea in his garden where he warned me that Harvard was implacably antimentalist and reductionist. Only Oxford was worse, in his opinion! I learned only later how rough a ride he'd had at Harvard.

Graduate School at Harvard

Early in the autumn of 1938, I arrived in Cambridge, Massachusetts, and enrolled as a graduate student at Harvard. I had spent the summer in a tiny French Canadian village, reading and walking and canoeing, often spending evenings talking with a militant railroad shop steward from Montreal, a man of enormous integrity named Cory Kilcupp. I had landed there by ordained chance. Wanting a summer to collect myself, I had started from New York with two suitcases—one with clothes, the other with books. I went as far as I could into the Laurentians, got off and found a family who would take in as a boarder for a month or so, Kilcupp's aging parents. I had with me Bechterev's *Principles of Reflexology,* Köhler's *Mentality of Apes,* McDougall's *Outline of Psychology,* Joyce's *Portrait of the Artist as a Young Man,* Coghill's *The Problem of Behavior.* What else? Bechterev was the one I struggled against most. It had a fierce finality about it, a reductionism that I found fascinating and enragingly detestable: much the same reaction I had had when, in the autumn before my first graduate year at Duke, I had attended my first APA meeting at Dartmouth College and heard Clark Hull deliver a paper on "Mind, Mechanism, and Behavior." In any case, when I arrived in Cambridge, I was full of psychology, very "ready," yet not quite knowing what to expect.

It was perfect. There was, first of all, our group of graduate students: Bill Prentice, Dorwin Cartwright, and Mason Haire from Swarthmore (who had actually studied with Köhler!); the studious and droll John Harding, Fillmore Sanford, Alfred Baldwin, Jack Levine, Don McGranahan, and a charming Alabama niece of the Bankheads, Jeannie Graves (whose grandmother had cautioned her that she should always spend as much on books and music as she did on her food). There was no proseminar going in those days, so we organized our own and prepared weekly papers in multiple carbons for each other. We lunched together every day in our own "enlisted men's mess" in Emerson Hall, much as "the faculty," in another room, had lunch of sandwiches of cheese and meat, and vile coffee—a custom that had become established when Boring had developed ulcers some years before and could not lunch at the Faculty Club. Then there was a set of "junior officers," the younger faculty, who would drift into our lunchroom to argue with us, having left the senior officers' mess a little early—Clifford Morgan, Smitty Stevens, Leo Hurvich, Irven Child. The big guys were always there, but rather at a distance of polite reserve: Gordon Allport, E. G. Boring, Jack Beebe-Center, Robert White; while some of the more "remote" members, like Henry Murray and K. S. Lashley, would come only occasionally.

What was extraordinary about Harvard psychology at that time was its cohesiveness as a community. The "teaching" took the form, principally, of an apprentice relationship, the debate was incessant and remarkably good-natured in spirit, and the sharing of interests was virtually complete—at least as far as the graduate students were concerned. Whatever we were to turn into later, we were psychological graduate students first: We all went together to Kurt Goldstein's seminar on brain and behavior, to Bob White's on "lives in progress," to Gordon Allport's on the life history, to Smitty Stevens' on operationism, to Köhler's William James lectures, to Professor Boring's on sensation and perception, to Kurt Lewin's on topological psychology. After hours, we argued, all of us, about Lashley's equipotentiality, Allport's functional autonomy, Boring's *Zeitgeist*, Stevens' attributes of tones, Murray's alpha and beta press, Bill Sheldon's somatotypes. In the manner of our mentors, we wrote endlessly at papers and, one year, were terribly "snob" when we totted it up and found that the graduate students had published as much as the faculty. We were sure, dead sure, that we were the chosen of the next generation of psychology, and the list of past doctorates posted at the center of the corridor only served to reassure us that this must be so: our own Boring, Stevens, Allport, etc., but also Thorndike, Tolman, Skinner, Hoagland, Wever, Bray, etc., etc. Nowadays, it would be considered a terrible elitist display. Then, it reinforced our sense that this was the place where the future of psychology was being shaped, as the past had been shaped before. It surely led to ideas being taken seriously, and it made a powerful impression on all of us that the senior members treated what we had to say with respect and commented on it in full, critically, and even stylistically. Boring and Allport, particularly, were watchdogs in their approach to language, the latter's celebrated "awk" in the margin being particularly dreaded.

Professor Boring proclaimed his famous dictum to us about the Harvard graduate student's "eighty-hour week." Indeed, so it was. After dining, we would often go back to the lab, usually to find the junior faculty there, notably Smitty Stevens and Leo Hurvich—reading in Robbins Library, analyzing data, running subjects, going to seminars of our own or of the faculty, visiting, or otherwise. We *did* spend an eighty-hour week, but it was more a club than a workplace. Smitty Stevens was a key figure in all this, and while we knew that some of the

senior members, notably Allport and Murray, found him de-
plorably "narrow" as a psychologist (and he probably was), his
enormous virtue was in bringing his marvelously crotchety enthusiasm (or peevishness) to bear on any subject anybody
would raise—intellectual, political, artistic. His consistency was
total and maddening. I recall his telling me, while we were
playing pool at Billings and Stover between dinner and the
lab, that my fondness for Bach was that it was all "second-
component music" just like me, good somatotonia! But Stevens would tackle any subject with you: nothing was beneath
contempt or above suspicion. His sneers were *ad rem*, never *ad
hominem*. In the interest of his point of view, he would bully,
bait, and even sulk. And he expected the same in return. He
was not everybody's dish, but he was a superb comrade in
arms.

The "prelims," the exams we took at the end of our first
year, forced us to go more broadly than we do now in psychology. It was possible then. And we were a close group. I
shared a flat on Oxford Street with Mason Haire, Willie Carroll (the physiologist), and "Flash" Bernstone, a witty but un-
decided Coloradan who was not to find his way into psychology and was probably put off by the zealots around him.

For all the internal scholarly (and social) intensity, the
world was coming apart during those idyllic three years of
study, discussion, and research. It may well have been in the
very nature of that situation that we, as a group, should have
been so close, "traveling lightly armed before the disintegrat-
ing sea." Hitler was going from triumph to triumph, America
was withdrawn in isolation, Europe seemed supine and cor-
rupt before the troubles. At Harvard, President Conant and
Ralph Barton Perry established the Committee on the Present
Danger, in which I became involved, as well as with the Harvard Teachers Union (for I was also a teaching assistant in the
introductory course given in alternate terms by Boring and
Allport, and the tutors as well). My flirtation with the Communist Party ended soon after my arrival in Cambridge. I was
very much Left in my sympathies and made friends with the
group around the Marxist bookshop in the Square. But aside
from F. O. Matthiesen and Granville Hicks, I found them
smugly self-satisfied with a line that, after a bit, could be al-

together too easily predicted at any turn of events. I drifted away and, perhaps because Gordon Allport served as my tutor to the local scene, found myself increasingly concerned that America take its place against Hitler and fascism. When it came time for my thesis, I was sufficiently involved in the war to choose as my topic the analysis of the propaganda broadcasting of belligerent nations, and I spent the summer of 1940 at Princeton with Hadley Cantril and Lloyd Free, establishing (on the model of the BBC unit in London) a foreign broadcast monitoring service that specialized in techniques for extracting intelligence data both from "spot" materials and from changes in trends (such as the shift from adjectives of "strength/weakness" to ones relating to "morality/immorality" in commentaries on communiqués as signaling changed estimates of battles going from good to bad). My thesis was a detailed analysis of several episodes—like the *Altmark* boarding by the Royal Navy in Norwegian waters, all but forgotten save by students of naval warfare —and the patterns of broadcasting of the opposing parties. We were able to get at the worldwide broadcasts of the contending parties because our venture included the setting up of a powerful monitoring station "well out in the Atlantic"—in fact, near San Turce, Puerto Rico. Within a week of finishing my thesis, I was on my way to Washington, D.C., to go to work for the group that had been set up officially to carry on the work there: the Foreign Broadcast Intelligence Service of the FCC.

That year of writing the thesis in Cambridge was a particularly rich one personally—my first year of married life. My wife was Katherine Frost, a gentle Maine Yankee with a genius for order. She was the department secretary and Gordon Allport's editorial assistant. Our courtship had been in the familial context of Emerson Hall and the nearby haunts of Boston—Symphony Hall, Jake Wirth's—and at the endless round of parties our "gang" seemed to generate. She quickly and easily won me over to ordered domesticity. Her background in literary history and her tastes had led her into editing: I have never seen a gift to match hers in rendering a manuscript into a form more directly expressive of the author's ultimate intent.

In the summer of 1939, after finishing a rather strenuous

statistical analysis, with Gordon Allport, of changes in psychology in the decade of the 1930s (for his presidential address to the APA), I went off to Europe for the first time with my good friend Leo Hurvich. It was a moving trip that summer on the edge of war, and it was for me something of a return "home" to the Europe I had heard discussed so much as a child. We followed a conventional enough itinerary: London (including a weekend with Oliver Zangwill and Pat Rawdon-Smith deep in the Hertfordshire countryside), Paris briefly, the south of France, and then Italy, where the war broke out around us. We departed from Venice with, of all things, an ensemble of Chester Hale dancing girls in our charge, found our way across Switzerland and an incredibly chaotic France—hopping rides on troop trains principally— and finally returned to the Paris of the phony war with its total blackout. We had met Isadora Duncan's brother Raymond who lived in the Rue de Seine, garbed always in a Grecian toga, full of contradictory proverbs celebrating either the gentle Christ, Henry Ford (whom he somehow had learned to idolize as a man of peace), or his sensuous sister. We lived in his "commune" for a month. I recall now with bemused pleasure a thirtieth birthday party honoring Leo Hurvich, given jointly by a certain "Countess" Monici (one of Raymond's more bizarre hangers-on) and myself. It was latter-day *La Bohème*. Eventually, we were rounded up with other tardy Americans, shipped to Bordeaux, and put on board the *S.S. Shawnee*, which had been diverted from the New York–Florida run to save the "American colony" of Paris. As *The New Yorker* put it, "Last week the *Shawnee* arrived in New York with the cast of *The Sun Also Rises*." Leaving Bordeaux, steaming out of the Garonne, I felt a little the deserter—not just as a Jew leaving the others to their fate, but also as a failed brother's keeper.

Looking back at those years of graduate study at Harvard— perhaps they were too narrowly psychological, but that in its way may have been a necessary element in their intensity—I realize how little we were aware of the revolution we were living through. Did Parisian students know in 1789? For all that, the place had an astonishing and graceful vigor. Harvard itself, as a community, was sufficiently self-assured, under

Conant's brilliant leadership, to explore to its full the role of a great university. Scholarship was its principal enterprise, but the models of scholarship provided to us were neither narrow nor defensive toward the other styles of using mind and taste. The great figures, rising or already fully resplendent, were Alfred North Whitehead, Ralph Barton Perry, I. A. Richards, Samuel Eliot Morison, Arthur Schlesinger, Sr., Joseph Schumpeter, Crane Brinton, F. O. Mattiesen, Walter Cannon among the fully resplendent; and Perry Miller, George Wald, Talcott Parsons, Harry Levin, W. V. Quine among the rising. They were models of excellence, to be sure; but perhaps more important for the impression they made on the young, they were models of diverse styles. And Harvard was a sufficiently small place (like the Oxford I was to come to know many years later) to be parochial at the same time that it was worldly. Gordon Allport used to say that each member of the Harvard faculty had two constituencies: Harvard and his fellow scholars, both important. There were, in consequence, many visitors, invited, so to speak, to bridge the gap between the two constituencies. We were forever awash in intellectual controversy, endlessly taking sides, trying out ideas for size and pattern, becoming involved in the "Walsh and Sweezy" tenure battle or the tense vote on whether the Harvard Teachers Union should donate one dollar symbolically to the campaign of The Yanks Are Not Coming, an isolationist movement in Boston. For psychology, this was its time in life when it had developed enough confidence in its own possibilities to be open and nonexcluding. Allport always seemed to have in train a rather bizarre string of German phenomenologists or Polish characterologists visiting him, devotees of Scheler or Dilthey who would have done better in the atmosphere of America thirty years later. Stevens would import astringent young British philosophers like Freddie Ayer or worldly acousticians like von Bekézy and Boring was constant host to the Psychological Establishment. Visiting lecturers included Kurt Goldstein, Lewin, Köhler, and Tolman. Saul Rosenzweig would come in from Worcester to offer a seminar, as would Hudson Hoagland. William Sheldon preached somatotypy under Stevens' unlikely wing, and Harry Murray's visiting friends preached the Jungian collective unconscious or straight Freud. And for all that, there was a prevailing atmosphere of conviviality, with all included—at the Allports, the Murrays, the Borings, even at Clinic parties where Silvan Tomkins and Robert Holt brought in the outsiders. Only Lashley remained remote—respected but impersonal.

There is a personal thing I should add about the early Harvard years—two strains reinforced in me that, I think, persisted.

One was a sense that psychology is an undivided subject. I was never happy with Gordon Allport's fond distinction of the *Geisteswissenschaften* and the *Naturwissenschaften*. Perhaps the experience of that particular group of graduate students made the difference. Somehow, however dim the vision might be, it seemed there should be a unified approach, within a single system of thought—though the form of that unified system was not clear, save that it should not be either a reductionism to biology or a form effected entirely by an "experimental method." There must be many approaches—both for finding and for testing hypotheses. I had been much impressed, for example, by Gordon Allport's seminar and then his monograph on the study of the life history.

The second strain reinforced in me was an uneasy feeling that the question of *where* psychology got its research ideas from that would lead it better to *understand* human behavior was very much open. In some sense, it seemed to me, we did not yet fully know the entire range of what had to be understood nor, for that which we had taken as the "subject" of "official" psychology, did we know clearly enough where to go for our explanations. In a way, we were competing (or collaborating) with other approaches to the explanation of human behavior. I had sat in on lectures by I. A. Richards on the interpretation of poetry, and these had given me a "feel" for cognitive processes that was not less compelling of study than what I had gotten from Beebe-Center's lectures on "higher mental processes." And the work of those anthropologists I read—particularly, their emphasis on culture—struck me as richer (though less manageable, so it seemed) than what I had encountered of traditional social psychology. And I recall the green-visored Alvin Hansen saying that economics was just as much about psychology as psychology was! I suspect that these conjectures were reinforced by the next period in my life.

The War Years

I arrived in Washington, D.C., the June before Pearl Harbor, in 1941. I was sure that it was only a matter of months before we would be in the war, as were all the motley crew at the Foreign Broadcast Intelligence Service. We were an odd lot: academics, newspapermen, political scientists. Our job was to glean intelligence from the huge output of broadcasting from every belligerent or potentially belligerent nation whose airwaves we could monitor. Besides myself, our group included Tom Grandin of CBS and Harold Graves of the *Providence Journal,* DeGrazia and Bernard Berelson from Harold Lasswell at Chicago, Eric Estorick (who had just published a biography of Stafford Cripps and was rather a flaneur), Audrey Menefee, and Donald McGranahan of rather straightforward psychological background, and William Carter (who came by family to his Far Eastern interests). Ted Newcomb and Goodwin Watson were later to join us. We did our thing in a secret and dingy hideaway tucked southeast of Union Station. It was here that I first encountered a new form of the old battle between the realists (who think the truth can be found right there in the content) and the conceptualists (who, like myself, thought it was in the deep structure and needed digging out). Each morning—and after Pearl Harbor, our mornings started at 6:00 sharp—we would arive to find the bulk output of the preceding evening's broadcasts translated and duplicated by our extraordinary staff of translators—almost all of them emigrés and as movingly engaged a group of people as I have ever met. The "news" realists would prepare their midday report on the basis of this "clue" or that "item" indicating that, since Field Marshall X or General Y had not been mentioned in despatches from the front, they might have been relieved of their command, failing in their salient on the Russian front. Our conceptualist approach rather spurned such directness. We kept track of key themes and their handling. We were tuned to shifts from emphasis on power and control to emphasis on moral issues. *That,* we were convinced, was how to read signs of self-doubt in the enemy mind. Why each faction felt so superior to the other now seems a little obscure.

As far as I can remember, we never received any feedback from the War Department, the State Department, or the OSS, to whom our midday reports would go. Perhaps our bosses did, at some higher level, but downstairs we had the sense of sending our daily offering into the void. Moreover, we had been briefed on how badly hit America had been in the Pacific and knew how "hopeless" the European scene looked to American intelligence. So, late in the gloomy spring of 1942, I was quite ready for the blandishments of Rensis Likert, who then blazed on the scene equipped with a mandate to establish, as part of Roosevelt's new Office of Facts and Figures, a bureau for studying how American public opinion was holding up, how it was responding to various war appeals, etc. Likert combined the charm, intelligence, and innocence to do that job superbly well. "His bureau"—the Program Surveys Division of the Bureau of Agricultural Economics, what more innocent!—was to be converted and yet keep its old locus in Agriculture. How did Likert manage to recruit such a staff so quickly? In a month or two, we were: E. R. Hilgard, R. B. MacLeod, I. Krechevsky, Dorwin Cartwright, Richard Crutchfield, Eleanor Maccoby, Ruth Tolman, Angus Campbell, to mention only a few. The "method" was the "open-ended interview," conducted nationally, carefully pretested in order to assure appropriate "filter" questions, with the final interview worked through for coding purposes by the field team, the study director, and the special coding unit. It was work superbly done. We worked for various agencies—for Treasury on the war bond campaigns, and for War Production on the effect of mobility and worker shortage, the absorption of women into the labor force, and the degree to which the American people were informed on war issues and post-war problems. (I was shocked at how poorly informed they were!)

One study I directed made a particularly strong impression on me. Skirting very close to the limit of permissible government research even in wartime, it was a comparative study of the readers of Colonel McCormick's *Chicago Tribune* and a "matched" sample of readers of other Chicago papers. We constructed a "barometer" of critical war issues that might differentiate between these readers: whether American participation in the war was "necessary," whether it would matter who won in Europe, all elements of the "Axis Line." It is hard to allocate cause and effect in opinion surveying—whether readers flock to a paper to confirm their own views or get them from reading a paper. There was, indeed, galling alienation from the war among the *Tribune's* readers, far more than we had expected and principally rooted in the profound distrust of "the foreign" so characteristic of the American Right. Later in the war, in Paris shortly after the Liberation, I gave a dinner party for Admiral Muselier, who, at de Gaulle's instructions, had "liberated" St. Pierre and Miquelon in the Gulf of St. Lawrence with a couple of corvettes, to the huge annoyance of Roosevelt, who, moved by the Monroe Doctrine and his intense dislike of de Gaulle, had used the unforgivable phrase in a public statement: "the so-called Free French have liberated St. Pierre." Muselier commented—a bit in his cups I think—that Americans despised foreigners and instinctively distrusted them. I thought of my *Chicago Tribune* readers as I tried to talk him out of his distemper. It ended by his assuring me that some of his best friends were American!

Another study, conducted in response to a request from General Hershey, head of the wartime draft, produced a different kind of echo later. The draft had begun to dig deep and was well past calling up the unmarried and unspecialized. Hershey wanted to know how people were taking the drafting of fathers, husbands, critical workers. Our study showed that dissatisfaction had rarely to do with the *amount* of sacrifice people were being called on to make. It was almost exclusively a reaction to sensed *inequality* of sacrifice. It was not until after the war that the principle of relative deprivation came clear. The American soldiers in Stouffer's studies reckoned their satisfactions and dissatisfactions in much the same way.

Wartime Washington, for all its excitement and derring-do, was a place riven with competition and rivalry for power and position, particularly where the information services were concerned. The Office of Facts and Figures went through reorganizations and became the Office of War Information. Power, in some curious way, became dissociated from function. Were the information agencies doing any good? Were we at Likert's shop helping to "win the war"? The relation between research and policy at times seemed more political than practical, research being used to justify a claim or to stake out a position rather than to expedite the joint effort. Our "shop" was cut drastically, for no better reason than it had been expanded. It may have been one of the most talented collections of social scientists ever to delve into a nation's public opinion, but that seemed not part of the issue. Hadley Cantril, very much the lone operator, appeared on the scene, offered me a job at Princeton, at his Office of Public Opinion Research, to work directly in an advisory role with the State Department on public opinion issues concerning State. I was tempted by Cantril's work metaphor, which was rather in the image of "Advisor to the Prince."

We came to wartime Princeton—my wife, my year-old son Whitley, and I. Cantril could not have been more generous. We were a small shop: Cantril, Fred Williams, Fred Mosteller, and some part-timers. The spirit of the work was very policy-oriented, either in the specific sense or the more general sense of examining public reception of Roosevelt's wartime policies. Each week I was off to Washington to consult with John Dickey (later president of Dartmouth College) at the State Department, staying Thursday nights at the Richard Tolmans and consulting the next day in the old State, War, and Navy Building. Meanwhile, Hadley "planted" our findings here and there in "backstairs" Washington—with Judge Rosenman, the President's confidant and speech writer; with the brilliant and admirable Oscar Cox, another White House intimate; and with Gerard Lambert, the retired St. Louis pharmaceutical manufacturer who kept a house in Washington and a house in Princeton and who lobbied tirelessly for his ideas, which were uncompromisingly internationalist, in favor of alliances with our wartime allies for postwar cooperation, and full of schemes for making the average American aware of what it was to be dependent upon the goodwill of the rest of the world. Cantril was a man of strong and genuine liberal convictions, greatly attracted to Roosevelt and his circle, yet romantically given over to a conspiracy theory of history that places far too much emphasis on whom one dined with and far too little on the inevitable flow of historical and economic forces.

And what was the burden of our message at the State Department? Mostly urging policy makers not to be greatly impressed by any surface resistance in American opinion to our participation in the postwar international plans then being born—Bretton Woods, the new United Nations, an International Monetary Fund, and so on. There were data, to be sure: the changeability of popular opinion regarding policies that, though initially resisted, would end up being accepted once they had been strongly enunciated by the President as necessary steps for securing the peace. I think the main function of my Friday visits to Washington was to give nerve to gifted men in the midst of negotiations that could only go in one direction anyway: toward increased American participation in multilateral efforts. It was a position I strongly supported myself. I doubt my advice was "objective." But even more strongly, I doubt whether the advice made much difference. I suppose it depends on one's view of history.

On Thursday evenings in Washington, I stayed with Richard and Ruth Tolman. She had worked with me at Likert's, and he was, quite unbeknownst to me, directing the Washington end of the Los Alamos project. They were two people I loved very dearly—as did others, for they were gifted friends. A frequent covisitor at the Tolmans on Thursday nights was Robert Oppenheimer—brilliant, discursive in his interests, lavishly intolerant, ready to pursue any topic anywhere, extraordinarily lovable. We remained friends until his death, and I shall come back to him later.

Something about Princeton goaded me into sorting out what was meant by "American opinion." Partly it was the archive of polling data Cantril had collected. But it was also the contrast of going each week to Washington and then returning to the old Dutch farmhouse outside Princeton where we lived that year—cutting cords of wood for our fireplaces to supplement our coal ration, raising chickens, attending the drama of the two elderly spinster neighbor farmers who for years had been caught up in the masculinity of their black farmhand. I collated the extant polling data and wrote a naive book on American opinion, *Mandate from the People.* It was naive as only a psychologist can be naive about public opinion—without a sense of the power of institutions as forces in political life and without sensitivity to deep historical trends that shape the thinking of a nation. Public opinion was a summing across a sample of the opinions of individuals. My historian and near-historian friends—Elting Morison, Perry Miller, Morton White—would not save me until later, if then! Nor had the anthropologists quite gotten across to me the concept of culture. Clyde Kluckhohn blew up at me not too many years after, accusing me of being "a typical psychologist" and of caring only for what went on inside the skin, what could be measured by "some bloody brass instrument." Later, *Mandate* seems to have provided fodder for historians working over the war period, but how different the data look in the pages of John Blum!

I had a bad case of restlessness. I wanted a more direct part in the war. The mood of patriotism is hard to reconstruct. I went to Trenton, tried to enlist, and was turned down for "insufficient vision." It was humiliating in one way, but a little relief of guilt as well. I then discovered that I could get into the Overseas Division of the Office of War Information, in spite of my substandard vision, by waiving certain insurance rights. I arrived in London shortly before D-Day, greeted by terrifying buzz bombs, and became part of the Anglo-American Psychological Warfare Division of Supreme Headquarters Allied Expeditionary Force Europe—PWD-SHAEF. Our job was to assess whether there would be any "troubles" behind the moving lines of our advancing troops in France. We were mixed civilian and military, the former (like myself) being put into bastard uniforms and given a week in Northamptonshire to learn how to handle the British M1 rifle and the Enfield carbine, neither of which I ever thereafter fired in anger or in fear. Our gallant little band could have qualified for the theater of the absurd! We were under Elmo Wilson, a New York commercial pollster (of all things!), and the British side included a charming Guards captain, Max Michaelis, gifted water-colorist and wealthy eccentric who had commanded Moors in Franco's army and had fought as a ski-trooper with the Finns against the Russians in the Winter War. Max was there, I always thought, to monitor us for MI5. I recall how smartly he saluted nuns and priests—"fellow officers." Our other British officer was a psychiatrist named Pierre Turquet, an RMC major, épée champion of Britain, and a delightful and intelligent man. A third was added as we approached Paris—Major Bryce Gallie, the biographer of C. S. Peirce, the American pragmatist. There was also a long-time American expatriate sculptor, Cecil Howard, who knew our territory very well indeed. Our group on the American side was quite accidentally very Harvard: Albert Guerard (a PFC), the critic; Perry Miller, the literary historian (thinly disguised as a cavalry captain); John Riley (with whose wife and children mine were staying), who had studied sociology at Harvard with Parsons.

We did not find much trouble in the newly liberated areas—save from the Free French. A certain M. Coulet had been appointed by General de Gaulle as High Commissioner for all newly liberated French territory. He was, as the British say, a very shirty type, and after his first round of complaints about the delay in bringing General de Lattre de Tassigny in with Deuxième Division Blindée from the Tchad, he focused on us. By what rights was there an Anglo-American team prying into the internal affairs of French local governments and political movements? (It is just possible that he had gotten hold of a report from our unit on the high respect in which the Franc-Tireurs Partisans were held, a stalwart Communist group, mostly of slum-tough Parisian teenagers who had stayed there in Brittany and fought the whole war in the active underground.) In any case, we were quietly and swiftly disbanded in the interest of Allied harmony.

I was to report to the Office of War Information headquarters, but it was en route to Paris, which was on the verge of falling, and so I took off for Paris, also hoping to find Jean Stoetzel (who had been running an underground poll and was to become France's Gallup). I found him in the midst of those zany few days when some arrondissements were having street dances and others were witness to the last rounding-up of fascist Milice Française diehards fighting from the roofs, fearing for their lives. Stoetzel became a lifelong friend, a man not quite French enough for French sociology and too French for the Anglo-Saxons.

I was duly assigned: to work under Lewis Galantière and Cass Canfield, the latter being our chief boss and a wise and kindly man. He was doing "cultural relations" with the "French university world" with a staff far more qualified than I, including Albert Guerard (who was, at last, in his medium of high French culture) and John Brown (who was to go on to become a crack diplomat). Our shop in Paris swarmed with amateur talent—including Galantière, a charming and irascible Franco-American intellectual, and Michael Bessie, now a distinguished New York publisher—and in time, the professional bureaucrats came. We organized literary fortnights, dined incessantly with "leading figures," and might even have done some small good in convincing French intellectuals that Americans were interested and involved. It was a slender reed on which to lean *amitié franco-américaine!* During this period, at Pierre Auger's invitation, I first became conscious of what "educational reform" entailed, for he invited me to come as an observer to meetings of the Commission Langevin, then rewriting the charter for French public education. John Brown and I wrote up the proceedings after the war as a piece for the *Harvard Educational Review.* It was then that I became aware of the political compromises needed to maintain both equality of educational opportunity and a special "track" for the evidently talented—a particularly tortured conflict in France, which so prided itself on the system of *les grandes écoles.*

Two memories are particularly intense as symbols of the end of the war in Europe. One was VE-Day. I had taken a British Wren to dinner at our billet, and we were then to proceed to the Place de la Concorde to see the lights turned on. She was in her early twenties, a charming and intelligent girl who was full of the prospective excitement of the occasion. At 9:00 p.m. sharp, as I recall it, the Place came alive in a glow of light. My companion broke into uncontrollable sobs. It was the first time as a grown-up she had seen a city lit up at night! Some weeks later in 1945, I was with a friend in the press room where the American journalists went for their briefings. These were signaled by a loud bell, the number of rings being in proportion to the importance of the news to be issued. Four bells sounded, and the briefing officer, a youngish man with a tortured face, came forward: "I wish to announce that the President died in Warm Springs, Georgia, at four o'clock this afternoon, their local time." We were all stunned into an endless silence. Finally, Janet Flanner of *The New Yorker* leapt hysterically to her feet and shouted angrily, "You ring four bells for any damned communiqué. Can't you do better than that when the President dies, Goddamm it?"

Some days afterward, I received a letter from Gordon Allport inviting me to an instructorship at Harvard starting the following September. In a few weeks, I was back in Belfast, Maine, reunited with my family, discovering my son, sailing an ancient little sloop around Penobscot Bay. I knew I had "changed": I discovered how much when we returned to Cambridge at the end of the summer.

Postwar Cambridge

Cambridge was full of excitement and stimulation. For one, there was an influx of extraordinary graduate students, the postwar "veterans" who, while they were my students, were also practically my contemporaries and, in many ways, my closest mates: Brewster Smith, Sheldon Korchin, Virginia Senders, Ray Bauer, Henry Riecken, Gardner Lindzey. And much the same faculty were there, augmented by Hobart Mowrer, who, though officially in education, was soon to become involved with Murray, Allport, Kluckhohn, and Parsons in the "plottings" that led to the famous split between "biotropic" and "sociotropic" psychology and the founding of the Department of Social Relations at Harvard.

One enormous change in Cambridge after the war was the shift in the "center" of Harvard—or better, Cambridge—psychology. Before, it had been very much a traditional, " experimentally" centered place, with perception, memory, learning, and sensory psychophysics at its heart. After, there was a far more "behavioral science" orientation. The Massachusetts Institute of Technology had its Center for Group Dynamics, led by the restless and brilliant Kurt Lewin, always ready to look to the puzzles of daily life as the starting point for psychological conjecture. He had with him there a lively crew, some of them my closest personal friends: Leon Festinger, Mason Haire, Dorwin Cartwright, Jack French, and Alex Bavelas. We spent much time together talking social psychology or whatever else happened to be at hand. We had all done "war psychology" and had ventured beyond the laboratory, Harvard psychologists as well as MIT. We also knew people outside psychology interested in "our" sort of problems and did not much care if Bob Merton happened to be a sociologist or Clyde Kluckhohn an anthropologist. Curiously enough, too, what might be called the "ideology" of the Tavistock Institute in London was known through visits by Bowlby and Dicks, and through their collaboration with MIT. Many of us were also members of SPSSI, then a lively ginger group mostly centered in Cambridge and New York, working for the application of psychology to social issues. This was a very different Cambridge from the very traditional psychology department of graduate student days.

It was soon to grow into a new grouping at Harvard, the Department of Social Relations, with the more "personality" and "socially" oriented members making common cause with anthropologists and sociologists. There were personal tensions at work as well, but in my view they only served as personal catalysts to a historical process that was very much a reflection of those times. Boring tried to hold the Department of Psychology together (I learned only some years later) by proposing that James Miller and I be elected to permanent posts in the Department. But the flood tide of "sociotropic" behavioral science had already risen too high to be stopped. There followed the appointment of Sam Stouffer to direct the new Laboratory of Social Relations—a sociologist of such empirical vigor and capacity as to bridge the gap between Parsonian theory and the ways of thought of the more traditional psychologists who had joined. On the psychological side, Dick Solomon then joined the Department, he and I started the proseminar, and there also began a decade of hugely invigorating cross-disciplinary work. Perhaps the most powerful force in holding attention focused in that diverse new Department was the weekly seminar in Social Relations where the members "did their thing" of reporting on their own research, trying to connect it not only to their own specialty but also to the joint interests of the Department. I think it would be fair to say that as a venture, the first decade of Social Relations was an enormous success in forming a new generation of behavioral scientists. And the credit goes principally, I think, to Sam Stouffer, Talcott Parsons, and Clyde Kluckhohn among the senior members, for they were the ones most intellectually committed to the "integration." Allport and Murray were both important presences, undoubtedly, but both of them were wedded to a psychology that, in fact, had not much theoretical maneuvering space for sociological and anthropological theorems—mostly for ideas about "personality and culture." And even at that, Gordon Allport was always wary of a view that held personality, as W. I. Thomas had put it, to be "the subjective side of culture."

What it did for me personally, this immersion, was to make me appreciate to what extent cultural and social forms and the rules that govern them become somehow internalized in the mental apparatus of the individual human being. I think that will become clearer in what I have to recount about my later work, and I quite agree with Jeremy Anglin's assessment in his introductory essay to *Beyond the Information Given* that the effect on me was considerable.

As for myself, I wanted various things on my return. One was to "bring back" and to "tame" what I had been doing in the war years. I was too innocent, really, to know how to look at the relation of public opinion and public policy or to grasp the meaning of "public information." My mind worked too naturally along lines of psychological theory, which, I surmise, has little to say on such issues. But I looked for the lost coin where the light was familiar!

Robert White and Brewster Smith hit on a project that was an interesting compromise. (More of that in a moment.) I also wanted to get back to what for me had been the chief entrance into the guts of psychology: the study of perception. That turned out to be solved by good luck. I was to find a powerful and extraordinarily energetic ally in this work in the person of Leo Postman, with whom I worked in harness for seven or eight years on the role of set, drive, and attitude as factors in perception. I also wanted to keep my foot in Europe: Could social psychology be given an international base? My good friend Henri Laugier, who before I had left Paris had become the Director General of Cultural Affairs in France, had now come to New York as the first Assistant Secretary General for Social Affairs. We were determined that there should be an international, U.N. sponsored Institute of Social Research. What a madly ambitious agenda, yet I was barely thirty and, perhaps neurotically, impervious to fatigue.

Let me try to capture the nature of the two main projects, on opinion and on perception. First, the one on the psychological foundations of political opinions. Upon my return to Harvard, I joined the political scientist Joachim Friedrich to teach "Gov. 25"—the course on public opinion that had been introduced many years before by Abbott Lawrence Lowell. I was to lecture on the "psychological dimension," Friedrich on the political–institutional. Friedrich's mind was of that brilliant, European analytic cast that lives midway between political philosophy and astute observation of the contemporary and historical scenes. For my part, initially rather cowed by our audience of students plus Nieman Fellows and a fair sprinkling of the junior faculty of the Government Department, I presented the view that an opinion must be considered partly a projection of needs, fears, and wishes; partly a summary of informational input, collated in the light of one's values; and partly an expression of historical modes of thought deriving from immersion in a culture. In fact, there was not much of a literature on any of these matters—save a few rare classics, like Walter Lippmann's *Public Opinion.* I leapt at the chance to start a project with Bob White and Brewster Smith, using a combination of clinical and survey techniques to establish the psychological roots of opinions on political issues. We chose the subject of attitudes toward Russia and Communism, partly because it was such an emotive issue and partly because, in cold-war America, it was so preoccupying. Ten men in the midst of life were to be studied intensively, seen by a variety of investigators who would attempt to plumb not only their political and social opinions but also their personalities to assess the projective routes by which their opinions were formed. True to the Clinic tradition, their records were then to be discussed by a "diagnostic council" (presided over spiritually by Bob White) and then written up by a member of the team on completion. Freed Bales even set up a satellite project to study *us!*

In addition, Brewster Smith was to devise a more or less open-ended questionnaire to be administered to a cross-section of adults in order to examine the manner in which, "in the field" so to speak, the dynamics observed in our smaller, intensive sample could be observed and found to be constrained by demographic factors. The talent and variety of the group at work on the project were unrivaled—Eugenia Hanfmann and Marika Rickers-Ovsiankina on the intuitive pole, and Sheldon Korchin serving as our doubting Thomas. It went on for years, with order in the company assured by a remarkable lady, Esther Smith, who saw to it that the records were in order, that subjects met their appointments, and that the research group remained not only friendly but happily convivial.

The outcome was an interesting, eclectic book, *Opinions and Personality*. There are bits in it—as on the functions that opinions serve for their holder in summing up social reality and in extending the range of his intrapsychic reality to contemporary events—that are useful formulations. And on the informational side, the distinction the book draws between "line sources" derived from one's reference-group "organs" and "filler sources" used for selective documentation of one's beliefs, is important. The book was politely received and had little impact—partly because the field of opinion research had gone stale, partly because the psychoanalytically inspired "personality" orientation of our project had become banal as a vehicle of explanation. As for the field studies, the difficulty lay in the complexity of the instrument employed and in the slow pace of the development of ideas from the clinical to the social side.

While the cumbersome "Clinic study" was going on, Sheldon Korchin, Ray Bauer, and I did a "quickie" sampling survey on the appeal of James Michael Curley to Boston voters—he was running for Mayor while under indictment for electoral fraud—and I think it turned out a richer harvest than the more elaborate study. The reason was simple: It was done in the context of a political event, an election, and was a case study that managed to preserve the ecological structure of an event in which political opinions express themselves. Curley's was the appeal of somebody who is "no worse than the next fellow" in political morals, but who gives the impression of getting something done for the city: an urban Robin Hood, an outsider making it in an insider's world, the closed Boston of those days. Curley gave people an antidote to helplessness: Something, it seemed, could get done. This was *election* behavior, and people "behaved election-like" whether they had unresolved Oedipal problems or not.

My interest was increasingly drawn to the study of perception. *How* one saw events would provide answers to questions that otherwise might be too complicated to unravel. Leo Postman and I in those days were like the twin protagonists in Santayana's *The Last Puritan:* Mario, willful, impulsive, and Italianate; Oliver, constrained, ordered, and classic. The "New Look" experiments grew from initial discussions about constant errors in psychophysical judgment—time errors, space errors, adaptation errors. In most perceptual experiments, such suspected sources of error were neutralized by randomizing the conditions that produced them. We published a paper in 1946, "The Reliability of Constant Errors in Psychophysical Measurement," criticizing this procedure. Shortly after, a gifted young undergraduate, Cecile Goodman, and I did an experiment on judgments of the apparent size of coins. The argument was straightforward. According to the theory of the central tendency of judgment, large objects in a series of objects that vary in size should be underestimated, smaller ones overestimated. The concept of central tendency is powerful and important. What would happen if, as sometimes is the case, the small end is low in value and the big end high? Would a new rule emerge that would supplant central tendency? Would small get smaller and big bigger? That was just what happened: Less valuable coins were underestimated in size; more valuable ones overestimated. Others repeated the experiment: Sometimes it came out our way, sometimes it produced no reliable effect, but in the main the yeas had it. There are ways of accentuating the "value" effect (by introducing slight ambiguity in the judging condition or by emphasizing the value aspect, as we had done by comparing "rich" and "poor" children). What was most plain, however, was that *various* "rules" could operate in judgmental phenomena for accentuating (or diminishing) symbolic value, the significance of stimuli, etc. To my total astonishment, these experiments made a great "splash," both among psychologists and in the public press.

What came next in the series represented a new departure. For one, we became more interested in selectivity than in distorted judgments of sensory attributes like size. We came to concentrate on recognition thresholds and the hypotheses leading up to correct recognition. Postman and I first found that words producing very long or very short reaction times in a word-association test were recognized either more quickly upon rapid tachistoscopic exposure or more slowly, on average, than ones that produced a normal reaction time. The words that were slow of recognition, moreover, seemed to produce rather weird recognition attempts from our subjects. Indeed, some of our subjects seemed to be "slowed down" in the recognition of associatively "hot" words, while others speeded up. We analyzed the data to within an inch of their lives, enough to embolden us to offer the hypothesis that there were crucial, "personal" factors operating in perceptual recognition and that these could, in our experiment, be roughly classed as governed by "vigilance" or "defense": the former a strategy for getting as quickly as possible to the source of emotional arousal, the latter perhaps being an as-yet-unspecifiable strategy of denial. The fat was in the fire! "Perceptual defense" became a battle cry. There were deep problems with such a concept, notably the argument of the Judas eye: How does the nervous system know what to defend itself against or what to let in neatly and swiftly? Again, a spate of research was set loose, including some very beautiful studies by Richard Lazarus and his colleagues, showing the tendency of "intellectualizers" to vigilance and "deniers and repressors" to defensive recognition patterns.

Our next series was aimed at the dilemna of the Judas eye. Postman, McGinnies, and I sorted subjects initially on the Allport–Vernon Study of Values scale, then presented them

value-denoting words controlled for Thorndike–Lorge frequency for tachistoscopic recognition. In the main, and with
very high reliability, the higher their score in a value domain,
the more quickly they recognized a word from that domain.
High-value words, moreover, were more liable to elicit
"covaluant" hypotheses—*church* would produce "steeple" from
a religious subject; *money*, "income" from an economic one—
while "contravaluant" ones emerged for words in the lower
value domains of a subject, *church* eliciting, say, "devil." By
now, the fever chart of New Look research was very elevated
indeed, and I recall a study by the APA in the late 1940s or
early 1950s (based on bibliographical reference citation) indicating that, next to Sigmund Freud himself, Bruner and
Postman were second on the list—sharing the fate of that
great master, being targets for attack as often as objects for
admiration. Davis Howes was on about the control of word
frequency, Chapanis pointed to the role of reconstruction
from fragments seen in the quick flash—all good methodological arguments, all eventually well controlled by us or others,
and none really prevailing against the main brunt of the argument about perceptual selectivity.

One of the major effects of this research—the period of
collaboration with Postman, as well as the period after, when
George Klein joined me at Harvard and then David Krech,
two men whom I deeply admired and in whose company I
felt most intellectually alert—was its role in creating and con-
solidating new intellectual alignments in psychology. Students
of personality, of social behavior, of classical perception, of attention met and argued together about their work: Tolman
and Krech and Brunswik from Berkeley, Fritz Heider from
Kansas, Lazarus and Chapanis from Hopkins, George Klein
from Menninger and Gardner Murphy from Columbia in
search of personality correlates, the Gibsons and Julie Gleit-
man from Cornell, Hans Wallach and Hochberg and Prentice
from Swarthmore (representing Gestalt theory), Hilgard from
Stanford, etc. I agree with Hilgard that the New Look, for all
its strident debate and turbulence, helped turn the tide of
American psychology toward a more cognitive emphasis—not
only at its classical, experimental center, but also in the field of

personality and social psychology. My former colleague Henri Tajfel argues that the present, phenomenological orientation of social psychology is directly traceable to the New Look.

I must say a word about teaching here, about "Psych. 148" on Cognitive Processes. It was our forum for trying out emerging ideas on graduate students and advanced undergraduates—what teaching in a "university college" should be about. Teaching it with Postman, with Krech and George Klein, and later with George Miller was a joy. Perhaps I was lucky in my colleagues!

What happened to the New Look? There has been one highly interesting retrospective review in the past few years (in *Psychological Review*, 1976) that does a fair-minded job of summing up its accomplishments and its weaknesses—emphasizing the degree to which it related perception as a process to other forms of processing activity by which information is acquired, retained, and transformed for future use. I can easily reconstruct what happened to my own interests. It became plain to me by, say, 1953 that there were two general programs of "readiness" in terms of which perception was tuned to "select" input for further processing. One was designed to minimize surprise: We are prepared for what we have learned is likely to occur, given the circumstances operative. We ride with the contingent probabilities of events in our immediate environment, based on the models of that environment that we have stored. As George Miller once put it, we spin the model a little faster than events unroll and use the outcome of the spin to predict events. It is reasonable to suppose that survival in a given biological niche is assured by an organism's capacity to construct a model for his type of environment and to spin it sufficiently in advance of events to be able to foretell them without lethal error. Call this the Principle of Minimizing Surprise. A further biological benefit of such a system, of course, is that it provides a baseline against which "surprise" can be judged—deviation from acceptable limits of likelihood. I was enormously excited by the work of Sokolov, of Galambos, and followed with great care the emerging work on the ascending reticular system as an alerting system—greatly aided by the enthusiastic tutorials of Karl

Pribram, then at Yale, and Bob Galambos, who had by then gone to Bethesda to work.

However, the spotting-and-minimization program could not suffice for *search*. There had to be a way by which the perceptual system could be tuned to search for targets related to some action program in force—regardless of probabilities. But a search program of this kind could not be so narrowly tuned that it judged and selected only in terms of a single criterion—the distance between target specifications and the actual objects present to sense. This would be little better than a projective screen. A search had also to be guided by processes sensitive to environmental likelihoods and "search routes"; else it would be rigid, stupid, and lacking in the forms of local opportunism for which perceptual search is justly celebrated. This was just at the period when Oliver Selfridge (later with Dick Neisser) was beginning to develop "Pandemonium" programs for simulating recognition—a set of recognition "demons" searching for different features whose relative weights would be determined in part by the programmed dictation of a centralized, "editorial" demon monitoring several feature-detecting demons and by the relative frequency or effectiveness of various "bits" of the different feature demons in a given editorial pool. It is all very crude in retrospect. I mention it here because it was one of the first instances in which the new computing metaphor began to affect my way of thinking. Perhaps from these models would come something complicated enough to search with high selectivity and, at the same time, to "keep track" of the environment. This, for me, was also the period in which I began to work with George Miller on informativeness and redundancy, following up some of his highly original notions about approximations to English and their use in studying the manner in which the perceptual system used the structure of the language as a basis for inference.

Renato Tagiuri and I were also working at that time on "social perception"—an extension of sociometry in which one asks members of a group to indicate not only with whom they would choose, say, to work, but also who they thought would choose them to work with. What dilemma! It became increasingly clear to us, in comparing actual results with various Monte Carlo models of how choices and perceptions of choice might be distributed, that our subjects were "wishful" (i.e., much in excess of chance, they thought that those whom they had chosen would also choose them), but that, on the other hand, choosing somebody had in fact the effect of increasing the likelihood of their choosing you back! There was no way of sorting out this mix of realistic pragmatism and wishful illusion—statistically or otherwise. Yet, there were many incidental findings in this work that were to lead Tagiuri and others into some useful work in social psychology.

I did not follow these, for I was becoming much more attracted to studies of the "models" we used for sorting out the world perceptually and conceptually. George Miller was probably as responsible as anyone for my choice. He is such enormous fun to talk to that one is lured into studying whatever he is interested in! At that time, in the early 1950s, Robert Oppenheimer had set up a committee to advise him on how the Institute for Advanced Study at Princeton ought to "get into" psychology. Miller, Hilgard, Hebb, Ruth Tolman, occasionally Edward Tolman, and I would congregate there once or twice a year to discuss the state of psychology, with Oppenheimer and such cronies of his as Niels Bohr or John von Neumann. They were interested in a psychology that could shed light on how people constructed "theories" or "models," and they were forever in search of dilemmas of indeterminacy in the nature of knowing. I recall Bohr asking whether it was possible to know somebody both in the light of love and in the light of justice at the same time! And this was the period, too, when Craik, in England, was beginning to make an impression.

The Institute and the Supper Club

In any case, by the mid-1950s, my interests were moving more explicitly toward the analysis of inference and the nature of the models in which the results of inference were stored for use. I spent 1953–1954 at the Institute for Advanced

Study—one of the richest years of my life. What a relief from the pressures of the modern university! My closest companions there were Oppenheimer, the physicist Bram Pais, and the classicist Harold Cherniss. The physicists were in their most optimistic and nominalistic theoretical phase, full of conjectures about the dependence of observation on the viewpoint and presuppositions of the observer. Von Neumann was brimming with amusing accounts of the alternative forms in which memory storage could be effected in computers. George Austin, who came back to Harvard with me later, was also there, and we talked endlessly about problems in reasoning and inference. Bartlett was beginning his work on thinking, and we entered into correspondence. I deeply admired his freedom from psychological dogmatism.

It has always been a weakness in my work that I do not like tightly modeled, hypothetico-deductive miniature systems that force one to test one's hypotheses on narrowly defined experimental paradigms. I know that I have worked with just such paradigms—be it in studies of the perceptual recognition process by the use of the tachistoscope, or anything else. But when I do, I have a fear of digging myself into an isolated tunnel. In an almost compulsive way I need to try out the generality of what I am doing and have always enjoyed trying to tell outsiders what psychology concerns itself with in a general way to see whether it makes sense to them. The Institute provided one such chance. I also had a "group" in Cambridge. From the late 1940s until the Vietnam War, I dined on the first Friday of each month with a group of companions in Boston. We all shared a streak of the generalist compulsion, all dozen of us. I was the psychologist. The others were lawyers, physicists, historians, whatever: Elting Morison, Myron Gilmore, and Robert Lee Wolff were historians; McGeorge Bundy was a political scientist; and Wassily Leontief and Max Millikan were the economists; Victor Weisskopf and Edwin Purcell were the physicists, as was Edwin Land of Polaroid; George Homans was the sociologist of the group; and Kingman Brewster was the lawyer. Julius Stratton was provost of MIT. Will Hawthorn, an English engineer, would come when he was in America. We never expanded the group, though we often invited guests, early on with a view to "looking them over," but it soon became apparent that we were like the Junta in *Zuleika Dobson,* perpetually blackballing all newly proposed members. We had no "program"—just conversations, and such occasional guests as we would invite pitched in. (Isaiah Berlin, Robert Oppenheimer, Ernst Gombrich, Walter Lippmann, or Serge Chermayeff). In the twenty years of our existence as a group of "regulars," we surely must have talked about almost everything under the sun! Though the Supper Club had no direct impact on my psychological thinking, so far as I know, its indirect impact and its reinforcement of generalism were very great. It surely kept me a little more secure against the kind of "psychological imperialism" in the explanation of human affairs that I had fallen into in my first book.

The Supper Club had come into being as a result of Project Troy, when a group of us from Harvard and MIT were brought together in the late 1940s to review for Secretary of State Acheson the state and objectives of American information policy. The project accomplished little, aside from provoking an internal review in Washington and perhaps getting the Policy and Planning Staff of the State Department to consider, for a while, what they had characterized as "iffy" questions. But I have always been grateful for its happy side effect in Cambridge.

Strategies of Thinking

When I returned to Harvard after the Institute, I started work on concept formation. Robert Oppenheimer and John von Neumann had argued the year before that any efficient system of information seeking could be characterized by a "strategy" that specified selectivity not only of what information would be taken up, but of how that information would be searched for. This was the germ of the idea that started us off on the experiments that went into *A Study of Thinking.* The period of work on that book was enormously engaging. The little house on Bow Street where we worked was buzzing as the problem expanded. The concept of strategy grew to take into account many more criteria—the requirement of economy dictated by limited processing capacity, the requirements of "checking" by sampling redundancy, etc. Jacqueline Goodnow and I collaborated, at first with George Austin, but it was a terrible shock when George, having scarcely gotten started with us, was diagnosed as having an advanced cancer and, in a matter of months, was dead. He was a gifted man, and he had hardly found his stride when he was stricken. Years later his daughter Carol spent a year working for me at Oxford.

Roger Brown had just joined the Department, and he and George Miller were patient and encouraging. Eric Lenneberg was a graduate student, as were Nathan Kogan, Michael Wallach, Renato Tagiuri, Molly Potter, and Lotte Baily. It was a splendid group. One graduate student in particular, Robert Seymour, was a restless, erratic, and brilliant contributor who soon left to pursue the study of law. I think it was he who saw most clearly the need to formulate the idea of an "ideal" strategy—how an ideal subject working on an unmixed strategy would operate, this pattern then serving as the basis of a discovery procedure in analyzing the hypotheses that subjects actually use.

In one respect, the study of categorizing is a very "dry" kind of psychology, but, in another, it is as ancient and classic as any of the approaches to "understanding rationality." The one-sidedness of the book (as Oppenheimer noted in his review of it) is that we worked exclusively on well-defined problems, fully determined concepts. At that, we were able to observe the appearance of thematic strategies—tying together information in a fashion more fitted to natural than to logical categories. The most exciting development in the study of categorizing and concept formation since then has, I think, been just in this direction—the work principally of Eleanor Rosch.

In the very last stages of writing *A Study of Thinking*, perhaps 1955, we had a visit in Cambridge from Dr. Bärbel Inhelder, her first visit to America. She arrived while I was off giving a class, and my secretary gave her a copy of the first three chapters to read. We talked over lunch and through the afternoon. It was the beginning of a continuing association with her and with Jean Piaget. I was in need of such a cordial exchange at the time. For though the book turned out to be a "success," it produced some hostile reactions from traditional learning theorists on the one hand, who disliked its ignoring of the role of reinforcement, and from "dynamic" psychoanalytic students of thinking, like David Rapaport, who found it too rationalistic.

The book done, I packed off to the University of Cambridge for the autumn of 1955–1956, taking my family and my assistant, Michael Wallach, with me. That summer, Bartlett and I (with a grant from Rockefeller) had been cohosts at a conference on thinking at Cambridge—with Zangwill, Miller, Oldfield, Pribram, Werner, Mackay, Gregory, and others interested in problem solving and thinking. It was one of those occasions of high exchange when many of us were encouraged to find that others shared what had seemed to be "private" or outlandish ideas. Under Bartlett, British psychology had been steadily becoming more cognitive than its American uncle. In Cambridge, I found Donald Broadbent, Norman Mackworth, Richard Gregory, and Oliver Zangwill, all of whom have remained close friends since. It was the McCarthy period, and I recall that, shortly before departing, Dick Solomon and I helped Leon Kamin review his defense before the infamous McCarthy committee in Boston, since he had been "charged" as a "fellow-traveler." Harvard had risen to his defense. My college, St. Johns, was just at that moment testing the legality of a will that had left money to the College to set up studentships for "white, Anglo-Saxon applicants." I was, I recall, very moved by the uprightness of both Cambridges.

It was also the time of my first visit to "Le Patron," Piaget, in Geneva. We struck it off very well. With Piaget, one can be as critical as one needs to be so long as one does not cast doubt on the underlying *approach* of his theory of development. Once a topic can be shown to be discussable in terms of that approach—can be shown, for example, to fit into his ideas about the conversion of sensorimotor into operative schemas, or to fit the doctrine of equilibration, or the underlying logical structures of operational and formal intelligence—Piaget will argue hard, well, and with enormous good humor. In any case, he saw *A Study of Thinking* as a blow for the common cause and wrote me an enthusiastic and encouraging letter about it, and in turn I was becoming much more conversant with and enthusiastic about his latest theoretical writing. We walked for hours through the mountains, in deep conversation, picnicking off stale bread covered generously with mayonnaise pressed from a tube and mixed with freshly squeezed garlic clove, a garlic press being part of the standard ware inside his rucksack. He particularly delighted in predicting where snails were to be found and, finding them, noting the marvelous and invariant regularity of their shells. I teased him, suggesting that his theory of development might be too closely modeled on the snail and might not take full enough account of how different motivational and experiential conditions affected mental growth. He was amused and a little shocked. And so was I—in retrospect! Six months later, he came back to the theme at a meeting of the Swiss Psychological Society in Berne where he had arranged a "debate" between us on the nature of perception: As he put it, he supporting "l'homme calme" and I supporting "l'homme agité." I recall Piaget saying, on the train returning to Geneva (for which we arrived characteristically forty minutes early), that he was first and foremost an epistemologist and secondarily a psychologist—that his admitted object has always been to find a psychological basis for an adequate epistemology.

I got back from Cambridge (and Geneva) to Harvard in the midst of a cold and unhappy winter. My marriage was breaking up. I was full of self-pity and full of blundering worries about my two children. To cope with my depression, as I have usually done, I threw myself into work with fiendish energy to blot the other worries out. Between 1956 and 1958, I published some twenty-two papers and a book! One wonders about the relationship between misery and productivity. My life was in a shambles, fermenting but disorganized.

Yet the work of that period is as good or better than that of any other period: papers on perception, on perceptual aspects of social behavior, on concept formation. I worked with rats, with tachistoscopes, with sociometric groups. I read broadly in the exciting new work on the ascending reticular system, wrote long and detailed reviews of new books by Bartlett, Piaget, George Kelley, Kenneth Spence, Ernest Jones. The French speak of a *daemon de midi* that attacks in mid-life, in the late thirties and early forties. I was having mine. The battle with it was tumultuous, at times glorious, and exhausting. I missed the easy contact with my children, their "visits" always being "set pieces." I think my friends saved me, nurturing me on the bounces as I tried to build a new life, moving cross-country, cross-ocean, cross-purposes.

Psychoanalysis and the Left Hand

I must say a word here about psychoanalysis and my experience with it. In the early 1950s, I was awarded a Commonwealth Fellowship, one of several that were established for behavioral scientists to go through analysis and then through training seminars offered by the Boston Psychoanalytic Institute. My analyst was Edward Bibring, a cultivated and kindly Viennese who had known Freud and worked with him. I had read quite widely in Freud and was later to write some essays on psychoanalysis that were admired by the "inner circle." As an interpreter of the human condition in the first half of this century, Freud must surely stand as a genius. But it must also be said, with respect, that as a therapeutic or, indeed, prophylactic tool, psychoanalysis as a treatment procedure does not seem in my case to have been a success. I know one cannot prove anything about the individual "case." Yet, in spite of analysis, I managed my own life during this crisis period clumsily, inflicted pain, and brought off some monumental feats of selfishness at the expense of others. I commented on the fact that my friends were the ones who managed to keep the pieces together with great perceptiveness. Yet, curiously, there is no place in psychoanalytic theory for the network of people who manage somehow to keep each other going—and not really in the manner of "object relations." Nor does analysis have enough to say about the institutional structures—be they a university, a bank, or a law office—that provide the lifelines to which one grabs while the storm is in full force.

I spent the stormy summer of 1957 in the London flat of wartime friends. It was the summer of Suez. I read and talked with old friends, gathered my wits. I read Greek mythology, had an orgy of the Pre-Raphaelites, and stayed away from psychology of the conventional kind.

That fall, I began a series of studies on aspects of cognitive development, stumblingly, for I found it difficult to get into. I wanted to work on the development of inference. But I wanted to work in more natural contexts than we'd used in the previous work on conceptualizing and categorizing. I ran badly into all manner of blocks. For one thing, I started by concentrating on individual difference—the contrast between inferential "plodders" and "leapers." Good experimental procedures eluded me. I was not used to working with children. And the study of individual differences, however important it may be, is not my style. I had splendid graduate students at the time, like Michael Maccoby who became a close friend as well, and a marvelously gifted research team including such people as Albert Caron and David Shapiro. But for a couple of years, in the late 1950s, I was rather adrift.

Much of my spare time went into "the left hand," following up the broodings of my London summer. I was divorced and living alone. My chief companion and confidante was a tumultuous, gifted painter and political activist, Elizabeth Weems. She presided over a household in Colorado, I was in Cambridge, Massachusetts; there was much traveling back and forth. I think our friends thought we exerted too much influence on each other! Perhaps so, but we ended up, I'm sure, the richer; and I a less single-minded, "experimenting" psychologist.

I began doing some therapy on children with learning blocks at the Judge Baker, which made me very aware of the difference between coping with problem solving (what children are supposed to do in school) and defending oneself against failure-producing learning tasks inherent in school work. It gave me a very good feel, indeed, for what school looked like to children. I also took a hand, with William Gordon, in an "invention group" at A. D. Little, the Cambridge engineering consultants—a precursor to his "synectics." The approach was to take the problem given (ours was the development of quick-off protective clothing for chemical workers) and to try reformulating it in the broadest, most metaphoric terms, then search the solution space from there, avoiding technicalities until their solutions were required. Gordon was flamboyant and informal, his principles a cross of slightly controlled free association, followed a day later by close listening to tapes of the session for hints. We began with a wild look at "opening and closing" and came out with what was not a bad technical solution. (I even invented a draft-proof sleeping bag en route!) Those months gave me a striking sense of the power of intuitive leaps in problem solving and, in an interesting sense, gave me a livelier sense of the limits of the sort of problem-solving tasks I had been using in my own work. In addition, the work was enormously good fun, and it, too, had its effect on what I was to be concerned with next.

Educational Reform

I cannot remember when I first actually met Jerrold Zacharias. He is a man of enormous self-assurance. James Watson said of Francis Crick that he had never seen him in a modest moment. Nor have I ever seen "Zack" with a flicker of doubt—unless doubt were the formulated line for the day. He was convinced that schools were a scandal and should be reformed. I recall driving my son Whit up to Exeter for the start of the school year in 1959. I commented (he has reminded me since) that somebody ought to have a fresh look at the field of education. Shortly after, I had lunch with Zack and Francis Friedman, both physicists at MIT, both at work on a physics curriculum for schools. They wanted to talk about the growth of thinking in children. They were very bright, very well informed about schools, and totally irreverent about "established truths" in the psychology of learning, thinking, perception—particularly dicta about what children *couldn't* do. Andrew Gleason, the Harvard topologist, had tried his hand, the summer before, at teaching a few children some mathematics and, perhaps in the manner of Plato in the *Meno*, reported that he had never been able to reach the limits of their comprehension, "So long as I made it clear."

I began seeing more of Zack and Franny; their kind of talk

was what my research on the development of thought
needed—not little "tasks" but connected structures of ideas in
which to operate. This had also been clear in the work on
learning blocks. Francis Friedman was, moreover, an absolute
revelation to me in his intuitive gift for grasping and criticizing psychological ideas—and for all his critical acumen, he was
one of the most generous men I have ever known. It was an
intriguing period, my first *real* go at applied psychology in the
best sense—in Donald Broadbent's sense of finding generality
in practical problems. But I had no idea of what we were getting into!

That summer, 1959, the National Academy of Sciences decided to hold a workshop to assess what all the ferment in
science curriculum was about—the so-called post-Sputnik
boom. I was to be in the chair. We were at Woods Hole, in the
rambling country house that served the Academy as a summer
headquarters. The curriculum makers were there—from
mathematics, physics, biology, history. From psychology, we
lured, for ten days, as disparate and gifted a group as imagi-
nable, bound together only by a willingness to consider what
was going on in education: Lee Cronbach, John Carroll, Bärbel Inhelder, Kenneth Spence, George Miller, Richard Alpert,
Donald Taylor—and B. F. Skinner for only a day.

What came out of this workshop was a "director's report,"
The Process of Education, written by me and circulated to the
members for comment and criticism before publication. The
book appeared in 1960. Contrary to our modest expectations,
it exploded. The ebullient Paul Goodman announced in the
pages of the *New York Herald Tribune* that it would be a "classic,
comparable in its philosophical centrality and humane con-
creteness" to Dewey's essays on education. It became "a cen-
terpiece in the debate on education in America." The National
Education Association asked me to give the keynote address to
their annual mass meeting in Madison Square Garden, where
the returning voice reverberates like memories of the an-
nouncer of the Tunney–Dempsey title bout. Educational
correspondents of the *New York Times* and the *Washington Post*
featured it, and my Senator, John F. Kennedy (with whom I
had campaigned in his first election as Congressman from our
11th District of Massachusetts), telephoned to inquire about

educational legislation. I was catapulted into the midst of the raging educational debate—flattered, bemused, and skeptical.

My skepticism did not stem from doubts about the correctness of the position we had taken at Woods Hole. The position, as Franklin Patterson pointed out some years later, was structuralist and intuitionist, proposed in opposition to a founding myth in American education that was empiricist and pragmatic. I argued in the book consistently with my own growing belief in the importance of "models in the head," that the nature of any body of organized knowledge (a "discipline") was that it consisted of an underlying structure of propositions from which the particulars could be derived and only in terms of which their meaning could be grasped. The object of education, looked at cognitively, was to assure that a learner go as directly as possible to the underlying structure. Coverage was not the issue; penetration was. Once the learner had mastered the structural principles, he could then use them to generate interesting hypotheses, good "intuitive" guesses. Drill should not be repetition but practice in generating reasonable and testable predictions. The motives for learning may initially be extrinsic, but in the end they become intrinsic as well—the intrinsic pleasure of mastery and the minimization of surprise. The young learner, then, should not be *talking about* physics or *about* history or *about* mathematics in a derived school language; he should be *doing* physics or history or mathematics. Knowledge truly mastered was knowledge in some way rediscovered. A curriculum involved successive passes through the same domain, learning the underlying structure (and a supporting body of facts) in more and more powerful, formulated ways—a spiral curriculum, as it came to be called.

Writing a preface to a new edition of *The Process of Education* nearly twenty years later (after it had been translated into twenty-two languages!), I commented on the climate of emerging structuralism in which the book had been written. Certainly, the idea of models or structures as factors in cognition was to the fore, and I have already mentioned my involvement in such ideas. Noam Chomsky's ideas about generativeness were already much in discussion around Cambridge; Piaget was also much in my climate, and I had shortly before written a lengthy and appreciative review of the Inhelder–Piaget book on the transition from childhood to adolescent thinking. Still another part of the climate was Claude Lévi-Strauss, with whom, over the years, I had exchanged reprints.

Life was coming back into a pattern again. One day, late in the autumn of 1959, a most gifted and delightful woman, Blanche Marshall McLane, came to my office, sent by a mutual friend to inquire whether I needed a research assistant. She was Adelbert Ames' niece and had worked with him on his perceptual displays in Hanover. I hired her to work on the studies Molly Potter and I were then doing on the manner in which low-grade input from defocused pictures interfered with their eventual recognition. We were married in January, a combined family of seven children. We worked together on various perceptual studies, but in time her interests returned to a variety of other concerns—especially painting. We began then, and have continued since, a life of great richness and, indeed, some rather high adventure. Like me, she is a "water rat" and, together or with children and friends, we have sailed the three boats we successively owned from the Bahamas and Bermuda to Newfoundland and the coasts of Norway and Sweden. We have sailed through some rough storms. It is impossible ever to describe a happy marriage, which may be what led even Tolstoy into thinking they are all alike. From the intellectual point of view, I think it would be fair to say of my wife that I have never seen her either daunted by an idea because it seemed complex or impressed into submission by the prestige of its promulgator. She makes splendid, independent-minded company. She is, by any standard, a model blend of sympathy and good sense. She served with me in the times of trouble at Harvard, as cohead of Currier House, to which we will come later.

The early 1960s gave a marvelous opportunity for pushing as hard as one could, both within university psychology and outside in education. The financing of research was generous, and the spirit of reform and "rekindling" ran high with the election of Kennedy. Robert Frost read a poem at the Inaugural, and American antiintellectualism seemed at last in retreat. Soon after the election, I was given another chance to discover that my allegiance was to the university. One afternoon during the "Hundred Days," I had a phone call from

McGeorge Bundy. Would I be at all tempted "to get involved in this rough-and-tumble we play around here?" I think I was right to stay at Harvard. I am much better, I think, at formulating and debating proposals than I am at grinding them through to their compromised conclusions. I stayed at Harvard, even if I did spend a fair amount of time in Washington, D.C.

Center for Cognitive Studies

The Center for Cognitive Studies had been founded in 1962 and soon flourished. Its founding is a tale of its times. George Miller was unhappy with the polarization of "Mem Hall," where Smitty Stevens and Fred Skinner (the one preoccupied with acoustics and psychophysics, the other with operant conditioning and its ideological extrapolation into the marketplace) were keeping anything from changing. I was chafing from the "sociologization" of psychology in Social Relations, where "system building" under the gifted leadership of Talcott Parsons came, increasingly it seemed to me, to a focus exclusively on psychological conceptions that would fit the requirements of a sociological theory. Initially, I had applauded the effort to bring psychological and sociological ideas closer together and, indeed, had participated in many seminars at which just that was the agenda. It had been a rich exercise with such colleagues as Kluckhohn, Stouffer, Parsons, Murray, and Allport. But what seemed to *us* the center of psychology—the cognitive processes viewed in the broad—was being neglected at Harvard. And it could only grow if connected with other fields concerned with the nature of knowledge—philosophy, linguistics, anthropology. A center was needed.

George Miller and I wrote a two-page letter outlining our ideas to John Gardner, then of the Carnegie Corporation. A visit followed. Foundations (and Carnegie particularly) were eager to take initiatives that might realign university departments, and Gardner had been a leader in this effort. In a very short time, we were given a grant of a quarter of a million dollars for five years. Not enormous, but unrestricted, funds for explorations.

We went to the Provost of the University—McGeorge Bundy, who knew both of us well. He shared with Gardner the new and invigorating belief that growing an intellectual harvest depended upon cross-pollination. He believed, too, that centers were a useful instrument for challenging the traditionalism of departments. His first response, when Miller and I had outlined our hopes, was to laugh! Was there much difference between our Center for Cognitive Studies and what the University as a whole was supposed to be doing? He then swung around in his chair to the desk behind him, withdrew from its bottom drawer a large map of the University premises, ran his finger over the map until it came to rest on a spot that turned out to be 61 Kirkland Street, the former residence of President Eliot, which had long since gone to seed as a temporary roost for married graduate students. We were in business.

We had a small core of "permanent" members—really just the two of us. Though we had hoped that Roger Brown, who remained our great friend and supporter throughout, would join us, he did not, for he is, in his graceful way, a very private person. And we had a succession of visitors, chosen by ourselves and a "board" that included Roger, the philosopher Quine, the historian Stuart Hughes, and the linguist Roman Jakobson. Imagine visitors that included: linguists Chomsky, Katz, Jakobson, Levelt, Bever, and McNeill; developmentalists Inhelder, Vurpillot, Brazelton, Bower, Greenfield, and Carey-Block; philosophers Goodman, Sheffler, and Dreben; psychologists Mackworth, Jonckheere, Kahneman, Twersky, Treverthen, Bregman, Toda, and Wood. It was, to an extraordinary degree, a self-educating community. The supervision of graduate students was, as child rearing is in some "primitive" cultures, almost a communal responsibility. After Bundy's departure, the University never liked it much. Centers *do* obscure lines of authority. Our financing came entirely from outside sources—save for space and our two salaries—and the overhead was generous.

At the start of the decade, I was working on, among other things, mathematical learning in children. Associated with a visiting fellow, the mathematician Zoltan Dienes (an irrepressible pedagogue), we set out to explore whether indeed any *mathematical* subject could be taught to any child of any age in some useful form. We proposed to try mathematical group theory and quadratic functions for starters, to see where they might lead. I was interested in the *teaching* for its own sake—as a theoretical problem. What indeed goes on in instruction? The psychologist's model of the learning process virtually always leaves the learner on his own. In real life, we are surrounded by teachers, hint-givers, urgers-on, and net-holders.

Dienes has a respect for anybody's mathematical hypotheses that is profound and genuine. His pupils come, in short order, to respect their own intuitions. He is also a genius at finding concrete embodiments for those abstract ideas he is trying to get across. A quadratic function is one in which things are "square." It may be presented first as a thing in which, quite obvious to the eye, there are the same number of things in a set of containers as there are containers to put them in—in all its varied manifestations. The embodiments change, the descriptive formalism develops almost like a natural language. As issues come up, they are grabbed and exploited. Such an approach requires some combination of mathematical depth and intuition about the pupil's performance so the teacher knows how to give information and when it is needed. I mention Dienes' feats at some length, for they have always puzzled me. Or rather, the nature of instruction itself does. Five years after, I wrote a book with the title *Towards a Theory of Instruction;* over a decade later, David Wood (then a fellow at the Center) and I did a study on what, in fact, a tutor does. Wood persists (and has won the Spearman medal of the BPS for his efforts), and now Ira Goldstein of MIT has developed a computer program for primitive tutoring. It is one of the issues that lies deep and virtually unexplored in education—the nature of instruction. How odd that it should have received so little attention!

Other matters of a more conventional type were also concerning me at that time. Early studies that Postman and I had done indicated to what an extent "wrong" hypotheses were a liability in perception. As already noted, we set out to study these interference effects. We chose blur as the means of degrading a picture in a fashion to tempt wrong hypotheses with a likelihood of their receiving low-grade confirmation. I recall two students, Gerry Davidson and Phil Daniels, trying me out as a subject in the "ambiguitor" that moved a picture gradually into focus. The picture was a reproduction of a Renoir painting of a mother and daughter in an opera box flanked by red drapes. I was full of premature hypotheses. The picture came fully into focus: I could not make it out for nearly a minute. After much more research, Molly Potter and I published a little paper in *Science* on the effect. We received an inquiry shortly after from the head of the union of American airline pilots; they had observed that accidents due to human error often started with precisely such a history of wrong hypotheses under low-grade visual conditions. The general idea, in its broader implications, was of course picked up by Thomas Kuhn in his intriguing book on scientific discovery, noting how inappropriate theoretical paradigms prevent discovery of what is right under the nose. The work on perception that followed had principally to do with the study of eye-movements. But let me pick up that subject in a later section where it can be in context.

For a psychologist interested in intellectual development in the 1960s, the starting point was Piaget. Rightly so, for his structuralist reformulation truly "reconventionized" and modernized psychology in our day. But his was a needlessly quiescent account of development. As I read more Piaget, three points of dissatisfaction began to emerge. The first was his indifference to the *specific* history of an organism's experience. Whatever the child did, whatever he encountered within very broad limits, the stages unfolded in their timeless, logical way. The environment, indeed, was simply *aliment,* which, in slang, is like our pablum. Second, the operative filter to experience was always stage-specific. Nothing could get past it save what conformed to the rules of organization of the particular "stage." Was there no way of tempting growth? Was there, in Marxist lingo, no liberating principle? And third, Piaget's central concept of equilibrium controlling the unfolding of stages struck me as so much hanky-panky. It seemed to me that there *were* forms of environmental "nutriment" that had more effect on growth than others and these somehow got through or under the filter. Equilibrium, or lack thereof, did not seem a sufficient explanation.

I recall a visit at about this time from Alexander Romanovich Luria. I discussed my doubts with him. He then propounded a theory of action based on Vygotsky in which man operated on and transformed his environment by the use of a language-based Second Signal System. I read Luria's little book on the pragmatic function of language in development. It seemed to me that the burden of evidence was on the side of linguistic recoding as a major factor in the child's development. In Vygotsky's sense, there was a "zone of potential intelligence" that could be brought into play by the use of socially transmitted concepts and language. And we do not know the depth of that zone!

There followed a lively period of exchange between Geneva and Harvard, financed by Ford. Bärbel Inhelder spent a year at the Center and then there were visits back and forth with seminars. Piaget presided over his seminars and discussions with the somewhat slow and determined direction of a glacier. Data were presented by an *assistant,* always framed in a fashion to fit the logically defined topic of the year, and each year had its topic. "Le Patron" would then set forth the interpretation in a magisterial fashion comparable to a flawless Landowska performance of Bach's *Art of the Fugue*. It was breathtaking and brooked no major contradiction. If fundamental objections were raised, questioning the general *viewpoint*, they were handled with a rather withdrawn respect and put aside as out of the spirit of the logical framework. If within the framework, Piaget is a superb and totally engaged protagonist. His response is never "oppositional"; it is invariably to show, in ever more "logical" detail, how *his* argument handles all the phenomena necessary to it. It is a magnificent single-mindedness and, I think, lies at the root of his singular systematic thrust. But it is not easy to live with theoretically. He ingests everything offered, and it comes out more Genevan than ever.

I think the research on which I was then at work reflected, perhaps too much, the struggle to come to terms with the corpus of Piagetian work, and the strong bonds of the theory in which it was interpreted. Jackie Goodnow, I recall, commented that I had let myself get drawn too far off the functional base of means–ends analysis on which my theory of hypotheses had been based: I centered, instead, on the problem of representation—how to characterize the nature of the models in terms of which information was stored and transformed, with too little emphasis on the *use* of models. Enactive, iconic, and symbolic representations were seen as ends rather than as means in problem solving. Like Piaget, we were asking ourselves how levels of representation were attained, not how they were used. There were fruitful research spin-offs —particularly as regards the role of language in development, the role of conflict in stimulating development, and, particularly, the role of cultural factors in shaping the course of cognitive growth (principally, Patty Greenfield's contribution). But I feel that the theoretical thrust of the work as a whole came from Piaget. We dedicated the book to him. I recall well the lunch at the Ukrayina Hotel in Moscow at the International Congress in 1966 when we presented it to him officially. It was rather a stiff lunch, for he did not like the book. Roman Jakobson eased the occasion with a remarkable wit that can make light of any intellectual heresy. Piaget and I have not been very close since, though I keep a close working contact with Inhelder, Sinclair, and others there. For all that, the research and the book that came from it have had useful reverberations.

Man: A Course of Study

I left off the discussion of educational reform at virtually its beginning. It continued through the 1960s. There came into being in Cambridge, Massachusetts, yet another offshoot from the fertile tree of Jerrold Zacharias. This time, instead of physics, it was to be a social-science curriculum. Zack shared with Franklin Roosevelt the charming but devious practice of setting up or encouraging lots of competing seedlings to see which would grow fastest—doubtless the sign of a generous and optimistic heart. Cambridge was suddenly full of social-science curriculum seedlings—some serious, some bizarre. It was the age of curriculum projects, and Cambridge (with its nonprofit but wealthy Educational Development Corporation under Zack) had the means. Soon a "little seminar" was called together to sort out the confusion. Eventually, there grew out of the discussions a plan for "K to 12," as comprehensive curricula from kindergarten to the end of high school had come to be called. The upper end, on major themes in social thought leading up to the present day (evolution, technology, etc.), was to be presided over by the philosopher Morton White; below that there was to be a unit on the transformation of the idea of the American, from subject to citizen, supervised by the political scientist Franklin Patterson; and below that, for children aged ten to twelve, was to be a unit on man, on the nature of our species looked at biologically and culturally. That was the unit I was to be in charge of, with the aid of anthropologists and zoologists like Irven de Vore, Robert Trivers, and Asen Balikci, with Sherwood Washburn as consultant. Elting Morison was to preside over the entire enterprise. The psychological principles that were to guide us were very much along the lines set down in *The Process of Education*. Considerable grants were obtained from the government, and what was to be the most ambitious school–university collaboration in the making of social-science curriculum got under way.

Putting together *Man: A Course of Study* (MACOS) was an extraordinary experience in combining psychological ideas about pedagogy to fit not only the major ideas emerging in the human sciences, but also the demands of different media—print, film, graphics, "kits," and a variety of exercises for pupil and teacher alike. The germ of the idea for the course had come from "Soc. Sci. 8, Conceptions of Man," a year-long course in General Education at Harvard that George Miller and I gave together for some six years—including the years when MACOS was being constructed. For those of us involved, the experience was extraordinarily rich—intellectually, artistically, indeed over the whole range of the Allport–Vernon–Lindzey scale of values! I lured Peter Dow from the "Quaker Kremlin" of Philadelphia, Germantown Friends, to keep us in touch with the reality of schools, and in time we had a staff of teachers, artists, scholars, and lively graduate students that made for a very yeasty five years from 1962 to 1966.

We decided early on to avoid the format of a textbook *cum* teacher's guide. The course should be framed around "obvious" questions about man—what is distinctive about him, how he got that way, and how he could become more so. To answer any of these questions required inquiry into knowledge that, while not well established, was at least well investigated by scholarly research. The pupils were to get a direct experience of the data from which inferences were drawn—film records, field notes, behavior records, whatever. We turned to Lévi-Strauss' human exchange systems: affiliation, goods and services, and symbols, as defining human society. For the emergence of man, we turned to primate studies. How did we choose other peoples and other species to examine in depth? Luck helped. De Vore had already begun his long-term studies of free-ranging baboons in East Africa. His films and field notes were superb. We needed an accessible culture whose technology and way of life contrasted sharply with Western culture. We found Asen Balikci, a Canadian anthropologist who knew the Netsilik Eskimo of Pelly Bay, and we managed to get the Canadian Film Board to do a series of films on them under his guidance. Historical good luck was with us. Decades earlier, the Danish explorer–anthropologist Knut Rasmussen had visited the Netsilik. His journals and his transcriptions of their tales and myths were splendid. And when the time came to translate them into felicitous English, the poet Philip Booth turned up.

The experience with film was intriguing. With the help of Kevin Smith, we made "sound" films that had no commentary: the message had to be carried by the action, *its* sights and sounds. There is one film, indeed, in which an old man in the winter igloo tells a hunting tale in Netsilik, his auditors spellbound around him. It is beautiful in its directness. Smith quite justifiably carried off all manner of prizes, and pupils could look and figure out for themselves. Charles Eames advised us, "Better to fail well than succeed poorly."

Perhaps the most exciting medium of all was the classroom. We tried teachers, actors, scholars, even psychologists; we used seminars, lectures, "open plan." The chemistry of classrooms still eludes me—whether it produces leaden gloom or total and concentrated involvement.

We had an interesting failure. We "tried out" one summer in a school that had been made available to us by Newton, Massachusetts, with a few dozen eleven-year-old volunteers. The summer school was a huge success. But we failed to get children (save a very few) interested in the nature of language—"baby linguistics" as an approach to the human symbol system, "baby Chomsky" more precisely. David McNeill and Roger Wales presided. They even had the actor–linguist Paul Schmidt working his magic. The children did not lack for interest in the *literary* uses of language: Their renderings of the myths or the "guessed dreams" of the Netsilik were extraordinary. Was "linguistic awareness" missing? Or was it the separation of structure from use? The difference between a well-formed sentence and an ill-formed one, "meaningless" or "meaningful," moved them little. I think in retrospect that, had we concentrated on speech acts—felicity and sincerity conditions on speech—we might have been more engrossing.

What I realize now, and did not then, is that the proper target for a curriculum is *not* the pupil but the teacher, equipping a teacher for informed dialogue about matters that are not cut-and-dried, about which the teacher maintains a sense of conjecture. Such success as *Man: A Course of Study* has had, whether in America or England or Australia, comes from its tonic value for teachers. We succeeded modestly, and failed well! There have been prizes, honors, and such—even widespread adoptions. The course also inspired, in 1972, a vicious campaign against it from the extreme Right of American politics—the John Birch Society. It raised too many tender questions about man and human society. It was attacked as antireligious, as "evolutionary"(!), even as advocating wife-swapping as an alternative (a prurient misinterpretation of an Eskimo legend). A member of the House of Representatives from Arizona even charged that MACOS was a subversive conspiracy of those left-wing Harvard intellectuals, B. F. Skinner and J. S. Bruner! The National Science Foundation had its funds cut off by Congress for a few weeks until that body, badly advised in the Nixon era, agreed to pass judgment on the suitability of all future curriculum material prepared under their auspices. Only in America. In no other country where it is used has there been anything but murmurs of appreciation.

There was one other attack, a worthy one. Richard Jones wrote a book attacking the course as being guilty of too much intellect, not enough affect. He believed, and still believes, that a course of study should serve a self-realizing, somewhat therapeutic function. And while working on MACOS, he certainly enlivened the course by keeping us true to the affective, impulse-ridden, and anxiety-tortured lives of people who live in a subsistence culture—for example, the Netsilik boy who is not punished for stoning a snared seagull to death (a very powerful film sequence, again without commentary). How can we know whether Jones is right about what schools should do? His point is an interesting and powerful one, although I would hardly agree that MACOS is victim of the danger of dryness.

By 1966, I was running out of energy. My research and teaching, work on the course, service on the Education Panel of the President's Science Advisory Committee, Presidency of the American Psychological Society—they all added up to the famous eighty-hour week that may be easier to sustain in one's forties and fifties than when one is twenty-two, but that leaves one worn nonetheless. I recall so vividly the sense of relief, sailing off to Bermuda with our little gang in a friend's yawl. We were bashed around for a day or two just off the island, but it seemed so self-contained. Perhaps contrast *is* all!

Return to Research

What a calm contrast to return to almost full-time work at the Center. But there were changes in the air. *Studies in Cognitive Growth* had just come out. I felt the letdown one does feel after a cycle of work is done. I wanted to get beneath the kinds of phenomena we had investigated in that book. The field of cognitive studies was itself in process of change. Detailed studies of information processing were to the fore—filter theories, masking phenomena, studies of meta-contrast. The work was interesting within its limits. I lectured on it, even tried my hand at it a little with the gifted Danny Kahnemann, but I was not grabbed. My interest in developmental problems was still very much in force. I started some research on young infants, not being completely sure about what I wanted out of it, save possibly that it might provide me a run-up into the accomplished psychological functioning we had found in older children in the course of the previous cycle of work. And at the same time, true to form as Henri Tajfel wrote me, I picked up the thread of the perceptual work where I had left it a few years before, going back to perceptual recognition under degrading viewing conditions, this time using the technique of eye-movement recording in collaboration with that marvelously persistent analyst of eye-movements, Norman Mackworth. We were later joined by Elaine Vurpillot, who came to visit us for a year from the Sorbonne.

My interest in eye-movements had been kindled by reading and discussing with Mackworth the work of Yarbus and Luria, and of Vurpillot, particularly that aspect of their work that looked at eye-movements as external indicators of an internal search program. I had known Mackworth at the University of Cambridge. We had even wondered in those days whether the tracking of eye-movements might not be the road to understanding more fully and continuously the nature of unfolding perceptual hypotheses. Now we would look at differences between children of different ages and adults. We took as our displays some of the same stimuli that Molly Potter and I had used in our studies of blur-interference. What we learned was that, even down to age three, humans do in fact deploy their line of regard in a fashion consonant with the information value of features of a picture as judged independently by other judges. Big transport saccades take them to high-yield areas, and small saccades are used to search around within the area. Obviously, major features of the display not at the center of regard are being processed peripherally, judging by the manner in which regard shifts to them after a prior area has been exhausted. And indeed, there turns out to be very little difference in the pattern of ordinary eye-movements (uninstructed) between adults and children. One of the major ones of these is in the ratio of small to large saccades, the former being closer inspections around a highly marked informational feature. Young children do less close looking linked to the big patterns of movement. But I think I am not exaggerating when I say that it takes a quite experienced eye to distinguish the child's from the adult's record. Indeed, when one sets instructed tasks for subjects—as when Vurpillot in her elegant work asks children to judge whether two displays are alike or different—one can certainly find differences in the overall program, *what* it is that the child compares in making his judgment rather than anything intrinsic about the oculomotor system. Research in this promising field continues and, indeed, becomes possible now by virtue of new techniques not only of recording, but also of analyzing data. Indeed, along with a research student of mine, Peter Coles, I am in the midst of just such studies at Oxford. That will have to wait until a later installment!

The work on early infancy, started on my return to the Center, also continues now. I knew nothing about infants— aside from the direct experience I had had of my son and daughter and nephews and nieces. The incomparable Berry Brazelton, Harvard pediatrician and (along with Richard Held) an old tennis partner, took me in hand. He must have been appalled at my initial ignorance, but I am not shy with infants and read speedily. We did clinic rounds, observed infants in various tasks, looked at research films together. I trotted off to Bill Kessen in New Haven and Lew Lipsitt in Providence to search for procedures. My research assistant, Ilse Kalnins, was doing her Ph.D. at Totonto, stranded in Cambridge by her postdoctoral zoologist husband. She knew far more than I did (though *I* ended up as *her* cosupervisor). Soon we had a group going—Colwyn Trevarthen, Alistair Mundy-Castle joined from Europe, and Hanus Papousek in flight from Czechoslovakia. Tom Bower came later, and Jerry Kagan was also on the scene, though his interests were somewhat different.

I was back on my own street, searching out the roots of inference. And in the six years from then till my departure for Oxford in 1972, we managed quite a few variants on that theme in a rather unsystematic way, ending up studying the growth of skills. I never dreamed then then that "infancy" would become all the rage!

It soon becomes apparent, when one studies infants, that there is far more there than meets the unaided eye. What one needs are behavioral procedures by which the infant can make his information processing accessible for analysis. We—Ilse Kalnins and I—began with sucking. Drew Marshall helped us develop a highly sensitive device for its registration. In successive studies, we discovered the extent to which the infant could regulate his sucking as part of a self-comforting system in response to changing environmental disrupters, could alter the burst–pause pattern to suit the requirements of an operant-conditioning task with milk as a reward (Don Hillman's thesis), could suck in order to bring a picture into focus or desist when sucking defocused it (and then reverse when the conditions were reversed, all the while coordinating his sucking with his viewing of the picture). Meanwhile, Brazelton and Main, and then Trevarthen and Richards, were showing the degree to which mother and infant coordinated their joint attention and joint arousal in face-to-face contact. And a few floors below us, Bower was getting on with his studies of the perceptual precocity of infants, and Kagan with his studies of the sensitivity of the infant to changes from habitual presentation patterns. Marshall Haith, then fresh from Yale, was demonstrating that infants in the dark with minimal stimulation actively searched out their domain and were anything but passive. My own further work with Barbara Koslowski showed us that infant skill developed in a quite predictably rational fashion, subroutines being mastered for particular tasks and, once mastered with the consequent freeing of processing capacity, combined with other subroutines to achieve more complex goals. Mundy-Castle and Anglin were showing the extent to which infants could follow a hidden trajectory of a vivid stimulus that disappeared *up* in one window and then *down* in another. And the great bulk of the research was done on infants in the first half of their first year. At later stages, Greenfield and Smith were examining the grammatical combining of holophrase with gesture and context in the one-word utterances of infants.

I think that it would not be parochial to say that, in those five or six years at Harvard, work at the Center and in the group around it helped turn the concept of "helpless infancy" a little on its head. Virtually all the players—and I have only named half of them—are still at it elsewhere, and it is still too early to say where it leaves things. We are all, I suspect, much too close to know.

For all the productivity, however, this was not a happy period at Harvard and in America. Vietnam, with all its desperate inhumanity, was beginning to tear the nation apart. It also released something extraordinarily parricidal in the youth culture that started out in the innocence of "flower people" and led eventually to the Weathermen. For the first time in my academic life, I felt active hostility from some of the postdoctoral fellows, veterans of wherever they had been involved in the Vietnam protest or in university uprisings. I was strongly opposed to the war. My son Whit was in Vietnam in the Army. He was no supporter, but he was there as were many thousands of others. And beyond Vietnam, domestic issues of inequality had finally been made ineradicably clear by the Blacks in America. It was a matter with which I had become deeply involved in Washington.

The Revolution of Rising Expectations

In the atmosphere of the latter 1960s, research felt almost like an escape from the miseries of the world—from those miseries close by, as in ructions in the universities; from those at a middle distance, as in the squalor of American ghettos; and from those at a distance, in Vietnam. Earlier in the 1960s, I had been somewhat involved in getting Head Start under way. By 1963, there was already a good deal of discussion about the "irreversible" loss in cognitive development in children with insufficient early opportunity for stimulation. The "deprivation model" was very much the leading metaphor. Various friends, notably Urie Bronfenbrenner, and I had lobbied together in Washington for the improvement of preschool provision, particularly, for "deprived" children.

One episode gives a sense of the times. Another good friend, Adam Yarmolinsky, a brilliant young lawyer and one of Robert MacNamara's "whiz kids," had just become Sargent Shriver's principal aide in the new Office of Economic Opportunity, established by President Johnson to lead the "war on poverty." When I told Yarmolinsky about the currently circulating ideas for something like a "head start" for deprived children, he arranged for me to see Shriver, whose wife and I had served together on the Board of the John F. Kennedy Center in Nashville. I broached the idea. Shriver's response was: "Are you *seriously* proposing that the *federal* government get into nursery schools when we hardly dare to poke a nose into ordinary public education in the States? It's political dynamite." I departed for the Boston plane.

About a week later, at cocktails before dinner, the phone rang. It was Shriver asking if I could come down to talk more about "that idea." The conversation was curious the next day. I had mentioned "pilot projects" to explore how such a program might be put together, having very much in mind the models that had been tried out by Susan Gray and Nick Hobbs in Tennessee and by Bettye Caldwell in Syracuse. Shriver was urging that in a matter as important as this one, pilot projects were "too fastidious." If the need is there, one plunges in. In the American political perspective of that time, I suspect he was right. So Head Start came into being. Julius Richmond and Nick Hobbs did an enormous job of attempting to give it shape. Meanwhile, a number of us worked in a White House committee, on a more comprehensive child-care bill to be guided through Congress by Representative Brademas and Senator Mondale. I recall a dark, wintry Sunday evening I spent with Urie Bronfenbrenner in the Executive Offices overlooking the White House, drafting part of a speech we hoped President Johnson would give, supporting the proposal for comprehensive child care. He did give it, but by the time the bill had worked its way through the Congress, Nixon was in the White House. He vetoed it. The *New York Times* invited Bronfenbrenner and me to write one of their "op-ed" guest editorials, which we did in the form of an open letter to the President on America's short-sightedness toward children. The ebullient Daniel Patrick Moynihan, then in transit from Harvard to President Nixon's circle of advisers, visited me in my office shortly after. Would I support the President's new proposal for an Office of Child Development? I told him I would anytime there was a sign that it was more than a paper promise. There never was such a sign. Instead, there was the Westinghouse Report alleging that Head Start (hardly off the ground) was a failure—even though, for example, it showed that almost 90 percent of the parents interviewed felt the program had helped their children (a finding that, it seemed to me, suggested that, surely now, steps could be taken to involve parents more in the program). Fortunately, Head Start survives, and it may take many years before such an institution takes a shape suitable to its task.

By 1968, Harvard erupted much in the same pattern as other universities. It seemed a unique event as it came upon us, but it was a familiar scenario. I had always been close to undergraduate life at Harvard, as a teacher, as a member of Winthrop House, and eventually as comaster of Currier House along with my wife. In one respect, I welcomed the new political consciousness among the Harvard undergraduates. Far better than the Eisenhower years! But I disliked the political bullying by the "Red Moles" of the ordinary, guilt-ridden, moderate undergraduates. It seemed to me that the best approach to the "troubles" was to take them up substantively on their merits as they arose. Let student protests be dealt with nor as irrational expressions of parricide (which doubtless they were for some students), but on their merits within the legal framework. I know this is nineteenth-century liberalism and not very fashionable, but though I know the arguments of Rawls on the monopoly of justice by those in power, I still believe in the rule of law and the process of legal change.

Not surprising, then, that I urged that if indeed the ROTC *were* at Harvard in violation of constituted procedures, then the procedures should be amended (for which there was no taste locally) or the ROTC should be phased out by legal means. It was an emotive issue. There was a strike, a mass meeting of ten thousand students in the Stadium with strike votes and the lot. Two members of the Faculty were invited to speak—Stanley Hoffman and myself, both of us political moderates by temperament and stance—and we both urged moderation, a not very appealing line in that atmosphere! The chemist Paul Doty and I finally worked out a compromise acceptable to the Faculty and the Harvard Corporation, and I was given the sad job of negotiating the three Services out of the University—sad, for I found their serving officers honorable, sympathetic, and innocent.

The storm was over, but there had been enormous damage to the University. I recall entering occupied University Hall, having asked permission as Master of Currier House, to see what my people were demanding. Something irreversible had indeed happened there in the hallowed Faculty Room where I had been so awed at my maiden meeting by the thought of William James, George Santayana, and the presence of Whitehead and Roscoe Pound. Now, like a Hogarth print, it seethed with students in debate. It was something as irreversible, psychologically and symbolically, as I have ever experienced. It ended badly with a police "bust," and that further divided the University.

I'm often asked how I could leave Harvard after all those years and all those commitments. When the troubles were brewing, my wife and I agreed to take on the co-mastership of the new Currier House. Like many others, I foresaw troubles and thought that Harvard should try to react by reexamining itself as a university community. The bitterness of the "bust" spelled an end to that. The President, Pusey, finally resigned, and Harvard returned to a self-protective and very "managerial" orderliness under a new President. It was made plain that the Center for Cognitive Studies should now rejoin the Psychology Department, that the rule of departments was being reestablished and strengthened. I had also been very put off by a high-handed veto by the President of a cherished plan that Jerry Kagan and I had worked out jointly with the Children's Bureau, the National Institute of Child Health and Human Development, and the city of Cambridge, whereby Harvard would join in establishing a new "model" daycare center as a pilot project in national, local, and university cooperation. The mood was very depressed. George Miller left for Rockefeller, Morton White for the Institute, Kim

Romney for La Jolla, Alex Inkeles for Stanford—all close friends.

Move to Oxford

It was in this atmosphere, in 1971, that I received an invitation to take the Watts Professorship at Oxford. My weariness with the local scene was doubtless added to by the state of the nation: Nixon had just been swept into office by the greatest majority in history. Another element I considered was my feeling of "Europeanness" in intellectual formation. And the Oxford invitation also had some historical roots. In 1955, a "caucus" of Stuart Sutherland, Gilbert Ryle, and several others at Oxford had tried to get me to put in for the Chair that Humphrey was then vacating. But I had wanted to raise my two children in America, and Isaiah Berlin had, quite inadvertently, put me off by commenting about the prospects for psychology in Oxford—that the University was "like treacle: if you press hard against it, it is like stone; if you press gently, it giveth sweet progress." Now that my children were launched, Oxford had finally accepted (or seemed to have accepted) psychology, and the Watts Professorship had few administrative duties attached to it. My wife and I could afford the cut in salary. However, the biggest factor was Oxford itself. Alan Bullock, the Vice Chancellor, Isaiah Berlin, then President of Wolfson College of which I was to be a Fellow, and Larry Weiskrantz, who presides administratively over the Department of Experimental Psychology, were extraordinarily welcoming and cooperative. It was a lively scene. It looked like a good place to launch into a new phase of work in a bracing environment. I am enormously fond of Britain. I knew the country well (though not Oxford), had always enjoyed the open quality of discussion and the British capacity for friendship. They are reticent but loyal, and extraordinarily "personal"—capable of great kindness and, perhaps the other side of the same coin, also capable of stunning bitchiness. To have an Englishman for a friend *or* an enemy is an awesome experience! Fair-mindedness and bloody-mindedness are their yin and yang.

Harvard could not have been kinder, nor Oxford more cooperative, during my year of transition, a year that I spent on two enterprises. I wanted a year to read as widely as I could on the evolution of immaturity among primates, and during the year, I wrote "The Nature and Uses of Immaturity." I also wanted to prepare to sail the Atlantic in our old 32-foot water-line yawl, *Wester Till*. The year done, my wife and I departed from Manchester, Massachusetts, on June 17, 1972, with a few friends. We broke the journey at St. Johns, Newfoundland, and landed in Lymington on the south coast of England on July 14. It was a beautiful and trouble-free passage with some excitement from iceberg hazard in the dense fogs of the Grand Banks. We had birds with us all the way—puffins, terns, gannets, guillemots, dovekeys, razorbills, and even a displaced carrier pigeon who joined us in the Western Approaches, rested an hour, and departed for France. At the close of a very courteous inspection by Her Majesty's Customs and Excise, the boarding officer asked casually, "You don't by any chance have any drugs on board?" Yes, I said, I had six ampules of morphine for emergency injury. "What a pity, for it will mean filling out endless forms." He paused. "You're going to Oxford, aren't you? You must surely know somebody in the medical faculty there? Would you mind terribly taking those ampules with you and just giving them to him? It will save so much trouble." I'm told I am the first Oxford professor in history to sail himself across the Atlantic to occupy his chair. A rather specialized distinction!

What a contrast, a few weeks later, to fly to the International Congress in Tokyo. My new colleague, Peter Bryant, had told me that no visa was needed for Japan, and none is—if you are British. Fortunately, I was rescued by the incredibly efficient and welcoming Japanese organizers of the Congress.

Oxford has two worlds—the world of Colleges and the world of the University. The world of an Oxford College is intensely personal in a ritualized way, and highly convivial. It is a lens that focuses both the loyalty and the bloody-mindedness of the British character. There is no subject too small to matter if somebody in the College cares about it. The University is represented by one's Department, and I can only speak of Experimental Psychology. In Experimental Psychology, one's specialty matters deeply. Psychology is often regarded in the University as an "upstart" and an "easy option." In Britain, it is a field that receives little love and recognition from the Establishment. Only three British psychologists have ever been elected to the Royal Society, and none has ever been elected to the British Academy. There is a fair amount of self-hatred among British psychologists, that most often takes the form of dismissiveness toward specialties down-market in rigor from one's own. Some British psychologists, for example, are never so flattered as when mistaken for a physiologist or pharmacologist or geneticist. But perhaps this is increasingly endemic to psychology around the world.

Oxford psychology is curiously compartmentalized, and the emblem of its compartmentalization is the seating pattern at 11:00 coffee, in which each specialty group sits—the "information processors" here, the "brain and behavior" people there, the social psychologists in that corner, the developmentalists in another. It can easily be said that Oxford is greater than the sum of its Colleges. Of the Psychology Department it can be said, curiously, that the whole is less than the sum of the parts. For, individually, it is a Department of first-class people: Larry Weiskrantz, Jeffrey Gray, Donald Broadbent, Ann Triesman, Peter Bryant, Michael Argyle, to mention only some of the better-known. The members are fiercely hard-working, both as teachers and as research workers, but turned in on specialties. It is difficult to get sustained conversation going on the shape of psychology as a whole.

My first six years at Oxford have been enormously rich for me. It did not start well. I cast around at first to find a fresh way of pursuing my interest in the earliest period of cognitive growth, in the years before the child began his career as a user of language. I had, so to speak, "brought a team" along with me—Aidan Macfarlane and Paul Harris had been with me at Harvard, visiting from Britain, and came back, and some students came as well. I very soon collected a group of research students and postdocs who could, in the Oxford manner, form their own little in-group—and a very talented lot they were. Drew Marshall, who had helped so much at Harvard in designing apparatus, came along for the first few months to sort out the technical problems of the laboratory. Work started on perceptual development, with apparatus designed by Stephen Salter, and the group was soon turning out studies on the effective visual field of very young infants, on mother–infant bonding, on the impact of early mother–infant separation occasioned by the infant having to be put in intensive care. It looked as if one of the outlets of the work on infancy was to be a collaboration between our group, the pediatric group at the John Radcliffe Hospital under Peter Tizard, and the Department of Psychiatry—with Aidan Macfarlane, a physician–psychologist serving as the bridging agent. The object of the research was the exploration of how various forms of early care, particularly the forming of a close and early link between mother and infant, affected the course of development. After spending much time formulating a joint project, we were turned down by the Medical Research Council. I think it was too "broad" for official taste. It was my first "turndown"! We lost our team.

My own interests turned increasingly to the study of early communication behavior in children prior to the onset of full lexico-grammatical speech. It was a surprising departure for me. I had never really worked directly on language acquisition before—though I had been close to Roger Brown, David McNeill, and George Miller. I think it was probably Patty Greenfield's work on the structure of holophrastic speech that got me directly involved. My previous reluctance to get involved in language work stemmed, I think, from the feeling that formal syntactic analysis was only indirectly related to the psychological processes that interested me. Syntax was a generative system whereby one could go powerfully "beyond the information given." In this sense, it was like mathematics.

Roger Brown's book had come out in 1973. I had read it with great admiration, along with the new Greenfield–Smith manuscript. But one particular paper led me to the path I now travel: Joanna Ryan's on the social context of language in the Martin Richards volume on socialization. It is a beautiful paper, and it guided me into a literature "endemically" Oxford—speech–act theory and, more generally, modern pragmatics. I read Austin's *How to Do Things with Words,* John Searle's *Speech Acts,* Grice's chapter on the "cooperative principle" from his William James Lectures. Then on to Harrison, Strawson, and Lyons on deixis. We began a longitudinal study of six infant–mother pairs. Michael Scaife began his work on the child's sensitivity to pointing as an ostensive precursor to later forms of reference; Andrew Meltzoff, who had come with me from Harvard, was beginning his work on early facial imitation during the opening weeks of life.

I had imported the weekly "coffee-and-doughnut seminar" that had been a feature of our research group at the Harvard Center. It was extremely lively. But there were differences between Oxford and Harvard. The Oxford tradition of cut-and-thrust can, at its worst, be appalling. It leads to point-scoring and to the shooting-down of new and interesting hypotheses by the immediate marshaling of the limiting or invalidating case. For those deft in debate, it is an exciting form of flirtation. But scientific productivity is not particularly correlated with deftness in debate. My research group was a mix of people from quite divergent backgrounds—English, Scots, American, Spanish, Swiss—and our visitors ranged from Eastern European linguistic philosophers to Australian enthusiasts reporting on infant perception. In time, we formed an extraordinarily lively group. Of all my students, I think the ones who have the least skill in collaborating are the English. They seem least able to resist savaging an exposed flank. On the other hand, they are perhaps the ones most capable of lone work and a high degree of self-direction.

I began straining toward a general theory of how young children acquired the uses of language. Communication involved conventional procedures for fulfilling various extralinguistic functions—calling attention to objects, demanding or requesting, forming social relationships, and so on. These communication procedures emerged and became conventionalized in well-practiced action formats cooperatively involving mother and infant. The procedures are, at first, highly controlled by the mother in a way to join her and her child in a net of contingent interactions, the mother operating by reliance upon an updatable theory of the child's performance. The first results of this work began to appear in early 1975 in a paper on "From Communication to Language" and in more specific technical papers since. To say more on this matter would carry us into the future—a future now taking shape, I hope, in the form of a book. It is to be called *Acquiring the Uses of Language.*

The more deeply I have gone into the psychology of language, the more impressed I have become with the absence in psychology of certain forms of psychological analysis that are needed in the study of language acquisition and language use generally. One such is the role of intention and the perception of intention in others. Language use is premised, in a massive way, upon presuppositions about *intentions* and the *reasons* why people do or say things. Yet psychology, or at least positivistic "causal" psychology, ignores the role of intention and assigns no interpretation to reasons in the regulation of behavior. Such matters are most often treated as epiphenomena. How then can psychology connect with linguistics and sociology and anthropology and jurisprudence, where the establishment of conventions is premised on intentions and reasons and even "responsibility"? In 1976, I was invited to give one of the Herbert Spencer Lectures at Oxford, and I used the occasion to voice these misgivings, urging that psychology should not cut itself off from the sciences of culture. I'm afraid that most of my Oxford colleagues in Experimental Psychology felt I had let their side down! When my lecture appeared in *The Times Literary Supplement,* there was a double-barreled barrage—fan mail from one part of the psychological community and brickbats from the other. Skinner and I—I had attacked the antiintellectuality of behavior theory as an instance of our illness in psychology—had a sharp and overheated and prolonged exchange in the correspondence columns of *The Times Literary Supplement,* and in the spring, there followed a Department seminar. If nothing was settled, at least the debates caused some buried presuppositions in psychology to come out into the open, where they belong.

Two other ventures were launched in these past six years in Oxford. They are rather of a piece. One is a publishing venture, *The Developing Child.* There is such a gap between current, scientific *knowledge* about human development and its *application* in daily life, either in affecting policies (as in education or child care) or, indeed, in guiding or alerting an individual parent. The arranging of the course of human development, whether private or public, is in some crucial respect a "policy decision" based on a hoped-for outcome. I' *should* have the benefit of the latest and most robust knowledge we have about human development. Several of us hit on the idea of a series of books, written for the intelligent layman and the nonpsychological professional, summing up the state of the art in various domains of developmental psychology. Michael Cole, Barbara Lloyd, and I, with the Harvard University Press in America and Open Books/Fontana in Britain were able to convince some of the top scholars in the world to write such books. More than a half dozen have appeared. More will follow.

The other venture is, in George Miller's generous sense, about "giving psychology away," in this case developmental psychology. It did not take me long after my arrival in Britain to get back on my old battleground—the adequate provision of care for young children. Something deep is happening in the economically developed world. In 1974, in Sweden (to take the most advanced case), slightly more than half the mothers of children of five years or less were in the labor force. (Britain lags behind, but is catching up fast.) Who looks after their children, and how? Another facet of the same problem: In London, the incidence of clinical depression among mothers at home with children under five is running at about 25 percent, treated mostly by tranquilizers and mild antidepressants. There are plenty of studies to indicate what the pressures are on mothers—economic and psychological—and what kinds of factors put young children at risk. Indeed, there are now quite a few good studies about how part-time and full-time care outside the home can be arranged and organized so as to help the child. But what is extraordinary in Britain, as in America, is how little impact such research has on the practice of child care. Practitioners do not know about the work, or they pooh-pooh it as not related to their situations, or (if it runs counter to their child-care "ideology") they dismiss it.

When the British Social Science Research Council asked me whether I would like to field some research on the state of child care in Britain, I chose this for my topic: How does one get research on human development into practice? We are studying Oxfordshire as a microcosm and are mounting cooperative local studies with key practitioners serving as collaborators. To narrow our range of concerns, we have centered on the development of sustained attention or "concentration" in preschool children. How can one get practitioners to improve their practices with this goal in view? The research literature points to a trinity of factors that seem to increase concentration:

1. Opportunity of playing and interacting with adults.
2. Challenging materials with intrinsic structure.
3. Play and games with considerably elaborated rule structures.

But this trinity, alas, runs counter to middle-class, liberal, nursery dogma that urges the adult to keep off the child's back, to provide materials (water, sand, clay) that permit expressiveness, and to see that the children's play is spontaneous and minimally constrained. It is *not* going to be easy to "give psychology away"! However, the study is in process and we shall see.

Some Sort of Summing Up

My theoretical interests have been strongly functionalist. Hypotheses in perception, strategies of thinking, functions of attitudes, uses of language—all of these mark me as following the tradition of James, Dewey, McDougall, Vygotsky, and Tolman. And, surely, my developmental studies express the same interests. I am also a mentalist and have always felt that the banning of "mental" concepts from psychology was a fake seeking after the gods of nineteenth-century physical sciences. Professor Boring, whose historical world tended to be structured in neat, bipolar category pairs, would surely have put me in the tradition of Act Psychology with Ach, Brentano, and the South Germans, rather than among those interested in the contents of mind, with Wundt and Fechner. I am interested in structure and in the explication of structural principles, but always as an expression of some function and in the light of criteria derived from an assessment of function.

I realized fully one evening in the company of the anthropologist Alfred Kroeber that, like him, I believed in the "supraorganic" status of culture, definable independently of individuals who "represented" it in various roles—what Karl Popper today calls "World Three." I see culture as a product of evolution, which, once emerged, changes the biological status of man irreversibly and makes the application of Darwinian principles false and misleading. Biological factors constrain what culture can be, but culture has laws of its own. In this respect, I have always found myself sympathetic to such diverse "culture-isms" as Vygotsky's Marxism and De Saussure's structuralism.

For all my theoretical interests, I am (as the record must surely show) attracted to action. That, too, must express my functionalist bias. I have never been, for more than a few months at a time, without a cause of some practical sort—from devising science and mathematics curricula for children in developing African nations, to trying to increase the use of human potential in a giant technical corporation (General Electric), and even to giving advice on how to turn the rich coffers of Time-Life Inc. to the publishing of good science and humanities, etc., etc. I have also done my turn, as so many have, on panels in Washington, in the Presidency of APA and several of its Divisions. Certainly, my involvement must derive in large measure from an interest in power and influence, which I take to be ordinary enough. I have never been much involved in electoral politics, except for the time when I helped John Kennedy run a poll of our 11th Congressional District of Massachusetts his first time out and even that was more out of friendship than political interest. Though the exercise of power as a phenomenon has always interested me, I have little taste for doing much more than advising about it. I have never wanted to enter politics or "go into government."

Neither have I ever hankered after a "pure" research job. I enjoy teaching, enjoy narcissistically the "hooking" of others on problems that move me. I have had a dazzling array of graduate students, and many of them do all manner of distinguished work and have come through the experience intact enough to hold distinguished chairs from St. Andrews through Princeton to Macquarie. It is not very difficult to have such students if you teach at places like Harvard and Oxford with an occasional summer session at Berkeley! I even like teaching undergraduates and must have lectured to thousands of them over the years. It has its function, lecturing, but it is not a very deep one pedagogically. I have worked extremely hard at preparing lectures all these years. Was it the best way to expend pedagogical energies? Like others of my kind, I have delighted in having postdoctoral fellows: You get all the benefits of collaboration after others have done the lowly work of preparing a collaborator for you! I have hugely benefited from their presence, as a perusal of my bibliography will show.

I have greatly enjoyed collaboration. My collaborators have been my major tutors: Leo Postman, Robert White, George Miller, David Krech, George Klein, Renato Tagiuri, Jackie Goodnow, Patricia Greenfield, David Olson, Norman Mackworth. I have also (or mostly) enjoyed supervising doctoral theses. I cannot keep sufficiently dispassionate to avoid battles of will from time to time, which pain me (and pain my suffering student far worse). I am rather "social" in most aspects of my psychological work—although I grow less so with age, I suspect.

One part of my intellectual life has, however, always been highly introverted and solo. I published a book of essays in the early 1960s entitled *Essays for the Left Hand*. When I am "playing" near the source, in literature and the arts, trying to turn intuition into something more communicative and ponderable, I become very much the loner. My left hand goes through unpredictable cycles, probably responding to what it can pick up in the "rag-and-bone shop of the heart."

Do I feel I've been "successful"? Yes, in some conventional way. I've earned the usual honors and medals and have a boxful of honorary degrees. But in some curious, rather distressing way, the extrinsic honors seem never to connect with the parts of my mind with which I think about problems, do research, teach, or get involved in public matters. The ceremonies of award always seem to be for a character who is not a member of my cast. So the question needs to be asked in some other form. I do *not* feel as if my work has brought off any profound revolution either in my own thinking or in the world of scholarship or human affairs. In certain crucial respects, I feel I have failed. I had hoped that psychology would remain a unity, would not become fragmented into rather incommunicative subspecialties. It has. I had hoped it would find a way of bridging the gap between the sciences and the humanities. It has not. I had hoped it could guide social or public policy to a better formulation of democracy. Perhaps that was my misreading of the nature of politics.

In one respect, I have been extraordinarily well provided for—in my friends, inside psychology and out:

> *Think where man's glory most begins and ends*
> *And say my glory was I had such friends.*

But having said that much, I must add a perspective toward the future. I think that the work on which I and my friends are now engaged, on the acquisition of language and on the manner in which language serves communicative functions, I think this work is beginning to take hold. It *is* concerned with many of the issues about which I expressed concern a moment ago—with intention, with culture, with the relation of structure and function. Perhaps a link with linguistics will even provide an arterial connection with the humanities. Psychology is divided and cut into pieces, but there are some fragments around that may regenerate a new and more interesting whole. In any case, the prospect is lively enough to keep me at the eighty-hour week with relish!

1977

Selected Publications by Jerome S. Bruner

(with J. J. Goodnow and G. A. Austin) *A study of thinking.* New York: Wiley, 1956.

The process of education. Cambridge: Harvard University Press, 1960.

On knowing: Essays for the left hand. Cambridge: Harvard University Press, 1962.

Toward a theory of instruction. Cambridge: Harvard University Press, 1966.

(with R. R. Olver and P. M. Greenfield) *Studies in cognitive growth.* New York: Wiley, 1966.

Beyond the information given: Studies in the psychology of knowing. Selected, edited, and introduced by Jeremy M. Anglin. New York: Norton, 1973. [This volume of representative articles also contains a complete bibliography up to 1973.]

From communication to language. *Cognition.* 1975, *3*, 155–267. (a)

The ontogenesis of speech acts. *J. child. Language,* 1975, *2*, 1–19. (b)

Other Publications Cited

Kalnins, I., and J. S. Bruner. The coordination of visual observation and instrumental behaviour in early infancy. *Perception,* 1973, 2, 307–314.

Ninio, A., and J. S. Bruner. The schievement and antecendents of labelling. *J. child. Language,* 1978, 5, 1–15.

Ratner, N., and J. S. Bruner. Games, social exchange, and the acquisition of language. *J. child. Language,* 1978, 5, 391–402.

Hans Jurgen Eysenck

Early Days

I was born in Berlin, Germany, on March 4, 1916—not a particularly happy choice. Germany was losing the war; inflation was to follow, then mass unemployment; this led to Hitler and World War II. The Chinese prayer: "Let me be born in uneventful times!" can hardly have been heeded by the fairies, good and bad, who surrounded me at birth. They managed a reasonable assortment of gifts, favorable and unfavorable; most of these, of course, derived genetically from my parents. Both were actors. My father was already a well-known star, playing juvenile leads and occasionally singing in operetta—he was always the prince, in Ruritanian uniform, who sent the various maidens in the cast (and the audience!) into a swoon. My mother was very beautiful, but only a starlet at the time; she fell in love quickly, but was equally quickly disenchanted. They were divorced when I was two years of age.

I lived with my maternal grandmother from then on. She also had theatrical blood in her. When she was young, producers prophesied a great career for her on the operatic stage, but she fell and dislocated her hip, which was then so badly set that she became a permanent cripple. Small wonder that I too was drawn to acting. At the tender age of five or six, I played a part in a film in which my mother was the star—I still vaguely recollect trundling my hoop through the Tiergarten, tearfully bringing my film parents together after some long-continued misunderstanding. My father wanted me to carry on, but my mother (much more sensible) was adamantly against it, and so the world lost a budding star of stage and screen.

On my father's side, I come from a family of Rhenish, Catholic peasants; on my mother's side, from a family of Silesian, Protestant doctors. Neither had any particular religious interests, and although I was christened and later confirmed in the Lutheran faith, I remember that I had to be bribed by the promise of a bicycle to attend the classes preparing me for this holy occasion. My grandmother was an ardent Catholic, and her faith stood her in good stead when, during the war, she was sent to a concentration camp where she died. When the armistice came, Lloyd George promised that he would squeeze the Germans till the pips squeaked; I was one of the pips and almost died of starvation. My mother ceased to be a starlet and became a star; older German readers, who still remember the silent films, may recall her by the stage name of Helga Molander. She married a Jewish film producer, Max Glass, who was one of the extremely talented group that made German films world-famous at that time. When Hitler came to power, he and my mother had to leave, of course, and he set up business in Paris and continued to produce and direct outstanding films.

I was told that if I wanted to study at the University, I would have to join the SS; this idea was so repulsive that I decided I would prefer to go into exile. I had no illusions about the disastrous lowering of living standards likely to follow such a move (the Nazis had restricted to a minimum the amount of money that could be sent out of the country) or the permanent alienation of being regarded as a foreigner in the country of your adoption. Also, there was the possibility (perhaps even the likelihood) that Hitler would catch up with those who had "betrayed" the Fatherland—at one time, it looked only too likely that Germany would win!

However, I did not feel that I really had any choice. To me, Hitler and Nazism in general were an abomination, liberty and free speech a necessity; I simply could not see myself living a life of luxury as the beneficiary of this tyranny. I have since sometimes blamed myself for not staying to join the underground, but that was easier said than done. I was only a schoolboy when I decided to leave in 1934; I had strong, left-wing sympathies (he who is not a socialist when young has no heart; he who remains one into middle age has no head), but distrusted the communists almost as much as the fascists. For that reason, I had not joined any party, and you cannot, in a dictatorship as ruthless as Hitler's, just go up to anybody and ask: "How can I join the underground?" I clearly foresaw the inevitability of war; nothing I could have done would have made any difference. So I left, first to study French literature and history in Dijon, then to study English literature and history in Exeter. Finally, I decided to settle in London, where I tried to enroll in the University of London. They required me to take the matriculation examination, which I did after a year's study at Pitman's Commercial College (where I also learned shorthand and typing). Then came the question of what subject to enroll for.

Beginning in Psychology

My childhood had almost programed me for the arts. My family was solidly concerned with literature, theater, films, opera, music, painting, and the arts in general. In the flat that my mother owned and in which I lived with my grandmother, there was a large library, containing all the classics of German, French, and English literature, and I had read solidly through most of them, making up the rest at Dijon and Exeter. I loved poetry above all other arts, and in part, my decision to go to England was because I preferred English poetry to French. (Later, I shifted my main artistic experiences to painting and, later still, to classical music.) But in spite of all of these environmental pressures—to which were added the expressed wishes of my parents, my grandmother, and Dr. Glass—I had, from the beginning of my conscious life, been quite decided that art was for fun, for emotional experiences, for enjoyment, and that my life's work would lie in science. By that, I meant physics and astronomy. I still remember my first reading of Max Born's *Umsturz im Weltbild der Physik,* which set me off on my quest. I read widely, all outside the school curriculum, of course, and became really quite knowledgeable in what was then the "new" physics, helped by a private tutor who was a Ph.D. student in that subject.

Therefore, when it came time for me to enroll in the University of London, I had no doubt about what to study and confidently put down: physics. Alas, the University of London is one of the worst places in the world as far as bureaucracy and red tape are concerned; I was told I could not study physics because I had taken the "wrong" subjects in my matric! I could not wait another year and retake the "right" subjects, so I asked if there was any scientific subject I could take. Yes, I was told, there was always psychology. "What on earth is that?" I inquired in my ignorance. "You'll like it," they said. And so I enrolled in a subject whose scientific status was perhaps a little more questionable than my advisers realized. Have I ever regretted my choice? Often. I am now resigned to it. However, looking back, I think that perhaps the choice made for me was for the best; in physics, competition is a great deal fiercer than in psychology, and I might never have got anywhere in that exalted company!

In any case, I enrolled in a department presided over by Professor (later Sir) Cyril Burt; Charles Spearman had just retired and was still occasionally to be seen and heard. The department was very small; the only two academic appointments in it were J. C. Flugel, a noted psychoanalyst who also taught "orectic" and social psychology, and S. J. F. Philpott, who taught experimental psychology and psychophysics and was, oddly enough, a believer in the racial unconscious of Jung. Burt himself was a founder–member of the British Psychoanalytic Society, and we were saturated with "dynamic psychology —quite contrary to the repeated accusations of noted Freudians that undergraduates in psychology were always presented with a hostile account of this particular religion. I didn't enjoy this teaching much, but I decided to take it all in at face value. After all, I had the examination to think of, and I knew that, as an alien (soon to become an "enemy alien"), I had not only to get a first-class degree, but to really impress my teachers.

I also studied philosophy (a compulsory part of the examination), sociology (a *pis aller* subsidiary subject—I had elected physiology, but the course was full of medical students and there was no place for me), and statistics (Egon Pearson gave an excellent course, which I attended). I learned some genetics from J. B. S. Haldane and L. Penrose and founded the University College Psychological Society, becoming its first president. Occasionally, I visited my grandmother in Berlin. The clouds of war were constantly getting thicker, and I felt very dispirited when all my Cassandra-like warnings were blithely disregarded by my fellow students, who thought I was getting paranoid on the subject.

I began my first experimental and statistical studies at that time. My first article appeared in 1939 (Eysenck, 1939a), just after I got my B.A. degree, before the war broke out, and after I married Margaret Davies, a Canadian girl who had a degree in mathematics and was working as a secretary in London at the time. She later took an M.Sc. in psychology and published several papers. Leo Thurstone's famous first monograph had just come out, factor-analyzing the correlations between fifty-six mental tests and concluding that there was no general factor, as Spearman had hypothesized. Burt asked me, a first-year student, to reanalyze the huge matrix, using his method of group factor analysis, and to write a review article with him. This was an offer I could not refuse, and I carried out the analysis (which on a hand-crank calculating machine was quite a big job), showing that there was ample evidence for both a general factor and a series of group factors in the matrix. Several other people followed suit, using different methods and coming to the same conclusion; Thurstone later concurred.

I was also busy with an experimental study of hypnotic phenomena (Eysenck, 1941) in which I showed that the fairy tales about the tremendous perceptual and other powers of hypnotized people were just that—fairy tales; the only difference that occurred under hypnosis was the partial abolition of pain sensations and muscular fatigue. The conclusions are still correct, I believe, and the paper is still occasionally cited. I also got busy on work in experimental aesthetics; I chose the subject partly because of genuine interest, deriving from my deep concern with art in general and visual art in particular (although I also experimented with poetry), and partly because there was no apparatus in the department worth having, and aesthetic preferences could be studied without such. In addition, I was becoming proficient in statistics, particularly factor analysis, and the data lent themselves to the methods of inter-correlating persons, instead of tests. I naively thought that I had actually invented this method; I only learned later that both Cyril Burt and William Stephenson, who came down from Oxford to lecture to us on psychometrics, had made the same discovery and were furiously disputing originality. I also thought I had invented the Spearman–Brown formula for my paper on the validity of judgments as a function of the number of judges (Eysenck, 1939b). Fortunately, I discovered, before publishing it in the *Journal of Experimental Psychology,* that it had been known for quite some time. (I was very ignorant in many respects then!) Some sixteen articles altogether resulted from my work on experimental aesthetics (including sense of humor), all published around this time; these formed the basis of my Ph.D. thesis, which was presented and accepted in 1940.

War and marriage together presented me with many problems. I tried to enlist in the Royal Air Force, but was contemptuously turned down as an "enemy alien." (I had just failed by a few weeks to beat the five-year requirement of residence for naturalization.) The other services followed suit, and indeed, there seemed no place at all for me to help in the war effort. I had little choice but to register for a Ph.D., although in wartime this seemed an odd choice. The department had evacuated to Aberystwyth, in Wales, where I could hardly follow as my wife was tied to a war job to London. I therefore had no supervision at all for my research, and, in fact, Burt fondly believed I was doing something quite different. I worked hard, read widely and voraciously, and settled down to a life of rationing, nightly bombings, and a feeling of utter uselessness, while England fought for her life—and for civilization. When France and Norway fell, and the facts about Quislings and the "fifth column" became known, there arose a clamor to intern all enemy aliens, and the government passed legislation to that effect. Twice the police came to take me away, and twice Margaret and I talked them out of it. Unlike the German police, these men were thoroughly ashamed of what they had to do (the whole episode is one of the more shameful ones in English history) and grasped at any excuse, even the excuse that I had to finish my Ph.D. The law was finally repealed, just in time to save me from the rather unpleasant fate faced by many refugees—that of being interned with genuine Nazis.

The Ph.D. finally obtained, all doors to employment were still closed to me, as an enemy alien. Psychology was effectively barred to me because of the odd battle between the Cambridge experimental school, under F. C. Bartlett, and the London psychometric school. Instead of each valuing the other as contributing to an important area of psychology, each looked down on the other as inferior; no psychometrics were taught in Cambridge and little experimental psychology was taught in London. This absurd situation extended to academic employment—you had to be either one or the other. It might be thought that Burt would have helped me, but in spite of his great qualities as a psychometrician, geneticist, and mental-test expert, Burt was a somewhat unstable person who distrusted any of his students whom he suspected of possibly criticizing or supplanting him in any way. His feelings toward me veered, from favorable (undergraduate) to ambivalent (graduate) to hostile (postgraduate), to such an extreme extent that—to take but one example—he opposed my professorship when that was considered by the University. I was forced to join the ARP scheme (Air Raid Precautions)—groups of trained personnel, who spent 24 hours on duty and 24 hours off, and who were skilled in dealing with the effects of air raids on London. I learned a lot about the British working class from this experience (I was stationed in one of the worst slum areas of London), but little else. They were extremely xenophobic, and I would have had a hard time except for the fact that, shortly after I joined, the cricket season started, and the very first ball bowled at me I slammed for a six over the nearby schoolbuilding. That produced a lot of genuine friendliness, and I became their star batsman. I have always been good at ball games, winning open tennis tournaments as a junior, playing football and handball for the school and for the BSV (Berliner Sport Verein). I later played tennis and boxed for the University.

Research in Abnormal and Social Psychology

I was rescued from this rather aimless life by Philip Vernon, with whom I had become friendly through our mutual interest in experimental aesthetics. Aubrey Lewis, a rising star in British psychiatry, was looking for someone to replace E. Trist, a psychoanalytically minded psychologist who held a research post at the Mill Hill Emergency Hospital and who was joining the army to work on the newly created War Office Selection Boards. Lewis hired me, although I knew nothing of psychiatry or clinical and abnormal psychology; thus accident again intervened to throw me into a field of study that I knew nothing about and did not particularly like. Again I had to make the best of it; there was no choice. I started my experimental work with studies on suggestibility in hysterics (Eysenck, 1943, 1944b) and a general experimental analysis of suggestibility (Eysenck and Furneaux, 1945). I also worked on such diverse topics as parotid-gland secretion in affective mental disorders, screening tests for neurotics, graphological analysis, memory tests, projection tests, drug effects on suggestibility, experiences of success and failure, the effects of motivation on intelligence, and the like. (I shall not reference these studies; space is too precious.) More important are two other studies, which both led to later book publication.

The first of these (Eysenck, 1944c) dealt with a large-scale factor analysis of patients' symptoms. It led to the theory that there are two major personality factors, neuroticism and extraversion–introversion, and that neurotic diagnostic groups did not constitute meaningful, qualitatively discriminated groupings, but were simply points in the two-dimensional space generated by these two axes, with hysterics being extra-verted neurotics, anxiety states and others being introverted neurotics. In my studies of hysterics and other diagnostic groups, I had become suspicious of the reliability of diag-noses and had made a special study of this reliability; I found it to be abysmally low, and this led to my rejection of the categorical, diagnostic method of classification and the prefer-ence for a dimensional framework (Eysenck, 1970a). I also de-cided that factorial studies were not enough to properly define these dimensions; there should be a linkup with experimental work, embodying psychological theories regarding the nature of these dimensions. These ideas led to the work described in my first book, *Dimensions of Personality* (Eysenck, 1947a), which contains the germs of many later experiments.

I was now in the position to ask for helpers in my work, and I was given funds to employ two charming and beautiful girls—Hilda Himmelweit and Asenath Petrie, both of whom carried out many of the experiments in the book and both of whom became quite well known in psychology through their later work. The war ended; we all went back to Maudsley Hospital from which the personnel of the emergency hospitals had been evacuated; and I finished my second book (Eysenck, 1952c), in which I added psychoticism as a third major dimen-sion of personality. It is only recently that I have carried out sufficient empirical and genetic work to make this concept very meaningful (Eysenck and Eysenck, 1976e, 1976b). How-ever, in trying to prove that psychosis was a quantitative, not a qualitative concept (i.e., that the dimensional approach was appropriate), I hit upon the method of criterion analysis (Eysenck, 1950) and applied it to psychotic disorders (Eysenck, 1952b) with very positive results. This is my only original con-tribution to psychometrics; it has been misunderstood by al-most all critics as to purpose and method, and I still believe it has an important role to play in the analysis of continuity or dimensionality.

The other important article I published while at Mill Hill dealt with social attitudes (Eysenck, 1944a; see also Eysenck, 1947b). This article suggested the idea that the right–left di-mension along which social attitudes had been traditionally analyzed had to be supplemented by another dimension which

I called "tough-mindedness," as opposed to "tender-mindedness." Political parties formed a horseshoe pattern, with fascists tough-minded and right, communists tough-minded and left, conservatives and labor-party members right and left, respectively, and both intermediate on tough-mindedness, and the liberals tender-minded and intermediate on the radicalism–conservatism axis. Much empirical work was done, including a special study of fascists and communists (Eysenck and Coulter, 1972c), and the main body of this work was published under the title *The Psychology of Politics* (Eysenck, 1954). I have recently taken up these topics again, demonstrating a powerful genetic influence on the determination of social attitudes (Eaves and Eysenck, 1977) and replicability in other cultures (Brunis and Eysenck, 1976). The book earned me the undying hatred of communists and militant left-wingers, and much of the savagery of the criticism with which it was received is probably due to such political animosity. Unfortunately, history was to verify, in no uncertain manner and sooner than I thought, that communists indeed had this quality of dogmatic, authoritarian, Machiavellian tough-mindedness in common with fascists (to use some terms that are in many ways similar to my conception of tough-mindedness).

However, I am anticipating. When the war ended and we returned to Maudsley Hospital, which was a teaching hospital with Professor (later Sir) Aubrey Lewis as Professor of Psychiatry, I was still employed, together with Hilda and Asenath, as research psychologist under a Rockefeller grant. My wife and I had just bought a house near the hospital when quite suddenly the grant was terminated, for no very obvious reasons. For several months, I had no income, mounting debts, and little prospect—only the vague hope that Lewis would succeed in persuading the University to create within the University Postgraduate Federation an Institute of Psychiatry in which I might find employment. He did succeed, and we arrived at an understanding that I would be working as Reader within his department, with the special remit to create a profession of clinical psychology in Great Britain— something that, oddly enough, did not then exist. I decided to go off to the United States to see what was being done there, and I was lucky enough to receive the offer of a visiting professorship at the University of Pennsylvania. I took this up in 1949–1950 and, with a travel grant from the Rockefeller Foundation, had the opportunity of traveling through Canada, to the West Coast, and other parts. I shall recount presently what I learned.

Just at this time, my marriage was breaking up. Incompatibility is one of those expressions whose psychological content is slight, even though its meaning is clear to all who have had experience of it. I had a son, Michael, who was just five years old then; he is now married and is making a career for himself in psychology. He has been Lecturer at the University of London for some years and has concentrated his research on the field of human memory, in which he has published quite a few articles. Recently, his first book, also on this topic, has appeared (M. W. Eysenck, 1977). His interest in memory has led him to investigate personality, among other independent variables, as a causal agent in producing individual differences in performance. His major concern has been to identify the actual part of the memory process affected, and he has demonstrated the strong influence of arousal and of extraversion–introversion on retrieval, in particular.

I married Sybil Rostal, daughter of the famous violinist. She had come to Maudsley to change over from the study of mathematics and chemistry to something more human and, in due course, obtained her Ph.D. under Philip Vernon and has continued working with me ever since. She is Senior Lecturer in the University of London and has specialized on the construction and validation of personality questionnaires (several of our coauthored papers and books will be found in the bibliography). We have been happily married ever since and have three sons and a daughter to show for it. The eldest son has completed his postgraduate training in electronic engineering, our daughter has just obtained a degree in English at Sussex University, my next son is working in computers, and the last son is still at school. Sybil came with me to the United States, and after war-torn England, with its blackouts and its rationing, it was as if the land of milk and honey had at last opened itself to our delighted gaze when we entered New York.

Clinical Psychology: Creating a Profession

In the United States, I started, among other things, on my *Structure of Human Personality* (Eysenck, 1952d). This textbook has gone into three editions and gives a historical account of the development of modern theories of personality. But for the most part, I looked at clinical psychology and, to tell the truth, I did not like what I found. There was emphasis on subservience to psychiatry and to medical models; there was insistence on diagnostic testing, mainly using projective techniques; and there was psychotherapy. I could detect no scientific evidence in favor of any of these, and I missed what to me seemed particularly important: the application of psychological knowledge and principles to the problems of abnormal psychology. This second-rate imitation of unfounded psychiatric beliefs and practices, unsupported by any empirical evidence worth looking at, did not seem to me the sort of thing to bring home—but what to put in its place? I published a number of articles at that time on this topic; my pamphlet on *The Future of Psychiatry* (Eysenck, 1975b) is the latest in that line. My conclusions were as follows:

1. Clinical psychology can only justify itself if it applies the laws of academic psychology and the findings of experimental study to the problems of psychiatric abnormality.

2. The psychologist must be independent; if he is dependent on the psychiatrist for his bread and butter, he will inevitably take over the latter's concepts and values.

3. Psychotherapy and projection tests do not derive from psychological theory or knowledge, and there is no independent evidence for their practical usefulness; until and unless this theory or knowledge is supplied, they should not form part of the training of the clinical psychologist.

4. The logic of the above approach leads inevitably to the development of new treatment methods of a behavioral kind, i.e., behavior therapy.

All this sounds mere commonsense now, but at the time it was wildly revolutionary. When I published my findings regarding the lack of evidence for the effectiveness of psychotherapy (Eysenck, 1952a; see also Eysenck, 1966b), the sky fell in. I immediately made enemies of Freudians, of psychotherapists, and of the great majority of clinical psychologists and their students. Even nowadays, when a research proposal of mine is discussed in some committee, there are inevitably several people who, never having forgiven me for that paper, will veto strenuously any proposal I make, however innocuous it may be as far as they are concerned. Yet the truth of what I then said is not really in doubt and is acknowledged today even by leading psychoanalysts (e.g., Malan, 1976.) Similarly, my condemnation of the Rorschach and other projective methods (Eysenck, 1958, 1959b) met with a lot more undisguised hostility than a factual summary of the evidence would normally elicit. Much the same happened when I read a paper on the theme of my 1952 paper at the Oxford meeting of the British Psychological Society. At the end of it, a noted professor of psychiatry raced down the aisle, shouting, "Traitor, traitor!" and attempted to engage me in fisticuffs; fortunately, he was prevented from doing so by some quick interceptive work on the part of some friends of mine.

On these points, and on the independence of psychology from psychiatry, I saw eye-to-eye with Sir Aubrey Lewis. After I returned from the United States, I got my own department, was appointed Professor in due course, and was put in charge of the training of clinical psychologists and of the clinical work we were to do for the hospital. The relation between the Institute of Psychiatry and Maudsley Hospital (to which was soon joined the Bethlehem Royal Hospital, better known in history as "Bedlam") was symbiotic—they furnished us with patients to test and treat, and we carried out psychological investigations for them. But the ultimate responsibility for these investigations was mine, as befits an academic department. My colleagues could carry out their work without having to worry about pleasing psychiatric overlords. There was much friction at first, but gradually my point of view prevailed—helped a lot by the fact that all the registrars had to sit examinations including, prominently, two papers on psychology, for which we undertook the teaching; in this way we had a chance to educate them to a proper appreciation of psychology and its contribution to psychiatry. I still believe that this absolute independence of the psychologist is a prime requisite for any reasonable relationship between the two professions; I would have bowed out altogether had it not been granted.

The question of behavior therapy is another, rather less happy, story. I have stated that I accepted the job as research psychologist at the Mill Hill Emergency Hospital knowing nothing of psychiatry (other than what Flugel had taught us about psychoanalysis); this was not quite true. I have told the story elsewhere of how I made friends with A. Herzberg, a refugee German psychoanalyst who had worked out a system of "active psychotherapy" in which he incorporated tasks that the patients had to carry out (Eysenck, 1979a, in press). From the apparent effectiveness of this system, the apparent ineffectiveness of psychotherapy and psychoanalysis, and my reading of Watson's case of little Albert and the work of Mary Cover Jones, I put together a theory of behavior therapy that was, for all intents and purposes, similar to that which I still hold. When I joined the Mill Hill Emergency Hospital in 1942, that might have seemed to be the time to put my theories into practice. Unfortunately, Aubrey Lewis was adamantly opposed to any therapy being carried out by nonmedical people; while he was the most reasonable of men on all other issues, I found him quite unreasonable and, indeed, irrational on this issue. With so much else to do, behavior therapy had to take a back seat.

When I got my chair and my own department, I began to recruit people to undertake the clinical work and teaching, and I tried cautiously to get them to try out some of the methods I had been thinking about. This proved possible, with the help of some brave consultants (such as my old friend Linford Rees, later to become president of the Royal College of Psychiatry), who sent us suitable patients for treatment. The general attitude was one of unrelieved hostility—not so much to behavior therapy, but rather to psychologists doing it. Nevertheless, we persevered.

In 1958, we had collected enough case studies to show that the approach was viable, and I had been doing enough reading and studying to feel reasonably confident. I also thought that the time had come to trail my coat. Accordingly, I gave a lecture to the Royal Medical Psychological Society (the major psychiatric association in Great Britain), at which I presented my general formulation for the discipline of behavior therapy (Eysenck, 1959a). This was attended by an overflow crowd, mostly psychiatrists; they were not amused. Several books followed (Eysenck, 1960a, 1964b; Eysenck and Rachman, 1965c), in which I tried to present the evidence, both scientific and clinical (see also Eysenck, 1976e); to these should be added my *Handbook of Abnormal Psychology* (Eysenck, 1961), in which I tried to collect together all the known experimental evidence about abnormal psychology. (The second edition of this *Handbook* came out in 1973). A long, drawn-out battle ensued to make the hospital accept behavior therapy and, in particular, psychologists as therapists; this struggle is over now, and there is no further opposition—at least not at the joint hospitals! There are still backwoodsmen in some of the provincial mental hospitals, who refuse to recognize the changes that have taken place, but their numbers are daily dwindling.

The establishment of a proper *modus vivendi* would have been much more difficult had I not been fortunate in being able to appoint as head of the clinical section M. Shapiro, one of my former students whose attitudes in this field were very close to mine, and who had the integrity and courage to stand out for a proper degree of independence from psychiatric pressures for such things as Rorschachs, psychotherapy, and the like. He has made his own contributions to both research and therapy, but of these no doubt he will tell himself in due course. He was succeeded by S. Rachman, who had to cope with great pressures due to the rapid growth of the clinical section. Psychiatrists have learned that psychologists can make a valid contribution in terms of their knowledge and expertise, and this contribution is more and more in demand. It is the resolution of our original (and probably unavoidable) quarrels with psychiatry that pleases me most about this tangled story. I took no delight in having to fight for the independence of our science or for its right to make its contribution on its own terms, and the present, very amicable relations existing at the joint hospitals make me very happy—even though the credit must go to the hard work and sturdy common sense of my clinical colleagues who demonstrated their worth once and for all.

It should not be thought that our department is concerned to push one particular orientation (other than the general scientific approach); quite a few of our students have become psychoanalysts, for example. Several of them are working at the Tavistock Clinic, the holy shrine of British psychoanalysis; one is a psychiatric consultant, with a psychoanalytic orientation; one became the editor of the *International Journal of Psychoanalysis* and various other "dynamic" journals. What characterized this particular group, all of whom went from research to psychotherapy? As far as I can determine, only their extraversion! Conversely, several took the clinical course and then went into research; dare I say it that all of them were introverted? Whether it may be justifiable to frame the hypothesis that applied work appeals more to extraverts, while fundamental research appeals to introverts, is neither here nor there; the observation is significant by chi squared, however we may interpret it. Although ambiverts should be in the majority, we have found few people who can successfully combine research and clinical work; perhaps that is the reason why clinical research is often of such poor quality.

Organizing a Department

It was not, of course, only the clinical side of my department that I had to get going when I started it; in my view, no clinical department was viable that was not associated with a strong research facility. My department accordingly had two divisions: one was clinical teaching, which also included responsibility for the clinical psychological work of the joint hospitals; the other was laboratory research, for which we accepted Ph.D. students interested in any of a large set of different research problems, most of which are not in any way clinical. This laboratory research is currently directed by Irene Martin on the human experimental side, D. Fulker on the animal side, O. White on the psychometric side, and G. Wilson on the social side. I introduced a special representative of statistics into the institute in my department, but he was found to be so useful in general that a special department was created for him; Professor A. E. Maxwell taught whole generations of psychiatrists how to design their experiments and how to analyze them. The difference in the quality of psychiatric work, comparing the state of the art when I joined the hospital and now, is almost unbelievable. To have future professors of psychiatry arguing about the virtues of cluster analysis, discriminant function analysis, and factor analysis is something that no one could have predicted thirty years ago.

When I started my department, there were three great lacunae in British psychology. There were no animal research groups (although there had been one in Cambridge before the war), there was no physiological psychology, and there was no behavioral genetics. To my mind, no department could be called complete without these facilities, and accordingly, an animal section was started as early as 1949, just before I went to the United States. I got Professor Roger Russell, later Secretary of the APA, to come over and set it up, as no one in England had the necessary background. He made an outstanding success of it and then left to take up Burt's chair at University College. The best-known of his successors was Professor Peter Broadhurst, who later founded the Department of Psychology at Birmingham University. We collaborated on the genetic work on emotionality in rats, an area that had always been close to my heart (Eysenck and Broadhurst, 1964d; Broadhurst, 1975). There are several other animal experiments of mine in that book (Eysenck, 1964c), to which might be added one or two later ones (e.g., Eysenck, 1963a; Broadhurst and Eysenck, 1965; Chamove et al., 1972; Sartory and Eysenck, 1976). The animal section is still very much concerned with the genetics of behavior; there are a number of purebred strains, such as our emotionally reactive and nonreactive strains, our high-and low-avoidance conditioning strains, etc., and recently the work has extended to include behavioral studies of *Drosophila* and their genetic determination. We have also, of course, looked at environmental determinants of behavior; Joffe's (1969) book on prenatal determinants of behavior, for instance, is still a classic in that field, and we have done many studies to test my theory of incubation of anxiety (Eysenck, 1968), which completely restates the law of extinction and has led to a new model of neurosis (Eysenck, 1976b).

On the physiological side, I got research going with the help, and then under the direction, of Irene Martin and Peter Venables, who later started the Department of Psychology at York University; their *Manual of Psycho-physiological Methods* (Venables and Martin, 1967) is widely known. Our most recent work is concerned with the relation between intelligence and personality, on the one hand, and evoked potentials on the other. We have also done research on habituation, conditioning, and other hypothetical correlates of personality. Martin and Levey (1969) provided a revolutionary impetus to the study of eyeblink conditioning (which does not yet seem to have percolated to the textbook level), and Eysenck and Levey (1972d) demonstrated the importance of controlling stimulus parameters in establishing the relation between conditioning and personality.

As regards the third lacuna, one of my major interests, since the early days of J. B. S. Haldane, has been the biological and, particularly, the genetic determination of human conduct. I have tried to understand the direction that modern genetics is taking and to apply the resulting methods of biometric genetic analysis to actual data collected in our department (Eysenck, 1976a). Our early work (Eysenck, 1956a; Eysenck and Prell, 1951) was followed by the collection of a large twin register now containing over 2,000 pairs of twins. Some of our work on this register has already been published (Eaves and Eysenck, 1975, 1976, 1977), but a lot more is in the pipeline, and all of it will eventually be published in book form, as a monograph on the inheritance of personality. Chapters on the genetic determination of psychoticism, and sexual attitudes and behavior, respectively, are contained in books dealing with these topics (Eysenck and Eysenck, 1976g; Eysenck, 1976d). In all the later work, I have worked closely with the Department of Genetics of the University of Birmingham, particularly with Lindon Eaves; such cooperation is essential if we are to avoid repeating the errors of earlier psychologists, whose ideas of genetics were—shall we say?—a little eccentric. The new formulas, which are extremely powerful and enable us to test complex models of genetic and environmental determination, seem almost unknown in the United States; there is no evidence of close acquaintance in recent texts by leading experimentalists. Such knowledge would obviate a good deal of the nonsensical arguments about genetic determination of intelligence, for instance; we are in the middle of a study of this variable also, but nothing has as yet been published on the topic.

Central to these studies was, of course, my theoretical conception of personality, which led to a large series of factor-analytic studies; a recent book by Eysenck and Eysenck (1969) gives a brief review and many detailed empirical data. We also continued the experimental study of the concepts of neuroticism and extraversion (Eysenck, 1960b; Eysenck et al., 1957b), and were working up to a causal theory of these concepts. My first effort relied too much on Hullian theory (Eysenck, 1957a) and was a partial failure; my second attempt, going back to biological factors like the limbic system and the reticular formation–cortex loop (Eysenck, 1967), was more successful, to judge by later studies summarized in *The Measurement of Personality* (Eysenck, 1976c). A three-volume set of *Readings in Extraversion–Introversion* (Eysenck, 1971a) has brought together a lot of little-known empirical evidence. I have always believed that the eclectic way in which most psychologists look at personality is wrong. If we want to get anything better than a series of mutually contradictory theories, none falsifiable, then we must try to integrate our theories of personality with what is known about the psychology and physiology of the human animal. My work has always been directed toward achieving such an integration, and in some directions, I believe we are now in process of achieving it.

I have sought integration along two other pathways. Having suggested a dimensional system of personality description, I realized that drug action on human behavior could be systematized along the same lines (Eysenck, 1963b). If, as I believe, introverted behavior is caused by a congenitally high cortical arousal level, and extraverted behavior by a low level, then CNS stimulant drugs, such as nicotine and amphetamine, should have introverting properties. Similarly, drugs can be found that increase or diminish neuroticism; others again that increase or diminish psychoticism. This hypothesis is capable of precise testing, and we have carried out many tests that, on the whole, have been successful (Eysenck, 1967). There are also implications for the differential susceptibility of different persons to drugs (as for instance in the so-called sedation-threshold experiment); these predictions also have been verified for the most part. I believe this is an important direction for research to take; unfortunately, psychologists have difficulties in working with drugs without medical supervision, and pharmacologists are not usually interested in personality or in individual differences.

The other direction my research has taken has been in trying to predict life experiences, such as sexual attitudes and behavior, from the personality model. I have already mentioned my most recent book dealing with this topic (Eysenck, 1976d). Other similar ventures have been my books on criminality (Eysenck, 1964a; most recent edition, 1977) and on smoking (1965b). In view of the complexity of real-life situations, motivations, chance accidents, and the like, the outcome has been quite promising; I believe that this constitutes a viable line of future research. The genetic determination of much of this behavior is of particular interest to me; Eaves and I are just completing the manuscript of a book on the genetics of smoking behavior, and the evidence on crime and sex is already considerable.

A good deal of our work has been devoted to the production of better questionnaires, specially constructed to take into account our psychological concepts of the personality dimensions involved. Most of the work on this has been done by my wife, who combines in a unique manner statistical sophistication and psychological insight. Our most recent inventory, the EPQ, although published in our joint names, is largely a monument to her skill, patience, and endurance; it took a dozen years and over twenty separate factor analyses of different forms and populations before a satisfactory inventory was finalized (Eysenck and Eysenck, 1976f). Earlier inventories, such as the EPI and the MPI, have been quite widely used in the United States; they are, I believe, the only alien corn that ever prospered in that inhospitable clime!

The London–Cambridge disagreement has already been mentioned. When I started in psychology, there was an absolute monopoly, like a feudal supremacy, of the "Oxbridge" tradition. Almost by divine right, chairs in Great Britain or the Commonwealth would be allocated to graduates from Cambridge. (Oxford came into this much later, having been prevented from setting up a proper "school" for a long time.) There were one or two exceptions, like Rex Knight in Aberdeen; such "colonials" were occasionally tolerated. But, for the rest, there was an iron curtain around academia that no outsider from London or Redbrick could penetrate. My own department and chair had to be created independently, and I went on to see twelve of my former students break through this *cordon sanitaire* and achieve professorial status in England. The feudalism is still there, but it is dying; that is an important contribution to a living democracy. Apart from these twelve, I have had another forty or so students who have become professors or heads of departments all over the world, from Germany to the United States, from Canada to Japan, and from India to Australia; others will no doubt join their exalted ranks. Our students, in general, have been quite productive and successful (Drewe, 1971); this may lend some support to ideas I have published about program research and the running of academic science departments (Eysenck, 1970b).

As explained there, I believe strongly in program research—i.e., fitting Ph.D. students (if they are willing!) into an ongoing series of research studies that help them to discover an orientation, rather than wasting their time on "one off" experiments that will never make a proper contribution to science. Such program research increases motivation, helps them to get started and select a proper project, and ensures that their contribution will not be forgotten. Spearman pioneered this approach in London, following such excellent examples as Pavlov, Wundt, and Kraepelin; it is difficult to think of many outstanding psychologists who did not practice program research to some extent. I also believe in persistence and in continuity; that is why I have, in essence, stuck to my original post and have never felt tempted to accept any offers to go elsewhere; to have gone elsewhere would have broken the continuity, both as far as working with valued colleagues was concerned, and also as far as the building up of apparatus, technology, and expertise was concerned. As head of a department, you invest in your colleagues: to leave them when they have reached a high degree of achievement is folly— quite apart from disrupting firm friendships and personal relations. The converse applies too: Colleagues who could have gone elsewhere, to earn much higher salaries and occupy much more prestigious posts, have stuck with the department. All this may sound old-fashioned, but a department only has value in terms of the people in it; either it is a team or it is nothing. This should not need spelling out to psychologists, but departments where all members are friends are not so numerous that the point does not need to be made. "Physician, heal thyself!" is an injunction that may also apply to psychologists.

Writing Books

Outside the research field, I have edited several books that had a more didactic purpose; the *Handbook of Abnormal Psychology* has already been mentioned. More recently, I edited, with Arnold and Meili (1972b), a three-volume *Encyclopaedia of Psychology*, which has been translated into five languages and has sold extremely well. More recently still, Eysenck and Wilson (1976h) published a *Textbook of Human Psychology*, specially aimed at people (like teachers, psychiatrists, social workers, and others) who need some psychology for their examinations and future work, but do not expect to take up the subject at a professional level. For them, much that is contained in a typical textbook is of little interest, and their limited time should be devoted to more relevant themes. This we hoped to achieve in our book. Inevitably, we gave short shrift to what we considered unscientific doctrines, like psychoanalysis; Eysenck and Wilson (1973c) have examined the results of *The Experimental Study of Freudian Theories*, with a not-unexpected outcome.

A similar didactic purpose led to the writing of another set of books. In recent years there had grown up a rather bad-tempered battle concerning the inheritance of intelligence, with particular reference to the racial problem. It seemed to me that an impartial survey of the evidence might be helpful, and accordingly, I wrote *Race, Intelligence and Education* (published in the United States uner the title *The IQ Argument*). This book (Eysenck, 1971b) attracted a good deal of undeserved obloquy; clearly, the critics had never bothered to read what I had to say, and students and others took their cue from newspaper discussions that were not always well informed and were sometimes deliberately misleading. In the United States, the Students for a Democratic Society (SDS) threatened booksellers with arson if they dared to stock the book; well-known "liberal" newspapers refused to review it; and the outcome was that it was largely impossible in the land of free speech to discover the existence of the book or to buy it! Some friends wrote in despair, asking me to send copies from England. The editor of a biological journal had his classes disrupted because he dared to allow the book to be reviewed (by someone else!) in his journal. In England, the reaction was equally hostile. I was due to lecture at the London School of Economics on quite a different topic when I was attacked and beaten up by some left-wing hooligans; the National Union of Students responded by banning me from addressing any student meeting or society, under threat of bodily harm. The cradle of democracy had changed considerably from the days when I sought refuge from similar threats by right-wing fascists; my theory of the tough-mindedness of left-wing extremists had been vindicated only too well! Of course, the whole affair was counterproductive; millions of people who had never heard of me, or of my book, woke up to banner headlines, pictures, speeches, arguments, and denunciations. I had become famous—but in a way that I cannot recommend to others. Students at the University of Birmingham daubed in large letters these immortal words on the outside wall of their library: "Save freedom of speech—stop Fascist Eysenck from speaking!" *Sic transit gloria mundi.* The irony was not lost on me.

I went on to write a more academic book on *The Measurement of Intelligence* (Eysenck, 1973b) because I thought that the paradigm underlying the IQ was not being properly presented in the typical textbooks (or, indeed, anywhere else); this naturally gave rise to all sorts of pseudoarguments. In yet another, popular book, *The Inequality of Man* (Eysenck, 1973a),

I discussed the whole genetic picture, not only of the determination of intelligence, but also of personality, of criminality, of mental illness, etc.; I also tried to show the sort of social consequences that might follow from the facts. This book, not dealing with the inflammatory subject of race, was much better received, although the usual extremist attacks on it were not lacking—always led by people who clearly had no academic knowledge of the subject under discussion. It has been suggested, perhaps more reasonably, that even though what Jensen (who had been with me as a postdoctoral fellow for several years) and I were saying was true, it was not right to say it. I have discussed the ethical issues elsewhere (Eysenck, 1975a); I would simply take my stand on the scientist's overriding duty to tell the truth, the whole truth, and nothing but the truth, to the best of his ability. As Thomas Jefferson said: "There is no truth existing which I fear, or would wish unknown to the whole world." We cannot help in the solution of social ills if we censor the truth; that, indeed, is the surest way of making things worse and of destroying mankind's faith in science in the bargain. This belief was clearly not shared by the large number of booksellers who refused to stock my books (particularly *The Inequality of Man*), or the professors and students who went in deputation to a number of bookshops to request the owners to boycott them.

I have always enjoyed writing; it was as a natural extension of this bent that I started to write popular books on psychology, beginning with *Uses and Abuses of Psychology* (Eysenck, 1953), going on to *Sense and Nonsense in Psychology* (Eysenck, 1956b), and ending that series with *Fact and Fiction in Psychology* (Eysenck, 1965b). These books all came out as Penguin paperbacks. They were joined by *Know Your Own IQ* (Eysenck, 1962) and *Check Your Own IQ* (Eysenck, 1966a); these too were translated into many different languages—including, of all things, Russian! Finally, there is *Psychology Is About People* (Eysenck, 1972a), which came out in hardcover, but is now appearing as a Penguin paperback; it is too early to say anything much about the likely success of this book. The Ethical Committee of the APA received complaints about the IQ books and only allowed them to be published in the United States after some correspondence. I believe that the effect has been good rather than bad; I have received many letters from people who woke up to their potential as a result of doing the tests in these books and went on to start (and successfully finish!) university courses and other advanced types of training. *Know Your Own Personality* (Eysenck and Wilson, 1975c) looks as if it will be as successful as the IQ books, but it is too early yet to say. I usually type or dictate these books directly and without later revision. I have tried to see what happens when I rewrite what I put down initially; the empirical result is that the text loses its spontaneity, its humor, and its readability ("compulsive readability" some kind reviewers have called it). This has convinced me that rewriting would not be a good idea. Natural laziness may, of course, also play a part in this decision.

One or two further items may be chronicled here. I started the first journal to deal exclusively with behavior research and therapy, now in its seventeenth year and acknowledged to be the leading scientific publication in this field. I can say this without boasting because the credit for the excellence of the journal belongs entirely to S. Rachman, who has borne the whole burden of selection of articles, of correspondence with authors, and of seeing it to bed. It is only his refusal to accept my suggestion of removing my name from the journal that allows the erroneous idea to persist that I am actually to be congratulated on the standard the journal manages to maintain year in, year out. Such congratulations should, in the future, go to the man six doors down the hall. In 1980 I shall be editing another new journal, a stablemate of *Behaviour Research and Therapy*, entitled *Personality and Individual Differences*.

Around the same time as *BRAT*, I started the International Series of Monographs in Experimental Psychology; this has published many outstanding books that might not otherwise have seen the light of day—from J. Gray's *Pavlov's Typology* to P. A. Kolers' *Motion Perception;* from Dutta and Kanungo's *Affect and Memory* to G. Claridge's *Personality and Arousal*; from J. C. Baird's *Psychophysical Analysis of Visual Space* to R. Lynn's *Personality and National Character.* (I have already mentioned the books by Joffe and by Martin and Levey that also appeared in the series.) I believe that such monographs are an essential feature of the scientific scene; unfortunately, modern publishing practices make production of them more and more difficult. I am happy to have done something to reverse this trend. Quite recently, S. Rachman and I started a review monograph journal, *Advances in Behaviour Research and Therapy;* I hope it will be no less successful than the parent journal.

Battling with the Zeitgeist

So much for an all-too-brief account of my life and at least some of my scientific work. Does all this throw much light on the author as a person? From a psychologist, albeit an unwilling one, one might expect a little more. In my own case, this "little more" is perhaps more necessary than usual because there appears to be a marked divergence between my public image and my private being. Students and visitors often comment on this disparity. They expect an abrasive, aggressive ogre—hypercritical, dominant, and autocratic. They are surprised to find a friendly, quiet-spoken, extremely tolerant head of a department that is probably the most easy-going, permissive, and helpful in the country. *Le style, c'est l'homme* may be true of novelists, but it may not be true of scientists; it would not be psychologically meaningful to use my prose as a projection test! I have definite opinions on many subjects, and I tend to give clear expression to these opinions; I have never learned the art of disguising my meaning under a cloud of honeyed but empty words. My 1952 article did not say anything in essence that others (D. Hebb, C. Landis, or J. Zubin) had not also suggested; it served the purpose of the little boy in the story of the emperor's new clothes by saying out loud what they had been implying. My way is more effective, but, of course, it does not make many friends. I am unrepentant; I think what I said then had to be said—just as what I said about intelligence and heredity, or about the Rorschach, or about a dozen other topics had to be said. To stand up and be counted is in the best tradition of nonconformism; if speaking what you consider to be the truth appears abrasive to others, that is too bad. The cost of being liked by everybody can be too high. But attacking the holy cows of the Establishment is quite different from dealing with colleagues and students;

they deserve as much help, encouragement, and guidance as you can give them, and personality estimates change accordingly.

Why have I been in constant battle with the *Zeitgeist* about which Boring has written so much? From the fascist right of Germany to the modern, militant, communist left, I have attacked the undemocratic suppression of freedom of speech so characteristic of both; their racial and class-inspired hatreds that can only lead to inhumane and, indeed, inhuman actions; their gobbledygook pseudophilosophizing and their pretence of "scientific" respectability. I make no excuse for these battles; I believe that they were waged in a good cause. Beyond this social field, I have opposed orthodoxy in psychology too often for this to be dismissed as a chance phenomenon. Perhaps Mitroff (1974) was right when he said that "in every social system there are those kinds of individuals . . . who have a compulsive need to make revolutions, to disagree, as strongly as possible, with established ways of thinking— paradigms, if you prefer. These individuals have an almost consuming need to produce radical ideas and theories counter to those currently in existence if not in vogue. They seem to need to go out of their way to produce extremely novel ways of looking at old phenomena." This was written as the result of looking in detail at a large sample of "moon scientists" during and after the Apollo flights; although not a very sympathetic account (and I don't like the psychiatric "compulsive" as applied to nonpsychiatric behavior patterns!), this would seem to characterize my attitude in the eyes of many people. My own reaction would be that most psychological theories are pretty poor and can do with some revamping; that when the facts show these theories to be wrong, then we should not stick forever with them.

As an example, consider my work on reminiscence. For many years, I struggled with the problem of accounting for the phenomenon of reminiscence in Hullian terms—i.e., dissipation of inhibition—and of relating it to personality. My students and I have published some fifty or more experimental studies, trying hard to apply the orthodox theory; we finally proved that the theory was wrong, and suggested another (Eysenck and Frith, 1977c). This must be one of the few cases where a personality theory generated precise enough predictions to be convincingly disproved! I would not say that this change from a traditional to a novel theory demonstrated a compulsive need for making revolutions—rather, it demonstrated a punctilious regard for the Kuhnian paradigm of change in science. I would claim the same for my other onslaughts on the premature crystallizations of spurious orthodoxy; they were motivated by demonstrable faults in the theories involved or in their alleged empirical support. Only the future can decide, of course, whether I am right or not. By then, unfortunately, I shall no longer be around; perhaps it is as well, therefore, that I have a firm conviction that my views are along the right lines, although, of course, likely to prove wrong in detail. In the words of Lakatos (Lakatos and Musgrave, 1971), I am busy with a "progressive research programme"; no scientist can claim more than that.

What is the nature of this program? It derived essentially from the thinking I had the opportunity to do at leisure during my early days at the Mill Hill Emergency Hospital during the war. It seemed to me then, and it seems to me now, that Kuhn was right in stressing the importance of paradigms for science; in those days, Spearman was expressing the same fundamental thought when he stressed the necessity for general laws in psychology. Such general laws should ideally lead to an integration of the different parts that now make up psychology and further the progress toward the unity of the subject so clearly lacking at the moment. I thought that healing the rift between the Cambridge and London schools, or, in more general terms, between what Cronbach (1957) later called the "two disciplines of scientific psychology," was an essential first step, and most of my work has been dedicated to this aim. On the descriptive side, I used factor analysis and discriminant function analysis to search out the major factors in personality (individual differences); on the causal side, I tried to develop hypotheses linking these factors to widely accepted psychological and physiological concepts. In my book on *The Dynamics of Anxiety and Hysteria* (Eysenck, 1957a), I tried to use Hullian concepts; in *The Biological Basis of Personality* (Eysenck, 1967), I made the attempt to dig even deeper and use physiological systems, such as the arousal and limbic systems, as explanatory concepts. Insofar as the attempt can be called successful (and I am, of course, aware of all the possible criticisms and pitfalls), my work would seem to build bridges between personality theory (psychometrics) and experimental psychology; it would also serve as an explanatory framework for a large number of social phenomena, including social-attitude formation, sexual behavior, criminality, mental disorders, and many more. It seems curious to me that the intention (whatever may be said of the execution) has hardly been recognized by critics or praised for what ought to seem a worthwhile aim for anyone concerned about the diversification, without unifying principles, of modern psychology.

No doubt the *Zeitgeist* disfavors ambitious theories spanning many different areas of expertise, and even disciplines (such as genetics, sociology, psychiatry, etc.). Yet surely the data we are confronted with in the behavior of human beings do not recognize arbitrary divisions made for the comfort and sole benefit of *Homo academicus.* If we confine ourselves to progressively narrower and narrower, more and more highly specialized subdivisions of subdivisions of relatively trivial, purely academic problems, we are leaving the field of truly human, integrated psychology wide open to outsiders with social and political aims with which we may agree or disagree, but which are pursued essentially without benefit of scientific method and which are unlikely to issue in true knowledge. This contrast between narrow specialization, increasing technical sophistication, and limitation of focus on the one hand, and wide interests, large-scale theories, and concern with speculative hypotheses on the other is, of course, endemic in all science; it has been well documented by Mitroff (1974.) In psychology, this conflict has assumed the character of an atomic fission process, threatening to blow the subject apart as a single, unified scientific discipline, with, on the one hand, trivial busywork being regarded highly because it can be carried out with impeccable scientific methodology (even though it serves no useful theoretical purpose) and, on the other hand, speculation running wild and being rewarded as leading to a "human psychology" that unfortunately lacks all restraints of scientific fact-finding and proper theory-making. In thus trying to combine scientific methodology with a more wide-ranging interest in larger, more important topics, I have managed to sit down squarely between these two stools, a position neither comfortable nor dignified. Perhaps our successors will be more successful in solving these important problems; even now, though, I could wish that more discussion and attention were given to the nature of these problems, the very existence of which seems to be denied by many eminent psychologists.

What of the future? I am concentrating on genetic studies of personality and intelligence, and I am carrying on with our work on the biological foundations of these two concepts. O. White and I are in the middle of effecting a breakup of the IQ concept into its constituent parts; I have given a general conspectus of this work elsewhere (Eysenck, 1973b; Eysenck, 1979c). and will not go into details here. Our work on behavior therapy is concentrating on obsessive-compulsive disorders at the moment, with considerable success, using "flooding" and "modeling" techniques; I am hoping to integrate our applied work with my new theory of neurosis (Eysenck, 1979b, in press). Sybil and I are in the middle of a long-term study of national differences in personality; unfortunately, it seems difficult to obtain research funds for such a project. Much work is going on with respect to the comparatively new concept of psychoticism; this is in some ways our "baby," and Sybil and I are very fond of the youngster and will try to help him grow to adulthood. I am just starting a book on *The Roots of Ideology,* which continues from *The Psychology of Politics* (Eysenck, 1954) and *The Psychological Basis of Ideology* (Eysenck and Wilson, 1978b). I am hoping to return to experimental aesthetics and produce a proper test of visual aesthetic ability that will not have the obvious faults of existing ones. We are continuing work on the real-life correlates of personality, such as criminality, sexual attitudes and behavior, smoking and drinking; we hope to link this up with prophylactic and therapeutic procedures to improve people's unfortunate plights in these directions.

I have a great interest in the philosophy, sociology, and psychology of science and have read copiously in that field; I hope someday to write something interesting and novel on the subject and may try to link this interest with the writing of a full-length autobiography, illustrating general points from my own experiences. Our animal work will continue to try to elucidate the interplay of genetic and environmental variables and to demonstrate the relevance of animal experiments to human psychology and to behavior therapy. I hope to continue writing popular books explaining complex theories to the layman in simple language; my latest book, *You and Neurosis* (Eysenck, 1977b), has just been published, hopefully giving the man in the street a chance to understand the causes and cures of neurosis. Another book, on *Sex, Crime and the Media* (Eysenck and Nias, 1978a), has just appeared; the title is self-explanatory. These are just some plans I have for the future; the Catherine wheel inside my mind keeps sparking away, and it is difficult to know just what it may set on fire!

In the meanwhile, I continue to play tennis or squash every day, enjoy an exceptionally happy family life, and watch the third generation of Eysencks growing up—possibly to continue the psychological tradition established by the proud grandfather.

1978

Selected Publications by Hans Jurgen Eysenck

Primary mental abilities. *British J. educ. Psychol.*, 1939a, *9*, 270–275.

The validity of judgements as a function of the number of judges. *J. exp. Psychol.*, 1939b, *25*, 650–654.

An experimental study of the improvement of mental and physical functions in the hypnotic state. *British J. Medical Psychol.*, 1941, *18*, 304–316.

Suggestibility and hysteria. *J. Neurology Psychiat.*, 1943, *6*, 22–31.

General social attitudes. *J. soc. Psychol.*, 1944a, *19*, 207–227.

States of high suggestibility and the neuroses. *Amer. J. Psychol.*, 1944b, *57*, 406–411.

Types of personality: A factorial study of seven hundred neurotics. *J. ment. Sci.*, 1944c, *90*, 851–861.

(with D. Furneaux) Primary and secondary suggestibility: An experimental and statistical study. *J. esp. Psychol.*, 1945, *35*, 485–503.

Dimensions of personality. London: Routledge and Kegan Paul, 1947a.

Primary social attitudes. *Int. J. Opin. Attitude Res.*, 1947b, *1*, 49–84.

Criterion analysis—An application of the hypothetico-deductive method to factor analysis. *Psychol. Rev.*, 1950, *57*, 38–53.

(with D. B. Prell) The inheritance of neuroticism: An experimental study. *J. Ment. Sci.*, 1951, *97*, 441–465.

The effects of psychotherapy: An evaluation. *J. consult. Psychol.*, 1952a, *16*, 319–324.

Schizothymia—Cyclothymia as a dimension of personality. II. Experimental. *J. Pers.*, 1952b, *10*, 345–384.

The scientific study of personality. London: Routledge and Kegan Paul, 1952c.

The structure of human personality. London: Methuen, 1952d (3rd ed., 1970).

Uses and abuses of psychology. London: Penguin Books, 1953.

The psychology of politics. London: Routledge and Kegan Paul, 1954.

The inheritance of extraversion-introversion. *Acta Psychologica*, 1956a, *12*, 95–110.

Sense and nonsense in psychology. London: Penguin Books, 1956b.

The dynamics of anxiety and hysteria. London: Routledge and Kegan Paul, 1957a.

(with G. Granger and J. C. Brengelmann) *Perceptual processes and mental illness.* London: Chapman & Hall, 1957b.

Personality tests: 1950-1955. In G. W. T. N. Fleming (Ed.), *Recent progress in psychiatry*, London: J. & A. Churchill, 1958, 118–159.

Learning theory and behaviour therapy. *J. ment. Sci.*, 1959a, *105*, 61–75.

The Rorschach test. In O. K. Buros (Ed.), *The fifth mental measurements yearbook*, New Brunswick: Rutgers University Press, 1959b, 276–278.

(Ed.) *Behaviour therapy and the neuroses.* London: Pergamon Press, 1960a.

(Ed.) *Experiments in personality.* 2 vols. London: Routledge and Kegan Paul, 1960b.

(Ed.) *Handbook of abnormal psychology: An experimental approach.* New York: Basic Books, 1961 (2nd ed. London: Pitmans, 1973).

Know your own IQ. London: Penguin Books, 1962.

Emotion as a determinant of intergrative learning: An experimental study. *Behav. Res. Ther.*, 1963a, *1*, 197–211.

Experiments with drugs. Oxford: Pergamon Press, 1963b.

Crime and personality. London: Routledge and Kegan Paul, 1964a. (3rd ed.: Paladin, 1977).

(Ed.) *Experiments in behaviour therapy.* London: Pergamon Press, 1964b.

(Ed.) *Experiments in motivation.* Oxford: Pergamon Press, 1964c.

(with P. Broadhurst) Experiments with animals. In H. J. Eysenck (Ed.), *Experiments in motivation*, Oxford: Pergamon Press, 1964d, 285–291.

Fact and fiction in psychology. London: Penguin Books, 1965a.

Smoking, health and personality. London: Weidenfeld & Nicolson, 1965b.

(with S. Rachman) *Causes and cures of neurosis.* London: Routledge and Kegan Paul, 1965c.

Check your own IQ. London: Penguin Books, 1966a.

The effects of psychotherapy. New York: International Science Press, 1966b.

The biological basis of personality. Springfield: C. C. Thomas, 1967.

A theory of the incubation of anxiety/fear responses. *Behav. Res. Ther.*, 1968, *6*, 309–321.

(with S. B. G. Eysenck) *Personality structure and measurement.* London: Routledge and Kegan Paul, 1969.

A dimensional system of psychodiagnosis. In A. R. Mahrer (Ed.), *New approaches to personality classification,* New York: Columbia University Press, 1970a.

Programme research and training in research methodology. *Bull. British Psychol. Soc.*, 1970b, *23*, 9–16.

(Ed.) *Readings in extraversion-introversion.* London: Staples Press, 1971a.

Race, intelligence and education. London: Maurice Temple Smith, 1971b. (Amer. ed. *The IQ argument.* New York: The Library Press, 1971b.)

Psychology is about people. London: Allen Lane, 1972a (London: Penguin Books, 1977).

(with W. Arnold and R. Meili) *Encyclopaedia of psychology.* 3 vols. London: Search Press, 1972b.

(with I. Coulter) The personality and attitudes of working-class British communists and fascists. *J. soc. Psychol.*, 1972c, *87*, 59–73.

(with A. B. Levey) Conditioning, introversion-extraversion and the strength of the nervous system. In V. D. Nebylitsyn and J. A. Gray (Eds.), *Biological bases of individual behavior,* New York: Academic Press, 1972d.

The inequality of man. London: Maurice Temple Smith, 1973a.

(Ed.) *The measurement of intelligence.* Lancaster: Medical and Technical Publishing Co., 1973b.

(with G. D. Wilson) *The experimental study of Freudian theories.* London: Methuen, 1973c.

The ethics of science and the duties of scientists. *British Ass. Advancement of Sci.*, New Issue, 1975a, *1*, 23–25.

The future of psychiatry. London: Methuen, 1975b.

(with G. D. Wilson) *Know your own personality.* London: Maurice Temple Smith, 1975c (Penguin, 1976).

Genetic factors in personality development. In A. R. Kaplan (Ed.), *Human behavior genetics,* Springfield: C. C. Thomas, 1976a, 198–229.

The learning theory model of neurosis—A new approach. *Behav. Res. Ther.* 1976b, *14*, 251–267.

The measurement of personality. Lancaster: Medical and Technical Publishing Co., 1976c.

Sex and personality. London: Open Books, 1976d.

(Ed.) *Case studies in behaviour therapy.* London: Routledge and Kegan Paul, 1976e.

(with S. B. G. Eysenck) *The manual of the Eysenck personality questionnaire.* London: Hodder & Stoughton, 1976f (San Diego: Educational and Industrial Testing Service, 1976).

(with S. B. G. Eysenck) *Psychoticism as a dimension of personality.* London: Hodder and Stoughton, 1976g.

(with G. D. Wilson [Eds.]) *A textbook of human psychology.* Lancaster: Medical and Technical Publishing Co., 1976h.

You and neurosis. London: Maurice Temple Smith, 1977a.

(with C. Frith) *Reminiscence, motivation and personality.* New York: Plenum Press, 1977b.

(with D. Nias) Sex, crime and the media. London: Maurice Temple Smith, 1978a.

(with G. D. Wilson) *The psychological basis of ideology.* Lancaster: Medical and Technical Publishers, 1978b.

Alexander Herzberg and "active psychotherapy." In A. R. Mahrer (Ed.), *Creative developments in psychotherapy,* Vol. 2, 1979a, in press.

The conditioning model of neurosis. *The behavioral and brain sciences.* 1979b, in press.

The structure and measurement of intelligence. New York: Springer, 1979c.

Other Publications Cited

Broadhurst, P. L. The Maudsley reactive and nonreactive strains of rats: A survey. *Behavioral Genetics,* 1975, *5,* 299–320.

Broadhurst, P. L., and H. J. Eysenck. Emotionality in the rat: A problem of response specificity. In C. Banks and P. Broadhurst (Eds.), *Studies in psychology,* London: University of London Press, 1965.

Brunis, P., and H. J. Eysenck. Structure of attitudes—An Italian sample. *Psychol. Rep.,* 1976, *38,* 956–958.

Chamove, A. S., H. J. Eysenck, and H. F. Harlow. Personality: monkeys: factor analysis in Rhesus social behaviour. *Quart. J. exp. Psychol.,* 1972, *29,* 496–504.

Cronbach, L. J. The two disciplines of scientific psychology. *Amer. Psychologist,* 1957, *12,* 671–684.

Drewe, E. A.. The fate of Maudsley psychologists. *Bull. British Psychol. Soc.*, 1971, *24*, 201–205.

Eaves, L. J., and H. J. Eysenck. Genetics and the development of social attitudes. *Nature*, 1974, *249*, 288–289.

Eaves, L. J., and H. J. Eysenck. The nature of extraversion: A genetical analysis. *J. Pers. soc. Psychol.*, 1975, *32*, 102–112.

Eaves, L. J., and H. J. Eysenck. Genetic and environmental components of inconsistency and unrepeatability in twins' responses to a neuroticism questionnaire. *Behav. Genetics*, 1976, *6*, 145–160.

Eaves, L. J., and H. J. Eysenck. Genotype—Environmental model for psychoticism. *Advances Behav. Res. Ther.*, No. 1, 1977.

Eysenck, M. W. *Human memory*. London: Pergamon, 1977.

Hewitt, J., and H. J. Eysenck. Structure of social attitudes after twenty-five years. *Psychol. Rep.*, 1977, *40*, 183–188.

Joffe, J. M. *Prenatal determinants of behaviour*. Oxford: Pergamon, 1969.

Lakatos, I., and A. Musgrave. *Criticism and the growth of knowledge*. Cambridge: University Press, 1970.

Malan, D. H. *Toward the validation of dynamic psychotherapy*. London: Plenum, 1976.

Martin, I., and A. B. Levey. *The genesis of the classical conditioned response*. London: Pergamon Press, 1969.

Mitroff, I. *The subjective side of science*. Amsterdam: Elsevier, 1974.

Sartory, G., and H. J. Eysenck. Strain differences in acquisition and extinction of fear responses in rats. *Psychol. Rep.*, 1976, *38*, 163–187.

Venables, P. H., and I. Martin. *A manual of psychophysiological methods*. Amsterdam: North-Holland Publishing Company, 1967.

Frank A. Geldard

Frank A. Geldard

Some lives are shaped in childhood, some acquire their purpose in early maturity, while still others, buffeted by ever-recurring vicissitudes, assume their character slowly and gradually and have their patterns set only very late. As I reflect on my own personal and professional development, I am forced to the conclusion that it is the last class to which I belong. Coming into the world near the beginning of the century, living through two world wars with their attendant dislocations, witnessing sweeping social and political changes, and experiencing radical technological alterations of the environment, there appears never to have existed a sole immutable influence that would impart a smooth and unmistakable trajectory to my existence.

I was born in Worcester, Massachusetts, at Hahnemann Hospital, on May 20, 1904. Three boys had preceded me in the family, Walter, Ralph, and Raymond. Of the three, Walter was the only one to survive infancy, such was the scourge of what went under the name of "croup" in those days. Until I attained maturity, I hardly knew my brother, there being a veritable chasm created by the nine-year gap in our ages. For all practical purposes, I grew up as an only child.

My mother and father were of sturdy British stock, my mother Scottish, my father English. My father, Arthur Geldard, had been brought to this country, along with his younger sister, Ada, from the little Lancashire town of Clitheroe when the children were quite young. Emanuel Geldard, my grandfather, was a stonecutter; he settled down in East Longmeadow, Massachusetts, where there was a brownstone quarry. One of the projects in which he was involved was the setting of stone at the New York Statehouse in Albany. I never knew him or much about him beyond the vivid fact that, by virtue of the daily pumicing of his teeth by the stone dust in the very air he breathed throughout his life, he was said never to have had occasion to visit a dentist! My paternal grandmother, Caroline Radcliffe Geldard, I did know, for, after being widowed, she lived with us until I was about ten years old. She was a perpetual faultfinder, in her late years at least; my behavior being the most convenient butt of that, there came to be developed an ever-renewed feud between us. Her ultimate transfer to a "home" near Springfield, Massachusetts, as senility took over, was a great relief to all concerned, especially me.

My maternal ancestors I know practically nothing about. My mother, Margaret Hardy Gordon, eldest of four children, as a young woman in the Glasgow shipbuilding suburb of Caron, suddenly found herself responsible for two young brothers, Will and Jim, and a younger sister, Jenny. How she ever managed it I never knew, but she decided to flee the "bad times" of late nineteenth-century Scotland and set sail with her young brood for Canada on a small steamer that literally took weeks to overcome the North Atlantic storms. All four young Gordons went into "service" of one kind or another in Ontario, then one at a time migrated to Massachusetts as they matured and found more responsible work. My mother did housework in Springfield, where my father met her. To her dying day, she retained the vestibular conditioning of the Atlantic passage; she could not so much as step into a rowboat without feeling queasy.

My father, as soon as he grew up to it, first became a grocery clerk in East Longmeadow's general store, then progressed to weightier jobs in the produce business. Indeed, the climax of his occupational career came many years later as manager of a large wholesale provision house in Worcester. He had a host of friends from all walks of life, some of whom were business associates but many of whom centered on church and various fraternal orders. His own formal education had been sufficiently meager to create a strong desire to see that his two sons got the benefit of first-class schooling. Both Walter and I went through the Worcester public school system, from first grade to high school graduation. Both of us went to Clark College, the undergraduate division of Clark University, and both of us received the B.A. degree from that institution. The spacing of our careers was such that neither constituted a prohibitive burden on the family finances. Moreover, both of us were given early encouragement to help earn our own way. From the age of eleven, I worked at odd jobs—shoveling snow, cutting grass, operating a paper route, tending furnaces, delivering packages for drugstores; later on, "running" books in the reference division of the public library (valuable training that lasted throughout the four years of high school), working summers in wholesale provision houses (candling eggs, lugging sides of beef, unloading refrigerator cars)—all of which brought in substantial earnings.

I should not like to give the impression that my youth was one of hardship. There was plenty of play and recreation. One of my earliest affective attachments was to my bicycle, provided by my Aunt Ada (whom I held in the highest regard). I organized a bicycle club, with materials and encouragement supplied by a tire manufacturer, and every fair Saturday morning we packed lunch and rode out—a group of six to ten of us—to some Worcester County town perhaps a dozen miles away. In the winter, there was frequent skating on the lake of the first public park in the United States, Elm Park, Worcester. In summer there were miniature boat races in the same park. There was also much healthful tennis and sandlot baseball. I was an enthusiast for Boy Scout activities and for the weekly swimming classes at the local Boys' Club. Moreover, my parents owned a summer cottage at a Methodist campground near Sterling Junction, near Worcester. I have a set of confused early recollections of sandboxes, swings, berry-picking, chestnut roasts, and, most vividly, evangelists exhorting converts to hit the sawdust trail to the hay strewn just under the pulpit of an open-air tabernacle. Some of the hardest work I did as a youngster was to fix attention, at least ostensibly, on the endless stream of preachers that entered my life in a most repetitious manner. My parents were devout, and they tried very hard to set a flawless example along religious lines.

Very importantly, my brother and I were given competent musical instruction from an early age. This also paid off in the critical years. Walter came to be a quite proficient church organist—and both his daughters have since done the same—while my six years or more of music lessons developed a set of skills and appreciations that found outlet in a variety of ways, not the least valuable of which was participation in dance bands and other musical aggregations during college years. I was able to cover much of my own educational and social expenses as a result. Later on, even into graduate school, I continued to earn, but then with classical music, in the main, and on the concert stage. The piano has been a more or less constant companion all my life. I cannot but feel that there must be an inherent predisposition to music. As a youngster, my father trudged the five miles or so to Springfield to take a music lesson (for which he paid fifty cents), then wearily dragged his feet back home. It was his only lesson; the price in energy was just too great. He got permission to "practice" on a local church organ and must have learned in precious few trials, for shortly he was the church organist. Indeed, he served for fully fifty years, mainly in Worcester, either in that capacity or as choir director or both. My mother had a fine natural voice; though completely untrained, it was true of pitch and of memorable timbre.

The college years would have been difficult even without the frequent nights playing in orchestras. When I started, Clark was a three-year college. It gave the B.A. degree on completion of 108 semester-hours of work, much of it representing requirements. That meant that the normal load was six concurrent courses. It was necessary to make an early commitment to a major. I had done well at North High School in chemistry and physics, taking extra courses in those subjects, and it was natural that I should continue along that path. My brother was already a successful chemist in industry, and such a choice naturally had the blessing of my parents.

So chemistry it was, and physics was a natural minor. I shall always be grateful for the latter, for my instructor in general physics was no one less than Robert H. Goddard, the father of rocketry. His course was a perpetual delight. By nature one of the shyest of men and modest to the point of self-effacement, he spent endless hours preparing demonstrations for a one-hour lecture. Talk about a picture being worth a thousand words! A Goddard demonstration, whether of a candle being shot through a two-inch board or of something less vivid, was worth a million of them. Few people live to see their college professor of physics pictured on a postage stamp.

I completed the chemistry major, endless laboratory hours of it that I remember well. Except for introductory chemistry (pretty much a repetition of my high school work, therefore easy) and a course in the history of chemistry (taught by the sainted Benjamin Shores Merigold), both of which I found entirely enjoyable, the field became increasingly boring as I went on. The "cookbook" instruction in qualitative and quantitative analysis was stultifying, and the unexplained, almost mystical procedures of the physical chemistry laboratory were only a little less so. I learned next to nothing about scientific method from my instruction in chemistry; this is a complaint I have encountered on the part of others many times in my academic career.

By the time I got to organic chemistry, complete disillusionment was upon me. Indeed, the course became a nightmare. The instructor, a retiree from industry, habitually mumbled at the blackboard, his back to the class. He seemed more intent on displaying his familiarity with both the old and new names of organic compounds—the Geneva nomenclature had just come in—than in acquainting us with the myriad chemical relationships among them. I was soon floundering and never completed the course. The dean advised a change of program. Indeed, though I did not know about it at the time, he must have been on the edge of urging a change of scenery as well. Many years later, long after I had gotten my teaching career well launched at the University of Virginia, he sent me as a Christmas card the file copy of a letter he had written years before to my father stating that I was doing so poorly he might have to ask me to withdraw. He also enclosed my father's reply, to the effect: "If Frank doesn't do better, please throw him out."

Two things happened to save the day: (1) Clark became a four-year college, thus changing over to the 120-hour degree (with a five-course load), and (2) I was beginning to acquire some interest in psychology, the introductory course of which I had already completed and a second one, in social psychology, that I was then taking. The first of these circumstances took care of the mechanics of the situation; I already had more than enough credits to put me in good standing. The second is of more interest.

Psychology at Clark, in 1923, was very nearly at its lowest ebb. The Scott Nearing incident, to which we shall return, had taken place the previous session. J. W. Baird had died a few years before, J. P. Porter had gone off to Ohio University, and Samuel Fernberger to his beloved Pennsylvania. To cap the exodus, Edwin G. Boring and Carroll Pratt had just been attracted to Harvard. The laboratory was locked up except for one concluding piece of doctoral research, that of Charles Dickinson, who was being directed by ex-President Sanford, already retired. The undergraduate curriculum in psychology was nearly extinct, though about to be revived as part of a general renaissance triggered by Carl Murchison's coming. My first course in psychology was with Kimball Young, a sociologist with psychological leanings, who was visiting from Wisconsin for one year. We used Woodworth's first edition. I remember most vividly Young's color-mixture demonstrations; up to that point, I had supposed that psychology dealt only in words!

At the time of my conversion to psychology, I was taking Murchison's course in social psychology, as unsystematic a conglomeration of contents as could be imagined. We studied William McDougall's *Social Psychology, Group Mind,* and *Ethics and Some Modern World Problems,* John Dewey's *School and Society,* Plato's *Republic* in the Jowett translation, and an amazing medley of Machiavelli, Walter Bagehot, Thomas Buckle, and Irving King! Not a bad course in political theory, but hardly what we think of today as social psychology. The trend toward experimental social psychology was a revolutionary one when it occurred only a few years later.

The next year I was to experience broader vistas, for Carl Murchison, if not a great teacher, was unexcelled as an organizer. He launched a dual attack on the problem of resurrecting a defunct department. On the one hand, he set out to acquire representatives of the more important lines of thought in the then-contemporary psychology. On the other, he made plans to capitalize on the very considerable prestige that had been Clark's in G. Stanley Hall's day. The first aim he implemented promptly by attracting John Paul Nafe, who, though mature, had just completed his Cornell doctorate with Titchener. This move got the laboratory open and brought to the community an outstanding teacher, one who was to be greatly loved by all his students. The next addition was Walter Hunter, brought from the University of Kansas, to take the newly created G. Stanley Hall Chair of Genetic Psychology. On the heels of this important appointment, which revived animal behavior studies and supplied a strong adherent of the behavioristic school, arrangements were completed to bring Wolfgang Köhler from Berlin for a year's visit.

Thus, the neophyte in psychology, as a college senior, found himself once more in a laboratory, taking experimental psychology with Nafe, animal behavior with Hunter, and an advanced seminar with none other than a founding father of Gestalt psychology! Another importation on a visiting basis was William Bridges, from McGill University, who taught a course in abnormal psychology and provided a modicum of clinical experience, accompanied as the lectures were by weekly sessions at the Worcester State Hospital. Vernon Jones, acquired from Columbia, taught us statistical method and familiarized us with psychological tests.

Carl Murchison's genius displayed itself most clearly in his journalistic ventures, and the second prong of his attack on the revival problem was to inject new life into Hall's *Pedagogical Seminary*, still the property of Clark University. The name itself was an antique one. Murchison gave the publication a new designation, *Journal of Genetic Psychology*. In successive issues, he gradually reduced the type size in the old name and raised that in the new. This kept library subscriptions coming and produced the vehicle for modernizing format. This first journalistic venture was so successful that it was not long before other journals could be brought on the scene: *Genetic Psychology Monographs*, for the longer contributions, the *Journal of General Psychology* (a name curiously not preempted before), the *Journal of Social Psychology* (with John Dewey's sponsorship), and finally the *Journal of Psychology* (even more curiously original as a designation!).

The journalistic empire was a development over the years, of course, but meanwhile there were important books and these, in turn, came out of significant educational and organizational operations. The first of the books, *Psychologies of 1925*, recorded the contributions made by a distinguished group of visiting psychologists, selected for their representativeness in psychological theory. The Powell Lectures, underwritten and named for Carl Murchison's father-in-law, proved so successful that a second cross-section of the "schools" was produced five years later and became *Psychologies of 1930*, now with twenty-five chapters as compared with seventeen in the first volume. Meanwhile, quite a different kind of lecture series was attempted, and there came to Clark a wide spectrum of speakers on systems of belief (or the lack of it) in the occult. The Psychic Research Series and the volume, *The Case for and against Psychical Belief*, with fourteen contributors, including the prominent spiritists, Sir Arthur Conan Doyle and Sir Oliver Lodge, was the result. Some spectacular speakers visited Worcester at that time, including Harry Houdini, Margery Crandon ("the witch of Lyme St."), Frederick Bligh Bond (with his weird account of the "discovery" of the foundations of ancient Glastonbury Abbey through automatic writing), Hans Driesch, the phenomenologist, and F. C. S. Schiller, the Oxford logician. It was the Murchisons' custom to have an after-lecture coffee session at their house on the campus. To this all graduate students were invited and were given an opportunity to meet and question the visitors.

In the autumn of 1925, I entered the graduate school at Clark, having been offered a laboratory assistantship with

Nafe. But let us return for a moment to two sets of under-graduate memories that are ineradicable for me. One had to do with the traumatic Scott Nearing incident of my freshman year, the other with G. Stanley Hall's death in 1924. Both had indirect but important bearing on the future of psychology at Clark.

There was in existence, when I entered college in the fall of 1921, a small and quite ineffectual undergraduate organiza-tion, a poor imitation of Harvard's influential Liberal Club and known by the same name. It had eight regular members, as I recall it; its president was an energetic young man of Scot-tish ancestry named Ross Fraser. The club prided itself on providing a public forum for opposing views on social ques-tions. One speaker that session was a local Baptist divine, ul-traconservative in outlook; for the next meeting, Scott Near-ing, then regarded in some circles as a "pinko," was invited to represent the other side of the coin. His appearance had been cleared with the university authorities, as all speakers had to be.

An interested audience of about 300 people, mainly from the city, were listening to Nearing when the president of the university, Wallace W. Atwood, entered the rear of the hall, listened for a few minutes—Nearing was quoting Thorstein Veblen on "The Higher Learning in America" at the time—then announced in a loud voice, "This meeting is dismissed." There was general puzzlement, for Nearing had been speak-ing well over an hour and had his audience with him. Silence descended. President Atwood announced again, "This meet-ing is dismissed." Still no one moved. The speaker was embar-rassed, the audience filled with consternation. Finally, the president directed the janitor to turn out the lights! Someone got them back on and thus probably prevented panic. At any rate, departure was orderly, and some remnant of the meeting eventually adjourned to the Kappa Phi house (Fraser's frater-nity and mine, off campus), where the lecture was finished in the living room.

The next day, many things happened in rapid-fire order. As was to be expected, most of the student body joined the Liberal Club. Classes were halted and a student strike was de-clared. The liberal journals of the country dispatched their reporters to cover this latest assault on freedom of speech. (I recall that I gave up my bed in the fraternity house for a week to someone from either the *Nation* or the *New Republic*.) The faculty, at least the hardier members, divided into two camps—those who supported the president's crusade against "licentious and seditious utterances" and those who were sympathetic with the students.

Just how long the strike lasted and how or why we ultimately wandered back to classes I do not recall, but the casualties were many and serious. The nationwide news coverage subsided, but in the wake of the ruckus we found ourselves faced with the resignation of a half-dozen professors (the more liberal ones, of course) and with an uneasy feeling that we were to live out our undergraduate careers under a hostile administration.

There is a gratifying sequel to this story. Many years later Ross Fraser, by then prominent in industry, was elected to the board of trustees of Clark University. It was at his initiative that the university, several administrations after Atwood, decided to right a long-standing wrong and awarded an honorary degree to the aging Scott Nearing. And it was Ross Fraser, erstwhile president of the Liberal Club, who read the citation and slipped the hood over Nearing's head!

I spoke of a second indelibly recorded memory from undergraduate days. This had to do with the death of G. Stanley Hall. He had retired from active academic life in 1919, as had Edmund Sanford. The latter "kept his hand in" and even taught a course in educational psychology in the dark days following the virtual closing down of the psychology department. Hall, slowly going blind and contemplating the sorry events on the nearby campus, became pretty much of a recluse, though he did mobilize his declining energies to complete his autobiography, *Life and Confessions of a Psychologist*, which was published in 1924. His "keeping up" consisted in engaging several undergraduates to come to his house and read the current psychological journals to him. I read French—he didn't insist on an impeccable accent—and there were other German and English readers. He devoured vast amounts of literature by dint of his asking only for titles and first lines of paragraphs, this until he encountered something he really wanted to pursue. Indeed, the reader did well to distribute his attention to include his peripheral vision, for there was only one signal by way of instruction; when Hall nodded his head, he meant he had had enough of that paragraph!

Hall's death came in April 1924. His funeral, at a large Congregational church in Worcester, was attended by many old friends, some of whom had come great distances to attend. The arrangements called for undergraduate students to serve as pallbearers, and during the eulogy those selected (of which I was one) sat in the front pew, to the side, where our attention was naturally drawn to the distinguished honorary pallbearers grouped in front of the bier. The officiating clergyman pointed out how extensive had been President Hall's contributions to the world's religious and moral literature, then uttered a fatal qualification: "But I don't think Doctor Hall ever really understood institutional religion." The reaction in his listeners was prompt and intense. I recall especially that of Howard Warren. Verbal expression being out of the question, his face reddened until it vied with his flaming red hair! When the service was concluded, it was an irate bevy of fellow psychologists who filed out. The audience gone, the coffin sides were let down, flowers were rearranged, and official photographs were taken (for fully an hour!) for the university records, I presume. During all this, the impressionable young men sitting in the wings had engraved on their mnemic systems a set of engrams that were bound to last as long as life itself.

To return to the graduate years—it must be obvious that Murchison's main thrust was in the direction of creating a kind of "melting pot" of psychological theory, and the graduate students became immersed in it as it developed. Nafe's students were indoctrinated in the Titchenerian system of thinking. I almost wrote "structuralism," for that is the accepted name for the classical Cornell influence, but the Titchener of the 1920s was a far cry from the author of the 1910 *Textbook*. He had ceased to think of psychological analysis in terms of "elements" and "attributes"; " dimensions of experience" much more nearly described the heart of the system. Indeed, had the epistemologists not already identified the term with various systems of rational philosophy, Titchener might well have called himself a "phenomenologist." In some of his later writing, he used the term "existential psychology," but that designation, too, was to take on a meaning quite foreign to his intent.

Hunter was then systematizing his thinking about behaviorism, and the students fell heir to his quarrels with the earlier "mentalistic" psychologies. Hunter was never the wild man in psychological theory that Watson was. He rejected no important content, but he believed that all psychological problems could be solved without recourse to the concept of consciousness. "Anthroponomy," as Hunter tried to rename psychology, was not so much concerned with a denial of consciousness as with an attempt to redefine it objectively. Introspection, far from being the "unique method of psychology," was to be understood simply as language behavior occurring in a particular setting and having a particular genetic history.

The third influence complicating our existences (and doubtless toughening our constitutions!) was that supplied by Wolfgang Köhler. Gestalt psychology was new in this country, and there was little appreciation of the intellectual commotion that was about to be created by the almost simultaneous invasions by Köhler, Kurt Koffka, Max Wertheimer, and Kurt Lewin—the "little German band," as Yale's Professor Edward S. Robinson derisively called them in a memorable review. For those of us just getting inured to the pitched battle between behaviorism and introspectionism, Köhler's lectures on *Gestalttheorie* were a disquieting influence. Talk about Buridan's ass and the limits on freedom of choice; we had no fewer than three bales of hay out there and seemingly equidistant! Gestalt psychology had points of conflict with introspectionism and behaviorism separately and still others with them collectively. The adherence of the older systems to an alleged atomism in analysis was Gestalt psychology's major and ever-recurring complaint.

It is not to be supposed that the three years of graduate study at Clark took place exclusively in an atmosphere of pure thought. The tradition in Boring's day had been "eighty hours a week for graduate students," and for most of us that continued to be the rule. The day began with an early morning seminar and ended with coffee and conversation in what we called the "graduate room" (off the shop) at midnight or later. There was much education of graduate students by graduate students. Everyone doing a thesis was busy with apparatus, observations, boning up on literature, and generally engaging vigorously and with good spirit in the scholarly life. It was somewhat easier to do in those days than now; few of us were married or had pressing responsibilities on the outside.

But it was not a matter of "all work and no play." A monthly dance was held in the laboratory to the music of the "big bands" on records. Faculty and students, wives and sweethearts attended regularly and looked forward to these relaxing affairs. Wolfgang Köhler, anticipating his first departmental dance and feeling somewhat "dated" with respect to his terpsichorean skills, attempted to remedy the situation by taking dancing lessons in downtown Worcester. At the next dance, he appeared in full possession of the intricacies of the tango! His German heritage didn't at first permit him to distinguish between North and South America culturally, and he was greatly surprised that none of us knew how to tango. He promptly taught it to us.

Another incident connected with the dancing evenings is worth reporting. In my last year there and with the doctorate about to be bestowed, my wife, then Jeannette Manchester, of Worcester, and I decided to announce our engagement. We picked a departmental dance as the occasion for it. A distinguished visiting lecturer that evening was Karl Bühler, who, upon hearing the news, strode across the room and kissed the bride-to-be. Many years later (1960), on the occasion of the International Congress of Psychology at Bonn, there was a trip up the Rhine to the ancient river town of Linz. We found Bühler on the steamer, renewed our slight acquaintance, and reminded him of his congratulations of thirty-two years before. He promptly took Jeannette in his arms and kissed her again!

As I look back on the graduate days at Clark, I cannot but feel that Hall's "little German university" (for that is what it was in spirit and style) was the best of all possible places for acquiring a professional outlook and preparing for a teaching career. Nearly all classes were conducted as seminars, and everyone was at all times expected to be thoroughly prepared on the relevant literature. Nafe occasionally asked me to lecture to the advanced experimental group, and this was the best possible training, requiring especially careful preparation. The class, nearly all graduate students, included several whose names were to become well known: Clarence Graham, Robert Leeper, Wayne Dennis, Luberta Harden, Norman Munn, Dorothea (Johannsen) and Mason Crook. Two years their senior academically, I hope I had a little to do with their later successful careers. The story of the interaction with Graham, whom I came to know best among these, I have recorded elsewhere (Geldard, 1972). The relation with Dennis was destined to develop further, as we shall see.

My research, for both the master's thesis and the doctoral dissertation, was in vision. The first experiment was one directed at answering the question as to whether color adaptation went to completion, i.e., settled down to a terminal gray, or some hue remained when "fatigue" was complete. This was a major point of dispute in the mid-20s and was critical for testing Leonard Troland's view on the kinetics of adaptation. My study demonstrated that a low-level equilibrium was inevitably reached, but that some hue always remained, provided a Ganzfeld was used. The doctoral dissertation, published in the first volume of Murchison's new *Journal of General Psychology*, resurrected and modernized an old method, devised as early as 1877 by von Kries, for measuring retinal adaptation. Had it eventuated only in a set of curves showing the course of the adaptation process, it would have been somewhat less than exciting. As it turned out, the measuring procedure itself was put under test as a methodological matter. A binocular matching method was introduced that tested the validity of the initially used monocular one, and a huge discrepancy between the results of employing the two procedures was revealed. This naturally led to some quite crucial questions about possible interactions in the visual system. Indeed, some of the questions raised back in the 1920s have never been answered satisfactorily, and the retinal interaction problem is very much alive today, a half-century later.

The summer of 1927, the last before coming into final candidacy for the doctorate, was memorable in several ways. No musical job having appeared, I cast about for some way to make money and found a fellow graduate student, Harry Ewert, in a similar unemployment predicament. We heard about a local agent for washing machines who was looking for commission salesmen and decided to try a hand at it. Picking up the spiel quickly, we canvassed one section of Worcester door to door and even arranged to give a certain number of washes by way of demonstration. In a three-week period, neither of us sold a single machine, but the free washes went smoothly, and we both became convinced of the efficacy of our product. Harry continued in this the rest of the summer and, I believe, did manage to keep the wolf from his door. My fortune was better. Just at the nadir of my foray into salesmanship and when discouragement was greatest, I had a phone call from Carl Murchison, who inquired as to whether I would be free for the rest of the summer to serve as research assistant to a distinguished psychologist. Would I? To anyone, doing anything!

The assignment proved to be one of the most interesting and valuable of my life, and I have long been grateful for the professional outlook it provided. The job consisted of going to Boston, there to live with Joseph Jastrow in Edward A. Filene's Back Bay house and to make daily trips to Harvard's Widener Library to gather material from which Jastrow could concoct a series of articles to fill a newspaper column. Jastrow, just retired from Wisconsin and more vigorous in mind than in body—he had just recently suffered a bad back sprain from a fall—had contracted with a Philadelphia newspaper syndicate to supply, by late autumn, one hundred short articles under the general title, "Your Mind and How to Keep It Fit." These little essays ultimately appeared as a book, *Keeping Mentally Fit* (1941), but at the time, the 300-word pieces comprising it formed the backbone of a syndicated column, with readers' correspondence supplying the remainder.

Meanwhile, the grist had to be ground. Inexperienced as I was with popularization of scientific material, I nevertheless had to learn to think in such terms and to assay psychological facts and theories as candidates for popular consumption. Each day I read scores of articles in psychological journals and books, always with an eye out for usable anecdotes or illustrations. Barring the psychology of the ancient Greek and medieval philosophers, I have the impression that I read everything in psychology and related fields that summer! At least, I consumed a vast amount of literature that I would never have approached for any other reason. At the end of a day of grubbing, I would return to Boston, content if I had full notes on as many as three articles out of which little essays could be fashioned. Over supper at a Charles Street restaurant, we would lay out the next day's campaign, the professor drawing on a lifetime of memories to suggest where in the literature a particular theme might be pursued. He knew the difficulty of the task he had assigned me, was invariably kindly and forgiving of minor stupidities, and taught me a lot I would never have acquired in any other way.

Toward the end of the summer, Jastrow found himself more and more involved in the intellectual world's reactions to the notorious Sacco–Vanzetti case, then being tried in Boston, and joined with John Dewey and others in a committee to consolidate the rising protest. Accordingly, I inherited more and more responsibility for our joint output of articles. The frantic effort to imitate Jastrow's free-flowing style did nothing for my conceit. He was master of the vivid aphorism, and his well-balanced sentences were a constant source of reading pleasure. From his early *Fact and Fable in Psychology,* a great classic, to his later *The House That Freud Built* and *Wish and Wisdom: Studies in the Vagaries of Belief,* he invariably informed while enchanting his reader with a well-turned, picturesque phrase.

In the spring of 1928, the job market for psychologists was not a vigorous one; indeed, teaching opportunities in all fields were hard to come by. I was finishing up my dissertation and preparing for my final oral examination when Vernon Jones told me of a somewhat routine inquiry made by his alma mater, the University of Virginia. They were looking for a "general" psychologist. I lost no time in contacting Virginia's only psychologist, George Ferguson, and arranging a visit "to be looked at." I stayed overnight at his home, met the senior philosophers, Albert Lefevre and Albert Balz—psychology was the responsibility of the Corcoran School of Philosophy—and had a generally satisfactory visit. To be sure, psychology's status at Virginia was not appealing. It was housed in one tiny office in Peabody Hall, the precincts of the Department of Education. Ferguson, then Assistant Dean of the College of Arts and Sciences and spending nearly full-time in that capacity, would obviously not provide much professional support. There was no laboratory, but I was told that I could establish a modest one if I came.

Despite the negative aspects of the general picture, I found myself eager to cast my lot with this old and beautiful university. Everyone I met seemed congenial. Moreover, it was painfully obvious that an energetic fresh start in psychology needed to be made. Besides, with a June marriage impending, I badly needed a job! There presumably was a hasty consultation of responsible parties, and on the way to the railroad station, I was offered a position. With one foot on the platform, the other on the Pullman step, I was asked whether I preferred to be an "assistant professor" or an "associate professor"! In explication of the query, it was pointed out that there was no established salary scale at the university and that the two ranks maximally overlapped in remuneration. My hasty reply was that elsewhere the distinction was real enough, and I therefore preferred, for reasons of prestige, to be appointed an associate professor. And that is the way it was settled, and that was how, a year later, my salary was suddenly increased by fully a third. The DuPonts, meanwhile, had made a huge gift to the university, a faculty salary scale was established for the first time, and assistant and associate professors now occupied nonoverlapping ranges on it.

My efforts, in the fall of 1928, to inject new life into the psychology curriculum centered on the establishment of a laboratory. Free space was not easy to come by, nor had there been budgeted anything like adequate amounts with which to acquire cases, tables, and apparatus. However, a foothold was acquired in Peabody Hall basement in the form of a large, low-ceilinged room previously used for summer courses in manual training. Some of the tools were even available, and our first laboratory had a fairly well-stocked shop in one corner of it. Little by little—and with a display of "scrounging" that only a Yankee would have been capable of—there were acquired desks, chairs, tables, and apparatus cases (all from the state prison system at the cost of materials) and the very necessary pieces of apparatus for an introductory course in experimental psychology. I had learned a good deal at Clark about "making do" with pins, string, and cardboard, so the extremely modest laboratory funds could be used for a chronoscope, color-mixer motors, a simple tachistoscope, a memory drum, and similar standard pieces. Nothing was bought that could be made by hand. I recall that my wife and I labored long hours constructing a James "waterfall" that was driven by a sewing-maching motor. Similarly, we put together a sound-reproducing system that would permit playing to classes the Bell Telephone Laboratory records of the "missing fundamental," the Seashore tests, and George Estabrook's recording of the classic Bernheim hypnotic technique—the latter because, despite my essentially nonclinical preparation, I had undertaken to offer an undergraduate course in abnormal psychology, much in demand. I taught it for many years, following chiefly the descriptive approach of J. W. Bridges. Scarcely a premedical student has passed through the college at Virginia who was not exposed to this course, either under me or, a little later, under Frank Finger.

The first important public occasion at the University of Virginia, as a new academic session gets under way, is the October convocation, replete with a colorful procession down Mr. Jefferson's historic Lawn and a ceremony capped by a distinguished visiting speaker. At the conclusion of my first convocation exercise, in the fall of 1928, I was taken by Professors Ferguson and Balz to meet President Edwin A. Alderman, who had been away from the university at the time of my spring visit. President Alderman was invariably impressive, a man of superb personal bearing and a Southern orator of the old school. We chatted comfortably for a few minutes about politics—Alderman, a loyal Democrat, had been out stumping the South for Alfred E. Smith. Then, quite precipitously, he said, "Young man, how old are you?" I had just turned twenty-four when I was appointed and told him so. "And you have been made an associate professor in this university?" "Yes, sir," I replied, wondering what was coming next. The ensuing pause seemed interminable. "Well, you'll outgrow it, I have no doubt" was his welcome rejoinder! I have told this story many times but believe that I have not distorted it; it was one of the most vivid experiences of my life.

By the end of my first year in Charlottesville, it became apparent that the seed planted by the establishment of the laboratory was beginning to sprout and that an expansion of courses in psychology was indicated. The field I had staked out for myself was naturally classical "physiological" psychology, with its emphases on sensation and perception. I already had a darkroom and was busy with an assortment of visual problems. It was apparent that the other important area of experimental psychology needing encouragement was that of learning and memory. I urged Dean Ferguson to have a look at one of Hunter's students, Wayne Dennis, as a promising man to develop the animal learning field. Dennis was still a year away from his degree at Clark, but Hunter assured me that he was sufficiently advanced with his dissertation work to permit his completing it *in absentia*. Accordingly, Wayne visited us, impressed everyone favorably, and was given an appointment as assistant professor. Upon his arrival in September of 1929, we pushed on into the recesses of the Peabody Hall basement, set up a rat colony (generally regarded, it must be admitted, as a bad neighbor by the School of Education upstairs!), and had an old furnace room renovated to house an extensive, elevated maze. Dennis' experiments on sensory control of maze behavior, an important component of the attack being made by Hunter and his student Jack Liggett in the Clark laboratory, were completed on this apparatus. For the next half-dozen years, experimental work in the animal laboratory was vigorously prosecuted. By 1939, Wayne Dennis published some eighteen papers, eight of them with graduate students.

Another early addition to the growing psychology community at Virginia was R. C. Davis, who took a postdoctoral appointment under the aegis of the local Institute for Research in the Social Sciences. We promptly found new laboratory space for him. While Davis had been completing his degree work at Columbia, there had been published the startling paper by Travis and Hunter in which it had been reported that a very high correlation (-0.87) existed between measured intelligence and latency of the Achilles tendon reflex (Travis and Hunter, 1928). This aroused worldwide interest and prompted immediate repetition by several laboratories. In particular, it caught the attention of R. S. Woodworth, under whom Davis was working. On coming to Virginia, Davis proposed to get at the vexing question of the native ability of our Southern mountaineers, back in the remote hollows of the Blue Ridge, by measuring their reflex latencies. He worked very hard at it, devising a portable cathode-ray oscilloscope, then novel and revolutionary in its use as a chronoscope, and carried it by muleback into the hills, overcoming with great tact "revenooer" suspicions and tapping as many Achilles tendons as he could get access to.

In retrospect, it has to be said that Roland Davis made a very considerable contribution to the growth of the laboratory at Virginia, but not exactly through the expected channels. The intelligence–latency problem blew up in his face, so to speak. Travis and Young, two years after the original report, published a lengthy paper in which it was revealed that the early findings had been in error (Travis and Young, 1930). Substituting the more precise Westinghouse oscillograph for the relatively sluggish phonelescope employed in the first study and measuring 250 individuals covering a wide range of ages, they now found no real correlation between speed of nervous conduction and intelligence as assayed by tests. Davis' more lasting contribution was to a succession of graduate students in whom he took a great interest. He was unfailingly helpful, especially with apparatus problems. For many years, I kept in my reprint file a copy of his monograph coming out of the Virginia work, *Ability in Social and Racial Classes* (Davis, 1932). It was filed under "Electronic Circuits"!

The fourth decade of this century was not, in general, a good time to be developing academic departments or expanding laboratories. The Depression was upon us, and retrenchment rather than expansion was the order of the day. There were some financial setbacks. Thus, salaries and laboratory appropriations were cut; the former in three relatively small decrements, the latter in one major one. Yet, as someone remarked, "We should be thankful we have a traditionally conservative administration; Virginia is always in a depression, and the cuts don't matter that much." Indeed, as one contemplated what was happening to our neighbor, North Carolina, where schools, roads, churches, nearly everything had been bonded and sharp slashes were suffered in all public enterprises, we did indeed have reason for being grateful for our conservative policy. Actually, we made steady progress throughout the Depression years by dint of greater effort if not more plenteous resources. To be sure, the laboratory had little about it that was of gleaming glass and nickel but, on the other hand, we were blessed with some outstanding students. One thinks of Haller Gilmer and Bob Wingfield, the first ever to receive the Ph.D. in psychology from Virginia (1934), of Rains Wallace, one of the most gifted, of Dick Sollenberger, and of several others, such as Jim Porter, Dick Henneman, and Charley Gersoni, who got their start at Virginia but ultimately sought greener pastures for their doctoral work.

Similarly, we were enriched by a minor procession of visiting faculty members. In 1936, Wayne Dennis, whose teaching interests had led him further and further into social psychology, made the decision to ask for a year's leave to go to Yale and there study anthropology. A replacement was needed, and of these there was no dearth during the Depression. It was a buyer's market. After considering a most promising field of candidates, we settled on Dick Wendt, just finishing a three-year stint in neurophysiology at the Yale Medical School. The courses we asked him to teach were somewhat remote from his recent (or subsequent) interests, but with arduous preparation and complete devotion to the task, he brought it off and became a real favorite with both graduate and undergraduate students.

The following year, Dennis requested an extension of his leave. A teaching opportunity had presented itself at our mutual alma mater, Clark University, and Dennis was anxious to combine this with continuing study at New Haven. Wendt, meanwhile, had accepted a call to Pennsylvania, and we were once more faced with the replacement problem. This time also we did very well for ourselves, getting Kenneth Spence, fresh from a sojourn at the Orange Park primate laboratory. It soon became obvious that we had a genius among us. But we also had an outstanding teacher, a constant source of inspiration to students and colleagues alike. Spence was just then working out with Clark Hull some of the fine points of what came to be called Hullian behavior theory (though many have since credited Spence with something more than a triggering role), and there was a more or less constant colloquium by mail and visits during that year.

Dennis returned the following session, and Spence moved on to Iowa, where he was to remain, much of the time as departmental chairman, until quite late in his career. Meanwhile, the war clouds were gathering, and shortly we found ourselves caught up in defense research. A committee of the National Research Council (Viteles' Committee on Aviation Psychology) undertook to generate a set of problems the solutions to which might be of value to the national defense effort. At the urging of H. M. Johnson, who had performed the classical study on sleeping positions and sleep behavior and whose sleep recorders were still available, I agreed to set forth on an investigation into the sleep motility of student pilots. We had a contingent of these at Virginia, all undergraduates taking primary flying training at the university's nearby airport. Twelve of these students agreed to have attachments to their beds that would record all changes of position during sleep. The questions to be answered were, of course: "How is sleep affected by the flight experience? Are student pilots 'restless' on nights preceding or following flight training?"

Servicing of the twelve recorders, borrowed from Johnson and modified to improve paper drive and inking arrangements, and especially minute-by-minute analysis of the daily flood of records were rather more than I could handle and get anything else done, and I engaged an excellent young man, Horace Manchester, Jr., to assume full responsibility for the machines and their records. He was my wife's brother and superb in both roles, research assistant and brother-in-law. Never was nepotism so fully justified. Horrie, as we called him, was subsequently killed in an aircraft accident during the war. He is still, after all these years, sorely missed.

What came out of the research, briefly, was a set of important methodological improvements in the recording of sleep movements and, in particular, a valuable comparison of possible ways of deriving indexes of motility (Geldard, 1944). However, it had to be concluded that individual differences in sleep behavior more or less completely swallowed up any nonflight–flight effects. A much larger population would be needed to obviate the influence of such differences.

One ancillary experiment, performed by Minter Jackson as an integral part of the sleep research program, has always impressed me as being of considerable significance (Jackson, 1942). Jackson undertook to obtain rather more intimate records of sleep motility by using a fast recorder, one on which a bedspring displacement would actually show up as a sloping line. On the same record there appeared pulse rate, taken from an electrocardiotachometer. Comparison of the two yielded the interesting relation that the heart anticipates, by about half a minute, any major sleep movement. Jackson recorded 83 trunk turnings in 12 nights of sleep. On the average, pulse jumped from 63 to 89 pulses per minute prior to the change in trunk position, then declined rapidly to a slightly subnormal level when the motion ceased—proof enough of the apparent causal role of blood congestion from sustained posture in the initiation of sleep movements.

This is perhaps as good a juncture as any at which to insert a flashback of Virginia's early history in psychology and to contrast it with what we were trying to accomplish just before and after the interruption occasioned by World War II.

Psychology of a sort certainly existed at the University from before the turn of the century. Noah K. Davis had been Professor of Philosophy there since 1873. He retired in 1906. As early as 1892, he had written his *Elements of Psychology*, a widely used book, especially in the South. According to Bruce Payne, who succeeded him in handling the psychology courses, Davis gave only a single half-year course in psychology, devoting his major effort to his greater love, logic. The building of a library collection for psychology was clearly not uppermost in Davis' plans, for Payne reported in 1908 that when he had come, in 1906, there were only two modern books on psychology in the university library! As Professor of Psychology and Secondary Education, Payne offered two full-year courses—one in general psychology (with stress on experimental and physiological contents), the other in social psychology ("one-third pure social, one-third the psychology of religion, and one-third the psychology of education")—and he undertook to remedy the book deficiency. He got together a little fund of $50 for this purpose, then spent $10 of it for visual perception apparatus!

Payne was at Virginia only five years but led a very busy life. He was, "on the side," director of the summer school, and he also canvassed the high schools of the state in the interest of augmented admissions. Professor Lefevre, chairman of the Corcoran School of Philosophy, complained that Payne was necessarily away much of the time and that an amplified staff was the only possible remedy. But, when he was home, Payne obviously prosecuted experimental psychology and worked hard at establishing a laboratory. Up to a point, he succeeded, for in his 1909 annual report to President Alderman he expressed his gratitude to the professor of physics for having made available to him a basement room in the Rouss Physical Laboratory on the Lawn. Something of the milieu in which Payne was working can be found in Lefevre's urgently repeated requests: "The laboratory is requisite for instruction in modern psychology, and without it the School of Philosophy must remain forever lopsided" (1909), and "The time has come when we can no longer treat the subject of psychology as a mere appendix to other work" (1913). Again, as late as 1919, Lefevre was saying, "The significance of modern psychology for higher education, apart from its relation to philosophy, need not be here reiterated. It is vital for the increased usefulness of the Corcoran School of Philosophy, no member of whose present staff is even eligible for membership in the American Psychological Association."

This was indeed true. In 1911, Bruce Payne was called to the presidency of the newly reorganized, relocated, and renamed George Peabody College for Teachers in Nashville, and for more than a decade (1911–1921) the two psychology courses Payne had taught were given exclusively by Albert Balz, first Instructor, then Adjunct Professor, then Associate Professor, then Professor of Philosophy. Balz was best known as a student of Descartes but, more than that, he was a great "team player" and taught what had to be taught, whatever the inconvenience to himself. Finally, just after World War I and after a chilly year in the environs of Hamilton, New York, where he found the climate uncongenial to his Virginia blood, George O. Ferguson came to be Professor of Psychology and Education. In 1922, he took over all instruction in psychology.

Ferguson apparently made an early abortive move to divorce psychology from philosophy, a step that Lefevre countered with a forceful, "It is unthinkable, both on historical and pedagogical grounds." Philosophy carried the day; the question was not to arise again for a third of a century.

Numbers of registrants, that statistical refuge of deans, cannot be used as an entirely satisfactory index of academic progress, to be sure, but something of a story is told by the figures on courses and numbers of students under instruction over the years. Fortunately, such data are available in the annual reports to the President of the University, these having been submitted near the end of each calendar year since 1909. A graph would show a gradually increasing number of students in the Payne and Balz years (28 to 91, average of 50) in the two regular courses, general and social, then an abrupt increase to 108 as Ferguson took over and offered the beginning course and one in "mental tests." In 1927, he had 241, all but 25 in general psychology. I came in 1928 and Dennis in 1929. Eight courses were then offered to 215 registrants. By 1941, there were nine courses, 329 students, and an additional instructor, Jim Elder. The war years presented special problems, naturally. Dennis and Elder left for Louisiana State University, Frank Finger was brought from Brown University, and Cecile Finley, our own Ph.D. of a few years earlier, was recruited as Acting Assistant Professor. By 1943, the general speedup affecting all educational institutions in the country was in effect, and the triumvirate of Ferguson, Finger, and Finley gave instruction to 368 students scattered over 15 courses during a twelve-month span!

But if the war years seemed hectic, they were order itself as compared with the postwar period and the demands made on colleges and universities by returning veterans. Registrations in psychology were: 610 in 1946; 1,474 in 1947; and 1,699 in 1948 (the peak year). I had returned from the air force in February of 1946 and became Chairman of the Division of Psychology in 1947. With the flood of students engulfing us, it was clear that help was needed, and we added the seasoned B. von Haller Gilmer as Associate Professor in 1946. However, he remained only a year, in the course of which he was called to the chairmanship of the department at what was then Carnegie Tech. Associate Professor Henneman replaced him, and Assistant Professor Willard R. Thurlow was also added in 1947. The next year, 1948, saw the addition of Assistant Professor Raymond Bice and, the following February, Assistant Professor Starling Reid. We now had a competent group of teachers to handle the staggering numbers. The great impediment to efficient instruction was no longer staff but space. This was felt especially in the laboratory course in experimental psychology, now with seventy students to be cared for in a space hardly suitable for a dozen. Our answer was to double the lecture portion of the course, halve the laboratory work, and institute four laboratory sections, each under a different faculty member but with a common array of experiments. Other courses went out of bounds, too, so much so that new (and distant) meeting places had to be found for several. Whereas there had been a 20 percent increase in enrollment in the college, psychology courses were up 40 percent. Except for the Commerce Department, Psychology now had the poorest instructor–student ratio in the college, a circumstance that worried us considerably.

Somehow we survived it, but not always with equanimity. We found the crowded conditions especially vexing when research plans were being made. In the postwar years, the military looked to the colleges and universities to help catch up on basic research, a trend that not only has continued but has been greatly amplified in recent years. Beginning in 1948, we made a contractual agreement with the Office of Naval Research for a study of the vibratory sensitivity of the skin, followed shortly afterwards by a similar contract between Professors Henneman and Reid and the air force for work on auditory and visual displays in message presentation. Research activities in the division expanded rapidly. To meet all the research needs of faculty and graduate students, we should have had about twenty research rooms; by the most liberal count, we had seven. As early as 1936, following a summer visit to Berkeley, where I had seen the cooperative venture between biology and psychology called the Life Sciences Building, I campaigned locally for a similar arrangement at Virginia. That year we actually got some primitive floor plans worked out with the School of Biology, but nothing came of it immediately. In the postwar crisis, we again took up the cry, persistently urging that classroom instruction, laboratory exercises, research, and testing activities all presented space problems that could be solved in no other way. The clamor was ultimately rewarded, for in the early 1960s—unhappily, a little late to be of any direct benefit to me—Gilmer Hall, the present home of the biology and psychology departments, became a reality. I had much to do with planning its internal arrangements but had left for Princeton by the time it was occupied in 1963.

I have skipped over World War II as if it were no part of my personal existence. On the contrary, and by certain standards, a case could be made out for the 1941–1945 period as having been the most useful one of my professional career. Shortly after Pearl Harbor, I received an inquiry as to whether I would be interested in being directly commissioned in the U.S. Army Air Corps as a major—object, service as a principal in the aviation psychology program being organized under the Air Surgeon. Dr. John C. Flanagan had already been on duty for about six months prior to the Japanese attack and, with an impressive background of training and experience in the testing field, was attempting to put together a program that would bring psychological tests to bear on the aircrew selection and classification problem. The sudden onset of the war had thrust this problem on a considerably unprepared military. The initial plan called for the application of *a priori* knowledge of aptitudes for pilot, navigator, and bombardier training, this having been derived largely from consideration of the reasons assigned for failure to complete training in these specialties. A battery of likely-looking tests of the skills involved was put together. But the limitations of this kind of knowledge were fully appreciated. Really, what was needed were job analyses of the three aircrew positions. The decision was made to undertake continuous test development and organize this around the four areas of intellectual ability, observational and perceptual skills, psychomotor coordination, and motivation—the categories most often implicated in instructors' reports of failure. Each area was to be worked on at a different cadet-processing situation—tests of judgment, reasoning, and information at Santa Ana, California (Major J. P. Guilford); those of coordination at San Antonio, Texas (Majors R. T. Rock and A. W. Melton); those of motivation, interest, and temperament at Montgomery, Alabama (Major L. F. Shaffer); and the perceptual-alertness area at Ellington Field, Texas. The last-named was, of course, to have been mine.

Military exigencies being what they are, it is not surprising that modification of the early plan came promptly. Ellington Field was never activated as a cadet center, leaving my unit temporarily homeless. Also, the task of devising and developing psychomotor equipment proved to be ever so much more complicated than it had appeared at first, and Melton moved to the School of Aviation Medicine at Randolph Field to take advantage of its facilities in this area. Moreover, a critical decision was made by the air staff early in 1942 that moved actual test operations out of the headquarters of what by now was the Army Air Forces and centered administration of classification tests in the newly formed Flying Training Command. The surgeon of that command, Colonel Charles R. Glenn, obviously needed to add a psychological section to his Office. It was clear that he had suddenly inherited what was destined to become a far-flung empire. As the most available and not otherwise heavily committed senior officer, I was assigned to be its chief. Accordingly, with the transfer of the Flying Training Command to Fort Worth, Texas, in July of 1942, my wife, small daughter Debby (then five), and I moved from Washington to Fort Worth, there to remain until near the war's end. The Perceptual Research Unit went with me and, for somewhat over a year, functioned under Captain J. J. Gibson's direction at Fort Worth; ultimately, much of that unit was absorbed into the Psychological Test Film Unit created at Santa Ana, California, in 1943, several perceptual tests on film having been devised meanwhile.

The details of the operation of the Aviation Psychology Program have fortunately found their way into print—indeed, into a great deal of print, for the record of performance of the 200 officers and 1,300 psychological assistants, about half of them enlisted men, is thoroughly documented in the nineteen-volume *Army Air Forces Aviation Psychology Program Research Reports,* prepared by program personnel and published by the U.S. Government Printing Office. The story of the testing of over 600,000 cadets processed through eleven different units scattered widely throughout the training command and of the additional research facilities set up to look into a variety of psychological problems related to aircrew, especially training problems, has wisely been preserved against future emergencies.

Shortly after the Japanese surrender, ending the war, I embarked on a project that turned out to have a twofold objective: (1) to assist the newly formed Philippine Air Force in its problem of selecting men for training in aircrew, and (2) to ascertain what methods had been used by the Japanese during the war for the selection of their aviators. On September 15, 1945, my little unit—PMP (Psychological Mission to the Philippines) it was called—set off from Hamilton Field, California. We were fourteen in number, three officers and eleven enlisted men, handpicked and assembled from the processing units partly on the basis of known skills, partly on the basis of desire to participate in this venture. With us were several hundred pounds of test booklets, answer sheets, and a complete line of psychomotor apparatus. Between the time of our arrival in Manila two days later and early November, we were able to administer the aptitude tests to several different Filipino groups—urban and provincial high school and university students, and trade school students—and thus standardize the Stateside battery for the purposes at hand. We also established a testing center at Camp Murphy, near Manila, and trained both military and civilian personnel to operate it.

The first objective having been met, the officer complement (Captain Chester Harris, Lieutenant Franklin Bacon, and I) set off for Tokyo, there to question the principals in military aviation concerning their wartime practices in selecting and classifying their aviation trainees. We also examined documents (what there were of them; they were supposed to have been burned just prior to surrender), made field trips to flying installations, and interviewed nonmilitary officials. The outcome of our inquiry was described in a paper prepared for

American consumption (Geldard and Harris, 1946). It is clear that the Japanese procedures both differed radically from our own, in that they placed far greater emphasis on qualitative features of test performance—they were primarily interested in weeding out the obviously "clumsy" people—and resembled our own, in that a composite index, made up of roughly weighted scores, was used. But, whereas we had given up personal interviews in favor of group tests and strictly administered apparatus tests, they were more concerned with the "pattern of response" as judged by a trained interviewer, and the final judgment about a man was essentially a clinical one.

I had promised to get the boys back home by Christmas, but I failed to reckon with the vast number of officers and men who had been poised in the Philippines for the final onslaught on Japan when the A-bombs at Hiroshima and Nagasaki forced Japanese capitulation. Getting home was thus going to take more than a little doing; only the highest priorities got one into a California-bound airplane. By the greatest good fortune, I learned that there was at the Manila headquarters General MacArthur's surgeon, who owed me a favor by reason of the fact that I had once gone to considerable trouble to supply an airplane lift to Washington, D.C., for him when he urgently needed to keep an appointment. I hunted him out, described our plight, and through some magic known only to him—though I think the stars on his shoulders had something to do with it—got almost immediate air transport arranged for my entire unit! There have been times in my life when special privilege has seemed fully as attractive a principle as democratic equality.

The transition back to civilian life was memorable for me. On arriving in Washington with separation from the air force only a few days away, I received an urgent message from President Newcomb of the University of Virginia to the effect that plans were afoot to establish a "university center" in the Richmond area. The General Education Board of the Rockefeller Foundation was interested in sponsoring such a venture and had arranged for representatives of the colleges and universities involved to visit each of the existing university centers already being aided by the foundation. To that end, a Pullman car had been chartered for the group of a dozen administrators to visit, in turn, Ithaca, Toronto, Nashville, and Atlanta. Would I represent the university on the trip? The two to three weeks required were more than the president's own schedule would permit. I assented and joined the junket on the very day I yielded my air force colonelcy! The visits to the four centers, under the genial guidance of Jackson Davis, the board's executive secretary, were highly informative, setting as they did the pattern for genuine interinstitutional cooperation and the elimination of needless duplication of effort by educational neighbors. I learned much that was to broaden my outlook and provide real inspiration for future activities at the university. In particular, I noted the tremendous boost to morale that was supplied to faculty of the participating institutions by the existence of research committees in the centers, and that feature I insisted on having included in any plan that might develop for Richmond. Indeed, the majority of the institutions that ultimately banded together to form the Richmond center had never had research committees, since the wherewithal to support them had been lacking. Ultimately, such committees were established in each. While I am not informed on their long-range influence, there is little doubt that they had an immediate beneficial effect, especially in the smaller colleges, triggering research efforts that never would have existed otherwise.

The return to teaching the following month was in the midst of the turmoil I have already described. It was not only a matter of faculty returning to their academic pursuits; great numbers of students, many of them veterans, descended on the university as well. And quite a few of the veterans were now married men, some with families started. They meant business and were, by all odds, the best students it has been my privilege to teach. Indeed, there was a sharp contrast in behavior between these seasoned and serious veterans and the youngsters fresh out of secondary schools, with their "interest-me-if-you-can" attitude.

I look on the decade of the 1950s as one of solid accomplishment, both intramurally and extramurally. Within the walls, there was a strong teaching contingent to care for the postwar "ground swell" that had already begun to move into the advanced courses. Research interests were firmly established as well and, with the remodeling of the animal laboratory and a new partitioning of the laboratory space, much was being achieved. The contract with the Office of Naval Research for study of cutaneous communication was in force continuously from 1948, with intensive summer speedups, for a period of fourteen years. Its final report, written in 1962, listed eighty-two contributions by a total of twenty-one people: published articles, papers read at meetings, theses completed, colloquia given, contributions to joint volumes, etc. Henneman's air force project on message-presentation techniques continued for six years, then was supplanted by a similar arrangement with the army surgeon general. In the middle of the decade, Finger and Reid were granted support from the National Science Foundation for a cooperative study of induced drive states.

Another event of some significance in the mid-1950s was the separation of psychology from philosophy, alluded to earlier. By 1953, both divisions had sufficient personnel to "stand on their own legs," so to speak. Giving departmental status to both, all agreed, would dignify both philosophy and psychology. The psychology division annual report said, "Philosophy does not need the doubtful aid of the 'bolstering' by Psychology, and Psychology is nowadays related in no peculiar manner to Philosophy. As Queen of the Sciences, Philosophy could be linked to Astronomy or Biology with precisely the same justification that brings Psychology into rapport with it." With this plea, the faculty in psychology asked for *de jure* recognition of what, for a quarter of a century, had been *de facto* independence of the two disciplines. On April 9, 1954, the university's Board of Visitors, acting on our petition and a matching one from the philosophers, granted the separation. We must have been one of the last of the major universities in the country to take the step.

Outside the walls, too, the decade of the 1950s was an extremely busy one. Indeed, looking back on that period and running an eye down the list of extramural affiliations in which I got involved, the correct adjective is perhaps "frantic." Had it not been for the good people of Virginia's psychology faculty, several of whom assumed unusual burdens during my enforced absences from the university, it is hard to see how the decade could have begun with me in the Pentagon, working full-time for a whole year on research program planning for the secretary of defense, assuming for the next half-dozen years the chairmanship of the Human Resources Committee of the defense secretary's Research and Development Board, then taking more than a year off (1956–1957) to go to Europe, there to serve as Scientific Liaison Officer in the Office of Naval Research, London Branch.

Of these, the London experience was, by all odds, the most rewarding, both scientifically and culturally. For many years, there has been attached to the American embassy in Great Britain a contingent of scientists, assembled and administered by the U.S. Navy, whose function it is to maintain close contact with the scientists of the several Western European nations. There is a systematic rotation of scientific fields, most of the incumbents spending one year visiting their opposite numbers in England and on the continent. On the one hand, they keep their European counterparts advised as to what is happening in science in this country; on the other, they gather information on European developments and report them back home. There are some other points of liaison, such as participation in international gatherings, but the primary purpose is to insure a two-way street with our scientific friends in other countries. This has been going on since shortly after World War II.

Several psychologists had preceded me in London, notably Clarence Graham, Dewey Neff, and Lee Cronbach, and they had progressively laid down the lines of access to European psychologists. It was largely a matter of giving a little advance warning that I was coming; invariably, I was received with open arms, such had been the felicity of past contacts. The navy encouraged family travel in the interest of congeniality. My wife, Jeannette, went nearly everywhere with me, and Debby, now a college sophomore, accompanied us whenever her course responsibilities at the London School of Economics would permit. The loose English system of university attendance seemed to "permit" much of the time! We established many firm friendships that year, some of which persist to this day.

Among the most memorable visits on the continent were those made to: Michotte (Louvain), who was doing extremely ingenious perceptual experiments prompted by his theory of "causality"; Piaget and Inhelder (Geneva)—the central topic then was Piaget's theory of geometrical optical illusions, and interesting experiments on development time of some of the common illusions were under way; Metelli (Padua), with his Gestalt-oriented perceptual phenomena; von Frisch and Renner (Munich), the fountainhead of work on the language of the bees; Duijker (Amsterdam), who was handling with great finesse the problem, nothing less than a form of political dynamite, connected with intelligence and educational accomplishment of the new residents of the polder lands; Ivo Kohler (Innsbruck), then in the middle of his perceptual retraining experiments. The list could go on and on, for everywhere there were live centers of psychological research— van Lennep (Utrecht), working on scientific creativity; von Wright (Turku), who assembled for us, at his attractive home on the shore of the Baltic, much of the psychological talent of Finland; Tranekjaer-Rasmussen (Copenhagen), genial perpetuator of the Rubin tradition, with his experiments on form and distance constancies; Bouman, with his busy institute at Soesterberg, the Netherlands, prosecuting several important studies of vision and hearing; and Fraisse with his laboratory at the Sorbonne, devoted to a systematic program on the psychology of time.

Liaison with our British confreres was especially close. Much time was spent with Oldfield, both at Reading and Oxford, and a similar visit was made to Hearnshaw and Heron at Liverpool. Talks were given at all three universities. I attended several regional meetings of the British Psychological Society, giving papers at most of them. At the large annual meeting, held in 1957 at St. Andrews, Scotland, I was invited to chair the section on Engineering Psychology and to organize a symposium on that topic. The visit to St. Andrews was made the more memorable by virtue of the opportunity it afforded for Jeannette, Debby, and me to visit the "Ancient and Honorable"; this we did with a round of golf early on Easter Sunday morning.

Back in London, following a Cambridge colloquium on cutaneous communication that I gave at the Applied Psychology Research Unit, where Sir Frederick Bartlett had carried much of the discussion, I received a cordial note from him asking if I would like to return to Cambridge, live "in college" for a weekend, and continue our friendly debate. I naturally took him up on this attractive invitation, arrived on a late train Friday evening, and made my way to St. John's. Sir Frederick greeted me warmly, showed me to my room, and suggested that it would facilitate arrangements if my order for breakfast were left on the porter's desk. Unclear about local customs, I replied that I wanted no special fuss made for me and that I would take "whatever the others were having." Sir Frederick explained that a man would appear in the morning, light the fire, draw my bath, shine my shoes, and lay my breakfast while I was dressing. He then asked if I liked orange juice (yes); porridge? (yes—that had the ring of inevitability about it); eggs? (yes, brightening); bacon? (that would be great!); toast? (fine); and tea, of course? (of course). Sir Frederick penciled "365" on a little slip of paper and placed it on the porter's desk. The next morning all the predictions were realized. As I finished the unusually sumptuous breakfast my "gyp" (or, perhaps, "scout"—I can never remember which species inhabits Cambridge, which Oxford) asked, "Will there be anything else, sir?" "Yes," I said, "Last night Sir Frederick left my breakfast order for you; the whole message consisted of the cryptic numbers, '365.' What did that mean?" "Oh, that's very simple, sir," he replied. "That's what an Englishman has for breakfast 365 days in the year!"

One absorbing visit with two outstanding scientists took place without the necessity of any travel at all. The Swedish otologist Gösta Dohlman was spending some time at the Royal Institute of Laryngology and Otology in London. I called on him and, in the course of our discussion, asked him if he had visited Löwenstein's Birmingham laboratory. (Dohlman and Löwenstein, quite independently, had years before performed entirely crucial experiments, both classic, that had revealed the basic functioning of the nonauditory labyrinth.) Dohlman said that he had the greatest admiration for Löwenstein's work but that he had never met him. A few weeks before, I had spent a day with Löwenstein in Birmingham and had asked him if he knew Dohlman. No, he replied, but he admired his work enormously. It was a simple matter to arrange a luncheon at the London embassy and invite the two to come meet each other. Introductions over, I simply sat back and listened to the two scientists, who, in a matter of minutes, became fast friends. Never was there a more instructive seminar on labyrinthine functioning or a more self-satisfied entrepreneur.

One coordinate activity accomplished during the London year stands out as central. Before I left home, it had been arranged that Professor Langfeld's Committee on International Relations in Psychology, on which I had been serving, would manage, under air force sponsorship, an international symposium in the field of military psychology. This had not been attempted before, and there was no experience to serve as a guide. The meeting was to take place in Brussels the following spring. Since I was to be "nearby" and would have access to possible contributors to such a meeting, I was designated as general chairman and was given carte blanche to arrange the program as I chose. I cannot recall ever before or since having worked on anything so intensively. I began by inviting appropriate advisers to meet with me at Strasbourg, France, on the occasion of the annual meeting of the French-speaking group (Société psychologique de la langue française). A plan was worked out to prepublish and circulate to all members of the conference the formal papers to be offered at Brussels. This arrangement is not uncommon in Europe, though rare in America, and there is much to be said for it. At the meeting itself, the author expands on important points or provides illustrative material, and he has the assurance that he has already entered the apperceptive masses of much of his audience. Discussants of the papers were programmed as well. Between the paper-presenters and the designated commentators, I was able to schedule speakers from nearly every country in Western Europe. The sessions were held in the beautiful Palais des Académies. On all counts, including the final publication of the proceedings (Geldard and Lee, 1961), the First International Symposium on Military Psychology has to be judged to have been a great success.

The American university, with its mixture of democratic and autocratic traditions, operates largely on the committee system. If I were to enumerate the committees on which I served over the years at Virginia, the list would be a formidable one. The most rewarding were those on research, lectures and public occasions, and long-range planning. Almost from the time of my arrival at the university—mainly because I represented a new departure in graduate work—and continuing throughout my entire thirty-four years there, I was a member of the Graduate Committee. Eventually, in 1960, upon being asked by President Edgar Shannon to take the deanship of the Graduate School of Arts and Sciences, I became its chairman and was able to give direction to its policies.

The assumption of the deanship brought with it a much more radical change in general outlook than I would have thought possible, in view of my long involvement in graduate affairs. In 1960, the graduate school, at least by contemporary standards, was small; there were fewer than 400 graduate students in all departments combined. Well-defined traditions concerning the administration of graduate studies obtained: all departmental recommendations for admission were carefully reviewed by the dean personally; on admission in the fall, each registrant was individually interviewed by the dean, who would welcome him and make certain that his living arrangements and course commitments were congenial; the dean sat as chairman of the committee on fellowships and, for those originating in other than local coffers, dealt directly with the foundation and federal granting bodies that awarded them; he maintained frequent contact with departmental chairmen on graduate matters; he represented the university at meetings of the American Association of Universities and other such bodies; he met often with the Graduate Committee on all major questions of policy and operation. And there was no assistant dean to whom some of these functions could be relegated. Had there not been the skillful manipulations of Elizabeth Purvis, secretary to several successive graduate deans, the conduct of the graduate school could easily have deteriorated into a shambles. There were brief periods of stress when I thought it might anyway.

Two years of this kind of living brought with it a firm belief that one could not possibly retain his professional standing—certainly not his self-regard as a professor and researcher in psychology—and perform conscientiously as a major administrator. It was at this juncture that there came an invitation to join the faculty at Princeton University as Stuart

Professor of Psychology, the chair formerly occupied by Baldwin, Warren, and my old friend Langfeld. This had not been the first attractive offer from outside the walls, but two considerations combined to give extraordinary weight to it. The first was that, years before, I had come to the conclusion that there existed just three institutions in the world that, all things considered, surpassed Virginia in attractiveness. Of these, Princeton clearly headed the list. The other was the realization, by now nearly a conviction, that I had played so many roles at Virginia over such a long span of years—more than a third of a century!—that my usefulness to the community was considerably attenuated. A fresh view of the world was indicated.

The years since my resignation at Virginia have, I think, vindicated my decision to cast my lot with Princeton. Whereas the ten years of teaching remaining to me when I transferred in 1962 were not always entirely tranquil (there having been intradepartmental crises that sometimes approached the level of upheaval), freedom to conduct classes and research in my own way and encouragement to attend to a variety of peripatetic interests have led to a rich experience and, I think, to a useful existence.

Research, especially, has benefited from the change. Not only was it possible to transfer to Princeton the National Science Foundation grant under which we had been working at Virginia, but, much more importantly, arrangements were completed with Princeton to obtain a permanent appointment there for my former student and, by then, research associate Carl Sherrick. He had taken his doctorate with me in 1952, working on a fundamental problem in cutaneous sensitivity, had taught for several years at Washington University in St. Louis, and had completed an enriching stint in research at the Central Institute for the Deaf. Returning to Virginia in 1961, he has since been uninterruptedly identified with the area of sensory communication. By now, he has become a major and indispensable leader in this field of ever-increasing importance, especially to the sensorially handicapped. Scarcely is there launched in this area any new effort in the form of symposium, workshop, or advisory committee that does not include him, so well known are his proclivities for conscientious preparation and unremitting effort in completing an assignment. For many years now, we have enjoyed a more or less continuous colloquy; if I gave him anything of importance in the formative years, he has more than repaid the debt.

I have spoken of my early interest in vision. This embraced the adaptation problem, the encountering of a rare case of total color blindness, retinal interaction, and various measurements of flicker fusion. It was the latter phenomenon that originally led to an involvement with cutaneous sensation. Specifically, the question was, "Does the skin have a critical flicker point?" Attempts to answer it led inevitably to the effects of mechanical vibratory stimuli and somesthetic reactions to them. Curiosity about these, occurring first in conjunction with Gilmer's and Wingfield's doctoral dissertations (Gilmer, 1935; Wingfield, 1936), precipitated an ever-expanding line of work, pursued both at Virginia and at Princeton over a span of more than forty years. This is not the place to review the program in detail; the record is ample and public. But something of its progressive ramifications should be indicated, for it epitomizes what for me is the only reasonable view of the scientific process.

Pure science and applied science, or technology, are often contrasted, as two intellectual spheres differing in aims, attitudes, and methods. There has been a good deal of nonsense written on this subject. Actually, the only distinction between the two I have ever found to be worthwhile concerns the matter of freedom in the manipulation of variables. The technologist faces his problems in practical situations, and these are as he finds them, with their variables "frozen," even though they can be manipulated. If he is to experiment, he does well to keep his independent variables in the ranges they occupy in the relevant practical situation. The pure scientist, on the other hand, is under no necessity to preserve such fixity; he is free to vary any and all factors he wishes. The result is that "pure" or basic research often results in highly impractical, even ludicrously unearthly, outcomes. I once had a colleague who spent much of his time during commencement exercises at Virginia amusing himself with the "outlandish" titles of master's theses and doctoral dissertations in the printed program. As a nonscientist, he found any academic effort not directed at solutions of workaday problems to be absurdly pointless.

This view of the matter, first worked out in the immediate postwar years with my wartime colleague, Paul Fitts, I expanded in a paper prepared for the dedicatory celebration at the opening of Mezes Hall, the home of the psychology department at the University of Texas (Geldard, 1953b). There it had a somewhat colloquial cast. The question was being raised as to whether military psychology, more often than not dealing in real-life situations, is thereby a technology. The conclusion was that it may be a science, too, depending on what is done about manipulating variables in ascertaining its facts. But, in my view, the idea is generalizable; it represents perhaps the only real difference—certainly the most important one—to be found between pure and applied science.

I have elaborated the above because it is such a firm article of faith with me that it has been a prime determiner of the direction of my research efforts. The forty-year-long program on vibratory research illustrates the principle. On the one hand, there were studied over the years the results of supplying repeated impacts to the basket endings surrounding hair follicles of the skin to determine, among other things, whether the perception of vibration is mediated by the same mechanism as that responsible for pressure sensations or whether, as David Katz maintained, there is a separate "vibratory sense." This was the purest of pure science. I doubt that the average blind man knows he has basket endings in his integument or would care whether they can mediate "pressure in motion." But, if that pressure in motion turned out to be the means whereby he could communicate intelligibly with the outside world, it would matter greatly to him.

Meanwhile, a technological problem remains and needs tackling. Bereft of sight, our blind man deserves to have every effort made to explore the cutaneous possibilities of communication. Now, he mainly relies on braille, an arbitrary and essentially nonpsychological language so difficult to learn that relatively few blind people ever really master it. With such a consideration in mind, the vibratory research program has sought to achieve a balance between pure science concerns and those of communication technology. Over the years, my research colleagues and I have gotten involved with many aspects of vibrotactile reception: the transmission of forced vibrations through the skin, but also with the discrimination of gross bodily tactual patterns as elements in a signaling system; with a dimensional analysis of vibratory stimuli, but also with the devising of a method whereby useful alphanumeric information may be encoded; with the psychophysics of tactual numerosity, but also with the development of an "optohapt" to transmute optical characters into tactual impressions; with the question of whether sensitive vibrotactile "spots" on the skin display the fundamental neural phenomenon of primary summation, but also with the concoction of a "vibratese" language for the deaf and blind. These are markers only, buoys on the forty-year tide of somesthetic research, and they by no means encompass the range of research topics. They merely suggest the basic science–technology juxtaposition or, better, the inevitable partnership of the two for those who would interest themselves in matters of pith and moment.

Much has been said and written about the role of "luck" in scientific experimentation, with the edge in the argument seeming to favor the view that "lucky experiments" come only to those who deserve them. Deserving or not, it was not until my final year of tenure in my Princeton professorship that something approaching a lucky experiment came my way. Thus far, it has occupied me fully for my five years in emeritus status and has resulted already in several publications, one of them a small book.

Briefly, the experiment, which was designed as a class exercise in my advanced undergraduate course in perception, involved resurrecting the interesting experiment of Helson and King (1931), in which they had demonstrated a trade-off relation between space and time, the so-called tau effect—three equidistant tactual stimuli are judged to have uneven spacing if the time intervals separating them are unequal. We planned to deliver to the forearm a series of three brief "buzzes," spaced about four inches apart. Duration of each was to be controlled by a succession of five sinusoidal waves (total time for 60 Hz about 83 msec) operating through a punched tape. Through an inadvertence, the 60-Hz source did not get plugged in, but a dc amplifier delivering brief square-wave pulses did. The result was a train of five sharp pulses at each of the three sites in turn. I was the guinea pig for the first trials. The surprise was great when, in lieu of the three expected buzzes, there came a train of sharp taps, some of the fifteen located where they were "supposed to be," but most at intermediate points over the eight-inch span. For all the world the overall impression was that of a tiny animal hopping up the arm. My immediate response was, "Who let the rabbit loose?" Then, "Let's do that again." We did do it again— many, many times. Always there was the vivid mislocalization. After a time, it became evident that the localization "error" was systematically related to time between pulses. It also proved to be partially governed by intensity but relatively unaffected by distance or direction; indeed, our woodland friend could be made to run up one arm, across the nape of the neck, and down the other arm.

The main facts about our newly discovered phenomenon have been set down in a book coming out of the inaugural MacEachran Lectures at the University of Alberta (Geldard, 1975). The leaping effect, which appeared almost comical when first encountered but which has turned out to be a general sensory phenomenon occurring, under suitable conditions, in vision and audition as well as touch, I have dubbed the "saltation effect" or "saltatory induction." There is not the slightest doubt in my mind that the essential locus of the action is central rather than peripheral, that it bespeaks a fundamental metastability of the perceptual process, and that it will become increasingly important as we are led to an appreciation of the basic role it must play in neural functioning. Among other significances is the certainty that any simple excitation, whether of the skin by a mechanical pulse, the retina by a light spot, or the ear by a click, must remain available in central limbo for as long as a quarter of a second, for its localization can be affected by a second stimulus coming *after* it within that time span. If the second pulse comes within the short period of 20 msec or thereabouts, localization can be so faulty as to make the two impressions spatially coincident at the site only the second stimulus would normally occupy. Intermediate times yield intermediate leaps.

In view of what has been said above about science and technology, it is interesting to raise the question as to whether saltation is of any "use." The indications are that it has at least two immediate practical applications; both are presently under investigation. First, it is a valuable ingredient of the recipe for graphesthesia, "skin writing." Place a small matrix of vibrators on an expanse of skin such as the upper thigh, activate successively the contactors so as to describe an "O," and at no rate of repetition will the impression of a full circle be created. Now, repeat the exercise, this time letting each vibrator be energized three successive times before passing on to the next. If the repetition rate is right, the second and third pulses, responding to the saltatory conditions, will fill in the gaps between stimulators. A "dotted" contour forming an unmistakable "O" will be felt.

A second "use" is more speculative, but is probably much more important. In widespread explorations of the body, the systematic mislocalization never fails to appear and by predictable amounts. That is, it never fails so long as the contactors creating it are arranged longitudinally with respect to the body axis. Let the contactors be disposed transversely, however, and if the span crosses the midline of the body, there is a prompt failure of the hopping sequence to complete itself. This is true on the thorax and abdomen, front and back, and on the forehead. The bifurcation of the nervous system creates a barrier to saltation unless a contactor is also placed at the midline location. Obviously, since the saltatory effect is central—and of this there is little doubt; the rabbit jumps right into and out of the blind spot, for example, and also completes when one stimulus lands on one retina, the other on the other (if on corresponding sides!)—there is a fundamental principle of nervous functioning at work here. The saltatory effect may be well on its way to becoming a "neurological sign."

If my recent efforts are largely centered on research, my earlier ones often took a different road to productivity. Over the years, I have done a fair amount of writing—four books authored, four edited, and a dozen chapters written for other people's books. By all odds, the most important of these are the two texts: *The Human Senses* (1953a, 1972) and *Fundamentals of Psychology* (1962).

The origins of the two books are quite different. *The Human Senses,* begun in the busy prewar years, was originally intended to be a general text in experimental psychology—in many quarters much needed, then as now. I started on vision, mainly because I knew more about it than I did other topics. The war intervening, with scholarly work hardly possible for me during that period, I returned to the "experimental" book in 1946. By the middle of the following year, I had gotten so far into vision and audition that it became apparent that some restriction of scope was going to be necessary. I was teaching in the summer school at Wisconsin that year and discussed the problem with my friends there. They, probably better aware of my limitations than I was, were univocal in urging that I confine the book to man's senses. As I now reflect on what I might have done with the topics of learning and motivation, had I stuck to my original plan, I conclude that the advice I received was eminently sound. The book took another half-dozen years to complete. Not only were the study and the laboratory in competition, but I was immersed in all manner of extrinsic developments, chiefly in Washington—chairing ONR's Committee on Sensory Psychophysiology, serving on NSF's first Committee on Biological and Medical Sciences, attending frequent meetings of the Research and Development Board's Committee on Human Resources, and somehow keeping up with the air force's Research Advisory Board and the Council of the Richmond Area University Center. But I was younger then, and writing could get done in the small hours when the house was quiet.

One other circumstance had much to do with completing the writing. In 1950, at the conclusion of a year in which I mainly inhabited the Pentagon, I was laid low by a coronary thrombosis. This was catastrophic for my family, terribly inconvenient for the Virginia psychologists, more than a little frightening for me, but a godsend for *The Human Senses*. The prolonged, enforced convalescence required by Dr. Tom Edwards, who had rallied around at 4:00 in the morning and had promptly gotten me into the hospital under an oxygen tent, provided perhaps the only set of conditions that would have brought the book to its conclusion. When the first copy appeared, I inscribed it to Tom Edwards, "Without whose timely help the author might have been finished before the book!"

If *The Human Senses* took an unconscionable amount of time to get produced, its general acceptance was entirely gratifying. Indeed, the first edition had an exceptionally long run and established itself as the standard text in its field. Finally, since the facts here as elsewhere never stand still, after nineteen years the publishers agreed with me that it was time for a new and expanded edition. This was accomplished in 1972 with somewhat greater ease and in shorter time than the original edition had required; by then, I was at Princeton, and the external pressures were fewer. Many mature psychologists have told me that they were "brought up on" the first edition; if it performs a similar service in its enlarged form, as it seems to be doing, I can wish nothing more for it.

The other text, *Fundamentals of Psychology,* came into being quite differently. I was "put up to it," so to speak. Just about as *The Human Senses* was being published, I was approached by an officer of Wiley's with the proposition that I undertake a revision of Boring, Langfeld, and Weld, a general psychology text that had already been through three editions (1935, 1939, 1948) and was widely used, especially by those of experimental persuasion. All three had been multiple-author books; I had myself done a chapter for the third edition. Boring, in a foreword to the *Fundamentals,* tells the story:

... a fourth "BLW" by Frank A. Geldard has at last become available. Early in the 1950's we three old editors selected him as our successor and secured his agreement to undertake the enterprise. We thought then that he would revise the BLW of 1948, but each of our own "revisions" had turned out to be a new book, and it is no surprise that this new volume emerged as all Geldard in style and in the imaginative insight that determines its choices and informs its pages.

Actually, when I accepted the assignment, it was with the understanding that BLW No. 4 would be a multiple-author book, that my role would be that of giving it unity of expression, and that all three of the original editors would be unsparing in their criticism and advice. Unity the book had, I think, based as it was in ringing the changes on the three central conceptions of modern psychology: motivation, learning, perception. Multiple authorship it had not, and it gradually emerged that

I was writing a book, not simply editing one. Advice and criticism there were in abundance, and I am eternally grateful for the thirty typed, single-spaced pages I had from Garry Boring in response to the rough draft of the finished manuscript.

The *Fundamentals* enjoyed brief domestic favor, then proved more popular in foreign markets. Like its predecessors, it was widely judged to be too "difficult," too "scientific." Boring gave as his prediction on publication, "It will be a good book for Harvard sophomores and the English!" However that may be, it still does quite well in Spanish, Dutch, and Afrikaans translations, and I am told that it is currently being translated into Hindi and Urdu.

As I look back over these pages, there appears to have been left a false impression that should be redressed. Because I have devoted so much space to details of research and writing, committees and teaching, the suggestion has perhaps taken root that life has been a bit too earnest, that work has completely preempted play. I hasten to put things back into balance. It was not only the year I spent in London that whetted my appetite for travel. Jeannette and I have often taken advantage of national and international meetings to "see the world" and, in particular, to increase our familiarity with the antiquities, in which we both have developed great interest. Especially memorable were the international congresses at Bern, Brussels, Bonn, Copenhagen, London, and Tokyo, partly because all permitted "getting around." The last was a real adventure, coupled as it was with visits to many of the beauty spots of Japan, then on to Hong Kong, Thailand, and the Hawaiian Islands before returning home.

While it is true that, ordinarily, a professional meeting provided the important nexus for associated travel, there was one considerably extended trip, taken during several months of sabbatical leave during which no paper had to be read, no committee meeting attended. It occurred in 1967, after several years of teaching at Princeton. The first few weeks of the free semester having seen the satisfactory completion of some exacting writing, we decided to try to fill in some important travel gaps, especially to areas representing the older civilizations. Accordingly, we headed for Egypt (the ancient pyramids, Luxor, and the Valley of the Kings and Queens), then on to the Holy Land (Jordan and the Arabian desert, including a horseback trip into the lost city of Petra), Syria (Damascus and the Roman ruins of Palmyra), Lebanon (Byblos, Baalbek, and the Krak de Chevaliers), Turkey (the great mosques of Istanbul), Greece (the Peloponnesus and the islands—with a somewhat exciting confinement in an Athens hotel in consequence of the military coup that overthrew the monarchy), Yugoslavia (the Dalmatian coast from Svaeti Stefan to Split), northern Italy (Venice, our favorite city), and home by a thirteen-day boat trip. Surely, these were changes of scenery enough for anyone, and, if sabbaticals are designed to secure refreshment of outlook, a guaranteed rejuvenation for the final five years of teaching.

Well, there you have it, the life of Frank Arthur Geldard laid bare for all to see. Perhaps not exactly bare, but possibly as much so as British genes, a New England birth, and a Methodist upbringing will permit.

1977

Selected Publications by Frank A. Geldard

A study of the sleep motility of student pilots. Washington, D.C.: Civil Aeronautics Administration Research Division Reports (No. 18), 1944.

(with C. H. Harris) Selection and classification of air-crew by the Japanese. *Amer. Psychologist,* 1946, *1,* 205–217.

The human senses. New York: Wiley; London: Chapman and Hall, 1953a (2nd ed., 1972).

Military psychology: Science or technology? *Amer. J. Psychol.,* 1953b, *66,* 335–348.

(with M. Lee) *Proceedings of the first international symposium on military psychology.* Washington, D.C.: National Academy of Sciences (National Research Council Publication No. 894), 1961.

Fundamentals of psychology. New York: Wiley, 1962.

Vision—from a wide mantel. *Perception and Psychophysics,* 1972, *11,* 193–197.

Sensory saltation: Metastability in the perceptual world. Hillsdale, N.J.: Erlbaum Associates, 1975.

Other Publications Cited

Davis, R. C. *Ability in social and racial classes.* New York: Century, 1932.

Gilmer, B. von H. The measurement of the sensitivity of the skin to mechanical vibration. *J. gen. Psychol.,* 1935, *13,* 42–61.

Hall, G. S. *Life and confessions of a psychologist.* New York: Appleton, 1924.

Helson, H., and S. M. King. The *tau* effect: An example of psychological relativity. *J. exp. Psychol.,* 1931, *14,* 202–217.

Jackson, M. M. Anticipatory cardiac acceleration during sleep. *Science,* 1942, *96,* 564–565.

Jastrow, J. *Keeping mentally fit.* New York: World, 1941.

Travis, L. E., and T. A. Hunter. The relation between "intelligence" and reflex conduction rate. *J. exp. Psychol.,* 1928, *11,* 342–354.

Travis, L. E., and C. W. Young. The relations of electromyographically measured reflex times in the patellar and Achilles reflexes to certain physical measurements and to intelligence. *J. gen. Psychol.,* 1930, *3,* 374–400.

Wingfield, R. C. An experimental study of the apparent persistence of auditory sensations. *J. gen. Psychol.,* 1936, *14,* 136–157.

Eleanor J. Gibson

Eleanor J. Gibson

I will abbreviate the beginning of this tale because my early life was so traditional as to make very dull telling. I did not escape from a bloody revolution or a wasting childhood disease or even a broken home. I was reared in an atmosphere of middle-class respectability among dozens of kindly, staunch Presbyterian relatives, all of English and Scotch-Irish ancestry. and all those ancestors had been long established in America. The only surprising thing to me is how I managed to break away so far from this background and emerge as an intellectual (an academic, at least), with ideas that would seem radical to many of my forebears. No one ever suggested that I was a bright child, or particularly wanted me to be bright. I began to ponder the matter when I went to high school at the age of twelve and found my peers generally older and more sophisticated than I. I wondered still more about my intellect when I grew interested in boys and found that it was essential, if I wanted any reciprocation, to conceal the fact that my grades were A's.

I grew up in Peoria, Illinois. (Quite literally, I "played in Peoria.") Grades of A were easily come by at the Peoria high school that I attended. But since I was destined, by family tradition, to go to Smith College where things wouldn't, presumably, be so easy, a couple of devoted teachers with high standards took me in hand during my junior year and put me to work. It is amazing to recall the number of hours and the effort they provided without any recompense except the hope of three pupils doing them proud on the College Board Examinations. I had two fellow pupils, another girl who was applying to Smith and a boy who was applying to Princeton. We read poetry, wrote papers, spent two afternoons a week after school doing Latin prose, and struggled with math every Saturday morning, doing all the old college board math exams for the preceding ten or fifteen years.

One of these self-sacrificing ladies (they were all ladies) was the Latin teacher, Miss Stewart. She had taught Latin and Greek to both my parents and felt privileged to turn me into a scholar, if possible, by any means she saw fit. She was notorious for cracking a ruler over the knuckles of lagging pupils, a method that, despite Skinner and his ilk, seemed to work pretty well. But she gave a really effective performance when she was occasionally driven to distraction by a bad translation. She tore her hair (red turning white), her pince-nez fell off, and she screamed, "Ye Gods, ye Gods, ye Gods!" It has just occurred to me that some of my awe of Miss Stewart has passed along, through a mysterious process of transference, to my husband, who sprinkles epithets, including "Ye Gods," over any manuscript of mine that he gets his hands on.

The efforts of the teachers were fortunately successful, and the three pupils went east to college. It was the first time any of us had lived outside the Middle West. Smith was a revelation and an instant joy to me, despite my provincialism. My roommate was nineteen, had attended an Eastern preparatory school, and had never been west of Northampton, Massachusetts. There was something comfortingly provincial about that, too. The greatest revelation was that Smith, a women's college, was a place where women were not only permitted but encouraged to be scholars, even scientists. That is said to be permissible today even at coeducational colleges like Cornell, but the atmosphere for real flourishing of an undergraduate woman who wants to be a scientist, in particular, still does not match Smith at that time.

During the first two years at Smith I wasn't much of a scholar, however. It was too important to absorb all the other wonderful and previously unattainable things: symphony concerts, mountains in the distance to be climbed, courses and books about things I had never heard of, and proms and houseparties at nearby men's colleges. But toward the end of my sophomore year, I discovered a profound interest in psychology.

I was assisted in my discovery by what now seems a rather unlikely person—Margaret Curti, from the Middle West and a confirmed dust bowl empiricist. She had taken her Ph.D. at Chicago with Harvey Carr. Her thesis, one of the first studies done on spectacle-wearing (with laterally displacing prisms), was in the tradition of the Chicago functionalists and emphasized the kind of S-R association theory that characterized Carr's theory of space perception—essentially the notion of linking, or relinking, local signs with localizing responses.

The idea as such was not so appealing to me—I doubt that I really understood it. What attracted me was the emphasis on experiment. The course was Animal Psychology, and we ran our own rats through our own mazes. The experiment was of no importance, but performing it was entrancing. I took Margaret Curti's course on Child Psychology, too. That wasn't so good; Chicago functionalism worked better for rats. But I was hooked, and I decided to major in psychology, instead of French as I had once intended.

My junior year was satisfactory, but not exciting. I had some good teachers, especially Harold Israel, who gave a year-long course in History and Systems, a hard and excellent course. He had been a student of Edwin Boring's at Harvard. He did no research at all, but he was a first-rate historian. He tried to teach us what problems a psychological theory should be able to handle, not just what any particular theory did handle—a valuable lesson. There was a course in Tests and Measurements, taught by Hannah Faterson, that I enjoyed a great deal, too, although not for the underlying theory of testing. During the second term, we learned to give Stanford–

Binets and went out to the schools to give individual tests. It wasn't exciting, and I determined not to continue in that area. But administering the test to a child was real, and I thought I would like to work with children almost as much as with rats.

At that time, the chairman of the Smith College Department of Psychology was William Sentman Taylor, a remarkable man. He had been a student of Morton Prince at Harvard, and Prince was his idol. He taught Abnormal Psychology and was interested in hypnosis. We read all about split personalities and the medium Marjorie, and we watched Mr. Taylor give rather unconvincing demonstrations of hypnosis in class. He did not hypnotize the students, of course. At a college for women that would be unthinkable, like not leaving one's office door open a few inches when a student was inside. For all the racy topics, Abnormal Psychology inspired no great interest in the students. I suppose Mr. Taylor, a very dull and prosaic man, made it dull. He had edited a book of readings in abnormal psychology that was used in his course. Each excerpt was short, ranging from a few pages down to a paragraph or even a sentence. The shortest excerpts had a proverblike quality, and evidently they were meant to, since Mr. Taylor's last publication before his death—apparently a lifetime's work— was a collection of aphorisms. Freud was seldom mentioned in the course, but when he was, the implication was clear that his ideas were unwholesome. The dynamics in what we were being taught were missing; but about the same time, they were introduced from a most unexpected quarter.

William Allen Neilson, president of the college, brought Kurt Koffka to Smith as a kind of professor-at-large. It was a time when many Europeans, especially Germans and Russians, were looking for a home in this country. Koffka brought with him a retinue of young psychologists—Molly Harrower (English), Fritz Heider (Austrian), and three émigrés from Soviet territories, Alexander Mintz, Eugenia Hanfmann, and Tamara Dembo. The latter three were known as "the Russians." Some of these people had been students of Kurt Lewin, and research began to burgeon on dynamic factors in perception and other cognitive processes, and even on emotions. None of Koffka's retinue gave a course, but naturally the psychology students were preempted as subjects, so the ideas filtered in.

Koffka himself did eventually offer a course, which I took my senior year. He read his lectures, which were notes for his book on Gestalt psychology, and the class seemed to me Germanic in style, just as he seemed dictatorial as a professor. He did not welcome discussion or inquiry from the students. I found him unattractive as a person and as a scholar, but I was an exception; for many students, including some of my most respected friends, were charmed by both the man and his ideas. I may have been rendered immune because I had just found the charm elsewhere.

James Gibson came to teach at Smith, fresh from a Princeton degree and only twenty-four years old. I had no contact with him until I met him at a garden party at the end of my junior year. It rained and we were happily stranded in a corner of a quadrangle where he was supposed to be shaking hands with parents of seniors as I offered them punch. He took me back to my dormitory in his ancient Model-T Ford, and next day I hurried to the class dean's office and changed the following year's schedule to include his class in Advanced Experimental Psychology. It was a wonderful course and I fell in love with experimental psychology and with the instructor.

The course was small—just nine students—and very time-consuming. Each person, with a partner, did four experiments each term, getting her own subjects wherever she could (Amherst was a favorite source) and writing up the experiments, complete with background. I made some of the best friends of my life in that course. Everyone in it went on to do graduate work. We did experiments on a wide range of problems—color constancy, aftereffects, conditioning, retroactive inhibition, adaptation to wedge prisms. One of the experiments that I did with Gertrude Raffel Schmeidler on bilateral transfer of a conditioned response (finger flexion to shock) was published (Gibson et al., 1932). It was very exciting and both of us felt we were budding scientists. We had our own laboratory in the basement of the psychology building. It functioned as a sort of club room as well as work place.

It was clear by that time that I wanted to do graduate work in psychology, but the Depression had hit. My family's finances were already strained from sending me to Smith, and there were no training programs and few fellowships in those days. I was in luck, however. Smith College did not give Ph.D.'s, but it did give a master's degree, and the Introductory Psychology course needed teaching assistants. I was hired with two of my friends, Hulda Rees and Sylvia Hazelton, to teach laboratory sections (they were given routinely as part of the course) while working for a master's degree. Hulda and I shared an attic apartment and were in seventh heaven. We were the best of friends (and still are), we felt terribly important hobnobbing with the younger faculty members, and we learned a lot. The students wrote one laboratory report a week, and we each had sixty of them to read, but even that wasn't too bad. We bogged down a bit once when an instructor in the department suddenly began to fancy that she was being poisoned by her colleagues, and we had to grade all of her papers, too. But we emerged from that episode with enhanced reputations for reliability and loyalty—very useful later.

During my first year as a graduate student, my exhilaration was compounded by my increasing intimacy with James Gibson. I took his seminar on William James, I began research for my master's thesis with him, and I drank bathtub gin and grapejuice with him and other friends. He was an ardent experimenter, among other things, and was doing his research on the aftereffects of exposure to curvature. Perversely, I was not particularly interested in perception at the time (learning was the stylish topic of the day). But I was interested in James Gibson, and we were married in September, after I had completed one year of graduate work. The wedding took place in Peoria, under the eyes of a large contingent of relatives, and we drove back to Northampton through the Adirondacks, carrying a suitcase full of books on social psychology. My husband had been assigned to teach that subject for the coming year, and I had been assigned as his assistant. Neither of us had ever had a course in social psychology, but things like that can happen in a college the size of Smith. I don't remember either of us reading any of the books on our honeymoon, but the course turned out pretty well. Taking a naive look at a field, if one has had good fundamental training in how to pursue knowledge that is desired, can pay off. My husband has always had a knack for that. The course even turned out to be popular.

I completed my master's degree that year, doing my dissertation research on retroactive inhibition (Gibson and Gibson, 1934). The experience was very instructive. I revised that thesis again and again under my husband's critical eye. Writing a thesis with one's own husband as director is definitely not to be recommended, but we survived.

It was time to go somewhere else to study, but the Depression made things difficult. I stayed on at Smith as an instructor, read widely on my own, and went to such seminars as were available. There was always Koffka's seminar, attended by his retinue, all the young faculty in the department, and the graduate students. Many of the people who came to Northampton with Koffka had left for other jobs by that time, but Fritz Heider remained, at the Clarke School for the Deaf. He and his wife Grace, also a psychologist, became our close friends. I think they were among the first psychologists in this country to study cognitive processes and linguistic development in deaf children.

Although the discussions in Koffka's seminar were on a very high level and were stimulating, I was not attracted by Gestalt psychology and yearned for what I thought of as "hard" psychology. I didn't like introspective methods. I wanted to be objective, as I thought of it then, and I wanted to work with animals and children. The time came when my husband had his first sabbatical leave coming up, and I applied to Yale, the antithesis of everything Koffka represented. I would go there alone for one term and my husband would join me for the other.

A Year at Yale

Yale was a lively place then. The Institute of Human Relations was new, and great things were to be done cooperatively with psychiatrists, anthropologists, and sociologists. Clark Hull had recently arrived. There were chimpanzees, which had come with Robert Yerkes from Orange Park, Florida. There were excellent people in neurology, a science that had been only minimally available at Smith. The idea of a big university with lots of research going on and famous people to study with was very attractive. I was not discouraged by the fact that I secured only a tiny scholarship that paid tuition and left me $25 to spend on other things.

What I did not realize when I departed for New Haven was how favored a life I had led at a women's college. It never occurred to me that a big university would not be quite as welcoming as Smith. I found this out in a hurry. After three days, I succeeded, with considerable effort, in making an appointment with Yerkes. A secretary let me in, and Yerkes invited me to sit down and asked why I had come. I answered that I had come to Yale to work with him. He stood up, walked to the door, held it open, and said, "I have no women in my laboratory." I was astonished and angry. I took my troubles to Carlyle Jacobson and Henry Nissen, who were both young professors in Yerkes' laboratory at the time. They said that was how it was and nothing could be done, but that they would find other opportunities for me to work with animals. Roswell P. Angier, who was chairman and a sort of kindly grandfather to the graduate students, just said it was only to be expected and I had better find a young faculty member to work with. Yale, as it turned out, did nothing for women at that time except tolerate a few as graduate students. The graduate school had a fine new building, with a library, refectory, living rooms, and so on, but women graduate students were not welcome. There was no place to live except for shoddy rooms and apartments that one had to locate for oneself. The institute was surrounded, for about an eight-block radius, by the most miserable slums in New Haven. They had to be negotiated on foot and alone at night because there was no place nearby to live and few students could afford a car.

Despite my original shock, I soon began to find Yale almost as interesting as I had expected. It consisted of small empires, each with its czar. Yerkes had the most impressive empire, or at least the most noticeable one, because of the chimpanzees. They had outdoor cages atop one of the buildings and, in fair weather, could be heard from every quarter of the institute. Arnold Gesell had a large institute of his own, with many subordinate faculty members—Helen Thompson, Louise Ames, Frances Ilg, and others whose names I have forgotten. Raymond Dodge had recently retired and was ill with

Parkinson's disease, but he appeared at his laboratory occasionally. Walter Miles had a large laboratory full of fascinating gadgets, but few followers. The dominant figure at that time was Clark Hull. His laboratory was large and he had many students. It was a lively place, although Hull himself was rather an awesome figure until one came to know him. There were younger faculty, too—Donald Marquis, Neal Miller, Richard Wendt, Carlyle Jacobson, Henry Nissen, Leonard Doob—excellent people, all very active and approachable. Marquis and Miller were both on leave the year I was there, but I became well acquainted with the others. John and Lillian Wolfe and Hobart and Molly Mowrer were at the institute as postdoctoral fellows, and my husband and I became friends with them as well.

Outside the department of psychology, in the Institute of Human Relations, there were Mark May, John Dollard, and some psychiatrists who participated with psychologists in an interdisciplinary seminar—but not one that was open to women students. Having been turned away from that endeavor, I made the best of necessity and explored what the medical school had to offer. I attended John Fulton's seminar and took a course in neuroembryology with H. S. Burr, both impressive and invaluable. I was permitted to watch and assist in minor ways when there was experimental neurosurgery on cats and monkeys, and I got involved in some research with a young neuroanatomist. The anatomists and physiologists were far more tolerant of women students than the psychiatrists, although they were not included in the institute. In the end, not much came of the interdisciplinary human-relations venture. Interdisciplinary cooperation apparently cannot be commanded. It can happen when a couple of people get together voluntarily with an idea (as Miller and Dollard did), but referring to some important scholars collected under one roof as an "institute" seems to be of little avail.

Graduate students as a rule educate one another. Yale was no exception. All the new graduate students (there were ten of us) had to attend a "proseminar." We moved rapidly from one area of psychology to another, the areas determined primarily by the interests of the senior professors. Each czar had his fortnight. But he himself didn't necessarily have to appear more than once. (I don't remember seeing Gesell more than once, for instance.) He could, and frequently did, send emissaries. We got little out of these meetings from the leaders, but the group of students became closely knit, and we learned a lot by arguing among ourselves, despite the vaudeville style of the seminar. Irvin Child, Helen and Vincent Nowlis, and Austin Riesen were part of the group, respected friends then and now. Older graduate students (although not older in years than I) included Carl Hovland, John Finan, John McGarvey, Adella and Dick Youtz, and Elliot Rodnick. Some of us had a supper club in the Youtz's tiny apartment at 80 Howe Street. The conversations with these friends were very influential in my final decision to work with Clark Hull.

When I approached Hull, he was somewhat standoffish, but not uncivil. He said that he already had a number of students working with him (as indeed he did), that he had large-scale plans mapped out for his own work, and that he was interested only in graduate students who fit somehow into those plans. By that time, he had published most of his justly famous series of articles on the conditioned reflex and its role in various animal learning situations, such as the maze, the discrimination box, and problem solving. He had introduced the concepts of the goal gradient and the habit–family hierarchy, and he had argued in the first and strongest of all these papers for the functional nature of the conditioned response and its properties of extinction, generalization, and spontaneous recovery. He was at the height of his interest in developing what he called "miniature systems" that applied principles of the conditioned response to more complex learning situations, using a rigorous deductive method to generate testable predictions from carefully stated postulates.

He lent me some of his more recent "notebooks" to see if I could find an idea for a thesis that he would approve. He wrote in these notebooks every Sunday, jotting down ideas for experiments, thoughts for future papers, goals to be achieved, and sometimes his personal feelings about people and events of academic interest (see Hull, 1952). They were fascinating reading, but I found nothing there that I wanted to work on. When I returned them, I said that I had previously worked on verbal learning and that I thought I could stay within his general plan by attempting to apply some conditioning principles—generalization and differentiation—to various phenomena of verbal learning and forgetting. The idea was "around" at the time—I had discussed it with Elliot Rodnick and with Carl Hovland—but it had not been exploited. He asked me to show, in a preliminary way, how I would do it and demonstrate that some productive experiments would be generated. I did this (actually as part of my "prelim" examination) and he acceded, with the stipulation that I would construct a miniature system, with axioms and derivations in the kind of logical format that he had himself worked out.

My time at Yale was limited to just one year, for both marital and financial reasons, so I took every examination going (including the two foreign languages required then) and strove to make the most of every moment. I left in September, with some regret, to go back to Smith to teach again and to work on my dissertation. Since I taught full-time, I spent two years on the dissertation, traveling to New Haven as often as possible to discuss progress with Hull. We gradually grew well acquainted and I became truly fond of him. He looked like my father, who even had a limp rather like Hull's, but I don't believe my fondness sprang from some Freudian depths. He was interested in what I was doing, read everything I sent him carefully before I came for discussions with him, and often talked freely about his own goals and worries (especially his fear that his health would not permit him to complete his "grand plan").

The dissertation was completed by the May 1st deadline in 1938. It included a long, theoretical paper—my "miniature system" linking the concepts of generalization and differentiation to paired associate learning, forgetting, and various transfer phenomena (see Gibson, 1940). There were also four experiments, testing some of the theoretical predictions (Gibson, 1939, 1941, 1942). Pavlov would probably not have recognized my definitions of generalization and differentiation. I thought of generalization as confusability, and of differentiation as a process leading to hitherto unachieved discrimination. I did not use the concept of extinction as inhibition that could be compounded, a possibility that was explored by others. I felt wary of it, as I did of the concept of reinforcement as Hull used it, though I didn't and couldn't make that clear at the time. I was not an S-R psychologist at heart, I suppose, for all my attraction to animal research. I didn't believe, then or now, that external reinforcement, in Hull's sense, was applicable to perceptual learning. I thought that differentiation, once achieved, was not extinguishable, even though a subject was commanded to learn new responses to whatever had been differentiated. However, it wasn't possible to say all this in so many words at the time.

Work and Family

Smith College had no nepotism rules and continued to employ both my husband and me as full-time members of its faculty. Full-time was really full-time, however. One taught three classes a term (sometimes only two courses, with one repeated) and had numerous advisees, committee duties, and so on. The atmosphere was that of a college rather than a university, but the faculty was excellent, a group of scholars carefully picked by the president, William Allen Neilson, certainly one of the great college presidents of all time. He was a Shakespearean scholar, so the arts were rather heavily emphasized. The faculty was about half men and half women, a balance that Mr. Neilson liked, but he saw to it that there were distinguished women on the faculty and that they were promoted at the same rate as the men. There were Mary Ellen Chase, Eleanor Duckett, Grace Hazard Conkling, Gladys Anslow (a physicist), and a number of excellent women in music, art, and philosophy.

A number of my own forebears had come from Northampton, including Eleanor Strong, whose first name was given to me, along with some of her silver spoons and a silhouette portrait. I felt at home there and loved the place, as I still do.

My husband and I had a son in 1940, I was finally promoted to assistant professor, we acquired a lovely, very old house with five fireplaces, and life was exceedingly busy. Trying to care for an infant and a house, teach a rather heavy load, and perform all the incidental duties of supervising honors theses, new laboratory assistants, and many advisees took all the time there was. My thesis was rewritten and published, but my only chance for research was via an occasional master's thesis or honors thesis, not actually performed by me. I did in that way get several more of the theoretical predictions in my thesis put to experimental test, but I couldn't do it myself. It seems to me that one can do two jobs at a time, but not three. The teaching and the family I could manage, but not the research, too. I am afraid that restriction may still hold, despite modern reorganization of family life, with the father taking more responsibility. It does not have to be frustrating, though, when there are plenty of rewards and when the period does not last too long.

War Years

During these years the Depression had been desperate, but Smith and its faculty came out of it unscathed and probably the better morally for attempts at forming a teachers' union and assisting local factory workers. It was the threat of war in Europe, and possibly our own involvement in it, that began to change the calm academic life. We had a number of refugees from European countries at Smith, the last one to arrive in the psychology department being Annalies Argelander, a German developmental psychologist. Her husband, Jerzy Rose, a physiologist, accompanied her. They arrived in the nick of time, having had to leave all their personal belongings, even books, in Poland. On Pearl Harbor Day, my husband was away at a meeting of the Psychological Round Table (a kind of Young Turks experimentalist group that excluded women), but he arrived home already wondering what he would do in the coming months.

Early in 1942, he joined a group of psychologists in the Training Command of the Army Air Force. They were to construct tests for selecting personnel for aircrews, and it was thought that a psychologist specializing in perception could help. He left for Washington, D.C., less than halfway through the second semester. I took over some of his experimental duties, Fritz Heider took over others, and the social psychology course was carried on by Richard Sollenberger, a social psychologist and good friend at nearby Mt. Holyoke College. But Sollenberger joined the Training Command too before the term ended, and I found myself grading examinations for social psychology again, little better prepared than I had been some years before.

When the Training Command was finally located in Fort Worth, Texas, I left in July with our son, then two years old, to join my husband. There were many psychologist friends there with their wives—the Geldards, the Kemps, the Sollenbergers, the Ghisellis, the Hennemans, the Deemers—and others came and went constantly. For a short time, I rather enjoyed the experience of socializing with the women and doing a not-very-useful job for the Army Emergency Relief. Our daughter Jean was born in Fort Worth in 1943, and a few weeks later, my husband was moved to Santa Ana, California, to an air base near Los Angeles. I followed again, after a while, and lived in a succession of temporary quarters in various areas of Orange County, a community so reactionary that the local newspaper featured editorials inveighing against free public education.

We stayed in California until April 1946. Again there were some good friends, especially Bob Gagné and his wife Pat. The young noncommissioned officer psychologists who worked with my husband and Bob were rather like a group of graduate students. They did research on aircraft recognition and space perception, and they made training films. The entire time was a kind of latent period for me; I discussed their research with them sometimes, but there was no way that I could be truly involved in it. As so many women have done, and still do, I wondered whether I would ever be able to make it back. But the rather empty life I led there taught me something useful. If I had ever had any doubts about the desirability of an academic career and the joy of research, as opposed to a life of feminine socializing, community service, and women's clubs, they were thoroughly dispelled. The boredom of it became awful. Teaching and research were glorious to contemplate.

Postwar Years

Although I did not have tenure, Smith College took me back, with my husband, and things returned to a new equilibrium. I taught better for the sure knowledge that I was doing what I wanted to do. Northampton was beautiful, a fine place for the children to grow up, and it was good to see the old friends again. I taught a heavy load, served on innumerable committees, and spent all the time I could with the children. It all worked pretty smoothly, because we located a young Japanese girl, fresh from an internment camp in Colorado, who came to live with us and help with the children. Sadako ("Sadie" as she wanted to be called because it sounded American) was wonderful and became a kind of foster daughter to us. She stayed with us for three years, until she went off to nursing school and we exchanged Northampton for Ithaca.

Although Northampton seemed like paradise after four years of uncertainty and life in unlikely places, it became clear within a year or two that Smith was no longer the right place for my husband. The students were still first-rate, and he had certainly never been a male chauvinist, but there was no emphasis on research or even much reward for doing it. The era of government-supported research arrived immediately following the war, and he quickly got a navy contract (as they were generally called at first) to work on problems of perception, such as gradients of surface texture and motion, that were leading him to a new theory of space perception. The problem was that there were few graduate students to work with him and, except for me, almost no one to talk to about his new ideas. Koffka was still alive, but he was interested only in his own views. Fritz Heider was there for a while, but he moved away to Kansas. My husband became a bit restless. Various places made tentative gestures, but none of them seemed an improvement. I asked him one day where, of all universities, he would most like to go. His answer was "Cornell," and like a miracle, a letter came the next day from Robert MacLeod, the new chairman of the psychology department at Cornell. Of course we went, but there was no job for me. However, it was not a repetition of the war years, since I would have the time and the opportunity to do research and to be part of the community of psychologists in a big university again. I was given the title (without pay) of Research Associate at Cornell.

Life as a Research Associate

Freedom to do research is one thing, but more is required—a laboratory, some support for equipment, and a source of subjects at the very least, plus of course some good ideas. Cornell did not give me the opportunity to seek my own outside support at first. In some desperation, I accepted an offer from Howard Liddell to work on his project at what was known as the "Behavior Farm," a laboratory in the country about three miles from the university. It was literally a farm. The laboratory was surrounded by fields and pastures, and the subjects were sheep and goats. Liddell's project was to investigate experimental neuroses by establishing conditioned reflexes based on shock in these animals. I was to photograph leg movements and monitor breathing and heart rate. In short, I was to become a "sheep shocker." Liddell had been at this project for some time, and I had often heard him speak at meetings. He was an exceptionally entertaining speaker, and I began my job without too many qualms, prepared to learn about experimental neuroses.

To my dismay, I found that Liddell himself almost never went to his laboratory and that the research was run by the farm manager, his brother-in-law Ulric Moore. Moore was a very pleasant man, an expert with apparatus, and a lover of gadgetry, but he had no training as a psychologist. The research had no clear aim except to produce neuroses in the animals. There were several show cases, always brought out as demonstrations for guests. One was Brown Billy, a mature goat who was a real performer. He lifted his foreleg and rolled his eyes for the visitors from the Rockefeller Foundation and was rewarded with cigarettes. We made miles of records of heart rate, breathing, and movements, but no one appeared ever to read the records. The animals obviously did not like to be shocked, but so far as I could see they were no more neurotic than I was, and even if they were, could one generalize from such a procedure to a human neurosis?

Although that aspect of the work seemed, frankly, humbug to me, I was interested in the theory of conditioning. Did a shock to an animal's foreleg produce a flexion that was copied, like a conditioned reflex, when a buzzer or some neutral stimulus had preceded it long enough and then was presented alone? Did the flexion come to anticipate the shock (the classic expectation), and why should it if the animal got the shock anyhow? What if the animal escaped the shock by anticipating it with leg flexion? Did the pattern of behavior resemble that of conditioning with inevitable shock? These questions were of popular interest at the time, relating to the dual-factor theory of reinforcement introduced by Hobart Mowrer. I trained kids (young goats) in a situation permitting free locomotion with varied conditions of shock (inevitable, avoidable, and random) and recorded their behavior in detail. I did come out with a two-factor theory, though not one very similar to Mowrer's. The shock had two functions: first, to reinforce an emotional state that instigated some kind of defensive response (locomotion backward always came first); and second, to suppress that response as it was found ineffectual. Inevitable shock did not increase the probability of recurrence of the same response, as a simple Pavlovian view would have demanded, but produced variable reactions, a kind of continuous trial and error (Gibson, 1952).

Perhaps that research had some implications for a theory of neurosis, but I did not think so, and I began to concentrate on something that interested me more: ethological observations of maternal–infant interaction in goats. A newborn kid is a very interesting animal. It gets up and walks almost at once, looking curiously at the world around it. I was interested in olfactory bonds in the maternal–infant relation, and so on one occasion I was taking the kids from the mother, before she could lick them, and bathing them in a detergent. I had bathed the first kid as its twin began to appear and wondered what to do with it, in a hurry, while I dealt with the newcomer. Moore was watching. He said, "Put it up on that pedestal"—a camera stand about five feet from the floor that we used frequently when filming behavior. The platform was only large enough to hold a camera, but the little animal stood there motionless, watching the scene. After all, he had evolved from ancestral cliff dwellers and retained some of their genes.

My second year at the Behavior Farm was devoted to this work, and with Moore's help, I made a nice motion picture of maternal–infant behavior in goats. I was engaged in a controlled rearing experiment (pairs of twins separated—some reared with the mother, some reared under other conditions of isolation or human companionship)—when my faith in the possibility of working in that laboratory was shattered. One of my groups was given away during a weekend absence of mine. The experiment was ruined. I looked for a new job, but working with the kids was instructive and rekindled my interest in development.

About this time, our old friend Bob Gagné joined Arthur Melton at an air force laboratory that had ample funds for supporting outside research. They were interested in perceptual learning, and so was I. My husband and I were the beneficiaries of a very generous grant from them, with my own projects to focus on perceptual learning, especially distance perception. Nothing could have suited me better. I began (at Bob's suggestion) by reviewing and putting together all the experimental literature on perceptual learning. It extended back to 1858 (A. W. Volkmann's experiment on the effect of practice on the two-point limen on the skin), and no one had ever got it together before. I could see a brand-new field for research and theory. The experiments I did at this time were fairly traditional psychophysics, involving special kinds of practice, mostly done outdoors in a very large field. I had some good graduate-student assistants, and the work was fun. We collected data all summer, while the weather was clement. The subject situation was any experimenter's answer to a prayer. Subjects arrived every day from nearby Samson Air Base via bus, attended by a sergeant. They were new recruits, since Samson did not train flying personnel. The trip to Ithaca was part of their indoctrination, and they were glad to get away from the routine of shots and tests. By the third summer, we had a whole series of experiments lined up for them and kept them busy all day, but they enjoyed it.

The "field experiments" were very straightforward investigations of the effect of training on all kinds of distance judgments—absolute, relative, and fractionation—over quite large distances (Gibson and Bergman, 1954; Gibson et al., 1955; Purdy and Gibson, 1955). Theoretically they were not terribly exciting, but I have always felt rather proud of them. A lot of important muddles got straightened out, such as the confounding of perceptual learning with response bias and the danger of generalizing from photographs to real space. It also became pretty obvious that young human adults are very skilled, without training, at making relative judgments of distance, even over a large area, and that perceptual constancy for stretches of distance over the ground is good. At the end of the three years this research occupied, I felt that a new field for learning—perceptual learning—had been staked out.

Meanwhile, the urge to theorize, acquired from all my mentors—my husband, Hull, and even Koffka—was still strong. My husband and I spent many hours arguing about perceptual learning, what it really was and how it happened. Generalization and differentiation—concepts exploited in my thesis—were prime candidates for describing the process. We thought that perceptual learning was a change in what was perceived, not in the association of a response with a stimulus, and that the change was best described as increasing differentiation or decreasing generalization. It could be described as a narrowing of the class of things or displays responded to in some predesignated way. I did an experiment with a set of scribbles, originally all very confusable, that we designed to serve as an illustration of our ideas. The experiment was developmental, too, with subjects of three age groups, and showed that the kind of change we hypothesized occurred developmentally, as well as with practice. The result was a paper, "Perceptual Learning: Differentiation or Enrichment?" (Gibson and Gibson, 1955), one of only five that we have written together. The results of our collaboration were apt to be good, but the arguments always got too heated.

I did work with my husband for two years after this, however, on a navy contract for which he was investigating the perception of motion. We did some nice experiments and I was initiated into the concept of detection of invariants (Gibson and Gibson, 1957), an idea that gradually came to fit very well in a theory of perceptual development.

A new colleague, Richard Walk, came to Cornell about this time and was assigned to teach the learning course. He was interested in perception, too, and we soon planned some collaborative experiments on perceptual learning in early life. The experiments were done with rats and involved rearing groups of them from birth with exposure to various cut-out shapes hung on the walls of their dwelling cages. When they were three months old, we trained them on an appropriate discrimination to see if there was transfer from the "early experience" of viewing the cut-out shapes. Aha! Early experience worked in our first experiment (Gibson and Walk, 1956), and the National Science Foundation gave us a generous grant to delve into the problem. Those experiments did not pay off very well. Sad to say, we never got results again that looked as convincing as the first experiment. I now think it is simply the case that one doesn't have to learn to see triangles and circles. Differentiating them was easy, even for rats that had been reared in the dark (Gibson et al., 1959). The work constituted a great learning experience for me, however, and I began thinking far more seriously about what must go on in perceptual development. Shapes do not get etched on the brain, nor do we learn to see them because somebody reinforces us for it. My urge to work on perceptual development grew very strong.

One of Walk's and my experiments produced some unexpected, serendipitous results. We were engaged in rearing a number of rats in the dark, and we decided to do something with them in addition to giving them the lengthy and boring discrimination training after bringing them out. A replication of Lashley and Russell's (1934) experiment on depth discrimination following dark rearing seemed a good idea, if we could find a way of testing the animals before they had experience in the light (as they necessarily had, with the jumping-stand method used in that earlier experiment). Walk had worked in the army with trainees learning to do parachute jumping from a high platform, and I had a long-standing aversion to cliffs, dating from a visit to the Grant Canyon with a small child. We decided to build a simulated cliff and see whether the animals would step off, even when they had never seen a drop-off or walked over one. My kid had stayed on a high camera platform, so something of the sort seemed a possibility. Thomas

Tighe (our research assistant at the time) and I hastily put together a contraption consisting of a sheet of glass held up by rods, with a piece of wallpaper under one side of it and nothing under the other side except the floor many feet below.

A few rats left over from other experiments got the first try. We simply put them on the glass and watched them. They walked around nonchalantly, apparently not caring what was under them or even looking to see. We had to make them look somehow. We put a board about three inches wide across the division between the surface with flooring and the unlined glass, and put the rats on the board. Would they descend randomly to either side?

What ensued was better than we had dared expect. All the rats descended on the side with textured paper under the glass. We quickly inserted some paper under the other side and tried them again. This time they went either way. We built some proper apparatus after that, with carefully controlled lighting and so on, to be ready for our dark-reared animals. It worked beautifully. They behaved like the light-reared animals. Rats (hooded ones), at least, didn't have to learn to see depth at an edge to avoid stepping over it (Walk et al., 1957). Of course, other animals might. The National Science Foundation was good to us again, and we proceeded to investigate various aspects of the problem and compared the behavior of many young animals, including human infants (Gibson and Walk, 1960b; Walk and Gibson, 1961). We couldn't very well rear the infants in the dark, and we had to wait until they could locomote on their own to use avoidance of the edge as our indicator of depth discrimination, but infants of crawling age did avoid the "deep" side. They may have learned something in the months before they could crawl; but whatever it was, it could not have been externally reinforced, since the parents never reported that the babies had fallen from a height.

An invitation to spend a year at the Institute for Advanced Study in Princeton seemed to present the perfect opportunity to go away and think hard about perceptual learning and development, perhaps to write a book about it. I got there full of determination. But first there were many things to finish and to write up. I wrote a few chapters, but they did not satisfy me, and I spent a lot of time reading. It is easy to collect material and summarize, but thinking is hard. I did some chapters for other books—one for Paul Mussen's *Handbook of Research Methods in Child Development* (with Vivian Olum) on methods of studying perception in children (Gibson and Olum, 1960a) and another on perceptual development for an NSSE year-book (Gibson, 1963a). Somewhat later I did an *Annual Review* chapter on perceptual learning (Gibson, 1963b). These all helped to formulate the field I was trying to think about, but I still needed time to let my ideas mature.

Something happened then that postponed the book for a long while, but provided the maturing time. Two Cornell friends, Alfred Baldwin and Harry Levin, both professors in the Department of Human Development, came to visit me at Princeton with the proposal that I join them in a kind of interdepartmental consortium to generate some theories about the reading process and do research on it. We were assured of support from the U.S. Office of Education, and the research could be basic, not necessarily oriented toward instructional programs.

The idea of working on reading had never crossed my mind, and I resisted persuasion at first with the argument that I had only recently got in clear focus the area of psychology that was going to be mine: how perception develops in children, what perceptual learning is, and how it comes about. Eventually the counterargument of my friends began to make a lot of sense. The point was that perceptual development and learning are absolutely basic to acquisition of reading skill, and that they could be investigated with profit in the setting of a task that was anything but artificial and was, in fact, of great relevance to society. It was a good argument and it succeeded. The next fall the consortium convened and arranged a schedule of meetings. The group included Harry Levin and Alfred Baldwin (then from the Department of Child Development), Charles Hockett from Linguistics, myself and my husband from Psychology (although I was still only a research associate), and a number of younger people—Rose-Marie Weber, John Watson, Anne Pick, Harry Osser, and others. The senior people had each prepared a fairly detailed research proposal, so the meetings began with presentations to the group of what we hoped to do and there was lively discussion. We brought in people from outside as well. The cross-fertilization between psychology and linguistics was very useful, at least for the psychologists. Most of us were only superficially acquainted with linguistics, but we studied it eagerly. "Psycholinguistics" was young then, and applying it to the reading process was quite new. It was a splendid breeding ground for new ideas.

Anne Pick and Harry Osser worked with me. We started out, as I had planned, on a study of perceptual development, choosing material appropriate for reading (Gibson et al., 1962a). The material was a set of graphic forms that were similar to real letters (we thought) in that they incorporated the same contrastive features that I thought were used to distinguish Roman capital letters. Later we spent a lot of time trying to find out just exactly what those features were, but in the beginning the choice was altogether intuitive. We planned ways of transforming our original set of forms that would be relevant or irrelevant for developing perceptual skill in visual discriminations required in reading. One relevant means was the obvious right–left reversal; one that we considered irrelevant was a transformation accomplished by photographing the original form at a slant. Preparing the material and getting data from five age groups consumed a great deal of time, but before the year was over, we began a new project not pre-planned but spawned from our growing interest in psycholinguistics.

It seemed pretty obvious that a good reader does not read letter by letter. Were words the ultimate units, as many educators have thought? Surely there is something that transfers to new words, and for an able reader, it did not appear to be a matter of decoding letters to sound, one at a time. We all became very interested in writing systems and in the nature of English orthography. That system, so despised by some as being unpredictable and even whimsical, surely had some order in it, even though the language contains spellings like "tough" and "wrought." We began to look for rules in the English monosyllable, getting help from a paper by Benjamin Whorf (1940) and a book that was just appearing by Charles Fries (Fries, 1962). Whorf had a formula for a spoken monosyllable, which appeared to have some applications to its spelling, especially when combined with Fries' analysis of consonant clusters in English spelling that are in so many cases constrained as to position in the syllable (for example, WR only occurs in initial position and GHT in final).

I came up with the idea that units might be constructed by predictable spelling-to-sound correspondences that were constrained by position in a syllable or word. We set out to test this notion by constructing a list of monosyllables that were not words, but could be, in that they were orthographically legal combinations. They began with a constrained consonant or consonant cluster, followed by a vowel or vowel cluster, and finished with another constrained consonant cluster (GLURCK, CLERFT, etc.). One could then exchange positions of the consonant clusters and—Voilà!—an illegal monosyllable would be created (RKUGL, FTERCL, etc.). These "pseudowords," as we called them, were presented to skilled readers (college students) with brief tachistoscopic exposures, the legal and illegal combinations randomly ordered. The experiment worked as expected: The legal combinations were far easier to read (Gibson et al., 1962b). Other methods of presentation were tried (obtaining thresholds, presenting choices for selection of the preexposed letter string, etc.), with totally replicable results. Arguments arose about the basis for the facilitation, with the pronounceable property of the legal combination surfacing as a favored theory. The subjects presumably pronounced the letter strings to themselves and then remembered better the ones that rolled easily off the tongue. Thus the "phonemic recoding" notion of word recognition emerged. I decided to probe it in the most direct way I could devise: to do the experiment with "pronounceable" and "unpronounceable" pseudowords with congenitally deaf subjects (Gibson, et al., 1970).

My assistants, Albert Yonas and Arthur Shurcliff, and I journeyed to Gallaudet College in Washington, carrying our equipment on our laps in a Lear jet. The college provided the utmost cooperation, and we tested a number of deaf subjects. Interpreters (signers) were provided, and I paid our way, since the college refused money, by giving a colloquium that was simultaneously translated into sign language. The experience and the experiment were interesting in more ways than one. The deaf students differentiated between the pronounceable and unpronounceable items quite as well as hearing subjects. If they had shown only a mild facilitation, one might have concluded that they were doing a little phonemic recoding, despite the fact that none of them spoke comprehensibly; but the whole effect was there. A puzzle thus remained: What did explain "pronounceability"? We analyzed our data carefully for the possible effects of sequential probability of letter sequencing, but in the counts we had available for use in a regression analysis, it did not appear to be playing a role. Our conclusion was that the legal constraints in the spelling patterns of English—beyond mere sequential frequency—provided a structure that could be learned even without hearing the pronunciation.

For many years, with the help of a number of graduate students, I tried to find out how children accomplished this learning. We found that teaching it to kindergarten and first-grade children by any kind of deliberate instructional intervention was remarkably ineffective. And yet, four separate experiments by graduate students of mine showed that the average child from a middle-class neighborhood knew a lot about it in third grade. I believe now that it is learned by a process of abstraction or induction, much as a child learns speech. Of course, we don't understand a lot about how a child learns speech, either, but what little we know applies pretty well to learning the structure of the English writing system. That children make a considerable beginning by themselves has been demonstrated (Lavine, 1977).

The parallel just drawn seems to apply to structural rules that are analogous to syntax in language. But there is the semantic aspect as well, and once again, I do not think meanings of written words are learned entirely by "coding" or association with their spoken counterparts. Children infer the meanings of some words from context as soon as they begin to read. The process continues and develops for many years as the learner begins to understand that English spelling is not simply phonetic, but is morphophonemic. There has been very little work on the latter aspect of learning the system (Chomsky, 1970; Gibson and Guinet, 1971), but it is a good guess that learning about morphology and roots in spelling only begins after third grade. When does a child learn that "mishap" is not pronounced like "bishop" because it contains two morphemes that must be treated as such? Or that one can predict the vowel spelling in many nouns by knowing their adjectival counterparts (factor, factorial; manager, managerial) and countless other generally unanalyzed relationships?

My life as a research associate lasted for sixteen years and culminated in an unforgettable year at the Center for Advanced Study in the Behavioral Sciences. Lee Cronbach, Richard Atkinson, myself, and a couple of others were supposed to provide a "cutting edge" to promote the application of sound, scientific, psychological principles to education. We did hold a conference on reading, and we had some discussions, both closed and open, but we were all busy on our own writing. I got back to my book on *Principles of Perceptual Learning and Development,* starting absolutely fresh and much the wiser for the experience of the years that intervened since I began it at Princeton. I went home in August with the book nearly half-completed and the whole plan in mind.

Professorial Dignity

During the following year, the big break really came. My husband won a Career Professorship from the National Institute of Mental Health, which meant that the university no longer had to pay him. The nepotism rules apparently had something to do with finance. But I believe the climate of thinking was changing, too, and when my friend Harry Levin made a strong effort on my behalf, the rule (if it was ever actually on the books) gave way and I became the (at that time) only female full professor on the faculty of the Arts College at Cornell. (I was not the first one, however; my friend Patricia Smith preceded me.) Of course, I was delighted to be appointed Professor of Psychology—only half-time, but still, a Professor! I could teach an undergraduate course, serve as a graduate student's thesis director and sign my own name, and enjoy other wonderful privileges and duties that a professorship bestows. I finished my book in the ensuing couple of

years, considerably aided by teaching a course in Perceptual
Learning and Development. The research continued, half-
time, still pretty much focused on reading, but the book represented better the breadth of my interests.

There were other "breaks" and honors in those years, too.
I was elected to the prestigious Society of Experimental Psychologists (the only woman); I was elected president of the
Eastern Psychological Association (a marvelous occasion, because EPA provided a free suite that must have been deco-
rated for Near Eastern oil barons and their retinues); I went
on a two-week, back-breaking lecture tour for Sigma Xi; and I
won the Century psychology prize for my book.

The last of these honors was especially precious to me.
The Century series included many of the "greats" in my
life—Hull, Tolman, Hilgard, Marquis, and many others. To
be part of it and to win its prize were more than I had dared
hope. Psychological themes and paradigms had changed
greatly since these mentors wrote, as another Century
winner—one by my colleague entitled *Cognitive Psychology*
(Neisser, 1967)—attested. But I had thought and worked very
hard on my book, and it seemed to me to represent something
new—the putting together of a field I considered very important and the search for suitable principles to organize it and
provide hypotheses for investigating it. I had long ago abandoned the old S-R concepts, since they seemed to be of little
use and to force one into double-talk when perception was the
matter of interest. Perceptual learning I conceived of not as a
change in a response, but as a change in what was perceived.
The description of this change during learning or in development I found was best viewed as differentiation, not enrichment (Gibson and Gibson, 1955) by the addition or association of anything—a response, or another "stimulus" (cf. S-S
learning). Indeed, I found that the concept of a stimulus was
not useful if one was truly concerned with how the infant
comes to extract the necessary information from a real world
that he must cope with in an adaptive fashion. He does not
perceive stimuli; he perceives people and places and objects
and events, and he acts in relation to them. Calling them
stimuli simply prevents a proper analysis of the information
that the environment affords him.

The information-processing revolution was with us at the time I published the book, and I tried my hand at a few experiments in this tradition, using reaction time for deducing what was going on "inside." But I found myself discontented with that approach, which made assumptions that I could not accept about the "construction" of the world and which seemed even more bent on contriving artificial situations for research than had the S-R psychologists. It also seemed to me to bypass everything we had learned about evolution and adaptation —ideas that cannot be disregarded when one contemplates development.

The recent years are hard to describe, since one cannot look back at them in a suitably contemplative fashion. I continued with research on the reading process (not the instructional process), placing most emphasis on learning to read, so I worked mostly with young children. When I won my first (and probably only) sabbatical leave, I applied for a Guggenheim fellowship, and my long-time colleague and friend (chairman and dean, too, but I play down those relations, as does he) and I set out to write a book on reading. It seemed to us badly needed, since the last book with a wide coverage of the psychology of reading had been published more than half a century earlier (Huey, 1908). That book had been good, and we borrowed part of its title, *The Psychology of Reading* (Gibson and Levin, 1975). It seemed to us that teachers, parents, and other interested persons did not need instructional programs nearly as badly as they needed an understanding of the reading process and the kind of learning that went into becoming a skilled reader. Needless to say, the book's approach emphasized description of the information that the reader had to extract, the rulelike structure that characterized it, and the role of the learner as a person with motivation to find out and to abstract order. The latter aspects seemed crucial to us, and we suspected that what happened in schools frequently discouraged rather than fostered them. The psychology department at MIT offered us a home for a semester of intensive writing. The welcome and assistance we encountered there cannot be exaggerated.

When that book was completed, a little change seemed in order; one gets a bit stale on a topic after 650 pages. I had always wanted an infant laboratory for my students (I had not had one since the work on the visual cliff), and the time was propitious for setting it up. It has been in full swing now for something over five years, with development of the perception of invariants in infants as its principal theme for investigation (Gibson et al., 1978). Several theses and a number of experiments have come out of it so far; and there my story runs out.

Epilogue

This is an epilogue in a sense, but not an epitaph, because there is so much more that I want to do. But some sort of ending, perhaps a moral, is called for. One moral comes to mind at once, cliché though it be: Nothing succeeds like success. After sixteen years of second-class citizenship, the honors, once the ice was broken and I had attained the dignity of a professorship, came one upon another. My old college, Smith, gave me an honorary degree. Cornell gave me an endowed chair, the Susan Linn Sage Professorship. That was a first, since no woman had held one before in the university's history. Named for a woman it may have been, but the chair had been occupied for nearly a century by men. My old graduate school, Yale, gave me the Wilbur Cross Medal. I was elected to the National Academy of Sciences, the National Academy of Education, and the American Academy of Arts and Sciences. I was awarded the G. Stanley Hall Medal by Division 7 of the APA and the Howard Crosby Warren Medal by the Society of Experimental Psychologists. I was elected president of Division 3 of the APA and awarded an honorary membership by the British Psychological Society. I have served and am now serving on some truly prestigious committees. Do I wonder, now and then, whether I am serving as the token woman? Yes, I sometimes do.

Of course, I don't refuse for that reason. Better to have a token woman in these things than none at all. I think I can truly say that I have never felt any real bitterness about my inferior status during those sixteen years that I did research and paid the university a large overhead on my grants and contracts. I do lift my eyebrows, however, when people tell me how lucky I was to have all that time to do nothing but research. The people who tell me that, of course, are never women.

What does a woman need to succeed in a profession that seems to have evolved chiefly for men? She needs all the obvious things like education and drive, of course. Some women have forgone the privilege and joy of a family in order to achieve academic success. I saw many of them at Smith and at Mt. Holyoke. I am glad I did not do that. The family may introduce some obstacles, especially if one puts them— husband and children—ahead of oneself. But it is certainly worth it, and it seems to me that it works out in the end, provided one's husband is tolerant of one's ambitions, encouraging, and recognizes one's worth. Mine has always been such, and I am glad I have this chance to say so publicly. Helpful colleagues and first-rate graduate students are very important, too. Here one has to be lucky, as I have been. Most of all, one has to want the kind of life that teaching, research, and scientific fellowship offer. I cannot imagine any other kind of life being so satisfying. Sometimes I have felt that I had two lives and that one was temporarily being short-changed, but I believe each is the richer for the other.

1976

Selected Publications by Eleanor Jack Gibson

(with J. J. Gibson) Retention and the interpolated task. *Amer. J. Psychol.*, 1934, *46*, 603–610.

Sensory generalization with voluntary reactions. *J. exp. Psychol.*, 1939, *24*, 237–253.

A systematic application of the concepts of generalization and differentiation to verbal learning. *Psychol. Rev.*, 1940, *47*, 196–229.

Retroactive inhibition as a function of degree of generalization between tasks. *J. exp. Psychol.*, 1941, *28*, 93–115.

Intra-list generalization as a factor in verbal learning. *J. exp. Psychol.*, 1942, *30*, 185–200.

The role of shock in reinforcement. *J. comp. physiol. Psychol.*, 1952, *45*, 18–30.

(with R. Bergman) The effect of training on absolute estimation of distance over the ground. *J. exp. Psychol.*, 1954, *48*, 473–482.

(with R. Bergman and J. Purdy) The effect of prior training with a scale of distance on absolute and relative judgments of distance over the ground. *J. exp. Psychol.*, 1955, *50*, 97–105.

(with R. D. Walk) The effect of prolonged exposure to visually presented patterns on learning to discriminate them. *J. comp. physiol. Psychol.*, 1956, *49*, 239–242.

(with R. D. Walk and T. J. Tighe) Enhancement and deprivation of visual stimulation during rearing as factors in visual discrimination. *J. comp. physiol. Psychol.*, 1959, *52*, 74–81.

(with V. Olum) Experimental methods of studying perception in children. In P. H. Mussen (Ed.), *Handbook of research methods in child development*, New York: Wiley, 1960a, 311–373.

(with R. D. Walk) The "visual cliff." *Scientific Amer.*, 1960b, *202*, 64–71.

(with J. J. Gibson, A. D. Pick, and H. Osser) A developmental study of the discrimination of letter-like forms. *J. comp. physiol. Psychol.*, 1962a, *55*, 897–906.

(with A. D. Pick, H. Osser, and M. Hammond) The role of grapheme-phoneme correspondence in the perception of words. *Amer. J. Psychol.*, 1962b, *75*, 554–570.

Perceptual development. In H. W. Stevenson, et al. (Eds.), *Child psychology*, Sixty-second Yearbook Nat. Soc. Stud. Ed., 1963a, 144–195.

Perceptual learning. *Annu. Rev. Psychol.*, 1963b, *14*, 29–56.

Principles of perceptual learning and development. New York: Appleton-Century-Crofts, 1969.

(with A. Shurcliff and A. Yonas) Utilization of spelling patterns by deaf and hearing subjects. In H. Levin and J. P. Williams (Eds.), *Basic studies on reading*, New York: Basic Books, 1970. Pp. 57–73.

(with L. Guinet) Perception of inflections in brief visual presentations of words. *J. verb. Learn. verb. Behav.*, 1971, *10*, 182–189.

(with H. Levin) *The psychology of reading.* Cambridge, Mass.: MIT Press, 1975.

(with C. J. Owsley and J. Johnson) Perception of invariants by five-month-old infants: Differentiation of two types of motion. *Dev. Psychol.*, 1978, *14*, 407–415.

Other Publications Cited

Chomsky, C. Reading, writing, and phonology. *Harvard Educational Rev.*, 1970, *40*, 287–309.

Fries, C. C. *Linguistics and reading.* New York: Holt, Rinehart and Winston, 1962.

Gibson, J. J., E. J. Jack, and G. Raffel. Bilateral transfer of the conditioned response in the human subject. *J. exp. Psychol.*, 1932, *15*, 416–421.

Gibson, J. J., and E. J. Gibson. Continuous perspective transformations and the perception of rigid motion. *J. exp. Psychol.*, 1957, *54*, 129–138.

Gibson, J. J., and E. J. Gibson, Perceptual learning: Differentiation or enrichment? *Psychol. Rev.*, 1955, *62*, 32–41.

Huey, E. B. *The psychology and pedgogy of reading.* New York: Macmillan, 1908 (Republished by MIT Press, 1968).

Hull, C. L. Autobiography. In E. G. Boring, et al. (Eds.), *A history of psychology in autobiography, IV*, Worcester, Mass.: Clark University Press, 1952, 143–152.

Lashley, K. S., and J. T. Russell. The mechanism of vision. XI. A preliminary test of innate organization. *J. genet. Psychol.*, 1934, *45*, 136–144.

Lavine, L. O. Differentiation of letter-like forms in prereading children. *Develop. Psychol.*, 1977, *13*, 89–94.

Neisser, U. *Cognitive psychology.* New York: Appleton-Century-Crofts, 1967.

Purdy, J., and E. J. Gibson. Distance judgment by the method of fractionation. *J. exp. Psychol.*, 1955, *50*, 374–380.

Walk, R. D., and E. J. Gibson. A comparative and analytical study of visual depth perception. *Psychol. Monogr.*, 1961, *75*, (15), 44.

Walk, R. D., E. J. Gibson, and T. J. Tighe. Behavior of light- and dark-reared rats on a visual cliff. *Science*, 1957, *126*, 80–81.

Whorf, B. L. Linguistics as an exact science. *Technol. Rev.*, 1940, *43*, 61–63, 80–83. (Reprinted in J. B. Carroll, *Language, thought and reality*, Cambridge, Mass.: MIT Press, 1956, 220–232.)

D. O. Hebb

The Scotch, who now prefer to be called Scots, have a name for the lad who sets out to be a preacher but does not make it: He is a *stickit minister*. I am a stickit novelist who came late to psychology and a stickit reformer of elementary schools. As an undergraduate, I meant to be a novelist but never got as far, after graduating, as even the draft of a novel. (Fred Skinner, who had similar ideas, could get the fiction out of his system with *Walden Two*; for me, as others have observed, it had to be *The Organization of Behavior*.) To earn a living while learning to write novels, and later while beginning the study of psychology, I taught school in Nova Scotia and Quebec. In Montreal, I became so interested in the problems of elementary education that I might have made a career in that field, but I was defeated by the rigidity of the curriculum in Quebec's Protestant schools. I had already begun the study of psychology at McGill University, part-time, but it was only in 1934, at the age of thirty, that I made a final commitment and borrowed enough to go work with K. S. Lashley at the University of Chicago.

My emphasis on this delayed start is due to a conviction that it had a lasting and, in some ways, beneficial effect on my later performance. When I got to Chicago, I found that my part-time study at McGill had left me ignorant of much current work in psychology. I was ill prepared and had to begin again almost from scratch. It might therefore seem that I had simply lost ten years or so in getting started on my career. I do not believe this is true, or at least not entirely true. I now knew exactly what I wanted to do. I was interested in psychology as a natural science, and I had clearer ideas about natural science than I might otherwise, partly as a result of long discussions with graduate students in chemistry at McGill. (I had actually written a paper on scientific method, though to no avail; I am a stickit philosopher, too.) I had, all round, a better sight of psychology than I could have had ten years earlier. I was also prepared to work harder. Much that I saw at Chicago and later at Harvard looked trivial to me (some of it nonsense), but I had burned my boats, I knew I had to get the Ph.D., and so I set out to learn what had to be learned to pacify certain instructors.

This probably makes me sound more sophisticated than I really was, but my attitude was something of the sort even if I could not have described it at the time. I wanted to *find out*, to add to positive knowledge, and to make a name for myself on that basis. I recall a conversation in Chicago with a postdoctoral fellow who told me about a "cute experiment" he had thought up. It turned out that the experiment had the sole purpose of embarrassing his theoretical opponents. I was a second-year graduate student and he had his Ph.D. and a fellowship and was much senior to me, but this still looked to me like a hell of a way for a scientist to spend his time. Controversy is bad enough when one is forced into it, but to seek it is waste time; one ought to be *finding out* instead. Such a view may have resulted simply from my own predicament and knowledge that I had to get busy and make up for lost time, but it served me well later, whatever its origin. In the long debate for example in the 1930s and 1940s between Clark Hull and Edward Tolman, I was not tempted to take part, though I had some data on place-learning by the rat that were better, I thought, than what Tolman's group were reporting.

I *knew* that Tolman was right and Hull wrong, but it was unprofitable, and moreover dull, to spend time proving the obvious.

Background and Early Education

To begin at the beginning, I reckon that I was conceived in October, 1903, at a time when the Wright brothers were getting that contraption of theirs into final shape for the airways. The airplane and I are of an age, true contemporaries, though I was actually born in July 1904, the first of four children. My father was a country doctor; my mother was a doctor also who practiced for some years in St. John, New Brunswick, while waiting for my father to graduate. Mary Clara Olding earned her medical degree at Dalhousie University in 1896, the third woman to do so in the Province of Nova Scotia. My father, Arthur Morrison Hebb, took his B.A. first, then the medical degree, which, with the necessity of taking repeated years out to teach school and earn enough to return to college, meant that he did not graduate till 1901 or 1902. He set up practice in Chester, Nova Scotia, my parents were married in 1903, and they maintained a joint practice till 1920, when the strain of country practice and twenty-mile drives by horse and sleigh in the winters became too great. At that time, the family moved to the town of Dartmouth and my father to an urban practice. My mother died of cancer within the year and thus did not share in the new practice.

My father's family is known to have begun on this continent about 1750 with the arrival of Adam Hebb, a twelve year old English boy. According to family tradition, he was orphaned and adopted by a German family, but it may be that only his father died and that his mother then married one of the German settlers who were brought out to Nova Scotia at the time of the founding of Halifax. These German Protestants were to be a makeweight to the French-Catholic settlers remaining in Nova Scotia when the province was ceded to the British. (It will be recalled that the expulsion of the Acadians, including Longfellow's Evangeline, occurred shortly afterward, in 1755.) My father was the fifth generation—the great-great-grandson of Adam Hebb—and thus of German stock, though the name is English. My grandfather was versatile and experimental, self-trained, a millwright, pattern-maker, and farmer, very capable but bull-headed (a family characteristic, according to my observations), and with no opinion of higher education. Grandmother however was his equal. She was of an "intellectual"—literary and sermon-tasting—turn of mind, and it was thanks to her that three of the four children went to college. One of them, Thomas Carlyle Hebb, went on to become Professor of Physics at the University of British Columbia.

I have less information about my mother's family, the Oldings, and whence came that flouting of popular attitude and the tremendous drive that must have been needed for a girl to get herself accepted to medical school in 1892 and go on to graduate. But the women on both sides of the family, Oldings and Wiles (my grandmother Hebb was a Wile), were an independent lot who were prepared to concede to men as much as might be necessary, but no more, and who thought for themselves on any question and lived accordingly.

We do know the beginning of the family in Nova Scotia. Nicholas Purdue Olding was English, an Oxford-trained lawyer who apparently lived in one of the thirteen colonies at the time of the American Revolution and came to Halifax as a refugee in the 1780s (these refugees are known in Canada as United Empire Loyalists). The family used to treasure a remark someone made, with what justification I do not know, referring to him as Father of the Nova Scotia Bar. The story also is that, in the days of the Duke of Kent in Halifax, Nicholas Purdue was seeing too much of the high life surrounding the Duke, and his wife engineered a move across the province to Pictou County, away from temptation among the Scottish settlers. After that, until my mother's generation, the Oldings were small farmers, though my grandfather (Nicholas Purdue's grandson) was a cabinetmaker as well. The name was English, the stock was now Scottish, or Scotch.

Then, for both sides of the family, came the period toward the end of the nineteenth century when a large proportion of the young in Nova Scotia, finding little opportunity at home, began to move out of the province to seek their fortunes as doctors, lawyers, engineers, ministers, and teachers—especially teachers. In 1914, when I was ten years old, I had one or more uncles or aunts in South Africa, Cuba, Saskatchewan, Montana, British Columbia, and Hawaii. Of a total of eleven siblings of my mother and father, just one lived in Nova Scotia.

I did not enter school till I was eight. This was partly because my mother had been impressed by Maria Montessori, a contemporary woman doctor as well as an educator, and wanted to teach my younger brother and me at home. Also, I had already learned to read without being taught. I was devoted to "The Three Little Pigs," wanted it read again and again, and, knowing it by heart, would look on while it was read and would correct any slip made by the reader. Presently it was discovered that I could read it myself. (At what age this happened I do not know—I remember none of it.) Being able to read, I started school in Grade II, within a month was moved to Grade III, and at mid-year was promoted to Grade IV. (This was, of course, a country school, with two lower grades in each room, and three in the high school.) The next year, I completed Grades V and VI. After that it was one grade a year till Grade XI, which I failed. Things came too easily, I had never learned to work, I was bored by school from the day I entered to the day I left (with the exception of algebra and geometry, which came as pleasant surprises in high school, but they filled only a small part of the day). On entrance to Grade IX at the age of twelve—much the youngest pupil there—what was important to me was the respect of my peers, not my ability to solve algebra problems, nor my extensive extracurricular reading, nor my ability to outspell the rest of the school, including the teachers. (The principal, one day, pitted me against two or three of the teachers when I was in Grade VII, at the age of ten.) Such things were no help in maintaining my status after school, which for me was vital.

As a consequence, I automatically resisted all adult pressure and held a low estimate of the value of scholastic achievement, attitudes that lasted into my college years and beyond. I might have been a physicist now if my father had not pressed (math and physics were my only marks "with distinction" at Dalhousie). For years and years I would read no novel recommended by others, even after I realized how silly this was. It did not take as long for me to realize that I needed a more structured task than novel-writing and that perhaps I was suited for the academic world after all.

However, I received a B.A. from Dalhousie University in 1925 and got an appointment as principal and high school teacher in the village where I had grown up and where the older students had known me by my first name. I managed to keep order, but had no idea of how to induce them to study. After some months, the Provincial Inspector arrived to inspect and, after doing so, took me to one side and said, "Never mind, Hebb, I wasn't worth a damn my first year either." Following this disaster I took out for the West, got a job as an eight-horse teamster for the summer harrowing wheatfields, and then worked on the harvest. It was before the days of the combine, and large numbers of itinerant workers got jobs stooking wheat (piling the sheaves to dry, waiting for the threshing machine). I went on to Vancouver, failed to get a job as deckhand on one of the freighters bound for the East, came back home, got a job as laborer in Quebec while I thought things over, and at that point made the acquaintance of Freud. Obviously a very interesting fellow but, it seemed to me, not too rigorous. At twenty-three, it might not be too late for me to enter the field, which evidently had room for further work. I decided, then, to see if a career in psychology would be possible.

I had, of course, to earn a living. I could get a job teaching in Montreal if McGill University would accept me for graduate work. The chairman of the psychology department, W. D. Tait, who was from Nova Scotia, turned out to have known my mother in college and was also of the opinion that anyone from Nova Scotia had to be intelligent. He sent me off in September 1927 to spend a year reading James' *Principles* (the chairman had been a student of Münsterburg's at Harvard when James was still there) and Ladd and Woodworth's *Physiological Psychology* (which was little more than neural anatomy). In spite of my worse-than-mediocre record at

Dalhousie, he then in 1928 accepted me for a qualifying year, part-time; and in 1929 I became a graduate student, also part-time.

Indecision

It was just at this point that I became involved in an exciting experiment in teaching methods in the elementary school and began to think of possibly continuing in that field. What I saw of psychology at McGill was far from exciting, and studying psychology elsewhere seemed out of the question for lack of money (my poor undergraduate record ruled out scholarships). Perhaps I could go on to the Ph.D. at McGill but stay in the teaching business. This was a period of indecision, of tentative solutions to the problem of finding a satisfactory career, given my financial situation.

The six-year period from 1928 to 1934 was an active one. I made a major revision of teaching methods in a school of which I was now principal, was laid up in bed for a year (1930–1931) with a tubercular hip, wrote a bad theoretical thesis while in bed (M.A., 1932), got married but lost my wife eighteen months later in a car accident, devoted the evenings and weekends of a year and a half to being trained in Pavlovian conditioning methods, and tried my hand at an essay on objective psychology and the scientific method. The essay concerned the philosophy of science, really, though I was not familiar with that term. It was not something that commended itself to the Department of Philosophy at McGill, though Warner Wick, a graduate student in philosophy at Chicago, later told me that it had some relation to the 1929 argument of C. I. Lewis in *Mind and the World Order* (which neither I nor, apparently, the Department of Philosophy had heard of). In 1934 I made a clean break with McGill and Montreal. The break was precipitated by the death of my wife but also came about because I saw little future for my innovations in teaching methods in the public schools. I managed to borrow from the bank and from my father to go to Chicago. (The debt was finally repaid in 1956—twenty years post-Ph.D.)

Two of these false starts need more detail: the school experiment and the Pavlovian training.

My first appointment by the (suburban) Verdun School Board in 1927 was as a teacher in the high school, but next year the board needed a man as principal of an elementary school in a working-class district and I was given the job. I knew nothing of teaching methods in the early grades and consequently spent my first year doing the necessary paper work, maintaining order, and simply observing the work in the various classrooms. I was appalled at what I saw of the means resorted to by the less successful teachers to get work done, means that were mainly suited to make school as unpleasant as possible. I resolved that there would either be a change or I would get fired, and I talked the staff of twenty-two into trying a ridiculous experiment—but one that, miraculously, worked.

At the beginning of the next school year, the children were told that no one would be made to work, that work was a privilege, and that the reward for good behavior was to be allowed to stay in the classroom and work. There was to be no punishment for mere idleness, but disturbing others would mean being sent to the playground to play, or being sent home. Success was immediate. It took the astonished children twenty-four hours or less to begin living accordingly. The inspector's report, later, was entirely favorable, and there was a lower failure rate in the citywide examinations at the end of the year. The children were in favor of the scheme in this first year, and most parents also. It helped not to have to fight a morning battle to get the kids off to school on time, to have them hurry to get there instead. But not all parents approved of the scheme: One mother told me that she was moving to another school district because her boy was enjoying himself. She didn't send him to school to enjoy himself but to work and be punished.

There is more to the story than that, of course. There was a great deal of behind-the-scenes work to make learning interesting. For example, plays were written (the plot usually a direct steal from a comic book) and presented before the class, with advice from the teacher on spelling and good English. But the main part of each day was simply schoolwork with a new attitude. Mostly the experiment helped the less skillful teachers to do what the skillful ones had been doing all along; none of the latter began a lesson with an attitude of "Now I am going to make you work at arithmetic," but took willingness to work for granted. What was really done was to dramatize that attitude to let it work for all.

Unfortunately, whatever approval the preceding paragraphs have won me from some of my readers must now be forfeited, as I report next that free use was made of physical punishment: to wit, the strap. Deterrents there had to be. They could not be the assignment of extra schoolwork nor "keeping in" after school, since schoolwork was now a reward, and staying to talk with the teacher or to help her was a privilege. No disorder could be tolerated during a fire drill, for example, in the movement of 600-odd children from their classrooms in a two-storied building. To maintain order where it was necessary, I applied a strap to the palm of the hand.

Let me say at once that I know what reason there is for a ban on such punishment. There are always those who abuse it, and I myself once had to forcibly take the strap away from another teacher when I was at the high school. He was a "screwball" and a sadist and was enjoying the pain he was giving a twelve-year-old boy. But there is moderation in all things, and there is another side of the coin.

The use of ridicule and public embarrassment in the classroom may do more damage to a child's mind than the infliction of moderate pain. I hit hard enough to hurt but not hard enough to make me feared. Sample evidence: A delegation of sixth-grade boys requested that I use the strap if the class did not get more arithmetic done. After asking their teacher to leave the room, they had held a meeting and reached a unanimous decision. This was in the third year of the program and directly contrary to its spirit, but I was finally obliged to agree, with the proviso that any boy could call off the bargain at the last minute. Nevertheless, I had to give out strappings on this account. In another case, a boy with an overprotective mother was well on the way to losing all self-respect on the schoolground; I managed to catch him in a very small peccadillo and gave him a very small strapping; and the two older boys with whom I was in cahoots reported afterward that he was doing a certain amount of boasting about the whole thing. Now he was one of the boys. Finally, I report that the pain was not all one-sided. One day I set out to strap a boy who flinched so that the end of the strap went by his hand and hit my trousers at the level of the glans penis. It hurt like the devil, and I said to the boy, "This hurts me more than it does you." But I don't think he understood the joke.

The first great success of the experiment turned out to be, in part, a Hawthorne effect, and by the third year, it was on the downgrade. Pedagogically, it was working as well as ever, in the sense that the pupils were still learning as we wanted them to, but there was less enthusiasm on the part of both children and parents. With the children, we were too successful; they had learned that work could be a good thing, and they now wanted us to push so they would get more of it done. Also, they had begun to think that this was a sissy school: no keeping in after school, no assignments of extra work, no real conflicts with authority compared to what they saw and heard about in the next school district. As for the parents, the problem was failure in examinations. One mother told me, when her son had to repeat Grade VI, that he had just managed to pass Grade V the year before and now fell short by a few percentage marks only—"Without any help from you, Mr. Hebb, when just a *little* push would have made the difference." That mother could not be answered with evidence that the overall failure rate for the school was down, statistically, and she would not have understood if I had said that more pushing of her son might have resulted in poorer motivation and worse instead of better performance.

The essential remedy did not lie in our hands; the curriculum badly needed revising to meet the needs of a larger proportion of the school population. However, I learned a great deal from these years, and so did the teachers. The extreme form taken by the experiment, thanks to my naiveté, had a dramatic value that helped to put it over, but the approach can be made in more moderate form, as good teachers have always done.

The second activity of this period that needs some description was my training as a Pavlovian. My M.A. thesis, written in bed, tried to show that skeletal reflexes are a product of intrauterine learning. This was nonsense, but no immediate disproof was available at the time. The outside examiner was Professor Boris P. Babkin, a student of Pavlov's who had returned to Pavlov's earlier field, the study of digestion. He was skeptical but passed the thesis and told me I needed laboratory experience, which was true. He arranged for me to work with Dr. Leonid Andreyev, who had just come from Pavlov's institute on research appointment to McGill. This was kindness in the first place, but not only kindness; like Pavlov, Babkin considered that American psychologists had bastardized Pavlov's methods. Andreyev was to provide me with a proper training, and I would be a proper psychological and North American representative of conditioning as it should be, Russian style.

In the next sixteen months or so, I conditioned two dogs and began a piece of research with one of them. This concerned Pavlov's idea of waves of excitation and inhibition passing over the cortex. I recall no detail now, but it caused mounting skepticism in me. Andreyev seemed ready to fit any result into the theoretical scheme and to put great reliance on small differences of one or two drops of saliva. Perhaps I do him an injustice here, but it is definite that he had no idea of the probable error of measurement—and when I then looked back at Pavlov's publications, I saw that he had none either.

I might have gone on, but the car accident in which my wife was killed also destroyed the car and made it impossible for me to continue the experiment, for lack of rapid transport from school to university. I spent the following school year running my pedagogical experiment (although in its third year the zip had now departed), finishing my paper on scientific method, and playing third-rate chess, while recovering from my personal disorganization and deciding what my future should be. About mid-year, I wrote to Robert M. Yerkes at Yale, and he offered me a $500 assistantship. This offer I owed to Kenneth Spence and his high level of performance at Yale. He, too, had an M.A. from McGill. But about this time I talked further with Babkin, who urged me to work with K. S. Lashley. This was an act of great disinterestedness, for Babkin and other students of Pavlov were as hooked on the master as E. G. Boring and the others were hooked on Edward B.

Titchener, and Lashley's criticism of Pavlov hurt Babkin more than it did Pavlov. Still, he said Lashley was an honest man; Lashley was wrong, according to Babkin—but at least when he had ideas about the brain, he tested them on the brain. If I was going to give up my job and bet on a career in psychology, I should go the whole hog (not his words). I wrote to Lashley, was accepted, and wrote again to Yerkes to decline the offer. I would like to say this for Yerkes, that he never held my behavior against me. Perhaps rather the opposite. But later, when I was at Orange Park in Florida, I learned something of Yerkes' relations with staff and students and was doubly glad that I had studied with Lashley. Yerkes was orderly and authoritarian in tendency. He was an organizer and systematizer, not an idea man. Lashley was unsystematic, but there were always ideas in his neighborhood—his own and those he stirred up in others.

Chicago and Harvard

So I went to Chicago, at the time I think the best locus for behavioral study in the country. I still have pleasure in recalling a brilliant lecture course with L. L. Thurstone, who was in the process of getting out his magnum opus of 1935, and a less-organized seminar with Wolfgang Köhler as visiting professor, who was making up his mind to leave Hitler's Germany. Lashley himself was a poor lecturer but excellent in the informal occasional discussion groups in the lab. I also recall with pleasure a seminar in neurology with C. J. Herrick, and the visit to Paul Weiss' lab and his demonstration salamanders with transplanted limbs. I took a course in physiology from Nathaniel Kleitman, the great authority on sleep, who read the most suitably soporific lectures I have ever listened to.

This was a period of hard study because of my poor preparation. Lashley gave me the use of an experimental room from 8:00 to 9:00 A.M. (Yu-Chuan Chang had it for the rest of the day), and most of the rest of my time was spent in class or studying, but much of the stimulation of the place was from other graduate students. Among them were I. Krechevsky (later David Krech), direct from Tolman's lab with an NRC fellowship, Walter Lurie, and Douglas E. Smith. They should be counted among my teachers. In the spring of 1935 Lashley accepted a professorship at Harvard. He was the reason for Doug Smith's and my presence at Chicago, so we asked if we could go with him. He managed to arrange it—no small feat, perhaps, given the attitude of Harvard at that time toward lesser tribes without the law. I was admitted to a third (graduating) year, provided that I passed a comprehensive examination, which normally would have been written at the end of the second year. I wrote it about a month after my arrival. I record this detail to acknowledge the generosity of the department.

Also, its tolerance. Despite my earlier resolution to take what was put before me, to learn what I was expected to learn, I was restive in an atmosphere of Fechner and Helmholtz, Wundt and Titchener; no Ebbinghaus, no Thorndike, Binet someone who had invented a test, behaviorism and Gestalt psychology off in the wilderness. I let my feelings show when, on the history paper in my comprehensive examination, appeared the question: "Evaluate the importance of the following names." The names included Fechner and Wundt. For Fechner, I wrote, "Greatly overrated," and for Wundt, who came next, "Rather less important than Fechner." I stand by that judgment today—What contribution to knowledge has Wundt left behind him?—but in the circumstances it was childish. In other respects I answered soberly, but now came another weakness. The paper on the history of psychology asked about the relation of factor analysis to faculty psychology, and the paper on systematics (set by a different member of the department, I presume) had a very similar question. Both were included for my special benefit, since I had just had a course with Thurstone, but I had written my heart out the first time and when, next day, I saw the same question, I found I could not face it. I answered, instead, one that I was less well prepared for, though I knew this was not sensible. I passed, with three B's and a B minus (I was supposed to make a B average).

Then came the thesis. I had been working on the problem of spatial orientation and place learning, and it appeared that the experiment could not be completed in time for spring graduation. Another year was beyond my financial resources. Lashley suggested that I take a problem he had been interested in, one that could be completed in the available time, provided that I then returned to my own problem. His proposal was to rear rats in complete darkness and compare perception in the dark-reared rats with that in normal animals. I assumed, as he did, that there would be no important difference, but either way the results should be of value and would make a thesis. As it turned out, I found no significant difference in the perception of size and brightness and wrote a thesis on the innate organization of perception. Pattern perception would have given a different result, but this was not included in the thesis work. After that experiment was over, I still had some dark-reared rats and tested them on various aspects of pattern perception. I got some dubious evidence of innately organized figure–ground separation. I also got good evidence of a similarity between normal and dark-reared animals in the perception of horizontal versus vertical patterns and of erect versus inverted triangles, as shown by transfer tests *once the perceptions were established.*

Now the incredible part. In this later work I did not run any normal animals for comparison of learning rates, and I was so preoccupied with my use of Lashley's ingenious transfer methods that I did not stop to think about the learning. Fortunately, the paper I published (Hebb, 1937a) included the number of trials to acquisition (thus the data were available later), but I just did not think about them. My dark-reared rats took six times as long as normal to learn to choose horizontal versus vertical stripes (according to data for the normal animals of the colony, with which I was perfectly familiar). Still unthinking, I wrote a second paper (Hebb, 1937b), reporting the original thesis results with size and brightness, and proved what is false: that perception does not require experience. It was nine years later, when I was trying to account for some of Wilder Penfield's brain-injury results and developing the ideas that led to *The Organization of Behavior,* that I went back to my own published data and for the first time saw what kind of beast they were. Amazing.

Thus in 1936 I got the Ph.D. from Harvard, indebted to

the Harvard staff but without becoming a genuine Harvard psychologist. (Lashley was my model—Lashley the biological scientist interested in the mind—and Lashley was clearly a foreign body in the Harvard department.) There was no sign of a job on the horizon. Lashley found $500 for me as Research Assistant and Boring $200 as Teaching Assistant for the two Radcliffe sections of his introductory course. My own time was spent completing the interrupted work on place learning and studying the structure of the diencephalon. The experiment on place learning was not conducted for its own sake alone but was part of a wider scheme. I thought there might be clues to the larger pattern of cortical organization in any behavior that was easily affected by cortical injury, as place learning might be; that is, I thought it might be the highest level of cognitive function in the rat and, as such, most easily impaired. The results were interesting (Hebb, 1938). In fact, they were very interesting, but the fact also is, as far as I can discover, that no one at the time ever looked at either of my two papers. That year, 1936–1937, was nevertheless well spent. The anatomy I worked up was valuable later, and my general psychological education was advanced by the two-semester, seven-days-a-week informal seminar consisting of the discussions of the motley group of pre- and postdoctoral students assembled to study with Lashley. Besides Doug Smith from Alberta and myself from Nova Scotia, there were Frank A. Beach from Kansas, George C. Drew from England, Edwin E. Ghiselli from California, and André Rey from Switzerland. A diverse group, with Lashley included—argumentative, friendly, critical, and constructive. Educational indeed.

Physiological psychology was in the middle of its long period of decline, between 1930 and 1950, and at the end of this postdoctoral year, job prospects were poor for a physiological psychologist. I heard of one possible opening, but another man was in the running and likely to be accepted. Then a great stroke of luck: my sister Catherine, taking her Ph.D. in physiology with Babkin at McGill, wrote to say she had heard that Penfield was looking for someone to study the psychological status of his patients after brain operation. Why not apply to him? I did, and was appointed a Fellow of the Montreal Neurological Institute for two years, 1937 to 1939.

Personal and Motivational

Before going on to the professional career that began in the Montreal Neurological Institute in 1937, we might look at some personal aspects and keep them in mind as background. One purpose of these autobiographical reports is to get at motivation. I don't pretend to understand myself, and the workings of my mind surprise me often enough, but I can describe if not explain, at least to the extent that it seems to be relevant to my professional characteristics. But if I don't understand, it's not for Freudian reasons. I am quite aware of motives that Freud assumed must be repressed, and if Freud is, as I think, the great man of psychology who taught us how complex mind and motivation can be—wholly unlike what Wundt's psychology implied, or even James'—then the sources he gave for the complexity are absurd. Freud is like Darwin. In each case, the big picture is right and important, while the explanatory mechanisms are best forgotten.

From where I sit, from this privileged vantage point of self-observation, it appears that research, for me, was an acquired need like tobacco and, like tobacco, self-rewarding. It was only after I had experienced it that it became a compulsion, and this was true of marriage, also. Even though it seems an abuse of language, I am inclined to say that I had three main addictions: tobacco, research, and marriage. The first I broke after smoking a pipe for forty years. This has more relevance for a psychologist than one might think, for it gave me some understanding of what an addiction can be. If those poor bastards trapped by alcohol or heroin have the hook sunk much deeper than nicotine did in me then I'd say—if this weren't a technical report, more or less—I'd say God pity them, and to hell with those pious nitwits who ask, "But if it's bad for you, why don't you just stop?" Tobacco taught me something I might have learned no other way. My second compulsion or dependency, doing research, I'll return to in a moment; it's one of the surprises to find it waning with age, and after this report is finished I expect to live more like a normal human being than I ever did between the ages of, say, thirty and sixty-five.

Now the third. I have been married three times. Once I found out what it was like—at least for me, with my luck—I became dependent on marriage, and this one lasts. It makes no sense to me, but if I am away from home for more than two or three days, my ability to plan and write is impaired. The evidence of writing is particularly clear when anything except routine letters is concerned. When my wife goes to visit relatives I become less organized, and this was true even when I was deeply into some research and even though, when my wife was home, I would return at night only to read some trashy book or sit uncommunicative, playing solitaire. My first wife was Marion Isabel Clark, a nurse, daughter of the Reverend Dr. John A. Clark of Halifax, Nova Scotia. As the common phrase is, I was in love, and her death in 1933 was a bad blow. Four years later, having got the appointment with Penfield in Montreal, I married Elizabeth Nichols Donovan, a lecturer in sociology at Colby Junior College and daughter of the Reverend Dr. Winfred Donovan of Newton Center, Massachusetts. (Ah, those ministers' daughters!) We were married for twenty-five years and had two daughters—admirable citizens and mothers now, but the very devil to deal with as teenagers. In 1962, their mother died of complications of a surgical operation, and in 1966 I married Margaret Doreen (Williamson) Wright, who had lived next door to us and whose husband had died two years before. Only a doctor's daughter (Dr. Sam Williamson, of Yarmouth, Nova Scotia), she was at least a minister's granddaughter.

Finally, the research compulsion. I had of course every intention of making a name for myself, but I had to do it my way. As a letter from Boring to be quoted later will show, the result was that I spent thirteen years in the wilderness, though more immediate rewards were available for more relevant research—relevant, that is, to current opinion. When I published the 1949 book I expected it would not have much of a welcome and was astonished by its reception. Some time in the 1950s a younger member of the staff said, when he heard that I worked six days a week and half a day on Sunday, "If that's what you have to do to be a success, I don't want to be a success." He missed the point; I wasn't working like that to be a success; I was working like that because it was the most interesting and sometimes even exciting thing to do. I love sailing a small boat; but when I went for a month in the summer with my wife and children to visit my father and stepmother and sail the boat they had given me, I became restless after two weeks and anxious to get back to the desk and the laboratory after three weeks. The work was done as much for its own sake as the tobacco was smoked for the sake of smoking.

Intelligence and the Human Brain

My research for the next five years, 1937–1942, turned on the effort to understand the status of Wilder Penfield's patients following surgical operation on their brains. I would have preferred to work with rats or dogs, since human beings are so complicated. Also, the patients usually keep on living and don't make their brains available for study. All the same, this was the right place for me, even though I could not see it at the time and even though my first six months at the institute looked to me like total failure. I went to the Neurological Institute with plans to measure the intellectual loss produced by brain operations—and I could find no sign of loss after large amounts of brain tissue were removed from the frontal lobe. It took time for me to realize that here I had a more significant problem than the one I had expected to attack. It was this problem that set the main course for all my subsequent work, and I would not have met it anywhere else.

Penfield's research on the pathology of cerebral scar had led him and his right-hand man, William V. Cone, to new surgical methods of treating Jacksonian epilepsy resulting from a scar in the cortex. Removing a scar can leave the rest of the brain in normal condition, unlike most operations for tumor (a growing tumor may damage the rest of the brain by compression; removing it cannot usually reverse the damage). Penfield was an innovator and a discoverer, a brilliant observer whose observations have fundamentally affected physiological and psychological thought, but he was not really a theorist and certainly not a psychologist, though in later years he lectured freely on the psychology of language. I think he had no great interest in finer physiological mechanisms, and his theoretical stance was a sort of phrenology. Taking for granted the separate existence of such things as memory and consciousness, he looked for their separate locations in the brain (memory in the temporal lobe, planning in the frontal lobe, consciousness in the brain stem). But he had the eye of an observer, he saw things that others did not see, and he saw that they were important and must be recorded. He was second only to Lashley as a formative influence on me, but, on the whole, I learned from his remarkable therapeutic results; he offered little guidance.

It was otherwise with Cone and the Fellows (particularly Francis McNaughton, Guy Odom, and Edwin Boldrey). I was a babe in the woods in that clinical setting, but a fortunate circumstance got me off on the right foot. I had studied the rat's diencephalon; now I wanted to know about man's. When I got stuck, I would consult one of the others. Their answers were vague at best, and presently I realized that none of my fellow Fellows—none of these young neurologists and neurosurgeons—knew one end of the diencephalon from the other. What *they* had to know was the gross structure of the brain, the shape of the ventricles, the course of blood vessels, and so on. But that interest in anatomy established my credentials. They proceeded to give me an intensive course in pathology and various clinical problems. This was invaluable in reporting my results and trying to communicate with colleagues elsewhere. The frontal-lobe work in Montreal was truly revolutionary, and I met frank skepticism in reporting, for example, that a young man made a perfect Stanford–Binet score after removal of the left prefrontal lobe (Hebb, 1939a) or that the removal of both prefrontal lobes in another patient had raised that subject's IQ from 80 to 95 (Hebb and Penfield, 1940). The latter result is readily explained, though it was a new development then: Subclinical epileptic activity before operation was impairing activity in the rest of the brain, and its removal allowed a rebound to a more or less normal level. The real problem lay in the first of those two cases, and in the repeated evidence from others showing that large lesions may have little effect on intelligence-test performance. (Of course, this is not true for all lesions. The speech areas are a different matter, and I also published the first report of the selective effect of injury to the right temporal lobe: Hebb, 1939b.)

The problem preoccupied me during the next three years at Queen's University as Lecturer and Assistant Professor (1939–1942). During this time I continued the development of some new intelligence tests for adults and got some research done jointly with students (Hebb and Foord, 1945b; Hebb and Williams, 1946), but my main product was a paper on the nature of intelligence, which was concerned with the brain-injury problem (Hebb, 1942). Somewhat to my surprise, I came to the conclusion that intelligence itself, and not merely the ability to do well on an intelligence test, must be a product of experience. It was a surprise because this conclusion ran counter to my own assumptions at the time, as well as everyone else's. I wrote better papers later but as an intellectual achievement—if I may use such high-sounding language—this, I think, was my peak performance.

Still lacking was any way of making the problem neurologically or physiologically intelligible. The paper proposed that experience in childhood normally develops concepts, modes of thought, and ways of perceiving that constitute intelligence. Injury to the infant brain interferes with that process, but the same injury at maturity does not reverse it. In other words, more brain tissue or more raw intellectual power is necessary to develop a concept than to retain it. What then is a concept, in terms of neural mechanisms? And at this point my thinking stalled, partly because, like everyone else, I was still thinking of the brain as a through-transmission device and partly because of difficulty in reconciling the facts of learning (which must be localized in specific synapses) and the facts of perception (which, it seemed, is not localized). I had given up thinking about the problem for two years or so, when Hilgard and Marquis (1940) drew my attention to Rafael Lorente de Nó's work and led me to write *The Organization of Behavior* (Hebb, 1949), which contained a theory quite different from any of my earlier ideas.

Yerkes Laboratories of Primate Biology

The book was really a product of the Yerkes Laboratories, though it was only finished at McGill after leaving Orange Park. In the spring of 1942, Lashley was appointed Director of the Yerkes Laboratories of Primate Biology, Orange Park, Florida, a chimpanzee breeding and research station, and invited me to join his staff. I had no desire at the time to study chimpanzees—I wanted to compare early and late brain injuries in dogs—but a full-time research appointment was not to be declined after three years of teaching four courses in the winter, marking extramural essays, and teaching summer school to make ends meet. Once more, circumstances were putting me on the right track whether I would or no. Exposure to the chimpanzee was broadening indeed, even though none of the work planned at first ever came to pass. Lashley's research program was that he and Henry Nissen (Assistant Director) would study various aspects of learning and problem solving, and that I would develop measures of temperamental variables. Then he would operate on the animals' brains, we would retest them, and thus we would see what sort of brain injury affected what behavior over a broad front. However, the first step in this program was for Lashley to train a large group of adult chimpanzees in about thirty different habits, which he expected would be easy to do, given the high intelligence of the chimpanzee. When he found instead that it took about three hundred trials to train a chimpanzee in a form discrimination that a rat would have mastered in sixty trials, the program was off. The first brain operation on an adult animal was made five years later, in the last month of my stay at the laboratories.

There is no basis for complaint in that fact. It is unlikely that any results of brain operation would have turned out half as interesting as the emotions and attitudes of the normal animals. I am accustomed to say that I learned more about human beings during that time than in any other five-year period of my life, except the first. After two or three months of daily observation, I found that the thirty adult chimpanzees of the colony were as distinctive in personality as one would expect of thirty human beings assembled more or less at random. The personalities were human personalities, too—combinations of attitudes and motives and sensitivities that are quite familiar in human society: Mimi upset on finding a worm in her biscuit; Pan neglecting Wendy in the cage with him in favor of the young, inexperienced, but sexually receptive Soda outside the cage; Wendy properly annoyed thereat;

Bimba fond of the human staff and liked by them, but not to be teased; Kambi jealous of attention paid to any other animal; and so on. Thirty human patterns, all the more interesting because of the lack of speech as a complicating variable. They were all afraid of snakes, even on first exposure, but not because they had been told by their mothers that snakes are dangerous. And on top of this came my accidental discovery that they were frightened—or better perhaps, horrified—at the sight of a clay model of a chimpanzee head or, as shown by subsequent testing, any recognizable part of either a chimpanzee or a human body (e.g., a head or a hand from a display mannequin). Given the difference of intelligence and the restricted experience of the caged animals, the parallel with human responses to a dissected body or a major operation is inescapable.

A bonus was the opportunity to look at the old problem of the recognition of emotion, in a new form. It was very interesting to see that the scientific staff and the caretaking staff agreed well in identifying anger and fear, friendliness and jealousy and even depression, in their chimpanzee subjects. How did they do it? What was the basis of judgment? I could show that the judgments were valid, by the criterion of subsequent behavior, but it also appeared that neither I nor the others knew how the judgments were made. I spent some time working this out; the main discovery was that the recognition involves perception of a temporal pattern of behavior and the relation of the present behavior to what has been usual in the past.

There were also opportunities to enjoy the dilemma of those hard-boiled visiting "learning theorists" who could not help recognizing behavior in the chimpanzee that they were already familiar with in man, but who could not talk about it without embarrassment—because it would require "mentalistic" language. To say that Pan's *purpose* was to frighten visitors or that he *enjoyed* doing so, or that Bimba was angry because she *thought* she was being teased, they regarded as anthropomorphism, and anthropomorphism was a sin, scientifically speaking. What should have been of interest, even from a radically behavioristic standpoint, was that identity of behavior in the two species that makes it impossible not to recognize, again and again, familiar human patterns in the chimpanzee. Here one may get a new sight of human beings and their social relations (Hebb and Thompson, 1968). What you can't see in your own species you may be able to see in another. ("Oh, wad some power the giftie gie us/To see oursels as others see us!")

It was in February 1944 that I came back to the problem of thought and the brain, when I found out that Rafael Lorente de Nó had recently shown: (1) that reentrant or closed circuits were to be found throughout the brain, which thus was no longer to be seen as a through-transmission, sensorimotor mechanism, but as one capable of a purely internal activity also, as a possible basis of thought; and (2) that one neuron by itself may not be able to excite a second neuron at the synapse, but can do so if supported by simultaneous action from another neuron. (That is, two presynaptic neurons can be effective when one is not, which, in principle, offers an explanation of the selective effect of attention, when some activity that is going on in the cortex provides such support for one sensory input but not for another.) The first idea offered a solution for my earlier problem, What is a concept?—namely, that it is a group of cortical neurons exciting and reexciting each other. The second idea was a fascinating one, for attention and set had been a complete mystery up to that time (Gibson, 1941), and now I had a possible solution. Exciting.

The excitement was short-lived, however, for there was still trouble with the subject of perception. It seemed implied that, without experience, there would be no pattern perception, that separate learning would be needed to perceive the same object in different parts of the visual field, and that wholes are perceived only after the perception of component parts. I could not accept any of those propositions. However, I then recalled, vaguely, von Senden's (1932) report of persons born blind and given their sight later, and then also Austin Riesen (1947) brought his dark-reared young chimps out into the light. Both Senden's data and Riesen's said that there is no pattern perception without prior experience. Was my schema right after all?

This sequence of events—an apparent difficulty that turned out to offer confirmation instead—occurred a second time and convinced me that the general line must be right, plausible or not. This concerned emotion. I was now looking at thought as a sequence of brain events, each excited jointly by the preceding event and by the sensory stimulation of the moment. The schema implied that thought must be disrupted in a strange environment with unfamiliar contingencies: *A* being accompanied by *C* instead of the usual *B*. How could I propose that one could not think clearly in a strange environment? Even if things should fall up instead of down, metals become soft, and dogs become able to talk, could one not observe and think about what was going on, even if it was incomprehensible? But then I recalled those puzzling fears of the chimpanzee, referred to above. They were produced by a lack, instead of a conflict, of the usual contingencies (such as a head without a body), but this also fitted the schema; and Austin Riesen and I had described infant fears in which an actual conflict disrupted behavior (for example, a familiar caretaker wearing another caretaker's coat terrified the year-old chimpanzee babies). It was reasonable to suppose that thought was disrupted also. Now the schema offered an explanation of those deeply puzzling results, in suggesting that emotional disturbance is a disruption of thought due to a conflict with environmental events or to a lack of usual sensory support, and this idea was readily extended to include humoral sources of emotion (from nutritional lack or endocrine disorder).

Up to this point, working with the schema had been rather like playing a game. Now it had to be taken seriously. Clearly, there was something in it. I went to Lashley and proposed that we work it out and publish together, since this would have to be a book-length job, which I was not ready to face by myself. Also, I hoped that he could devise a better treatment of perception (I thought this part of the schema was wrong, but could find no alternative). Between us, a much better job was possible, in both theory and presentation; and with him as joint author, the book would get a hearing that I did not expect I alone would get. But Lashley was entirely uninterested and remained skeptical of the whole thing. (Criticizing a draft of a later manuscript that said a bridge was being thrown across the gap between physiological detail and molar psychological conceptions, he wrote in the margin, "Lacks the central span.")

This led me for the first time to a realization of how completely Lashley's interest in theory was negative and critical.

The realization was reinforced by another incident that occurred about the same time. No one seemed to have taken my frontal-lobe papers seriously, including the paper published with Penfield. So when Kurt Goldstein published an ill-thought-out paper saying that the negative results obtained with the small number of my few frontal-lobe cases could carry little weight, in view of the larger number with positive results, I was irritated enough to do what I had avoided before: I went down the line and showed the defects of data and method in every one of those papers reporting positive results (Hebb, 1945a). This was the only paper of mine that Lashley praised wholeheartedly. He told me he wished he had written it, which was praise indeed—but also, this was the only one of my papers that was entirely devoted to criticizing other work. I once told Harry Harlow of my surprised discovery that Lashley was so interested in criticizing others' theories and so little interested in developing one himself. Harry, I think, had the right diagnosis: "It's hard to get over having been a genius at twenty-five." That was not the right age—Lashley's reputation was at its peak in his late thirties—but his tremendous experimental success between 1921 and 1930 (from age thirty-one to age forty) was at a relatively early age and it was entirely destructive, mostly destructive of Watsonian connectionism, but also including a foray into neurophysiology to cast doubt on current ideas about the monkey's motor cortex. He made a career of finding things that were hard for others to explain, and he was fond of saying that he had destroyed all theories of behavior, including his own.

As director of the laboratories, Lashley was a good man to work with. Yerkes, the first director (when the laboratories were the Yale Laboratories of Primate Biology), wanted things done in an orderly way. When I first arrived at the laboratories, I found in my desk a booklet for investigators in that earlier regime that said, at one point, that originality in research is, of course, important, but . . . and went on to list some rules and regulations concerning experiments with the animals. Lashley was at the other extreme. Housekeeping detail was left mostly to Nissen, and I saw no sign of any control of research by Lashley. Having assembled a staff, he left it to them to get to work; he provided what material support was possible in wartime; he argued vigorously for his own theoretical views, but he did not force them on the rest of us. It was not necessary to agree with him, and in fact I never did persuade him that I was not still a Pavlovian, though I had gone to work with him explicitly because of his different views. He had curious lapses of memory in some respects. Very flexible in discussion, he would admit the force of contrary argument on some point—but if one came back to the same point a month or two later, one would find him back at the old stand, ready to be persuaded again, and forget again. A different sidelight on his character was provided by an old friend of his, W. N. Taliaferro, when I was still at Harvard. He talked to me while waiting for Lashley to return from some meeting and asked what Karl was doing experimentally. I had to say I didn't know that he was doing anything just then. Taliaferro, with a sort of grin, then asked if he had said anything about being all washed up experimentally and thinking about going to the medical school to make cell counts in human brains. As a matter of fact, he had, and Taliaferro told me that Lashley's repeated pattern was one of furious work for eight or ten or twelve months, followed by a longer period of no ideas, feeling all washed up, and thinking of falling back on the cell-counting project (which he never did).

Free as he was in academic discussion and theoretical give-and-take, he maintained a careful distance personally. Apart from Taliaferro, I knew of no one who called him Karl, and he always addressed us younger colleagues by our surnames. I think he had been a shy and socially uncertain youngster who found safety in professional discourse and could admit to intimacy only a few close friends. He still had some of the mannerisms of shyness. None of this could impair his effectiveness as a teacher in the laboratory or in the outdoor luncheon meetings in Florida: a teacher by example and by undogmatic argument, evidently deeply convinced but arguing with students and junior staff as one among equals.

Return to McGill

At the end of my five-year appointment in Florida, I was lucky again. Robert B. MacLeod was appointed chairman at McGill

and offered me a professorship (for which I suspect I had
Penfield to thank, since Penfield was by now a power in the
university and held a favorable view of my work with him).
The prospects were poor otherwise. Positivism and the black
box were the style, Hull avoiding and Tolman and Skinner
denouncing any involvement with the brain. Apart from
Lashley's lab, only Frank Beach's and Harry Harlow's that
I knew of did much physiologically. At that, Harry once
told me the reason for working on the monkey's frontal
lobe was that that was what he could get grants for. No one
was looking for a physiological psychologist, and as for me it
seemed that even my nonphysiological papers, eleven years
post-Ph.D., hadn't made much of a dent on psychological
thought.

To confirm that impression, E. G. Boring wrote me one of
his famous I-should-tell-you-frankly letters. On December 14,
1946, he wrote to ask me to teach summer school at Harvard.
His second paragraph began: "I had better be frank with you.
We tried to get a man who is better known than you because
we thought the Department, after the recent fission, needed
the publicity. We tried So-and-so, So-and-so, and So-and-so,"
but they had all declined, so the department had voted
"unanimously" to invite me. Boring's estimate agreed with
mine, so it came as no blow—in fact, I was pleased to be the
possessor of one of those letters, which were really famous
within a certain circle. It is a pity that later, when Boring
(1961) published a selection of his letters, only one of the
"frank" ones could be included (to Sir Frederic Bartlett, telling
him how lousy British psychology was). There was certainly no
malice, and Boring could not have been kinder when asked
for help. He read ninety-eight pages of a first draft of my
book, for example, and offered useful, detailed criticism. I
learned much from him *after* leaving Harvard: an important
influence in my poststudent development.

At the end of my first year as professor at McGill, Bob
MacLeod went to Cornell, and I had to take the chairmanship,
but I was able to set up a triumvirate with E. C. Webster and
G. A. Ferguson (each of whom subsequently took his turn as
chairman). Sharing the burden made it possible to organize an
animal lab and get a research program under way during the

following two years (1948–1950) and became still more important after my book appeared late in 1949.

I will come to that in a moment. First let me note my dependence also on younger members of the staff—Dalbir Bindra, W. R. Thompson, and John Zubek, particularly—and on two graduate students who were *de facto* instructors before they graduated: Woodburn Heron (Ph.D. 1953), who ran the sensory-deprivation experiment, so-called (Bexton et al., 1954) from 1951 to 1955, and Peter Milner (Ph.D. 1954), who had taken over instruction in surgical and histological methods by 1952 or 1953. For example, when Jim Olds came with a post-doctoral fellowship to study physiological method in 1953, I sent him to work with Milner, the result being the dramatic discovery of the pleasure areas of the rat brain (Olds and Milner, 1954). It was in a way embarrassing to delegate responsibility to such an extent—it's scarcely ethical to have students who know more than you do—but they were after all capable students, and I had many things to attend to, including the early-environment program (e.g., Hymovitch, 1952; Thompson and Heron, 1954; Melzack and Scott, 1957). This program was less dramatic than the sensory-deprivation work, but perhaps more important. It was a major influence in persuading psychologists that the IQ is not built-in at birth, and so a factor in such things as the Head Start program.

In fact, I finally learned that I was trying to do more than I could. Reading a paper in the December 1951 *Journal of Comparative and Physiological Psychology*, I thought, this is important, I must make a note (for some work we were planning). Then I turned over the page and there at the end was a penciled comment to that effect. This was something new and frightening. I was quite used to forgetting unimportant things, but it was something else not even to recognize after starting to read the paper that I had already read it—still more so when the subject was of immediate concern. Such a lapse, surely, was not normal. I thought seriously of a possible early onset of senile dementia. It occurred to me, however, that I was covering a lot of ground (teaching three courses, one of them an evening seminar, organizing a research program, and handling the detail of departmental administration) and, in particular, was reading twice as much technical material now because of letters from people who had just looked at my new book and thought I should know about such-and-such a paper or So-and-so's work. Could that be the explanation? Why not turn over a new leaf? I determined to stop doing any work at night and to read not as much but as little as possible. I would scan the journals and read only what seemed imperative. (As this worked out, I also read what the graduate students thought was imperative and insisted on my reading.) Memory gradually came back to its normal degree of unreliability.

The Organization of Behavior was published by Wiley in 1949 as the first volume in a series in clinical psychology. (It turned out, also, to be the last volume of this series, which never got off the ground—I can't imagine for what reason.) Publication followed two prior rejections that disappointed but did not surprise me. I expected that years of research with graduate students would be needed to get a hearing for the book once it did appear, and its immediate success was quite astonishing. The result was a difficult personal adjustment to have to make, from being an unknown to being known everywhere (or so it seemed). "Jack" Hilgard was once thoughtful enough to tell me I was being too deprecative. I needed the advice, he was quite right, up to a point, but I had more to be modest about than he realized. It would have been false modesty to talk as if the book were not a success (it was indeed, beyond expectation), but it was not modesty to keep in mind and to have others keep in mind the limitations of the theory. The arousal system, fundamental to cognitive function, was discovered by G. Moruzzi and H. W. Magoun in the year the book was published; a year or two later J. C. Eccles and collaborators finally established the existence of inhibition, which I had been afraid to postulate. These facts in themselves meant that the physiological basis of the theory was wobbly. I had had to make a number of arbitrary assumptions in detail, so its details could hardly be correct, and as I have said my account of perception looked improbable to me. (Ten years later, Roy Pritchard and Woodburn Heron found evidence showing that it was pretty sound after all: Pritchard et al., 1960.) All round, it is still surprising that the general line, at a behavioral level, turned out to be as solid as it has.

In my paper on brain injury and intelligence (Hebb, 1942),

written when I was thirty-seven, I noted certain parallels between brain injury and old age. In both cases there is a loss of
brain substance, and it appeared that, while there is a loss of
what may be called raw, naked intellectual power, there is also
a surprising retention of intellectual function in one's own
special area of thought. In recent years I have begun to gather
first-hand data relevant to that hypothesis, in private investigation. It is pleasing to find some confirmation of the earlier
view. That is, I can still think, more or less, and in the past
twelve months for example I have seen how to make an important revision of the conception of the cell-assembly (as a
mechanism that must shut itself off promptly, rather than one
that can maintain its activity), which also suggests a solution
for the long-standing problem of the extraordinary efficiency
of the human brain. This is briefly outlined in a recent paper
(Hebb, 1976).

However, the signs of age are clear. The most surprising
one is, as I said above, a waning of the compulsion to stay
involved in research, even armchair research. From now on, I
regard myself not as a psychologist but, like a past-president,
as a past-psychologist.

1976

Selected Publications by Donald Olding Hebb

The innate organization of visual activity: I. Perception of figures by rats
reared in total darkness. *J. genet. Psychol.*, 1937a, *51*, 101–126.

The innate organization of visual activity: II. Transfer of response in the
discrimination of brightness and size by rats reared in total darkness. *J.
comp. Psychol.*, 1937b, *24*, 277–299.

Studies of the organization of behavior: II. Changes in the field orientation
of the rat after cortical destruction. *J. comp. Psychol.*, 1938, *26*, 427–444.

Intelligence in man after large removals of cerebral tissue: Report of four
left frontal lobe cases. *J. gen. Psychol.*, 1939a, *21*, 73–87.

Intelligence in man after large removals of cerebral tissue: Defects following
right temporal lobectomy. *J. gen. Psychol.*, 1939b, *21*, 437–446.

(with W. Penfield) Human behavior after extensive bilateral removal from
the frontal lobes. *Arch. Neurology Psychiat., Chicago*, 1940, *44*, 421–438.

The effect of early and late brain injury upon test scores, and the nature of normal adult intelligence. *Proc. Amer. Philosophic Soc.*, 1942, *85*, 275–292.

Man's frontal lobes: A critical review. *Arch. Neurology Psychiat., Chicago*, 1945a, *54*, 10–24.

(with E. N. Foord) Errors of visual recognition and the nature of the trace. *J. exp. Psychol.*, 1945b, *35*, 335–348.

(with K. Williams) A method of rating animal intelligence. *J. gen. Psychol.*, 1946, *34*, 59–65.

The organization of behavior. New York: Wiley, 1949.

(with W. R. Thompson) The social significance of animal studies. In G. Lindzey (Ed.), *Handbook of social psychology*, 2, Cambridge, Mass.: Addison-Wesley, 1968, 532–561.

Physiological learning theory. *J. abnorm. Child Psychol.*, 1976, *4*, 309–314.

Other Publications Cited

Bexton, W. H., W. Heron, and T. H. Scott. Effects of decreased variation in the sensory environment. *Canadian J. Psychol.* 1954, *8*, 70–76.

Boring, E. G. *Psychologist at large.* New York: Basic Books, 1961.

Gibson, J. J. A critical review of the concept of set in contemporary experimental psychology. *Psychol. Bull.* 1941, *38*, 781–817.

Hilgard, E. R., and D. G. Marquis. *Conditioning and learning.* New York: Appleton-Century, 1940.

Hymovitch, B. The effects of experiential variations on problem solving in the rat. *J. comp. physiol. Psychol.*, 1952, *45*, 313–321.

Melzack, R., and T. H. Scott. The effects of early experience on the response to pain. *J. comp. physiol. Psychol.* 1957, *50*, 155–161.

Olds, J., and P. Milner. Positive reinforcement produced by electrical stimulation of septal area and other regions of rat brain. *J. comp. physiol. Psychol.* 1954, *47*, 419–427.

Pritchard, R. M., W. Heron, and D. O. Hebb. Visual perception approached by the method of stabilized images. *Canadian J. Psychol.*, 1960, *14*, 67–77.

Riesen, A. H. The development of visual perception in man and chimpanzee. *Science*, 1947, *106*, 107–108.

Senden, M.v. *Raum- und Gestaltauffassung bei operierten Blindgeborenen vor und nach der Operation.* Leipzig: Barth, 1932.

Thompson, W. R., and W. Heron. The effects of restricting early experience on the problem-solving capacity of dogs. *Canadian J. Psychol.*, 1954, *8*, 17–31.

Quinn McNemar

At the turn of the century, my first screams burst into the quiet air near Greenland Gap, a gap in New Creek Mountain which is a range that parallels the Allegheny Front in West Virginia. Between these two, which have elevations up to some 3,000 feet, there are two series of hills: one called Walker's Ridge, the other a succession of nameless knobs. As one would expect, there are little valleys and hollows "betwixt and between." Hillbilly, hollow folk area. Rivulets became runs, which became creeks (called "cricks" by the natives). That did not happen in Dry Hollow because of a series of sink holes. The sites of springs invited farm dwellings. The tillable land, once cleared of trees and brush, was mostly hillside, rocky, and seldom suitable for meadow (hay growing). A strip of limestone land along the top and eastern side of Walker's Ridge was, relatively, prime for farming and grazing. Lucky for some farmers.

The farm I grew up on was large, about 350 acres ("Dem dar hills was cheap" to buy), but the soil was clayish and typically lacking in fertility even before it became "worn out" because of overuse. The farm animals were the only source of fertilizer, which had to be spread too thinly. Actually, two-thirds of the acreage was wooded, some of which we cleared to have firewood and more land for crops. The plowing of such "new" land was a struggle with the stumps and roots, the roots of locust trees all too frequently taking revenge by snapping back from the plow onto the shins of the plower; my shins did not escape this.

Our farming was general: hay, corn, oats, sometimes wheat and buckwheat, potatoes, apples, peaches, and pears; a large vegetable garden, along with the fruits, led to much home canning. As to animals: two work horses, eight to ten milk cows, sixty sheep, a few hogs, chickens, a dog, and a couple of cats. Except for sugar and salt, the farm was self-sufficient foodwise.

The cash needed for buying clothing, farm equipment (rudimentary, believe me), and for sundry other things came from the sale of wool, lambs, calves (or yearlings, sometimes two-year olds), eggs, butter, and a few hams (hickory-smoked in our own smokehouse). These trickles of cash were supplemented a bit by the sale of bark peeled from felled chestnut oaks at sap-flowing time and hauled twelve miles to a tannery and by the sale of lumber from trees on the wooded areas. The lumbering job was made possible by an itinerant with a sawmill, pulled about by a steam tractor, the engine of which supplied the power for transforming the logs into lumber, which could be sold in the town of Keyser, twenty miles distant or seven hours away over a dirt road on a horse-drawn wagon. That sawmill and its wood-fired steam engine was great stuff for the boys in the neighborhood up to a point, i.e., up to the time they were expected to tote and stack the newly cut lumber, a job for which I developed a dislike.

The only favorable thing that I can say about the long hours and hard manual labor on a farm such as ours is this: there was variety. But as a skinny, nonmuscular teenager, I found the variety, even when interspersed with no-work rainy days, was an insufficient incentive to become a dirt farmer. Negative motivation? Reinforced by an outhouse when air-conditioned by subzero weather?

Let's turn to that span of family life for which I have some recollections. These include little about my father, who early in my life passed away. When I was seven, my mother became the wife of a widower, J. W. Ebert, who owned the farm described above. Whereupon the household came to consist of my mother and maternal grandmother, a stepdad, a step-grandma, a stepbrother (a year older than I), a stepsister (two years younger), and, some time later, a foster stepbrother who had been taken in temporarily as a baby when his mother died. His father quickly remarried, but never reclaimed his child.

If you think the foregoing mix of persons might have been conducive to domestic strife, read on. I had been spoiled rotten by my grandmother, who dominated my mother. Stepdad was a second-generation German, hard-driving, impatient, and blustery, a great worrier, a strict disciplinarian with a never-known-to-break hickory switch always available. Step-brother was a real bully, particularly toward his sister, me, and eventually mother. Nearly every day I fought with him, either defending myself or his sister from his tormenting. Having been spoiled, I was easily provoked. If my stepdad couldn't ascertain who started a scrap, both of us were whipped. Was I always innocent? Which of us fibbed the most during interrogation? Anyway, I had to share a bed with a stepbrother who increasingly seemed to stand for nothing decent and for all the bad things that characterize the real hillbilly. I was motivated to avoid being like him, the "good" (me) versus the bad boy.

Our farmhouse somehow accommodated the eight of us in four bedrooms. There was a seldom-used "spare" room, a little-used "parlor," and a room that served as a dining room during the warm season and, when colder, as a living room with a potbellied stove brought in and the dining table somehow squeezed into the kitchen. Frame house, wood outside and inside, with no insulation; no running water, no fireplace; kerosene lamps with light-stingy wicks, until that marvel of marvels came along: the kerosene-burning Aladdin lamp with its light-producing magic mantle.

This farm spread did not provide a family of eight with an abundance of the material things of life. Patched and re-patched clothing. Kids barefoot (not by choice) half the year. Scraps of paper saved for writing and "figuring." No butter when it could be sold at a "fair" price. An orange at Christmastime only. Small servings of meat. Many times nothing but milk (blue John) and corn mush for supper with the leftovers fried for the next morning's breakfast. Any kid who grumbled about the food received a dire warning from my stepdad: "Wait till you get your feet under your own table."

All four of the adults were members of the Church of the Brethren, a denomination that was (and is) akin to the Mennonite sects. The only way to get to heaven was via the CB; membership in any "progressive" church was a chancy way to achieve salvation, i.e., avoid hell. It was nearly inevitable that my sins, as a youngster, were to be washed away by a three-dip baptism in a waterhole of the nearby creek. Later, the members of the church congregation, sure that God was acting through them, tried to convince me that God was calling on me to become a preacher. Somehow the message didn't reach my heart. Perhaps my willingness as a teenager to teach the adult Sunday school class had been misleading to some on earth or Someone on high. My inculcated faith in religious mysticism received a blow when it was reported that the only avowed atheist in the area had never been struck down, even though he cursed the heavens repeatedly, challenging God, if He existed, to strike him dead. We kids were assured by all the God-fearing folks that He would do that to the wicked chap, but there was that escape clause: God is forgiving (even when forgiveness was not sought?).

Out of a strict religious background, the golden rule has survived as a guiding principle of my life.

Despite the physical and mental hurt imposed on me by my stepdad, in retrospect I suspect that he was the dominant influence in shaping me. Despite his harshness and bluster, he was fundamentally a kind man with a healthy sense of humor, a leader in the community, and a healer of frequent domestic strife in neighboring households. His most frequent "client" (no fee) was the farm family a half mile up in an adjacent hollow. We kids were never told anything about the cause of friction in this family, which was headed by a part-time preacher, the nominal head of the local flock. The rumor trickled down that there was a husband–wife problem some-how associated with a practice-what-you-preach idea that was connected with the preacher's frequently used Biblical text, "Multiply and replenish the earth."

And that reminds me of the fact that, despite an abun-dance of birds with their cheerful chirping and bees with their stinging stings, my puritanical stepdad somehow never got around to a frequently promised discussion of what is now called the story of the birds and the bees. But an adolescent growing up on a farm could not help making observations that answered the basic query and led to additional questions. Why were that "bulling" cow's crazy antics so quickly calmed by a ten-second bull service? In contrast, why did the sow, all the while issuing apparently appreciative oincks, require ten min-utes of the boar's action? And if it was all that much fun, why did the pussycat scream to the heavens during the act? Page Frank Beach! Observations of such things could be embarrass-ing and hazardous. Consider the time I was assigned the task of coaxing the sow to journey a mile on foot to the nearest farm possessing a boar. I arrived to discover that the only per-son at home was a girl about my age . . . enough said. Admit-tedly, my early environment did provide glandular stimula-tion, but what about intellectual stimulation?

There were many things to perk one's curiosity and/or imagination. The list could be long, therefore I offer a sam-ple (nonrandom). The trailing arbutus blossoms emerging as the snow melted away. The movements of clouds, sometimes in opposite directions. The changing wind pattern before, during, and after a thunderstorm. Why did rattlers and cop-perheads exist? Why did weeds grow faster than crops? What was the source of the folklore that next year's tomatoes and corn can be improved by selective choice of seeds from this year's crop? What use was made of the ginseng roots we boys searched for in the woods to sell for a few cents? Why was there such a great variety of trees in the woods? And what caused that breathtaking waving and pulsating display over the entire night sky of what was called "northern lights"?

Were the animals as dumb as they appeared to be? What of the seventeen red ants (half-inchers) that marched some thirty feet down a hillside, disappeared under a flat rock, then emerged, each with an oval-shaped egg, and proceeded back up the hill to go under another flat rock? Why the move? I turned over the first rock to discover no eggs. How come exactly seventeen ants knew to go and move exactly seventeen eggs?

Community (human) activities were mostly confined to the local school district, with a spillover into adjacent districts. One-room schools were spaced about four miles apart in the area between the two mountain ranges. We had little contact with people beyond these ranges. As usual, our one-room schoolhouse served a dual purpose: education (?) from the first of October through March, and Sunday school and church services with the inevitable "revival" meeting(s) in September.

Although the elders in my family had never finished grade school, they stressed the importance of "getting an education," with only the vaguest idea as to what that meant beyond the three R's plus spelling. Some readers may need a briefing on the "education" that was available in the one-room country school with thirty to forty pupils, grades 1 through 8, plus "postgrads" who continued in attendance to age eighteen solely because there was little else to do during the six-month school period. There was a seat-desk assignment, boys to right, girls to left (as one entered from the back), with the youngest in front. The "teaching" procedure involved a nearly steady stream of "recitations," each a stand-up-in-front affair of some two to five minutes of questioning by the teacher, plus help with difficulties. When not reciting, the pupils were supposedly studying for the next recitation period. That was a time for mischief, which forced the teacher to divert her attention from the reciting pupils. One thing some of us learned was how to display an innocent-looking poker face following any and all misbehavior.

The textbooks, which parents had to buy, new or used, varied in their interest for me. I lapped up the arithmetic, geography, and reader texts but found the book on state history downright boring. I did not, nor could I ever, believe that the "great" state of West Virginia had ever been populated with so many, many "great" men—the chief concern of that textbook. In a way, it was surprising that I liked geography as a subject, since I was required to know such minutiae as the county seat for each of the fifty-five counties in the state.

There was no library within twenty miles. The privately held books in the community were few, mainly Biblical works, some Gene Stratton Porter novels, and Horatio Alger books. Such barrenness placed the main responsibility for education on the teacher, but unfortunately all but one of my grade school teachers were poorly equipped for the challenge. Typical of the time, a girl (or boy) could become a teacher by attending a one-room, six-months-a-year grade school, and then passing a written state examination. With the exception of one who had had three years of high school, my teachers were not overburdened with an excess of knowledge. But none of them was handicapped by pedagogical trappings!

The subject matter that bothered my teachers most was 'rithmetic. So, I got my foundation therein by working my way through the eighth-grade level of the text by the end of my nominal fifth-grade year. My reward: The next year I found myself teaching (?) the eighth-graders their arithmetic, a task which the then-teacher had abysmally failed.

By current standards, and in current jargon, I most certainly grew up educationally and culturally deprived. Lucky me, the Stanford–Binet was not yet available. As a farm lad with little farmwork to do during the school months and no high school within twenty miles (six hours by a pokey workhorse), I continued attending the grade school until I was eighteen. The overlearning helped me pass the state teachers examination—I had decided that, of two choices, my brain qualified me better for teaching than my brawn fitted me for farmwork. I contracted to teach in a nearby (three miles away) school at $30 per month. I would live at home and get to and from school by shank's pony. The "I would" indicates that I didn't. The year was 1918. In Europe there was a war, about which we hill folks were downright ignorant except for what we read in a sheet called the *Toledo* (Ohio) *Weekly Blade*. Some boys in our area had been drafted, a fact that worried my folks. Was there a way to keep me from being drafted? Well, as members of a church that had long been recognized for C.O. status, it would have seemed natural for the family to attempt, via that route, to save my hide. But a cousin on C.O.

assignment had been killed in France. When someone said that being in school might at least postpone the evil day, my parents decided to let me go to the tuition-free Preparatory Branch of West Virginia University in Keyser, twenty miles away. I wiggled out of the teaching contract, accepted the thought of teaching the next year so as to reimburse my parents, and found myself in another world, where at the age of eighteen-plus I first encountered a flush toilet, "pull the string" type.

Growing pains were not over. As a country hick, completely ignorant of ordinary amenities, dressed in much too short hand-me-downs from a stepuncle who had become a banker near Philadelphia (not until my senior college year did I have a new suit), unread, etc., etc., I had to survive the taunts of the local high school boys ("beanstalk," "hayseed," and much more) and snubbing by some fellow "prep" students. Not exactly a cure for a feeling of social inferiority that was to plague me for many more years.

At that time, the school consisted of a dormitory (boys and girls in separate wings, common dining room between), one classroom building, and teachers oh-so-knowledgeable and sympathetic. Although loaded with extra courses, I breezed through the first year with a record that so impressed the principal, in whose algebra and Latin classes I had excelled, that he insisted I return for the second year. No state aid was available, but he said he could get me a job on a building-construction project. For the magnificent pay of thirty cents per hour, I found myself pushing a wheelbarrow loaded with sand, or gravel, or cement up ramps much too steep. At the end of the second year, the principal said I could earn my room and board by hashing and firing (stoking) the dormitory coal furnace. By the end of the third year, I had finished enough courses for the secondary diploma, and the state had upped the prep school by providing for freshman college work. The principal, now "college" president, urged me to return by offering again the hashing and coal-shoveling jobs.

That freshman college year whetted my intellect for more and more, but there was an incident that was innocently trivial and that may come as a surprise to readers who know me: I was involved in a student strike. For some silly cause, which escapes my memory, the students had demanded a holiday. Although refused by the prexy, all but a couple of students deserted classes for the town. The local town paper screamed that the students were Bolsheviks (the year was 1921) and demanded that the college punish the "radicals." Two things happened. First, the student leaders rounded up one of the boys who chose to go to classes instead of to town and literally paddled his bottom so fiercely that the poor guy couldn't sit for a week; second, the prexy scheduled an assembly to demand an explanation and apology from the leaders of the strike. Although I had not been one of them, the leaders persuaded me, as student body president, to defend the action of the students. (Actually, the ringleaders had chickened out, cleverly duping naive me into an effort to save their hides.) After my impassioned, and likely stupid, defense speech, the prexy firmly informed us that we were "striking against the *great* state of West Virginia," a state that would tolerate no such nonsense. The affair cost me my fair-haired status with the principal–prexy, who did not encourage me to return for the sophomore college year. No hashing, no furnace-firing, no more schooling.

A representative of Juniata, a Church of the Brethren college in Pennsylvania, happened by our farmhouse and persuaded the family that I should not take a teaching job yet. Having prospered a bit, the family made the necessary small loan for a second college year; then ditto for a third year and a fourth.

At Juniata, I completed a weak major in mathematics. My effort to round up the required six students for an advanced course in math failed, as did an attempt to get a third course in psychology (beyond general and educational). My interest in psychology was sparked by the teacher of those two courses, Charles C. Ellis, who had a Ph.D. minor in psychology. He was by far the best teacher I ever had—a master of oral exposition, with an uncanny way of popping a question at any student who showed the faintest sign of inattention. Perhaps one measure of his influence is the fact that from little Juniata College, with graduating classes of forty to fifty, six students went on for the doctorate in psychology during a decade.

A few courses in education and "practice teaching" of a

low-level math course at the college qualified me for a West Virginia secondary teaching certificate. The then Juniata prexy, M. G. Brumbaugh, formerly commissioner of education for Puerto Rico and one-time governor of Pennsylvania, casually remarked one day that if I were interested in teaching in Charleston, West Virginia, he would drop a line to the city superintendent of schools, a friend of his. That settled my worry about finding a job. So off I went to the West Virginia state capital to try my hand at the thing I had kept promising to do but had postponed seven years. About halfway into a second year of teaching math and science in a junior high school, I began to raise my sights—maybe I could better myself.

A brief digression. I was then twenty-seven and still hoping the time would come when I could afford marriage. Prior to that time I had been more or less serious about a couple of girls. In prep school, I had placed Mabel high on a pedestal— the ideal girl. The trouble was that another guy had done the same thing *and* he could afford to get married. In my senior college year, I fell for Betty, a statuesque, personality-plus freshman who hailed from Southern California. She was the first girl that I, age twenty-five, ever kissed, an event that may have created an illusion of deep love. An informal engagement followed. She went back to California, did not return to college, and at the end of my first teaching year, I hitchhiked west to see her. Shortly thereafter, she called it quits. Absolutely no scars or regrets on my part, but a bit of travel in California was to influence a later decision to go to Stanford.

Love-at-first-sight engulfed me during the following year in Charleston. Lorene was pretty and a natural charmer, with interests in music, drama, and literature. I am greatly indebted to her for inspiration that raised my level of aspiration. I came to Stanford the following (1927) autumn, and returned to the East (1929) at which time she said yes, she would marry me after I had finished the doctorate. By the end of the following year, our correspondence had not kept the love fires blazing. Then along came Olga, a Stanford senior whom I met (July 1930) under rather funny circumstances. Within a few weeks, we became inseparable, and in September 1931, we got married on a financial shoestring (I still needed a year to finish my dissertation). And we are still together, thank heaven. Now back to the main story.

I was considering engineering school when I happened to read an article in either *Harper's* or the *Atlantic Monthly* on the role of psychology in criminology, which sparked my interest (later to be killed by a course in abnormal psychology at Stanford). Where to go for graduate work in psychology? I wrote for several university catalogs, including that of Stanford. Why faraway Stanford? Mainly accidental. Three sons of the well-to-do but old-shoe Democratic Carskadon family in Keyser had gone to Stanford as undergraduates. One became a San Francisco Bay Area realtor; another became a writer, via journalism, for the Twentieth-Century Fund; the third, who had returned to Keyser to manage the family business, gave me glowing accounts of Stanford. I applied to Stanford, which to my surprise, accepted me. I was to learn later that admission to graduate school was then far easier than survival in it.

A digression about finances. My two years of teaching had enabled me to pay off most of what I owed my family. A hitchhiking trip in search of a 1927 summer job led me to New York City. There I contacted a Juniata classmate, Miriam Dugan, whose father owned a bakery business. I had no intention of asking her help in finding a job, but when I told her that I was looking for one, she quickly learned from her father that a house-to-house delivery route was available. Would I like to try it? Indeed, yes. Then, for ten six-day weeks, I found myself up at 5:30 A.M., harnessing a horse and taking on a wagonload of bread, pies, cakes, etc., for a seven-mile, nearly two-hour trek from Lynbrook to Long Beach, Long Island. Once I reached my assigned eighteen-block-long, two-block-wide, territory, I soon learned that selling the Dugan products was easy: just bark "Baker Dugan" and the natives and summer residents would emerge with cash in hand. Some dames seemed to be suggesting trade, but who would mind the horse? Saturday was the big day—big in sales and in length—I was seldom back in Lynbrook before 9:00 P.M. Compared to teaching, it was a lucrative job. As a result, I arrived at Stanford with enough cash for a first year of full-time study. How did I get to Stanford that 1927 autumn? Well, by hitchhiking, except for a miserable cool overnight ride in Nevada on a freight car loaded with, of all things, pig iron! Slightly less comfortable than the gravel roads between Topeka and California.

In essence, that first year, aside from three courses in statistics and measurement from Truman Kelley, was study in competition with those smart Stanford undergraduates. I managed a C in Comparative Psychology, but my overall record for the year was not a disaster. I earned my way as a research assistant during the next three years and as a sort of floating statistical adviser during the fifth graduate year. Actually, the second year was my first graduate year. Not until then was I allowed to participate in graduate psychology courses.

Before any of my possible detractors start raising questions about my "slow" (five-year) progress in graduate school, they should know that, aside from making up undergraduate work, I had to earn my way for four of the five years, I completed the course work in math for a second possible minor, and I spent eight months in the field running down and testing twins for my dissertation (McNemar, 1933). Nevertheless, there was time for rap sessions with other graduate students, some of whom later gained national visibility. Some names include: Roger Barker, Bob Bernreuter, Ray Carpenter, Harry Harlow, L. P. Herrington (via physiology at Yale), Lowell Kelly, Don Marquis, and Floyd Ruch. During 1929, the grad group adopted a precocious senior whose name was Bob Sears.

Typically, the number of admissions then was about ten per year, with two to four surviving long enough to attain the doctorate. Instead of cutthroat competition, there was helpful cooperation among the students.

The faculty at that time consisted of John Coover, Paul Farnsworth, Maude Merrill, Walter Miles, Calvin "C. P." Stone, Edward Strong (half-time), and Lewis Terman, all with open office doors. Truman Kelley was in the School of Education. Owl-wise Coover was known mainly for his giant (641 pages) monograph on psychical research (Coover, 1917). Terman once remarked to me that Coover had files of excellent data on learning (never published because he was overly meticulous). I, and a few others, found Coover a most helpful chap on logically knotty problems. One had to be patient while his mind, and discourse, wandered far and wide, seemingly forgetful of the question at hand. Coover had, on oral examinations, questioned a number of doctoral candidates about Chauvenet's criterion. I suspected that it had something to do with statistics and felt sure I would be the next one to be victimized by the question. I spent hours chasing the thing down, finally finding it in an old, circa 1860, astronomical journal. I arrived at the orals all primed, only to be let down: Coover didn't ask the question.

Farnsworth, whose undergraduate lab course (which I had to take) was anything but inspiring, redeemed himself in a graduate course entitled Modern Viewpoints, which many fellow students have said was their best course. Merrill, though scholarly, was shy in the classroom. She was at her best in office conference. One course from Miles was enough: Memory and Perception was naught but eye movements.

Stone apparently forgot (or forgave) the C in Comparative Psychology when he gave me a chance to be coauthor on a couple of papers. He called me in to say that he did not like my introductory paragraph to one paper and that he had written a better one. I would have submissively accepted his judgment, except for the fact that when he moved to point out the faults in my version, he mistakenly picked up his own and proceeded to tear it apart sentence by sentence. Mine was published!

I never had a course from Strong. As a member of my dissertation committee, he boosted my ego by telling later students to read my opus as an example of how a dissertation should be organized and written. (More later about my earlier nonskill in writing.) As a colleague, I came to appreciate Strong's penetrating mind. Somewhat lacking in formal statistical training, he frequently sought me out for help on ticklish statistical problems he was encountering, and had attempted to solve, in connection with his Interest Inventory. Generally, he had arrived at acceptable solutions—he just needed a little reinforcement.

Obviously, Truman Kelley, who was based in the School of Education and whose statistics courses were more populated by psychology than by education students, had a lasting influence on my career. Of twelve starters (1927–1928 year), I was one of three who finished the sequence. I managed to write a good set of notes, get A's, and really not understand much of what had been going on in class. During every lecture hour, he filled (1) the blackboards on three walls of the classroom with derivations, and (2) the students with a "Well, what was that all about?" One day he quickly reached the end of the blackboard space before noticing that something was wrong. For about twenty-five minutes, he scratched his head and vainly studied the text, *Statistical Method* (Kelley, 1924), which he himself had authored. No sign of embarrassment. Later it seemed that I was destined to do my dissertation with Kelley, but Harvard swiped him and Terman came to my rescue.

Actually, close contact with Terman did not begin until my second year, when I enrolled in his year-long, three-quarter term sequence in educational psychology. It was not a lecture course. Terman spent the first hour outlining the area under the traditional Thorndikeian subheads: nature of man, learning, and individual differences. Then he passed out a list of topics of current interest, with the instruction to choose one, dig up all the library sources, and be prepared to deliver, orally, a written report, one or more hours in length, to the class four months later. "Class dismissed, see you then." This was a blow to the few education majors who had ventured over to sit, with note-taking pencil, at the feet of the master. (At that time, Terman, as executive head of the department, signed the study lists of all graduate psychology students and saw to it that each took this course, usually in the first year.)

The delivery of these reports was typically a traumatic affair for students who knew or suspected that their candidacy for the doctorate hinged thereon (as was true). One petrified chap told me he knew throughout his two-hour report that he was saying the wrong things. I must admit that my persistent lack of self-confidence did not aid my presentation, but, after I had finished, my weak ego ballooned when Terman quietly remarked that the second half of my paper was worthy of publication . . . maybe an appropriate introductory paragraph and a little polishing—bring it to him; he would recommend it to an editor. I walked out on air, amid the congratulations of fellow students. Aha, I had it made, or had I? Well, not quite—read on. Terman called me in, three weeks after I had handed him the copy for my supposed second publication. (My first had been as a coauthor with statistician Kelley, an award for a small idea plus hours at an old-fashioned desk calculator.) Terman flipped through the first three pages on which the markings of his editorial red pencil were abundantly evident, looked up, and calmly said what I have never forgotten and so can quote exactly: "How can a person think if he can't write?" This was a real deflator because I had naively thought the write-up could not be improved. An educational psychology major, Ruth Thomson (later, head of psychology at San Francisco State University), who had an M.A. in English and whom I had helped in statistics, came to my rescue. In a short time, I learned more about the basics of clear writing than I had from all my English courses. She also helped me with other papers, but later I was to learn yet more from Olga.

Without doubt, Terman was an important influence in shaping my career. I suspect he was overly impressed by my A's in Kelley's stat courses and by my ability to talk stat at a level he could understand. He had, I believe, been overawed by Kelley's stat wizzardry—Kelley had his expository difficulties. Speculation about personality dynamics notwithstanding, I honestly believe my emergence as a critic had its roots in Terman's insistence that the literature of psychology should be approached with skepticism and a critical eye—that, and the critical atmosphere in his courses and the weekly evening seminar at his home, a seminar that included faculty.

The critical attitude planted by Terman reached into soil that had been made receptive by my early experience working on the farm. My German stepdad insisted on "doing it right," a goal that was shared by the other adult family members. As a critic, I have been concerned with how well (or badly) research has been done, leaving it to others to say whether the research should have been done at all.

The monograph on "Sex Differences in Variational Tendency," coauthored with Terman (McNemar and Terman, 1936), was essentially a critique of methodology in an area populated with fuzzy studies. My next critical venture was prompted by John McGeoch, who asked me in 1937 to prepare, for the *Psychological Bulletin,* a special review of the

Newman-Freeman-Holzinger book on twins. I had reason to believe that McGeoch was skeptical of this book, essentially a report of research, because he regarded Freeman as a soft-headed psychologist and because some people thought of Holzinger as a mathematician with little common sense. (Newman was a highly respected biologist.) My review (McNemar, 1938) was somewhat devastating since the book involved plenty of fluky methodology, which was soon to be outdistanced by that of the famous (infamous?) Iowa IQ studies.

When Terman asked me to look into the latter, I came up with so many faults that he and Florence Goodenough had overlooked that he suggested I prepare a separate evaluation (McNemar, 1940a), not a part of the projected Yearbook of the National Society for the Study of Education. Apparently, it was easy to overlook flukes in those Iowa studies: When I assigned one monograph to a couple of Stanford undergraduate students who wished to sharpen their critical powers, they came up with difficulties that Terman, Goodenough, and I had overlooked.

Two further points on those studies: (1) Following a talk by George Stoddard at Stanford on the research findings, I tried to pin him down on certain flaws. This effort led me to believe that he was not familiar with the contents of certain monographs for which he had prepared glowing prefaces. (2) At the 1939 APA convention, held at Stanford and Berkeley, Kurt Lewin (who was then at Iowa, but whom I had come to know at Stanford during his first American year) attempted the role of peacemaker by bringing me and Beth Wellman together. The prolonged dinner meeting was a model of congeniality, with Kurt asking about this and that point and Beth calmly responding to my questions and objections. I felt elated until our return to the campus. As she stepped out of my car, she suddenly turned emotional, bitter, and formal and, among other things, said: "Dr. McNemar, you should realize that Lewis Terman has poisoned your mind." I did not scurry to find either an antidote or a psychiatrist.

A word about my training in statistics and my experiences with mathematical statisticians may be in order. I had an introductory course at Stanford from a mathematician-turned-educationist who required the India-ink drawing of many,

many graphs. In addition, I almost learned what "standard deviation" and "critical ratio" meant. Kelley's courses, as of 1927–1928, dealt mostly with correlation, plus a bit on standard errors (sans much logic) and chi square only as a test of "goodness of fit." (Other uses of chi square, small sample techniques, and Fisherian methodology had not yet percolated an area long dominated by Karl Pearson.) I decided to take more math courses, including Uspensky's Probability and Harold Hotelling's Introduction to Mathematical Statistics, both tough courses for one (me) with a limited and rusty math background.

Hotelling, with a Ph.D. from Princeton's math department (which was then so pure that his degree was in analysis situs instead of statistics), had come to Stanford as a statistician in the Food Research Institute. As a practical statistician, he was such a flop that the institute eased him out. The math department reluctantly came to his rescue but restricted his stat teaching to just one course because the department head wished to keep math pure. (I took advanced calculus from said head; once he disdainfully remarked to me, "Oh, the correlation coefficient—I could easily invent a hundred of them.") Hotelling, who is usually considered the first and most important American in the "new" statistics, soon escaped from the restraints of the Stanford math department to establish, at Columbia, the first American Department of Mathematical Statistics.

In 1933, I was awarded a Social Science Research Council postdoctoral fellowship for further training in statistics. The stipend of $2,500 plus $300 for travel permitted me to spend the summer at the University of Chicago studying factor analysis with L. L. Thurstone, the academic year at Columbia auditing Hotelling's expanded courses and reading the literature (with his help), and the following summer at Ann Arbor, where a couple of statisticians operated within the math department. Olga and I drove across the country in a seven-year-old Chevy roadster that I had bought from Lowell Kelley in 1930 for $50 (sunburn in Yellowstone area; broken axle near Rapid City; car stolen, and recovered, in Chicago; gapingstock on Fifth and Park Avenues).

Early in the summer at the University of Chicago, I stumbled onto a meeting in which four "giants" were discussing factor analysis: Spearman and Holzinger on the defensive against Thurstone and Hotelling. Contacts with Kelley at Stanford had led Hotelling to develop his principal components solution, which was very similar to the principal axes solution developed, and rejected, by Thurstone. My own interest in the area had been spurred by the hunch that my doctoral written examinations might include a question on the "nature of intelligence," à la Spearman. My thorough reading and organizing of the literature paid off: I learned a lot and I did receive a three-hour question on the topic. Late in the summer of 1929, I had hitchhiked from California (my fourth and fifth transcontinental "hike") to Yale for the International Congress of Psychology, at which Spearman, as the first speaker in a symposium on the nature of intelligence, pontifically led off with "Now that the existence of g has been universally accepted, it remains to determine its nature." The second speaker, Kelley, immediately put Spearman on the defensive by denying the universal acceptance claimed by Spearman. Thereafter, such sputtering I have never heard from a person as cocksure as Spearman. Parenthetically, there was another event at the congress that impressed not only aspiring Ph.D. candidates. It was a statement by E. L. Thorndike (and I paraphrase), "I am about to say something never said before at an international congress: I was wrong." This from *the* featured speaker.

During the summer of 1933 at Chicago, I learned enough about factor analysis to make me something of an expert in the eyes of some psychologists I met in New York City during my SSRC fellowship tenure at Columbia. When I returned to Stanford, I encountered, in the course of hammering out on a desk calculator a series of factor analyses on Stanford–Binet items (published in McNemar, 1942b), a couple of as yet unresolved problems: sampling errors of factor loadings and the question of when to stop factoring. This led me to an empirical study of the former (McNemar, 1941a) and a derivation of a criterion for the latter, with empirical checks (McNemar, 1942a). It is safe to say that practicing factorists paid little, if any, attention to these two papers. They were too busy being psychologists to worry about what sampling errors might do to the deification of factors. Incidentally, I patted myself on the back when I learned that a mathematical statistician (Lawley, 1942) had concurrently proposed a similar criterion, based on the variance of residuals thought of as partial correlations, but I kicked myself lower down for not having the sagacity to see, as he did, that this variance could be tested via the chi square distribution. Oh, yes, he had additional precision by allowing for the degrees of freedom for the variance estimate.

While on the topic of factor analysis, I should remark that my enthusiasm for that subject was gradually diminished by what seemed to me to be anything but clear-cut results from its applications by every Tom, Dick, and Harry who happened to have available a table of intercorrelations (or file data for computing such a table). Even the few who developed a factor research program, maybe with hypotheses, were producing results that were too often just plain fuzzy.

My skepticism led me to a careful analysis of seventy-three (all I could locate) factor studies that had been reported in the literature during ten years, 1941–1950. What I found was an astonishing batch of nonsensical doings, which I subsumed under ten headings and which provided the basis for some fun in my presidential address, "The Factors in Factoring Behavior" (McNemar, 1951a), before the Psychometric Society in 1951. Since I had great admiration and respect for Thurstone, I was somewhat worried about his reaction as I spoke. Afterward, his wife Thelma whispered to me that Leon was tickled pink by my address because I was saying many critical things that he had wished to say.

Now back to the 1933–1934 year at Columbia. I accumulated pages of notes on the stat literature but despaired because so much of the stuff was mathematically over my head. In the literature, I found frequent references to a monograph by R. A. Fisher entitled "The Mathematical Foundation of Theoretical Statistics" (Fisher, 1922). I acquired a copy and soon found my bonehead against a wall of mathematics. I went to Hotelling for help, with the hope that he could bring it down to my level. It was a relief, but not an edification, to hear him say he had gone to England to get a first-hand explanation from Fisher.

In retrospect, that SSRC fellowship period is still full of

surprises. The $2,800 was stretched for travel from and back to California, summers at Chicago and Ann Arbor, the academic year in New York (during which time Olga acquired an M.A.—$300 for tuition—from Columbia with Carney Landis), and $350 for a used car (a most comfortable, air-cooled Franklin with a propensity for burning out connecting rod bearings). How did we do it? A sleeping room, with break-fast kitchen privileges, on Broadway near 104th Street. Eating at the nearby Automat, with an occasional splurge for a com-plete (55 cents each) dinner at Child's. This lean living re-duced my 6' 3" body to a lean 144 pounds.

That fellowship year was a godsend for me upon my re-turn to Stanford: the dire effect of departmental inbreeding had been stalled by the fact that I had received training elsewhere. Actually, I was stepping into the vacancy, still un-filled, created by Kelley's departure for Harvard. I made up for my lack of Kelley's brilliance by developing a knack for simplification in the classroom and in statistical advising. (Af-ter all, I had learned the hard way.)

The 1933–1934 year did not end my contacts with mathematical statisticians. A small stipend from SSRC for work on sampling in psychological research (McNemar, 1940b) permitted me to spend the autumn of 1938 at Prince-ton, where I hoped to pick the brain of Sam Wilks, who had a reputation for being able to descend from the lofty mathemat-ical clouds to the level of the practical guy. He had published two papers (Wilkes, 1931; Wilkes, 1932) on "matched" sam-ples, and I had developed a simple algebraic derivation that showed that the degree of correlation between matched pairs, needed in the standard error of the difference formula, would equal the square of the correlation between the experimental and matching variables. Not being sure of my derivation, I asked Sam to look it over. His quick response: "Okay. Why didn't I think of that?" At another time, he whacked me down on an intuitive deduction: "You cannot rely on intuition in mathematics."

In 1949–1950, I spent a sabbatical year at Columbia in an effort to retool my statistics in the best (at that time) stat de-partment in the United States. Hotelling had departed for North Carolina, but the department was populated by such lights as Ted Anderson, Henry Scheffé, Abraham Wald, and

Jack Wolfowitz. I was extended the privilege of auditing courses.

Scheffé was then developing a course on the analysis of variance, which effort, I deduce, led to his definitive book on that topic (Scheffé, 1959). Wolfowitz, in a course on correlation, kept making cracks, with sort of an apology to a "visiting eminent professor of education" (me), about the misuses of correlation. Having had my fill, I nabbed him one night after class only to discover that he was fairly ignorant of usage. He seemed to welcome the corrections, and thereafter I found myself at his side after class, trudging the cold and snowy streets of Morningside Heights. He was high-strung and needed to unwind after lecturing. Wolfowitz was a high-powered statistical theoretician, but his lectures left the students asking each other, "How in the heck does one apply this stuff?"

In contrast, each of Wald's lectures on design was an exemplar of clarity, delivered without notes and with ample blackboard usage. I had just gone through a little controversy involving my note on Latin squares (McNemar, 1951b). In a three-way correspondence, Wendel ("Tex") Garner and I were battling David Grant, and there was a rumor from the Pacific Northwest that Allen Edwards was going to sink McNemar. When Wald presented and discussed the model for the Latin square design, I asked about the omission—indeed nonmention—of interaction terms. He impatiently snapped, as though I should know, "Oh, they are assumed to be zero." (Which I had claimed in my note.) Students in the class, sensing my apparent embarrassment, informed me that Wald, perhaps in Old World tradition, did not want interruptions from the floor. I mention this incident as a reminder that, in statistical model writing, what is specifically included and what is unspecifically and specifically excluded are the terms that definitely restrict valid usage.

When Albert Bowker arrived at Stanford in 1947, he scanned the existing faculty personnel for possible inclusion in an emerging Department of Mathematical Statistics. (There had been a committee, on which I had served, for administering a doctoral minor in statistics.) It was a surprise and an honor to receive a courtesy appointment in the new department. At least, I felt free to pester the "basic" chaps with grubby questions about applications. As the department grew, I learned that some members were pure mathematical types who couldn't care less: they were *mathematicians*. Even those who were inclined to applications seemed unable to look for simple approaches. For instance, when I wrote my first of two notes (McNemar, 1957) on the Wilson distribution-free test for analysis-of-variance hypotheses, I succeeded only in pointing out, by seven numerical examples, that something was fundamentally wrong with the test. A year later, I spotted a fallacy so unbelievably simple (see McNemar, 1958b) that I sought out a member of the stat faculty, who had also been concerned about Wilson's test, to check on my reasoning. The response: "Correct. Why didn't that occur to me?"

My faculty membership in the stat department has had an amusing and deflating aspect. As per Stanford practice, my name appears at the top of the faculty listing in stat as a "professor emeritus." It has been reported to me that faculty newcomers to the statistics department have asked, "Who in the hell is McNemar?"

When I first taught elementary and so-called advanced statistics, I encountered a paucity of satisfactory textbooks. Kelley was much too difficult (Kelley, 1924), and the others were too cookbookish. Convinced that, without a text, the scramble of note-taking during lectures was a deterrent to learning, I supplied the students with a set of succinct notes. As frequently happens, this syllabus-type effort eventually evolved into a textbook, *Psychological Statistics* (McNemar, 1949), which appeared in 1949, and later, with much needed revisions (1955, 1962, and 1969). This venture was better received than I had anticipated.

Not surprisingly, a few things I have done emerged from consulting situations. As a statistical adviser to Terman and Merrill on the 1937 revision of the Stanford–Binet, I was asked, and given a free hand, to analyze the files of data that had accumulated on the standardization group. The results were published in 1942 (McNemar, 1942b). As a "consultant to the Secretary of War" (whom, of course, I never met), from 1941 to 1944, I was early involved with Sam Stouffer on the problem of soldier morale. My main contribution to this effort was persuading Carl Hovland to join the group, thereby shifting his career interest from learning to social psychology.

When he began considering before–after designs with dichotomous (or binary) dependent variables, I hit upon the needed formula for the standard error of the difference between correlated proportions (McNemar, 1947). This minor discovery was not nearly so surprising as the fact that it had not been found before.

My contacts with Stouffer's group led directly to my 1946 monograph-length critique of opinion–attitude methodology (McNemar, 1946). This paper, which has had a gratifyingly large distribution, was prompted by some who had become skeptical about claims being made that the morale group's work would have marked fallout effects on social science. It was hoped that I could provide an objective framework against which the claimed contribution could be evaluated, then appraise the then (early 1944) available army studies. Let me hasten to say that the later published books on the American soldier, by Stouffer, Hovland, et al., did bear out the optimistic claims.

My various stints (1948–1968) as a consultant to the Veterans Administration, the Office of Naval Research, the National Science Foundation, the National Institute of Mental Health, and the U.S. Office of Education were, in general, satisfying to my ego. My role in the VA was that of statistical-methodology adviser on research projects. Two observations may be in order. First, the earlier the chance to advise, the more beneficial to the advisee (and the more satisfying to the adviser). Attempts to salvage data based on faulty design are not rewarding. Second, the going consultant pay was then $50 per day or a fraction thereof, but my puritanical upbringing led me to question whether, say, two hours of consulting plus twenty minutes of travel was sufficient for a day's pay. So I simply submitted two half-day visits as one day, a practice that annoyed some fellow consultants. Why? I don't know, but I did and still do feel that a certain San Francisco Bay Area professor who regularly collected pay for seven days a month (no weekend consulting) was taking advantage of either his university or the taxpayer or both. Perhaps it would not have been so galling to me had he not been so loud in mouthing social and liberal causes, or was this a smoke screen for liberally helping himself?

My consultantship with the other governmental organizations had to do with evaluating grant applications. In retrospect, my days with ONR, NSF, and NIMH were heady doings for a one-time hillbilly, in that the panels I served on dealt out millions of dollars for research. During my time on these panels, the remunerative policies of NSF differed from the other two in that NSF atypically allowed three days' pay for homework prior to each meeting, a practice that likely resulted in more and/or better homework than was accomplished for ONR and NIMH. Actually, I usually needed far more than three days for a couple of reasons: frequent lack of content knowledge of research areas, and the realization that the panel members had come to rely on me to evaluate the statistical aspects of research proposals. In general, the panel members I served with were conscientious, objective, and tough but fair-minded. I can recall no instance of an agency representative not following his panel's recommendations. I hope that the current squawks about the government spending too much for consultants is not generalized to include NSF and NIH, both of which, in my opinion, are getting excellent value for the consultant dollars.

Now to the teaching function. As mentioned earlier, when I was faced with what seemed at the time to be a binary choice—farming or teaching—I opted for the latter. When I entered graduate school, my goal was to teach at the college level, but I soon realized that my less naive fellow graduate students had aspirations for university jobs. Though I raised my sights a bit, it never occurred to me that I might qualify for a major-league position. It was some time before I realized that getting ahead involved more than teaching.

I was given two tries at teaching introductory psychology. A flop! Introductory statistics? Well, I have kidded myself into believing that I did, over some thirty-five years, an above-average classroom job, even though the students' math backgrounds varied from the two-year high school level to, and including, calculus. Typically, a similar range in math training held for the graduate students in my two so-called advanced stat courses. This sad sitaution may remain hopeless at the undergraduate level, but could be alleviated at the graduate level by simply requiring calculus for admission. Aside from aiding the learning of statistics, such a requirement should not handicap the student as a future scientist, if that be his or her goal.

The teaching business went fairly smoothly. Yet I always had a queasy feeling at the first meeting of a new class. Twice I encountered open hostility. One time, with the influx of GI students following World War II, I found myself faced with a graduate class of ninety, much too large for the necessary blackboard work and for the individual help some students need in statistics courses. Many members in this particular class were highly competitive and combative. A storm of protests occurred when I passed back their midterm quiz papers—challenges not only to the assistant's grading, but also about my questions. I called the papers back, spent hours regrading them, found a correlation in the .90s with the assistant's grading, returned the papers, and gave the class a rather stern lecture to the effect that I would tolerate no further bellyaching.

The second instance occurred during my 1965–1970, post-Stanford retirement tenure at the University of Texas in Austin. In one class, also graduate level, there were a few students who never could come to believe that statistics should have anything to do with their training to become clinical psychologists. This malady had affected some students at Stanford, but at Texas it was exacerbated by the general student protesting during the late 1960s. The anguish imposed on me was somewhat alleviated by an influx of some bright students from the School of Education (educational psychology) who found my teaching more palatable than that in their own department.

My role in another area began in 1941, when Maud Merrill and I edited a volume of research papers by former students of L. M. Terman in his honor. Some time later, Donald Paterson invited me to serve on the editorial board of the *Journal of Applied Psychology,* in which capacity I served under four of his successors (Jack Darley, Ken E. Clark, Ed Fleishman, and John Campbell). This time span may not be a record, but my 98 percent rejection rate likely is. Lest any reader convert that 98 percent to the bad end of an S.O.B. scale, he should consider the likelihood that the editors were passing on to me the worst manuscripts. (I would hate to think that worse ones existed.) The rejectees may not agree that my recommendations helped maintain standards, but I am sure that a sizable number of them received from me a lesson in practical statistics. I also served on the editorial board of *Psychometrika* from its beginning (1936) until 1965, by which time that journal was passing me up mathematically.

In 1953, C. P. Stone (perhaps recalling that poorly written introductory paragraph for a joint-authored paper, mentioned earlier) asked me to become the associate editor of the *Annual Review of Psychology*. Here the task was entirely different in that there was no rejection of manuscripts authored by those who had been invited by the editorial committee to prepare chapters. My allotment contained a few that needed a lot of rewriting. Some required a lot of library work to check on what seemed to be (and frequently was) faulty reporting. As to questions on written exposition, I received much help from Olga. Following Stone's death, Paul Farnsworth became editor, and soon thereafter Olga was brought aboard as an associate editor. (I vigorously deny that husband–wife nepotism was involved in her appointment, and I shout to the world that she was better qualified than I.) From then on, two-thirds of the manuscripts had the benefit of the efforts of both of us.

While on the topic of editing, I feel compelled to report what I found a few years ago when I made a search of some twenty psych journals (APA and others, "hard" and "soft," first third of the 1970 decade) for possible examples of faulty statistical usage that might be assembled, in brief form, as a sort of "What's wrong with this?" booklet of statistical exercises. (For a title, I toyed with "STAT: DAT DON'T, DAT DO" or "STIX: NIX, FIX.") Our editors would be amazed at the many examples I found, ranging from elementary to complex.

Job-wise, my career was at Stanford, with a few exceptions. During 1937–1938, I taught in the Department of Educational Psychology at Fordham University (Woolworth Building "campus"). This was a pleasant year, especially because we could afford to indulge in some of the cultural advantages of New York City. That year had an amusing aftermath: Some years later, correspondence with psychologists at a "Big 10" Midwestern state university was such that I definitely expected the next mail to bring a job offer. It did not materialize, and months later via the grapevine I was to learn why. A "power" in the department had put two facts together: McNemar has a "Mc" name and he taught at Fordham. Ergo, he is a Catholic, and we don't want a Catholic. So I was axed by a false deduction and a prejudice.

I spent the years 1941–1943 (plus the winter of 1944) on the staff of the Social Science Research Council, with the fellowship program and grants-in-aid as my major responsibility. For three successive seasons, I interviewed almost all of the fellowship applicants, then had some fun outguessing tentative committee decisions before tossing in my bit. Unbelievable as it may sound, the experience of those years was to boost my self-confidence, still lagging at age forty-one. In addition to the advantages of being in New York City again, this period gave Olga the opportunity to pursue graduate study at Columbia to the point that, during our next stay (1949–1950) she attained the doctorate, thereby competing for the record as to length of time between A.B. and Ph.D. And before she had completed her dissertation, I had learned a lot about critical flicker fusion, a topic about which I had been totally ignorant. I have already mentioned my stay at the University of Texas, 1965–1970, after Stanford kicked me out because of old age. Pleasant five years, intellectually and financially rewarding.

In closing this narrative, I wish to become more personal and mention a few of the satisfying aspects of my career and life. (Self-appraisal can delude the self!) I have reasons for believing that many students benefited from my stat courses. I know that, as a member of dissertation committees, I have sometimes had a greater impact than the content-area chairmen. It would be easy to give the names of Stanford Ph.D.'s who later swung away from their dissertation-major area to statistics and/or measurement.

I am too realistic to think that I have made any major contributions to knowledge. Perhaps some minor ones. I can say that I never had a manuscript rejected, though it nearly happened once when an editorial consultant to *Psychometrika* said I was wrong on a basic point. It took me years to hit upon an algebraic proof that I was right, with the result that a record (?) five years elapsed between "Manuscript received" and "Revised manuscript received" (McNemar, 1958a).

The honor of being elected as the 1964 President of the American Psychological Association was as much a surprise to me as it was to a few of my detractors. Audience reaction to my presidential address (McNemar, 1964) was gratifying, as is the fact that this address has been included in fifteen books of readings and has appeared in a French translation (McNemar, 1965). My criticism, in that address, of some of the test doings at the Psychological Corporation nearly cost me some warm friendships but perhaps resulted in my becoming a member of its board of directors.

A life of all work and no play? At times, yes, but Olga and I have had the fun of a considerable amount of traveling. Forty-nine of the states, plus two trips to Canada and five deep into Mexico, all by car. Six weeks each in South America and in Africa; around the world in fifty days; and four sojourns in Europe for a total of sixty-six weeks, all but four of those weeks by car. Itching for more!

Leisure-time activities? Hooked on bridge playing until it was infringing on work time. Tennis until an elbow problem. Gardening until age slowed stooping. Reading and reading. Enjoy theater, opera, and symphonic music, despite not knowing a sharp from a flat. Actually, I have often been moved to tears by classical music. Perhaps, down deep, I have always had a stratum of soft sentimentality.

1977

Selected Publications by Quinn McNemar

Twin resemblances in motor skills, and the effect of practice thereon. *J. genet. Psychol.*, 1933, *42*, 70–99.

(with L. M. Terman) Sex differences in variational tendency. *Genet. Psychol. Monogr.*, 1936, *18* (1), 1–65.

Special review [of] Newman, Freeman, and Holzinger's Twins: a study of heredity and environment. *Psychol. Bull.*, 1938, *35*, 237–249.

A critical examination of the University of Iowa studies of environmental influences upon the IQ. *Psychol. Bull.*, 1940a, *37*, 63–92.

Sampling in psychological research. *Psychol. Bull.*, 1940b, *37*, 331–365.

On the sampling errors of factor loadings. *Psychometrika*, 1941a, *6*, 141–152.

Terman–McNemar test of mental ability, forms C and D, and manual. Yonkers: World Book, 1941b.

On the number of factors. *Psychometrika*, 1942a, *7*, 9–18.

The revision of the Stanford–Binet scale. Boston: Houghton Mifflin, 1942b.

The mode of operation of suppressant variables. *Amer. J. Psychol.*, 1945, *58*, 554–555.

Opinion–attitude methodology. *Psychol. Bull.*, 1946, *43*, 289–374.

Sampling error of the difference between correlated proportions or percentages. *Psychometrika*, 1947, *12*, 153–157.

Psychological statistics. New York: Wiley, 1949 (Rev. eds., 1955, 1962, 1969).

The factors in factoring behavior. *Psychometrika*, 1951a, *16*, 353–359.

On the use of Latin squares in psychology. *Psychol. Bull.*, 1951b, *48*, 398–401.

On Wilson's distribution-free test of analysis of variance hypotheses. *Psychol. Bull.*, 1957, *54*, 361–362.

Attenuation and interaction. *Psychometrika*, 1958a, *23*, 259–265.

More on the Wilson test. *Psychol. Bull.*, 1958b, *55*, 334–335.

On growth measurement. *Educ. psychol. Measmt.*, 1958c, *18*, 47–55.

Lost: our intelligence? Why? *Amer. Psychologist*, 1964, *19*, 871–882.

Perdue, notre intelligence? Pourquoi? *Rev. Psychol. appl.*, 1965, *15*(1), 1–23.

Moderation of a moderator technique. *J. appl. Psychol.*, 1969, *53*, 69–72.

On so-called test bias. *Amer. Psychologist*, 1975, *30*, 848–851.

Other Publications Cited

Coover, J. E. *Experiments in psychical research*. Stanford: Stanford University Press, 1917.

Fisher, R. A. On the mathematical foundation of theoretical statistics. *Philosophical Trans., Royal Soc. London*, 1922(A), *80*, 309–368.

Kelley, T. L. *Statistical method*. New York: Macmillan, 1924.

Lawley, D. N. Further investigations in factor estimation. *Proc. Royal Soc. Edinburgh*, 1942, *61*, 176–185.

Scheffé, H. *The analysis of variance*. New York: Wiley, 1959.

Wilks, S. S. The standard error of the means in "matched" samples. *J. educ. Psychol.*, 1931, *22*, 205–208.

Wilks, S. S. On the distribution of statistics in samples from a normal population of two variables with matched sampling on one variable. *Metron*, 1932, *9*, 87–126.

Charles E. Osgood

Charles E. Osgood

Following the habits of a lifetime, I had assumed that even one's autobiography must have a title. After some debate with my alter ego, I settled on *Focus on Meaning: In Individual Humans, Across Human Cultures, and for Survival of the Human Species.* The first line I wrote was, "This title may seem a bit dramatic, but it does capture what have been the three major themes of my professional life." And so it does, as I hope the following autobiographical sketch will demonstrate.

MUDDLING THROUGH CHILDHOOD

I was born in Sommerville, Massachusetts, a suburb of Boston, on November 20, 1916, to Merrill White Osgood and Ruth Madeline Egerton—as the names suggest, coming from old New England stock. We moved almost immediately to an upstairs apartment in Alston, Massachusetts (another suburb of Boston), where we stayed for my first six years of life—a period about which I have only the vaguest memories and near the end of which my parents were divorced. The arrangement was that I would live with my mother in Brookline (yet another suburb of Boston) most of the school year, spending every other weekend and the summers with my father—but, as it turned out, my summers were mostly spent at Camp Becket in the Berkshires. The point where young Charlie was "traded off" between his mother and father was an old building on Commonwealth Avenue, where both my Grandfather O (dentist) and my Uncle Herman O (X-ray specialist) had their offices.

Both my mother and my father were remarried within a year or so—mother to an occulist, who died a few years later, and father to a woman from Providence whom I always called "Brownie." Except for a half-brother via father and "Brownie," I was an only child, and on my weekend visits I felt more like a rather unwelcome guest than a member of the family; the saving grace was my Aunt Grace O, who was really my only confidante. She was then a student at Wellesley College, heading for a teaching career at Thayer Academy, and living with her parents near my father's house in Wollaston, Massachusetts. The occasional weeks at Lake Sunnappee, New Hampshire, where my Grampa and Gramma O and Auntie Grae had a summer cottage, were the happiest of my young life. Otherwise, right up through high school, my life seemed to be one continuous shuttle from place to place and from people to people (I must have gone to no less than four grammar schools in Brookline as my mother kept changing apartments)—all of which may explain why I have always been sort of a "loner," uneasy with people on a purely social basis, but easy with people on a task-oriented basis (something I got from my father, who, at a very young age, became business manager of Jordan Marsh, the largest department store in Boston).

INTRODUCING MY ALTER EGO

To enliven the monotonous parade of first person pronouns (*I*'s, *me*'s, *mine*'s, and *my*'s) in an inevitably personal document, an introspective little dinosaur (there were little dinosaurs, you know) will be a main character in this story. Not only will this serve as a reminder that we shouldn't take ourselves *too* seriously, but I was to discover that I *was* a kind of dinosaur!*

The baby dinosaur teethed on meaning during those visits to Lake Sunnappee by his Grampa O, a graduate of Harvard University in the 1880s who was a successful dentist but had always wished to become a college professor. He played all kinds of word games with baby Dino, feeding him rare words and then giving him pennies to buy jelly beans when he used these words spontaneously and correctly in sentences. Auntie Grae was a participant–observer in these little games, sometimes lending a helping hand behind the scenes, and on Dino's tenth birthday, she gave him Roget's *Thesaurus*—perhaps to even the odds a bit with Grampa O! He remembers spending hours and hours exploring the *Thesaurus*—not as a tool then but as an object of aesthetic pleasure—and he repeatedly had vivid dreams about multicolored, jelly-bean-like, word-points distributed in clusters all about an endless space. During weekend visits to his father's home, Dino picked up his first hobby, Hobby I: devouring all of the fantasy, horror, and science fiction he could lay his hands on—an appetite acquired from his father and appeased during long morning hours in the attic while everyone else was asleep.

AN AWAKENING AT BROOKLINE HIGH

Brookline High School in the early 1900s was acknowledged to be one of the top public high schools in the country (and maybe it still is). My memories of the first two years there are pretty dim. I had a marvelous teacher for Spanish (the only language I can still handle a bit, with some warm-up) as well as a dedicated young lady in English Literature, and I did beauti-

---

*In this autobiography, I must draw heavily on the version of "Exploration in Semantic Space: A Personal Diary" that appeared in *The Psychologists*, Vol. 2, T. S. Krawiec, ed. (Osgood, 1974), and on "A Dinosaur Caper: Psycholinguistics Past, Present, and Future," an invited address at a New York Academy of Science conference (Osgood, 1975b), both of which were autobiographical in nature.

fully in geometry (with my highly visual mind) but terribly in algebra. My father died, when I was sixteen, of stomach cancer at the age of only thirty-nine, but since I was at camp, the Osgoods didn't bother to bring me to the funeral.

In the third year at Brookline High, our young dinosaur came wide-awake: He became editor of both the weekly newspaper and the monthly magazine—founding the latter and becoming its most frequent contributor! Wealthy Grampa Egerton (supporter of his daughter and grandson) contributed a second-hand Royal #10, on which Dino soon became skilled at typing reporter-style with a few fingers and the thumbs of both hands (this, by the way, was the same machine that, many years later, was to write my *Method and Theory in Experimental Psychology*). Beginning with horror stories about oozy monsters rising from the crypts of ancient castles and armies of giant ants sweeping the earth, he then turned to more psychodynamic themes—about his own budding romances and the strangely puritanical ways of the Egerton family. (In one true-to-life scene, Grampa E gives his daughter holy hell for leaving the shaker with leftover soap chips soaking in the hot dishwater!)

Needless to say, Auntie Grae's *Thesaurus* came in very handy here. I collected my full share of rejection slips from editors of short-story magazines, a few of which I prize because they were intimate and encouraging. The summers at Harvard, Massachusetts (Grampa E's lovely home), and at Camp Becket were very different now: In the summer of 1934 (in Harvard), with my Aunt Bea as pianist, I designed and directed a minstrel show (and played as one of the end men), which was very successful in that little community (and had old Grampa and Gramma E laughing themselves fit to die). In the summer of 1935, along with Larry Hayford (who could not only play a mean piano but also read and write music), I directed the camp jazz band and even composed some pieces for it. A couple of years later, when I had become a counselor (tent "leader") at Camp Becket, I composed and produced a musical comedy with Larry, which, having been kicked out of camp for smoking on the sly a few days before the performance, I had to get special permission to sneak in and see!

The Setting of My Three Themes

In the late summer of 1935, young Dino traveled north to Hanover, New Hampshire, riding along in a little truck that was carrying a few bits of furniture, the faithful Royal #10, and some clothes and things. I don't exactly know how he managed to get admitted to Dartmouth College, but Gay Gleason (Grampa E's lawyer and a Dartmouth graduate) had a lot to do with it. Anyhow, young Dino went off to college convinced that he was destined to become, not a dinosaur, but a newspaperman and a novelist—and maybe a composer on the side!

THE FORMATIVE YEARS AT DARTMOUTH, 1935–1940

The notion of a concept-studded semantic space lay dormant until I had been at Dartmouth for a couple of years. My original plan was to get experience working on the campus newspaper while studying English literature and creative writing; then I would support myself by newspaper editorial and feature writing, while creating The Great American Novel. But during my sophomore year—after I'd spent some time trailing American Youth in a massive baby-raccoon coat, a hand-me-down from Grampa E (if you can imagine a dinosaur so attired), as a date-less reporter of the winter carnivals and spring proms for the *Daily Dartmouth*—I happened to take Introductory Psychology from Professor Charles Stone. Then came the real eye-opener—an advanced course with Professor Theodore Karwoski, later to be affectionately known on campus as "The Count" (for me, he soon became just "Ted"). I had found in psychology just what I didn't know I'd been looking for—the right combination of demand for rigor and room for creativity—and I forgot about writing The Great American Novel.

Ted Karwoski was a most remarkable person—quietly insightful, capable of thinking simultaneously on several levels and moving freely among them, warmly supportive of students from whom he felt a returning spark—and thoroughly disorderly! Although I didn't realize it at the time, Karwoski became for me the intellectual goad that Grampa Osgood had been and the intimate confidant that my father had never been. At the point when I moved into his life, Karwoski was doing casual experiments on color–music synesthesia—along with Henry (Hank) Odbert, a fresh Harvard Ph.D. and co-author, with his mentor Gordon Allport, of "Trait-Names: A Psycho-lexical Study." More importantly, Karwoski was thinking deeply about the implications of synesthesia for human cognition generally. Others at Dartmouth who were influential on my life were: Chaucey (Chintz) Allen, with whom I produced my first published paper; Irving (Irve) Bender, a warmly supportive person in personality and social psychology; and, later, the man who was to nurture my concerns with social issues, Ross Stagner. It would be hard to imagine an intellectual environment better suited to a young dinosaur with visions of semantic sugarplums in his head!

Out of my apprenticeship with these men—an undergraduate apprenticeship much more intimate and exciting than most graduate students in these crowded days are likely to enjoy—came five studies. One on appeals in advertising was published while I was still an undergraduate (Osgood, Allen, and Odbert, 1939), and the others were published during my years at Yale: one on synesthestic thinking (Karwoski, Odbert, and Osgood, 1942), one on scaling that anticipated the semantic differential (SD) technique (Osgood and Stagner, 1941b), one with Stagner that anticipated both the SD technique and my concern about international relations, with U.S. involvement in World War II just over the horizon (Stagner and Osgood, 1941), and one under my very own name, titled "Ease of Individual Judgment-processes in Relation to Polarization of Attitudes in the Culture" (Osgood, 1941a). I was pursuing a minor in anthropology under Professor Robert McKenna, and my undergraduate thesis at Dartmouth (I think the undergraduate thesis should be a more common procedure) combined laboratory studies of visual/auditory–verbal synesthesia with an attempt to determine the generality of such parallelisms across cultures, using firsthand ethnographic reports. Much of this early work at Dartmouth is summarized in Osgood, Suci, and Tannenbaum (1957c, pp. 20–25). A later paper of my own, "The Cross-cultural Generality of Visual–

Verbal Synesthetic Tendencies" (1960c), carries this strand along a bit further.

My undergraduate thesis was a fusion of Theme I (Meaning in Individual Humans) and Theme II (Meaning Across Human Cultures) of my professional life, and my work with Ross Stagner on nationalistic frames of reference was in anticipation of Theme III (Meaning for Survival of the Human Species). So, clearly, the major themes of my entire professional life had been set in motion during my undergraduate experience—and I've often wondered whether this is a fairly common or a rather unusual experience.

On June 27, 1939, soon after graduation from Dartmouth—and contrary to predictions of many Hanoverites about relations between students and towngirls—I married Cynthia Luella Thornton, a very attractive young lady who used to trot by my rooming house on her way to high school during our junior and senior years. We spent the following year in Hanover in a tiny little house next to an old country graveyard—a kind of intermezzo during which I served as everything from research associate to mimeograph operator in the psychology department and got used to being married. This is when I did much of my work with Ross Stagner. But it was also a very happy year, with parties 'till dawn and dancing on the lawn (beside the graveyard!) to jazz records from my collection—my Hobby II, which had been rapidly expanding during the Dartmouth years. Hobby I (science fiction) also had been intensifying during these years, along with yet another, Hobby III—playing jazz piano, composing jazz tunes, and also composing and playing a few rather Debussyan nocturnes, which Hank Odbert very kindly transcribed into readable music.

THE WAR YEARS AT YALE (AND ELSEWHERE), 1940–1946

The research and the prepublication papers I already had under my belt led to offers of research assistant positions at both Harvard (under Gordon Allport) and Yale (under Robert R. Sears). I don't recall now just what my reasons were, but I chose Yale—undoubtedly a major choice-point in my life. I was Bob Sears' RA and, for two years, was the "observer" behind a one-way mirror while high school students, with histories of either success or failure, played a dart game with Bob (in which they either "beat the Ohio high school record" or did so poorly they never even got on the graph!) and then were left alone, for five minutes or so, to rehearse the game, jab darts into the faces of Hitler and Mussolini, or just daydream. I also got swept up, just like everyone else, into the monumental edifice of learning theory that Clark L. Hull was building. I had the heady feeling that here, with appropriate elaborations designed to bring *meaning* to the fore, lay the key to even the most complex human behaviors, including language and social behavior generally. Visions of semantic space (Theme II) receded, but the problem of dealing with meaning in learning theory terms (Theme I) came to the fore.

My doctoral thesis, titled "Meaningful Similarity and Interference in Learning," was designed both to resolve the Similarity Paradox in the retroaction paradigm (A − B; A − X; A − B, where the A stimuli were nonsense letter-pairs and the B/X responses were adjectives having similar, neutral, or opposed meanings) and to demonstrate that meaning can be brought into the behavior laboratory (Osgood, 1946, 1948, and 1949 were all spin-offs from my thesis). I owe debts of gratitude to Donald Marquis (technically, my thesis director, but away in Washington much of the time) for keeping my interest in language alive, to Irvin Child for day-to-day critiquing as the writing of the thesis progressed, and to Charles Morris, who came to Yale as a Visiting Professor just in time to help me defend it.

During the years at Yale, I also worked with Walter Miles (doing some intriguing, even if never published, studies on shifts in meaning while observing the Miles' Kinephantoscope and the "filling in" of meaning of faint points of light to create lines, or squares, or faces) and with Arnold Gesell (even making a wire-tape recording of the first-year-of-life vocal expressions of our first child). I profited mightily from the exciting "Blue Room" sessions atop the Institute of Human Relations (in which the psychology department was housed), where extentions of Hullian learning theory into linguistics (Bloomfield and others), anthropology (Malinowski and others), language

(Mowrer and others), and social behavior (Miller, Dollard, Sears, and many others) were the main themes.

But the Yale years were also the war years. By 1943, many of the faculty were on leave in Washington, D.C., much of the time, and, as a third-year graduate student, the youthful dinosaur (who had never taught a course in his life) suddenly found himself teaching *all* of the introductory psychology course at Yale—two large lecture sections (one for regular Yalies, another for Navy V-12 students) and eight smaller discussion sections on the Thursday and Friday of each week. Dino was always just one little hop and skip ahead of the students, and since he was younger than many of the V-12's, he generated the little mustache that you can still see today—if you look closely enough. But his science-fiction, record-collecting, and jazz-playing/composing hobbies were still elaborating during these years. And his first small jazz combo—including Don Marquis on clarinet, Marve Herbert on trumpet, Al Pepitone on sax (I think), one or two others I can't recall, and ole' Dino himself on key-of-F piano by ear—used to get together every once in a while for a session in his little house in Short Beach, just northeast of New Haven.

I was also just a little hop, skip, and jump ahead of the draft board—first by one child (Philip Thornton Osgood, February 10, 1941) and then by another (Gail Ruth Osgood, July 31, 1943) when one wouldn't do. When no number of children would do as an excuse, I was teaching Navy V-12's, and at last when *nothing* would do, I had my Ph.D. and was whisked off to the Smoky Hill Army Air Force (SHAAF) base in Salina, Kansas, by Bob Sears and Wolfe Brogden to do research as a civilian on one of the projects out of the Office of Scientific Research and Development (OSRD).

Herein lies a tale of frustrated experimental genius (!) that I can only highlight here: Don Purdy (long-held Ph.D.), Bert Knauft (en route to Ph.D.), and Charlie Osgood (fresh Ph.D.) were that part of the Brogden–Sears project that was supposed to train B-29 gunners to hit the target (incoming attack planes on typically S-curved flights) by adjusting the size-of-frame/direction variables of their sights—these adjustments, via computer, remotely controlling each of eight (as I recall) rapid-fire guns on the B-29. We used cameras on each sight to evaluate gunner performance, but we found little relation between performance there and performance in knocking down dummy planes in an outdoor mock-up. We came up with the idea of putting *synchronized* cameras on the computer dials and the guns, as well as the sights, and we discovered that, if the gunners performed exactly as instructed, they were practically certain *not* to hit the incoming target! On their next visit, we excitedly showed Bob and Wolfe our data on this and were told that it was, indeed, a brilliant idea, and they would immediately relay it to their team in Laredo, Texas (I think it was), which was supposed to be working on the sights/ computer/guns relations—*but that we should keep on training gunners as before, i.e., to miss targets!*

FROM YALE TO CONNECTICUT TO ILLINOIS, 1946–1949

I wish more present-day graduate students could have the experience I had—certainly not of "draft-dodging," but of *independent* teaching while still in graduate school. I think that teaching is at its best when the ideas are being freshly molded by instructor as well as instructed, and there is no better way to discover what you really don't understand than to try to teach it to someone else. After I'd done a stint at the New London Submarine Base during the winter and spring of 1946—as a statistical analyst, of all things, on a project under Bill Verplanck, studying night vision with various kinds of binoculars, telescopes, and the like—I got a most welcome job offer from Wes Bousfield, department head at the University of Connecticut in Storrs. I was to teach a graduate-level course in experimental psychology (along with a couple of undergraduate courses) to just a handful of advanced students. I combined this with writing chapters of what was to become my *Method and Theory in Experimental Psychology,* and I discovered that the same rule applies to writing textbooks as to teaching—that another good way to discover what you really don't understand is to try to write about it. During the years at Storrs, I kept very busy, and productively happy, with this combination of teaching to and writing for graduate students.

Then in the spring of 1949 came one of those academic bonanzas that all young scholars hope for: a chance for an associate professorship with tenure *and* a half-time research appointment to work on problems of one's own devising. (I must remind you that those were the days when we had many bona fide Ph.D.'s as instructors.) From faraway Illinois came a "feeler" about just such a position, along with an invitation to pay them a visit at their expense. So, onto the overnight sleeper and off to the cornfields went the youthful dinosaur. There he discovered that his old friend, Ross Stagner, and his more recent friend, Hobart Mowrer, along with a good friend-to-be, Wilbur Schramm (director of a newly established Institute of Communications Research), were looking for a young social scientist who could develop both research and teaching on the psychology of language—in short, a *psycholinguist* (although it would be several years before that title came into vogue).

Needless to say, the people at Illinois were interested to know just what I might do by way of research in their new institute—should I, in fact, be offered the position. So, back in Storrs, I began trying to put together and down on paper, first *a behavioral theory of meaning* (based on Hullian learning theory, but with a generalized representational and componential mediation twist), second *a measurement model* (based on earlier attitude scaling with Stagner, but now multidimensional in principle and tuned to what were then new developments in multivariate statistics—in which I had discovered Illinois to be a hotbed of activity, what with Lee Cronback and Ray Cattell on the scene), and third *an image of semantic space* (based on my childhood explorations of Roget's *Thesaurus* and drawn from wherever one stores such things).

My original "vision" of a space studded with clusters of variously colored concept-points was refined to specify an *origin*, defined as "meaninglessness" (analogous to the neutral gray of the color space), and to conceive of concept meanings as the end-points of *vectors* extending out into this space, with *lengths* of the vectors indicating degrees of "meaningfulness" (analogous to saturation in the color space) and with their *directions* indicating the "quality" of meaning (analogous to both

345

the brightness, vertical dispersion, and hue, horizontal dispersion about the circumference, of the three-dimensional color space). Thus, two concepts might be quite similar in quality of meaning (same general direction in the space) yet be quite different in intensity of meaning (distance from the origin), like HATRED versus ANNOYANCE; or two concepts might be equally intense in meaning, yet be very different in quality of meaning, like GOD and BEGGAR. And one could also specify adjectival opposites, like *hot* versus *cold* or *hard* versus *soft*, as points equidistant and in opposite directions from the origin of the space, with imaginary lines always connecting them through the origin—this analogous to complementary colors that, when mixed in roughly equal amounts, cancel each other out to a neutral gray (semantically, to meaninglessness).

Focus on Theory and Measurement of Meaning in Human Individuals (Theme I)

Well, I got the job at Illinois and have been there ever since. The decade of the 1950s was devoted primarily to Theme I: (1) extension of Hullian two-stage behaviorism to Osgoodian three-stage, componential neobehaviorism; (2) development of the semantic differential (SD) technique with American English-speaking subjects; and (3) involvement in the renaissance of psycholinguistics as a research field and scholarly discipline. But in this busy decade there were other and diversified activities, including, early on, finishing my graduate text, *Method and Theory in Experimental Psychology* (published in 1953), and later, research excursions in a variety of directions. There were also some first steps toward Theme II (cross-cultural studies of meaning) and some anticipations of Theme III.

EXTENSION OF HULLIAN TWO–STAGE BEHAVIORISM TO OSGOODIAN THREE–STAGE (AND COMPONENTIAL) NEOBEHAVIORISM

The evolution of behaviorism can be viewed as a series of increments in the number and complexity of the theoretical mechanisms that were put into what might be called the Little Black Egg. In revulsion against what could fairly be called the "junkshop theorizing" that characterized much of late-nineteenth-century psychology, around the turn of the century a group of American behaviorists (Watson, Weiss, Kantor, and later Skinner) went to the other extreme: *There is nothing whatsoever of behavioral relevance inside the Little Black Egg!* Such primitive single-stage ("empty organism") behaviorism not only couldn't account for symbolic processes in humans, it couldn't even handle such a simple phenomenon as secondary reinforcement in the humble rat. The classic two-stage ("mediational") behaviorism we associate with Hull and Tolman (whose versions, I tried to show in *Method and Theory* [1953], were functionally equivalent over the range of phenomena investigated) put into the Egg *a mediating process* (an "anticipatory response", $r \longrightarrow s$, for Hull and a "sign-significate expectancy" for Tolman). In effect, the S-R relation was broken into two, *separately manipulatable* associations ($S \longrightarrow r_m$ and $s_m \longrightarrow R$ in comprehending and expressing, respectively), and the explanatory/predictive power of behavior theory was greatly amplified.

In the early 1950s, as my involvement in psycholinguistics increased, I became convinced that there were two very general, and significant, insufficiencies with the two-stage models of classic behaviorism, both of which came down to the fact that the theories could only deal with S-R associations: (1) inability to handle the phenomena of *perceptual organization,* so amply documented in the literature of Gestalt psychology (e.g., the phenomenon of perceptual closure), which stressed innate determinants, but also apparent in the extensive evidence for an inverse relation between the frequency-of-usage of words and their tachistoscopic thresholds—which depends on experience; (2) inability to handle the phenomena of *behavioral organization,* the formation of central motor programs for rapid and complex skills like piano-playing and talking—as so forcefully argued by Lashley in his 1951 Nixon Symposium address. Since it is S-S learning in (1) and R-R learning in (2) that is involved, no strictly S-R theory could be sufficient.

In the mid-1950s, I postulated, on both sensory and motor sides of the equation, an *integration level* between the projection level (solely utilized by single-stage theory) and the representational level utilized as well by two-stage theories), along with a functional S-S and R-R learning principle: *The greater the frequency with which projection-level icons ($\dot{s}|\dot{s}|\dot{s}$) or motons ($\dot{r}|\dot{r}|\dot{r}$) have co-occurred in input or output experience, the greater will be the tendency for the elements of their integration-level percepts (s-s-s) or programs (r-r-r) to activate each other centrally*—i.e., a learning-theoretic basis for the acquisition of perceptual and motor skills. Despite the introduction of this extension of my version of neobehaviorism to a three-stage (level) process, with both S-S and R-R learning, in two papers two decades ago (Osgood, 1957a, 1957b), most of my behaviorist colleagues seem to have remained oblivious to it—perhaps "conceptual blindness" due to the incongruence of a Hullian behaviorist espousing S-S and R-R association principles!

In any case, this extension has made it possible to incorporate both Gestalt-like perceptual phenomena and Lashley-like motor programming phenomena. Furthermore, with what I now call the "Emic Principle" of neobehaviorism, one can account for both the functional equivalence of different signs having the same significance (e.g., constancy phenomena in perception; synonymity and paraphrasing in language) and of different programs-for-behaving expressing the same intentions (e.g., saying, "Hi there!" and offering an upward bobbing of the head to express the same "interpersonal recognition" intention). Similarly, using what I now call the "Ambiguity Principle," one can account for both the ambiguities experienced when the same percepts are near-equally associated with different significances (e.g., ambiguous figures in perception; polysemes and homonyms in language) and when different intentions are near-equally associated with the same expression (e.g., a tight-lipped smile along with shaking a fisted hand to express either a threat *or* the successful completion of an arduous task; the question, "Can you open the window?" to express either a request *or* an inquiry about the listener's competence). These matters are elaborated in a recent paper (Osgood, 1979b, in press).

Probably the most distinctive, and critical, thing about Osgoodian neobehaviorism lies in making explicit what was only implicit in Hullian behaviorism—*the componential nature of representational mediation processes*. It is critical theoretically because, if my argument is right, the *bipolar mediator components* of global mediation processes are strictly analogous to the (typically) *bipolar semantic features* of linguistic and philosophical theories of meaning—hence this is the entrée of neobehaviorism to a theory of meaning and reference and, with structuring of the representational system, ultimately to a neobehavioral theory of sentencing. The global mediation processes—r_M in comprehending, and s_M in expressing (note capital subscript M's)—are thus *summary symbols* that are exhaustively analyzable into sets of mediator components—i.e., we have (note lowercase subscript m's) $r_M = [m_1, m_2 \ldots m_i, \ldots m_n] = s_M$. In other words, just as the total behaviors made to things signified are typically a *set* of overt reactions, which together constitute an "act," so also must be the mediation processes derived from these behaviors (and now elicited by the signs of things) be a *set* of mediator components. Such components function as *distinctive semantic features,* and a shift of a single component can be sufficient to change meaning.

FUSION OF BEHAVIOR THEORY WITH MULTIVARIATE STATISTICS IN THE DEVELOPMENT OF SEMANTIC DIFFERENTIAL TECHNIQUE

The refined "vision" of semantic space that young Dino brought with him from Connecticut both lent itself naturally to factor analysis as a mathematical means of bringing order out of the chaos of lines (defined by qualifiers) and points (defined by substantives) and implied a natural method of measurement—the bipolar, seven-step, scaling procedure developed with Ross Stagner (but at that time mainly attitudinal rather than multidimensional). When a sample of *native speakers* rates a sample of *concepts* against a sample of *scales*, a cube of data is generated in which, given the definition of the bipolar scale positions

TORNADO

fair ____: ____: ____: ____: ____: ____: ____ unfair

$$+3 \quad +2 \quad +1 \quad 0 \quad -1 \quad -2 \quad -3$$

as *slightly, quite,* and *very* in both qualifying directions, each cell represents a particular kind of "sentence"—NP is Quantifier

Qualifier, here *a tornado is very unfair*—produced by a particular "speaker". In the semantic differential (SD) technique, NP's and Qualifiers keep shifting, but the type of "sentence" remains constant. (My example here deliberately produced a "sentence" that American English speakers could only use metaphorically, since only concepts coded +Human can be *unfair*, a significant point to which we'll return.) This cube of data can be factored by scales, by concepts, and by subjects, but in our early SD work we concentrated on the scale structure.

I have been accused, by some associates as well as by some dissociates, of being schizophrenic as far as my SD measurement model and my neobehavioristic theory of meaning are concerned. There is no obvious relation, they claimed, between loadings on factors and little r_M's. This was disturbing, of course, to a young dinosaur who considered himself reasonably neat and internally consistent. What the critics hadn't taken into account was the *componential nature* of the representational mediation processes in the theory. The global r_M's representing cognitively the meaning of a concept-point (e.g., COWARD) and of the termini of the scales (e.g., *kind* and *cruel*) were analyzed into (at least) the three affective E, P, and A (see below) features as bipolar r_m components—and it is these components that correspond exactly to the primary dimensions of the semantic space revealed by factor analysis. There is no claim being made here, of course, that my componential, representational mediation theory is the *only* theory of meaning that could account for the SD model and the data produced. As noted earlier, this behavioral theory of meaning is not incompatible with the views held by many linguists and philosophers, although it differs from most (all?) others in (a) its specification of *continuously graded features* as the general case, and in (b) its derivation of semantic features in the *learning history of the organism* from actual behavior toward things signified.

Aided mightily by George Suci, the first research assistant I ever had, and abetted by interested students and staff like Percy Tannenbaum, Al Heyer, and Larry O'Kelly, Dino began exploring in earnest the semantic space he'd dreamt about as a youngster. He began, of course, by demonstrating—in a *Psy-*

chological Bulletin article (Osgood, 1952a), titled most bombastically "The Nature and Measurement of Meaning"—the abject wrong-headedness and futility of all previous psychological attempts to measure that elusive thing called "meaning," and he set forth both his theory and the fragile beginnings of SD technique. Chapters 2, 3, and 4 of *The Measurement of Meaning* (Osgood, Suci, and Tannenbaum, 1957c) describe the early set of varied factor analytic studies, the rationale of the SD as a measuring instrument, and an evaluation of the technique, respectively; the remaining chapters report on its use as a generalized device for measuring attitudes and its application to research in personality and communications research.

To cut a long story very short, all three of the major factor analyses yielded nearly identical evidence for three massive factors easily identifiable as Evaluation *(good, nice, beautiful, honest, etc.)*, Potency *(strong, big, thick, tough, etc.)*, and Activity *(active, quick, excitable, hot, etc.)*. The write-up of these analyses was submitted as a paper to the *Journal of Experimental Psychology*, and it was promptly rejected by the editor. Two underlying reasons for its rejection were given: (1) that "meaning" was hardly a suitable topic for "this Journal," and (2) that experiments are supposed to be tests of hypotheses, and factor analysis can hardly be viewed as an hypothesis-testing procedure. The irritated young dinosaur gave his first defense of "meaning" as perhaps the most significant topic in human experimental psychology and of replicated factor analyses—*where the subsequent samplings from the domain are completely independent of the results obtained in prior analyses*—as hypothesis-testing of the highest order! Dino is happy to be able to report that the paper was then accepted for publication in the *Journal of Experimental Psychology* (Osgood and Suci, 1955a).

In these days, when so much of research is "administered"—which means that relatively senior people have practically nothing to do with it between the original designing and the final writing up—it is a real pleasure to look back on those days when we literally lived and breathed our research from morning to night. Dino used to be his own first guinea pig in every experiment, to try to get a seat-of-the-pants feel for what might go on in the real subjects' heads. In the midst of doing an experiment, several other experiments were always aborning—over coffee, over sandwiches and beer, and even over cocktails and dinner, much to the amusement but never irritation of our spouses. I am reminded of an enlarged photograph on the wall of my office that caught Percy Tannenbaum and myself, glasses in hand, in animated mid-flight on something or other; a caption had been appended, reading, "BUT THERE MUST BE A MEDIATION PROCESS!" And I remember one full weekend spent with Al Heyer constructing a three-dimensional distance model of colored rubber balls and wooden dowels to represent the semantic similarities among forty facial expressions of emotions. With practically no sleep, we reached that point in exhaustion where every comment, every move, every facial expression of our own would reduce us to helpless laughter. I still have that old distance model in my office, but ANGER and CYNICAL BITTERNESS have fallen off and SURPRISE has somehow gotten attached to ADORATION—by a bemused janitor, no doubt. And it wasn't all work and no play: all three of Dino's hobbies were developing nicely—science fiction and record collections (now classical as well as jazz) were expanding rapidly, and our Illinois jazz band (with Don Dulany, trumpet; Al Heyer, trombone; Stan Roscoe, saxes; Kelly Wilson, clarinet; Alex Williams, violin; Bob Grice, gut-bucket bass; Larry O'Kelly, snare drum; and Dino with his key-of-F piano) even played for a big departmental party in the Illini Union Ballroom!

In 1955, I became director of the Institute of Communications Research (a position I was to hold for a decade), Wilbur Schramm having resigned after our fine university president, George Stoddard, was fired by a pack of trustees with (of all people!) Harold "Red" Grange at the head. In the comparatively brief period from 1950 through 1955, some seventy studies—some separately published, many not—had been completed, and in the summer of 1955, Dino and family departed for their first sabbatical in Tucson, Arizona. Packed in the trunk of the second-hand Buick Roadmaster (freshly painted in Dartmouth green) was just about everything about meaning and the measurement thereof that he could lay his hands on, including all the reports of our own studies in various stages of polish.

The main job during that sabbatical year was to put into one document all the diverse things we had been doing with the monies from the University of Illinois Research Board and, later, the Social Science Research Council. As each section was drafted, it was sent to George Suci and Percy Tannenbaum—by then, my closest colleagues in this exploration—for commentary as well as for additional analyses and even new experiments that had been suggested in the course of scholarly composition. They showed copies of some early chapters to the editor of the University of Illinois Press, and he suggested making a book out of it. So *The Measurement of Meaning* was published in 1957.

To the enduring amazement of Osgood, Suci, and Tannenbaum, this little book proved to be one of the bestsellers on the list of the University of Illinois Press. It also got some solid reviewing. Psycholinguist Roger Brown ("Is a Boulder Sweet or Sour?") took us to task for not adequately defining the meaning of "meaning" we were trying to measure, but he also anticipated our cross-cultural research, observing that "just over the horizon lurks the contra-Whorfian generalization [that] the various languages of the world operate with the same basic semantic dimensions." Psychometrician Harold Guilliksen ("How to Make Meaning More Meaningful") suggested that our seven-step scales were too gross and that twenty- or even thirty-step scales would be better (though impossibly cumbersome for ordinary language users), and he also raised the bogey of concept/scale interaction (of which we were acutely aware but unable to resolve). The late linguist Uriel Weinreich ("Travels Through Semantic Space") lambasted us for claiming to offer too much for the linguist–lexicographer but in fact offering very little (our claim was minimal, but the failure to deliver was maximal, for reasons we now know) and also for claiming to measure "meaning" when we were measuring "affect" and not meaning at all. (My "Semantic Space Revisited" [1959a] was a reply to Weinreich.) And, finally, psycholinguist Jack Carroll (simply titled "The Measurement of Meaning") very fairly criticized us for choosing too grandiose a title *(THE Measurement . . .)* and for using too few concepts in our factor analyses (corrected in our later cross-cultural studies). But he concluded by characterizing our book with the kind words, "It is *good*, it is *active*, and it is *potent*."

The notion of a quantifiable semantic space apparently caught the imagination of others—perhaps because it offered at least the possibility of measuring some important aspects of a very important variable in human affairs—and the two decades since its publication have witnessed a minor explosion of studies about or applying the SD technique. *Semantic Differential Technique: A Sourcebook,* edited by Snider and Osgood and published in 1969, appends a bibliography of nearly 1,500 items, and by now it must be at least double that number. However, I must confess that sometimes I feel like the Geppetto of a wayward Pinocchio who has wandered off into the Big City, and Lord only knows what mischief he is getting into. Some people think Pinocchio is a specific standardized test (he is not, of course, necessarily being modified for every particular application and being subject to concept/scale interaction); others think he is a measure of meaning-in-general (he is not, reflecting primarily affective meaning by virtue of the metaphorical use of his scales). However, in 1960, Geppetto received one of the APA's awards for distinguished scientific contribution to psychology, and it was based primarily on his research into the nature and measurement of meaning: his 1962 address in appreciation of this honor (Osgood, 1962d) was titled "Studies on the Generality of Affective Meaning Systems."

THE RENAISSANCE OF PSYCHOLINGUISTICS IN THE 1950s

The pre-1950 history of relations between linguists and psychologists concerned with language could be characterized as having been largely nil or contentious—witness the exchanges between linguist Paul and psychologist Wundt around the turn of the century (as described by Blumenthal in 1970). During the early 1950s, however, there was a drawing together of descriptive linguists and behaviorally inclined psychologists on a more cooperative, interactive basis. Olmstead and Moore, in 1952, and John B. Carroll, in 1953, both called for this development. Looking back after a quarter of a century, I began my "Dinosaur Caper" address (1975b) by saying that "my theme for psycholinguistics . . . is frankly *marital*—engagement, marriage, divorce, and reconciliation"—and the 1950s decade was nearly all a period of "engagement."

But first, a confession: At this time, except for the work of philosopher Charles Morris in semiotics, this young dinosaur didn't have the foggiest idea of what scholars in other fields were thinking and doing about language and meaning. Specifically, as to linguists, he had only the vague notion that these were strange, bearded, birdlike creatures who inhabited the remoter regions of libraries, babbling away in many exotic languages and constructing dictionaries for them—hardly fit companions for a robust, rigorous, and objective young dinosaur! The a-linguistic state of his awareness is evident from a perusal of the last chapter (titled "Language Behavior") of his graduate text (1953); it is devoid of reference to the works of linguists (the possible exception being Benjamin Lee Whorf).

His awakening came in the summer of 1951 when— sparked by Jack Carroll (attuned to linguistics by virtue of his tutelage under Whorf) and supported by John W. Gardner (a psychologist, then with the Carnegie Corporation of New York, later to become secretary of HEW, and still later organizer of Common Cause)—the Social Science Research Council sponsored a summer conference of linguists and psychologists at Cornell University. By some fluke, perhaps because he had just been awarded an SSRC Research Fellowship for support of the semantic differential work, the youthful dinosaur was invited to participate; and he readily accepted, in part because of the attractiveness of a summer in the hills and by the lakes of Ithaca. (I often wonder how the course of my own scientific life would have run if this fluke, and all that followed from it, had not happened.) In any case, that summer was an eye-opener: Not only were the linguists there neither polyglots nor lexicographers, but they were robust, rigorous, and objective—maybe even a bit more so than the young dinosaur!

As a result of that summer's meeting, the SSRC established a new Committee on Linguistics and Psychology in October of 1952. The initial membership was as follows: Charles E. Osgood (psychologist and first of a series of rotating chairmen); John B. Carroll (psychologist, Harvard); Floyd Lounsbury (ethnolinguist, Yale); George A. Miller (psychologist, MIT); and Thomas A. Sebeok (linguist, Indiana). Joseph H. Greenberg (ethnolinguist, Columbia) and James J. Jenkins (psychologist, Minnesota) were added in the fall of 1953. This turned out to be a very lively little committee.

One of its first steps was to plan and sponsor a research seminar on psycholinguistics, held during the summer of 1953 on the campus of Indiana University—when and where, not by chance, the Linguistic Institute was also having its summer session. The monograph that resulted from this seminar was *Psycholinguistics: A Survey of Theory and Research Problems* (Osgood and Sebeok, 1954b). According to one impartial chronicler, A. Richard Diebold, Jr. (writing in 1965), "within a year or two of its appearance, this monograph became the charter for psycholinguistics, firmly establishing the discipline's name. It so successfully piqued the interest of linguists and other behavioral scientists that the volume itself was soon out of print, and also became notoriously difficult to obtain second-hand, or even in libraries." And he noted that one of the graduate-student participants, Sol Saporta, was in 1961 to edit the first "long awaited reader, *Psycholinguistics: A Book of Readings* . . . [which was] also a testament to the fact that there [was] an ever-growing number of university courses variously titled 'psychology of language,' 'psycholinguistics,' 'linguistic psychology,' etc."

The thrust of the continuing SSRC Committee on Linguistics and Psychology is evident in the other projects and seminars it supported during the 1950s: a Southwest Project on *Comparative Psycholinguistics* (centered at the University of New Mexico, summer 1954); a conference on *Bilingualism* (Columbia University, 1954); another conference on *Techniques of Content Analysis* (University of Illinois, 1955);* another on *Associative Processes in Verbal Behavior* (University of Minnesota, 1955); yet another on *Dimensions of Meaning—Analytic and Experimental Approaches* (1956) (it was at this one that Dino first met

---

*The starred conferences culminated in published volumes.

young Noam Chomsky and got the impression that he was brilliant, but, alas!, *not* convinced that meaning was the central problem for students of language); a very impressive, large-scale conference on *Style in Language* organized by Tom Sebeok (Indiana University, 1958);* a summer seminar on *The Psycholinguistics of Aphasia* (Boston Veterans Administration Hospital, 1958);* and a conference on *Language Universals* (Dobbs Ferry, New York, 1961).* Ah, happy, eager dinosaur! Now reaching maturity (dinosaurs mature late, you know), he had participated in the full kaleidoscope of these SSRC activities, and spring was turning into what *had* to be a golden summer.

OTHER ACTIVITIES DURING THE 1950s

The first decade at Illinois was also a period of some rather diversified research activity. Some of this activity was stimulated by my attempts to resolve theoretical issues that had come up in writing my graduate text in experimental psychology. A paper that I wrote in 1952, with Al Heyer, offered "A New Interpretation of Figural After-effects" (an alternative to that proposed by some Gestalt psychologists). Other research papers were direct outgrowths of our ongoing major theme. "A Blind Analysis of a Case of Multiple Personality Using the Semantic Differential" (1954a, with Zella Luria) was made possible by J. McV. Hunt, then editor of the *Journal of Abnormal and Social Psychology*; since this paper dealt with the to-be-famous case of *The Three Faces of Eve*, reported by Thigpen and Cleckley (and came out so well), it gave our SD research some publicity. Another seminal paper, as it turned out, was "The Principle of Congruity in the Prediction of Attitude Change" (1955b, with Percy Tannenbaum), which became one of three "competing" attitude-change theories, along with those of Fritz Heider and Leon Festinger. And papers stimulated by my involvement with the SSRC Committee on Linguistics and Psychology and its various activities included the following: With Sol Saporta and Jum Nunnally in 1956, I wrote a paper titled "Evaluative Assertion Analysis," which combined semantic differential notions with a form of content analysis.

Finally, in this period there were also some anticipations of Theme II: As part of the Southwest Project on Comparative Psycholinguistics (SSRC-sponsored in the summer of 1954), George Suci had made "A Comparison of Semantic Structures in American Southwest Culture Groups," which wasn't actually published until 1960, however; in 1956, Heidi Kumata and Wilbur Schramm published a paper titled "A Pilot Study of Cross-cultural Methodology," which was actually an SD comparison of American English and Japanese; in 1958, Harry Triandis and Dino combined to produce "A Comparative Factorial Analysis of Semantic Structures in Monolingual Greek and American College Students." And at least bordering on Theme III there were two studies completed near the end of this period: One of these took off from the Heider/Festinger/Osgood–Tannenbaum theories of cognitive interactions ("psycho-logic") and was titled "Cognitive Dynamics in the Conduct of Human Affairs" (Osgood, 1960b); the other took off from Charles Morris' "Ways to Live" (a variety of styles of life), applied the SD technique to whole paragraphs on each "way" as concepts, and was published by Osgood, Ware, and Morris in 1961.

Intermezzo

From graduate school at Yale until I came to Illinois in 1949, I had had no interest whatsoever in politics or international affairs. My reading of newspapers was confined to the headlines and the funnies. I can thank—literally—the late Senator Joseph McCarthy for reawakening my concern with Theme III. With his attacks on intellectuals and his pet phrases like "Fifth Amendment Communist," he was trying to destroy everything that I had thought was sacred about our kind of society. However, for about seven years after McCarthy began his war on "communists," all I did was growl at the news and at the irrationalities of human beings. I didn't see what a psychologist could do about it. (This paragraph, comes from a "conversation" with Elizabeth Hall for *Psychology Today*, November 1973 issue—which, by the way, provides a kind of counterpoint to this autobiography.)

But in the fall of 1958, I went out to the Center for Advanced Study in the Behavioral Sciences at Stanford for a year. My original plan had been to use the year to start writing a book to be titled *Method and Theory in Psycholinguistics* and, appropriately enough, I found myself assigned to "cell" #10 (I think it was), with George Miller to the left of me in #11. But to the right of me, in #9, was someone who was to have a great influence on my future life—Jerome Frank. As a psychiatrist, Jerry *had* been doing something about it. He had testified before congressional committees and written articles for popular magazines. With his example right beside me, I forgot about writing my book on psycholinguistics—although I did polish off a few other things, including editing (with Murray Miron, then a graduate student on our Institute staff at Illinois) a book based on another SSRC conference, titled *Approaches to the Study of Aphasia* (Osgood and Miron, 1963d). Instead, I joined Jerry in organizing Center seminars on Survival in the Nuclear Age (or some such titles), and I wrote my first paper dealing directly with Theme III, "Suggestions for Winning the Real War with Communism" (Osgood, 1959b, published in *Conflict Resolution*).

Also, in the spring of my year at the Center, I began drawing up definite plans for research on Theme II. As a Fellow, I had the time to sit back and look at the larger pattern of things, and it became clear that the next step in our exploration of semantic space must be a shift from *ethnocentric* research with American English-speakers to what might be called *anthropocentric* research, with the focus on mankind in general and the hope of discovering some things universal in human semantic systems. By the end of my stay at the Center, I had rough-drafted the design for conducting such cross-cultural research with the SD technique—a design that, quite closely, has been followed, first with support of the Society for Investigation of Human Ecology (1960–1963) and later, on a larger scale, with joint support from the National Institute of Mental Health and the National Science Foundation (1963 to the present). Dino's earliest hobby, avidly collecting and reading science fiction, lost some of its charm in 1945 when the first atom bomb was dropped on Hiroshima, and by the end of his year at the Center it had quietly faded away. The real world had itself become an unfolding Weird Tale.

Focus on Universals of Affective Meaning Across Cultures

The decade of the 1960s was if anything busier, but it was also more focused on my three major themes. The greatest effort, time-wise, went into Theme II—cross-cultural explorations in semantic space—and during this period our sample human communities around the world went from zero to over twenty. But paralleling this worldwide enterprise was my intermittent involvement in Theme I—theory and research in psycholinguistics—where a crisis in the Kuhnian sense had developed. And throughout this decade (again, intermittently), I kept plugging away on Theme III—meaning and survival of the human species in the nuclear age—and trying to bring a strategy for reducing international tensions, based on psychological principles, into the awareness of the public at large and people in government in particular.

FROM ETHNOCENTRISM TO ANTHROPOCENTRISM IN STUDYING AFFECTIVE MEANING

By the end of the 1950s, the generality of the Evaluation/Potency/Activity (E-P-A) structure of affective meaning had been amply demonstrated for American English by many replications across various factoring methods, a wide diversity of types of subjects, and with many varied samples of concepts and scales. But there was a serious limitation on any claim for universality of this E-P-A structure in human cognizing: The research to date had been highly ethnocentric, limited almost entirely to American English-speaking subjects, and it was at least conceivable that the dominance of Goodness, Strength, and Activity was attributable to something peculiar about American culture or the English language or both. So, in 1960, Geppetto and his Pinocchio set out across the world looking—not for fame and fortune—but for friends in foreign lands who might catch some of their excitement and join in the exploration. And in *these* wanderings, at least, Geppetto has been able to keep his hands on the puppet's strings.

On the Strategy of Cross-cultural Research   There is much that I could say here about the nitty-gritty of cross-cultural research, but I have said it elsewhere (Osgood, 1964, 1967). There are the trials and tribulations of long, complicated, often round-the-world trips, as well as the shocking (at the time) events that sometimes occur and become humorous anecdotes (in retrospect). For example, there are difficulties that reflect language barriers:

I awake on the first morning of a visit to my Italian colleagues in Padova and phone the hotel desk for my breakfast. I say, "This is Mr. Osgood in room 412 and I'd like my breakfast, please" all very slowly in crisp Bostonian English. A long pause is followed by "Un momento, un momento!" There are strange noises and then a female voice that says what sounds like "Buon giorno! Disa elana gibsa!" So I say, "Look, habla español? Yo quiero mi café y . . . ." And then, I hear, "Charlie! This is Eleanor Gibson in 414!"

The hotel personnel had assumed I was trying to contact my fellow countrymen, the Gibsons, Eleanor and Jimmie, who were on a lecture tour!

And there are those difficulties that reflect cultural incongruities:

On my first visit to Tokyo, a delegation of Japanese psychologists is visiting with me at the International House, and they invite me out for *sushi* at a nearby restaurant. We start out, and I discover, to my egalitarian horror, that, being a Distinguished *and* Visiting Professor, I must *lead* a hierarchically ordered train of Nipponese through the busy streets of Tokyo, with only the light taps and polite smiles of the senior professor right behind to guide me. We did reach the restaurant, however, and I did enjoy the raw seafood on beds of rice.

All I can say is that I'd hate to have been a monolingual Uzbek-speaking psycholinguist from Tashkent trying to initiate the same twenty-five-plus culture project!

Here are a few comments on strategy:

1. Ideally, cross-cultural research should be *planned* as cooperatively as it is executed; though, given the vast differ-

ences in theoretical and methodological traditions, this is usually just not feasible, at least in the early phases.

2. All research *procedures* must be carefully piloted in one's home community before they are "exported" to others—e.g., our decade of indigenous American English research with the SD technique.

3. One must always be aware that he is working in a *socio-political context* and be alert to the possible political sensitivity to—and even misuse of—the information he is collecting. In general, we have tried to work on a professor-to-professor basis, leaving matters like obtaining informed consent to the foreign colleague in question.

4. And, of course, there is the absolutely critical business of locating *the right senior colleague* to work with in each location. I consider myself most fortunate in having developed a "network" of some sixty colleague–friends across the world in the course of this research.

The internal staff at our Center for Comparative Psycholinguistics has been equally important. Murray Miron and Sharon Wolfe were major contributors during the formative years; Leon Jakobovits functioned as codirector during the middle years; and I refer to Bill May fondly and accurately as "my right hand"—acting in the capacities of programmer, data processer, business manager, tutor and confidant of our research assistants, and since 1970 codirector. Over the nearly twenty years of this project, some thirty graduate students have also helped shape this research, while earning their bread and their degrees, and at least half of them have been from foreign countries, many serving before as field workers and some becoming, afterward, particularly sophisticated senior colleagues. It is these people who have handled the computerized processing of the masses of data that this research has generated, who have helped to prepare reports and continuation proposals, and who have shared the really amazing load of correspondence.

The cross-cultural research falls rather naturally into three phases, which we may call the "tool-making phase," the "tool-using phase," and the "data-interpretation phase." I can be appropriately brief here, since I have covered these phases in several publications—particularly "Exploration in Semantic Space: A Personal Diary" (1971b), which accompanied my acceptance of the Kurt Lewin Memorial Award, and "Probing Subjective Culture" (1974). The fine details may be found in Osgood, May, and Miron (1975a).

Tool-Making Phase In each community, 10,000 qualifier *tokens,* generated by having 100 teenage males give single adjectival responses to 100 culture-common nouns, were processed by our computer so as to generate an ordered list of the 50 most productive qualifier *types,* and these were made into bipolar scales by opposites-elicitation. The same 100 translation-equivalent nouns were rated against these 50 scales in the usual SD fashion, and both *indigenous* and *pancultural* factor analyses were run on these data—both yielding highly consistent evidence for affective E-P-A structure, and the latter making possible the selection of maximally comparable short-form SD's across our communities.

Tool-Using Phase Pruning and translation-checking of a large number of culture-common nominals yielded 620 concepts for an *Atlas of Affective Meanings.* These were rated against the short-form SD's by more teenage males (about 40 contributing to each concept), and these data were computer-analyzed to yield, for each community, the basic E-P-A and standardized Familiarity, Meaningfulness, Polarization, and Cultural Instability measures for all *Atlas* concepts.

Data-Interpretation Phase With the 620 *Atlas* concepts organized into some 50 conceptual categories, chain-linked computer programs yielded a sequence of analyses for all categories (CATANS)—correlations of communities on each measure, ranks of concepts on each measure for each community, componential analyses of these ranks, and both *intra*cultural (among concepts for each community) and *inter*cultural (among communities for each concept) distances. Our staff marked all CATANS for statistically significant Universals, Subuniversals and Uniquenesses, and, finally, group meetings among geographically close subsets of community-informants were held on *Atlas* data interpretation.

On the Powers and Limitations of Semantic Differential Technique The SD was my first vehicle for exploring semantic space, and she proved to be a spaceworthy ship—but she does have her limitations. Let me now say something about her virtues and vices—which I can do without embarrassment, since she responds only to feeling, not to reason! The strength of the SD technique lies, first, in its natural adaptability to the very powerful techniques of *multivariate statistics,* in which factor analysis is a means of discovering semantic features and distance measures provide a rigorous metric for specifying semantic similarities and differences among concepts. Second, the strength of the SD technique lies in its being a *componential model,* describing the meanings of large numbers of concepts in terms of a small number of distinguishing features. Its power lies, third, in providing a *systematic sampling* of the distribution of terms rather than the somewhat haphazard "compelling examples" characteristic of most linguistic and philosophical semantics.

But *why* such massive E, P, and A—and so little of anything else? The answer comes in two parts:

1. We really are—Chomsky and the rationalists to the contrary—a kind of animal, and what is most important to us now about the signs of things, as it was in the days of Neanderthal man, are $\pm$E (Do they signify things *good* or *bad* for me?), $\pm$P (Are the things signified *strong* or *weak* with respect to me?), and $\pm$A (Do they refer to things that are *active* or *passive*—things that I must fight or flee, or things I can simply avoid or ignore?). These "gut" reactions to the signs of things are crucial for individual survival (see Osgood, 1969).

2. The SD technique literally forces the *metaphorical usage of scales* since *every* concept must be rated against *every* scale. This means that, in many (in fact, most) concept/scale pairings, the judgments must be metaphorically determined (thus TORNADO must be judged *fair* or *unfair,* MOTHER must be judged *hot* or *cold,* and SPONGE must be judged *honest* or *dis-*

honest) with shared affect the only guide (so TORNADO is *un-fair*, MOTHER may be *hot*, and SPONGE probably *dishonest*).

The "why" of E-P-A is simultaneously the reason that the SD is an insufficient vehicle for discovering all features of semantic space—metaphorical use of scales amplifies E, P, and A at the expense of the many and subtler denotative features of meaning. Both the pair NURSE and SINCERITY and the pair HERO and SUCCESS have nearly identical locations in the E-P-A space. One can say, "She's a cute nurse," but not, "She's a cute sincerity"; and one can say, "Our hero defied them," but hardly, "Our success defied them." It was for these reasons that, in the mid-1960s, I began designing a new vehicle for exploring semantic space—the Semantic Interaction Technique. Briefly, the SI technique utilizes the rules of usage of words *in systematically varied syntactic combinations* (noun or verb phrases, or even sentences) as a means of inferring the minimum number and nature of features necessary to account for exactly those rules of usage. So far, SI technique has been applied to only a limited set of conceptual domains—with Kenneth Forster, interpersonal-verb/adverb combinations—e.g., *meet suddenly* (acceptable) versus *console suddenly* (anomalous)—and with Marilyn Wilkins, adjective/emotion-noun combinations—e.g., *sudden surprise* (apposite) versus *sudden melancholy* (anomalous). Only the work with Forster has been published so far (see Osgood, 1970), but I have high hope for the new semantic spaceship.

PENDULA SWINGS VERSUS REVOLUTIONS IN LINGUISTICS AND PSYCHOLINGUISTICS

By the end of the 1950s, the distant mutterings of a scientific revolution were in the air—impelled by Chomsky's (1957) transformational and generative grammar—certainly for linguistics and possibly for cognitive psychology, too. In the preface to his *Psycholinguistics* (1961), Sol Saporta was to say that "all attempts by psychologists to describe 'grammaticality' exclusively in terms of habit strength [etc.] . . . seem inadequate . . . to account for some of the most obvious facts of language" (p. v). In 1959, Chomsky wrote a carefully documented and scathing review of Skinner's *Verbal Behavior* (1957)—which Skinner never responded to—and this was to have cumulative impact on many psycholinguists. Perhaps because our dinosaur was confidently mature, had a much more complex behavior theory, and, indeed, had written a highly critical review of Skinner himself in 1958, he was not particularly disturbed and kept right on nuzzling among his semantic daisies.

At the Center in Palo Alto in 1958–1959, George Miller, Eugene Galanter, and Karl Pribram were working on their *Plans and the Structure of Behavior,* to be published in 1960. It was heavily influenced by Chomsky and included a chapter on "Plans for Speaking." This was followed by Miller's important 1962 paper titled "Some Psychological Studies of Grammar" and soon thereafter by a small flood of papers by Miller, his students, and others testing the psychological reality of grammatical structures and transformations. The consummation of this intimate relation between linguistics and psychology was symbolized in 1963 by two chapters in the *Handbook of Mathematical Psychology,* written jointly by Chomsky and Miller: "Introduction to the Formal Analysis of Natural Languages" (Chomsky and Miller) and "Finitary Models of Language Users" (Miller and Chomsky.).

The distant mutterings of revolution were now becoming heavy rumblings of immanent paradigm clash. As Bever, Fodor, and Weksel concluded their debate, in 1965, with Martin Braine over the learning of grammatical ordering of words in sentences, they felt themselves able to say: "As the empirical basis for assuming an abstract underlying structure in language becomes broader and the explanatory power of that assumption becomes deeper, *we recommend to all psychologists that they seriously question the adequacy of any theory of learning that cannot account for the fact that such structures are acquired*" (p. 500, emphasis in original).

By 1966, the conflict between competing psycholinguistic paradigms had reached what in 1962 Thomas Kuhn had called the "crisis" stage in scientific revolutions. In 1965, Fodor had published a paper titled "Could Meaning Be an r_m?" explicitly aimed at O. Hobart Mowrer, but obviously including me, to which I replied (Osgood, 1966b). It claimed to reduce neobehaviorist two-stage mediation theories to single-stage

Skinnerian theory, hence rendering them heir to all of the inadequacies claimed by Chomsky in his review. In the spring of 1966, there was, at the University of Kentucky, a conference with an innocent-enough-sounding topic, *Verbal Behavior and General Behavior Theory*. This was published in 1968 under the same title (Dixon and Horton, editors). Particularly in the session on psycholinguistics, the prepared papers by "revolutionaries" Bever, Fodor, Garrett, and McNeill constituted a frontal attack on behaviorism and associationism generally. As discussant of these papers, I found myself in the unfamiliar and unenviable role of defending the Establishment. The title of my discussion, "Toward a Wedding of Insufficiencies," is indicative of my ambivalence in this role. And I was beginning to realize that I *was* a dinosaur!

This is not the place to go into any detailed analysis of scientific revolutions (however, see my *Lectures on Language Performance*, 1979a, in press), but I have come to the conclusion that, although the impact of Chomsky on linguistics was certainly a revolution in Kuhnian terms, this has not been the case for his impact on cognitive psychology (or even psycholinguistics). Why? Because it has not met the criteria that distinguish revolutions from mere pendula swings in the competition between viable paradigms:

1. There has been no attempt to incorporate solutions to problems successfully handled by the old paradigm.

2. The old paradigm has not been shown to be insufficient *in principle*.

3. There has been no new paradigm to shift *to*—in the sense of a well-motivated, internally coherent alternative theory of language *performance*. There has been shift *away from* behaviorism in any form but, in the absence of any alternative paradigm, this would be better termed "revulsion" than "revolution."

Maclay noted in 1973 that the responses of

psychologists who had a vested interest in research on language . . . fell into the three familiar categories of AVOIDANCE, CONVERSION, and COMPROMISE . . . their overwhelming response was conversion . . . [and] the quasi-religious nature of scientific conversion required that those who had seen the light should condemn everything connected with the erroneous views they had previously held.

Maclay also points out that, in a clash between paradigms, the middle ground becomes very insecure, and he very kindly comments that

Osgood was the only major psychologist who continued to take linguistics seriously but who rejected some of its implications for psycholinguistics . . . [particularly] the assumption of the centrality of grammar. While acknowledging the success of transformationalism as a linguistic theory and insisting that his students be trained in linguistics, he continued to argue that a revised version of behavior theory was, at the least, an essential component of an adequate *psycho*linguistic theory.

Nevertheless, it was a rather lonesome dinosaur who kept offering his daisies at the shrine of a near-deserted (even if still viable) paradigm in the late 1960s. The aging Dino even sent some of his best students (after helping guide them to their Ph.D.'s) to serve at the shrine of the opposing paradigm at MIT—first, Merle Garrett and then, for briefer periods, Ken Forster and John Limber. But this period was another busy one on the home grounds, and the dinosaur didn't have much time to brood about a possible paradigm lost.

DISILLUSION AND DIVORCE IN THE LATE 1960s

The *marriage* between linguistics and psycholinguistics in the 1960s might better have been called an *elopement*—or perhaps even an *abduction*—because it was a very one-sided affair. The intuitions of generative linguists were to provide a theory of competence, and the wifely psychologists were to cook up experiments on performance designed to demonstrate empirically the validity of such a theory of how the mind works in sentencing. This presumed a direct correspondence hypothesis—that the derivational history of a sentence linguistically corresponds, step by step, to the sequence of psychological operations executed when a person processes the sentence. Learning a language was equated with the acquisition of its

syntax, and semantics took a back seat. Since it seemed in-
conceivable that such an incredibly complex system as a transformational grammar could be learned in the short period of
four or five years, it was assumed by many that much of it
must be innate—universal to humans and specific to language.

Although the early psycholinguistic studies of sentence
processing, carried out by George Miller and his associates,
seemed to give credence to such a correspondence hypothesis,
sufficient contrary evidence had accumulated, even by the
mid-1960s, to lead Fodor and Garrett in 1966 to say that "an
acceptable theory of the relation between competence and
performance models will have to represent that relation as
abstract, the degree of abstractness being proportional to the
failure of formal features of derivations to correspond to performance variables." In the absence of *any* characterization of
this "abstract" relation, of course, all this does is to remove any
competence grammar from the danger of being disconfirmed
by performance data!

Although in the early 1960s even the middle-aged dinosaur in his Illinois daisy patch had been eyeing the ominous
storm in psycholinguistics with some concern, he was still
eager and busy. And, as such things are measured, he was
successful in his profession, having been elected in 1961 to be
president of the American Psychological Association in 1963.
He was, therefore, quite confident. In 1963, however, he
began to worry about what he should say to his fellow psychologists in his presidential address. He went through a
period of intense ambivalence about this: on the one hand,
since his year at the Center at Palo Alto he'd been giving high
priority to strategies of international relations in a nuclear age
and he knew that most of his potential audience hoped for a
tough policy speech on this major social issue; on the other
hand, he felt a strong urge to follow the tradition of most past
presidents of APA and talk about the most crucial scientific
issues in his own specialty—even if the audience for such a
talk would be smaller in terms of concern or comprehension.
In the end, he took the latter course, and the title of his
address—"On Understanding and Creating Sentences"—indi-
cates what he thought was the most crucial issue for psycholinguistics at that time.

Oh, how the dinosaur worked on that APA address! By the middle of the summer of 1963 (and only a few weeks before the convention) he had pounded out a small book of 204 double-spaced pages, and that had to be paired down to about thirty-six deliverable pages. The full version was never published (I was not really satisfied with it), but much of it was predictive of the path I would be following in psycholinguistics through the next decade.

In my opinion, the denouement of the competence/performance distinction came in two papers published in 1970. One of these, titled "On Two Hypotheses Concerning Psycholinguistics," was by William C. Watt; after demolishing to his own satisfaction (as well as mine) the hypothesis that a Competence Grammar (CG) could be isomorphic with what he termed a deep Mental Grammar (MG), Watt suggested that an *Abstract Performance Grammar* (APG) would be isomorphic with the MG, but he had little to say about such an APG's nature. An abstract performance grammar is precisely what I have been working on for the past near-decade (see Osgood, 1979d, for an anticipation). The other 1970 paper was by Thomas G. Bever and was titled "The Cognitive Basis for Linguistic Structures." His main theme was that *performance,* at least in part, determines ultimate linguistic *competence,* and he demonstrated this in a variety of language-processing situations; he concluded that we must "reject the claim that a linguistic grammar is in any sense internal to such linguistic performances as talking and listening."

Focus on Meaning for the Survival of the Species

In 1962, I received an honorary degree as Doctor of Science from my alma mater, Dartmouth College. The honor was bestowed on me primarily, I am sure, for my having become president of APA, but also for my having continued the thrust that Ted Karwoski had begun and (as the statement went) for my concerns about the future of Mankind. Interestingly, John Glenn, one of our first astronauts, also received an honorary degree at the same convocation. Being president-elect of APA during the early 1960s, I found all kinds of opportunities—via media invitations, college colloquia, consulting opportunities, and the like—for pushing the GRIT strategy (Graduated and Reciprocated Initiatives in Tension-reduction) and psychological factors in international relations more generally. Since I was simultaneously initiating the cross-cultural project on human affective meaning systems *and* keeping my hand in the developing crisis in psycholinguistics, these were *very* busy years.

EXPLOSION OF PAPERS AND BOOKS ON GRIT IN THE EARLY 1960s

After returning to Urbana from the Center in Palo Alto during the summer of 1959, I went to work with a vengeance on the theme of survival of the species in a nuclear age. I began writing what I call my "basic book" on GRIT, titled *An Alternative to War or Surrender*—to be published as a paperback by the University of Illinois Press (Osgood, 1962a). In course, I generated a slew of papers of varying length, which I tried to distribute over as wide a range of both academic and popular media outlets as I could reach. Some of the more important, as I look back, were the following: in the *Bulletin of the Atomic Scientists*, a paper titled "A Case for Graduated Unilateral Disengagement" (1960a); in the *Journal of Social Issues*, one titled "An Analysis of the Cold War Mentality" (1961a); in a collection titled *The Liberal Papers* (edited and with an introduction by James Roosevelt), a paper titled "Reciprocated Initiative" (1962c); and in a collection titled *Preventing World War III: Some Proposals* (edited by Q. Wright, W. M. Evan, and M. Deutsch), one titled "Graduated Unilateral Initiatives for Peace" (1962b).

In the year of my APA presidency, I was invited by the editor of *Taboo Topics* to contribute a quasi-autobiographical account (along with references to other psychologists working in the area, of course) of my activities related to GRIT, which I titled "The Psychologist in International Affairs" (1963b). For a quite different audience, and in a different direction, I wrote "Questioning Some Unquestioned Assumptions about National Defense" for the first volume of the *Journal of Arms Control* (1963c).

371

BUTTONHOLING, CONSULTING, AND TESTIFYING FOR GRIT

During the early 1960s, by virtue of both APA committee business and consultations with people in the Human Ecology Fund, which was then supporting the beginnings of our cross-cultural research, I was spending a lot of time in Washington, D.C., and New York. I went out of my way to visit various senators and congressmen when opportunities arose (or could be induced), but it was usually young people on their staffs with whom I actually talked. Early on, I developed close contacts with both Richard Barnett and Marcus Raskin—then among the bright young men on the new President Kennedy's staff, across the street from the White House, and later to be founders of the lively Institute for Policy Studies in Washington. On my visits to the capital on APA or HEF business, I usually arranged some GRIT-related business as well—for example, leading discussion groups at meetings of the American Friends Society chapter there. For several of these years, I served as a consultant to both the Air Force and the Navy—an experience that I found most educational but not particularly gratifying! And a bit later, I became a consultant to the fledgling Arms Control and Disarmament Agency—a position that was at once gratifying (knowledgeable people to talk to) and frustrating (nothing ever seemed to happen further up).

On the morning of Wednesday, May 25, 1966, Jerome Frank and Charles Osgood testified before the Committee on Foreign Relations of the United States Senate on "Psychological Aspects of International Relations." The session was chaired by Senator J. W. Fulbright—a most remarkable human being—and he led it off with some interesting excerpts from letters (of which I had been completely unaware) exchanged in 1932 between Einstein and Freud on "deliverance from war." Jerry and I had planned a division of labor—with Frank (the psychiatrist) emphasizing aspects like "the self-fulfilling prophecy" and "the ideological character of the Vietnam war," and Osgood (the communications psychologist) emphasizing "calculated escalation and de-escalation strategies" (and how they can't be mixed) and "the communication and interpretation of intentions" (vis-à-vis the United

States and particularly the Russians and the Chinese). Besides Senator Fulbright (who had asked us there via Jerry, whom he already knew), Senators Sparkman, Hickenlooper, Gore, Church, and Case questioned us thoroughly. Senator Case put some tough questions to us, but I think we fielded them reasonably well. As I reread our testimonies and the extended interactions with these senators to prepare this autobiography, I was intrigued by the interplays. Toward the end of it, after Senators Case and Church had gotten into a debate, I couldn't resist saying, "For a moment here I had a feeling that we [Frank and Osgood] were graduate students on their final thesis examinations, where it's a fine thing when the examiners begin to debate among themselves"—which drew laughter from both senators and onlookers.

IMPACT?

During late 1959 and early 1960, Dallas Smythe (on our Institute of Communications Research staff) and I organized and conducted three conferences on public policy at the Gould House in Dobbs Ferry, New York. We called them "tripod conferences" because at each, by design, there were several academics in the international relations area, several people in government at various levels, and several people in the mass media. I particularly remember long evening hours at one of these conferences spent with John McNaughton (who was soon to become Assistant Secretary of Defense for International Security Affairs) debating the fine points of GRIT—and he would keep asking me, "But what would you do in Berlin?"

In June of 1963, President Kennedy initiated a very GRIT-like strategy, which, in a very carefully documented 1967 paper by Amitai Etzioni, has been called The Kennedy Experiment. The President began his strategy with his speech on June 10 at the American University, in which he outlined "A Strategy of Peace," praised the Russians for their accomplishments, noted that "our problems are man-made . . . and can be solved by man," and announced a U.S. initiative (we were stopping all nuclear tests in the atmosphere and would not resume them unless another country did first). The speech was published in full in both *Izvestia* and *Pravda,* with a combined circulation of 10,000,000, and on June 15 Premier Khrushchev announced that he had ordered production of strategic bombers to be halted. A series of reciprocative initiatives followed, and there was no question but that a marked thaw in the Cold War was developing. But then, on November 22, 1963, The Kennedy Experiment came to an abrupt end in Dallas, Texas.

When one is wandering around in a desert, he is liable to have mirages of the reinforcement he so desperately wants. Was The Kennedy Experiment inspired by GRIT? In late 1962, I had sent the President a copy of *An Alternative to War or Surrender*, autographed and embossed with a note urging him to seriously consider this strategy, along with some other short summary-type papers on GRIT. In the spring of 1963, I did get a little note from his personal secretary, thanking me and saying that the President had read the materials. But earlier, at the height of the Berlin crisis, when U.S. and Soviet tanks were lined up snout-to-snout, there was an explicit graduated and reciprocated pull-back and accompanying reduction of tension. And then there was the Cuban missile crisis (at a time when I was a consultant to the Air Force and knew that Kennedy was being pressured to aggressively escalate by bombing the missile sites before they could become operational): the setting up of a naval blockade was a beautifully calculated move. (GRIT says that, if an opponent escalates aggressively, one should shift from the carrot to the stick—but only to the precise level required to restore the previous status quo.) A few days later, Khrushchev began removing the missiles, and a couple of days after that, I got a note from John McNaughton that said, "What did you think of our use of GRIT in Cuba?"

What about the impact of GRIT generally? As far as the academic community is concerned—if one can consider as evidence the frequency with which my *Alternative to War or Surrender* and other GRIT papers have been cited in the then-developing field of laboratory simulations of conflict situations in particular and in the social science literature generally—then the impact has been gratifying. As just one example, in 1968 I was asked by Gilbert Abcarian to give a lecture at Florida State University on the psychology of politics; the paper I prepared (later to be included in a book to be titled *Social Psychology and Political Behavior: Problems and Prospects*) was a "funpiece" (but also very serious) with the ridiculous title, "Conservative Words and Radical Sentences in the Semantics of International Politics" (Osgood, 1971a).* However, as far as impact on politicians and people in the military establishment is concerned (except for the possible influence in The Kennedy Experiment), I seem to have run up against a pretty solid wall of (often ridiculing) resistance. This reaction is typified by the characterization of my "Reciprocated Initiative" contribution to *The Liberal Papers* (1962c) by the Republican National Committee as "surrender on the installment plan"—to which, in the context of my "Semantics of International Politics" (above), I guess I can only say, "Touché!"

I was traumatized by the assassination of John F. Kennedy—almost literally glued to the television set for several days—and was not satisfied then (or now) that it was the work of "a lone assassin." (Not only had the President and his brother Robert tromped heavily on some government agencies—e.g., the CIA, with its plan for a *second* invasion of Cuba—but there were many powerful people in what President Eisenhower had called "The Military–Industrial Complex" who stood to lose power, and profit, if The Kennedy Experiment continued and succeeded.)

In the late summer of 1964 (the end, thank goodness, of my year as Past President of APA), I left for a sabbatical year in Hawaii, where I planned to write up all those studies that had been patiently waiting on the sidelines during my three presidential years, as well as to extend my graduate course in psycholinguistics from one to two semesters. Some of the paper-drafting did get done—e.g., "On the Dimensionality of the Semantic Space for Communication via Facial Expressions" (Osgood, 1966a, based on data I had actually collected as an instructor at Yale), two papers with Al Hastorf and H. Ono on predicting the meanings of stereoscopically fused facial expressions, and a paper with Murray Miron for

---

*Actually, this lecture-to-paper was based on two BBC Third Programme lectures I taped while in England in the fall of 1965, attending the first meeting of a group with the title *Mankind 2000*!

Ray Cattell's *Handbook of Multivariate Experimental Psychology,* to be titled "Language Behavior: The Multivariate Structure of Qualification" and based, of course, on our cross-cultural tool-making Phase I.

However, soon after taking over as President, Lyndon B. Johnson began to escalate in Vietnam, from the small army of "advisers" that Kennedy had sent there to a full-scale miltary operation. There had been his quick decision to bomb the mainland bases of North Vietnamese gunboats when one of our naval patrols was attacked in the Tonkin Gulf (and damaged to the extent of one bullet hole, as I understand it). And then, in early 1965, right in the middle of my sabbatical, there was a massive escalation of civilian bombing in the north. So, I dropped everything but my teaching and dug into another pocket-sized book, *Perspective in Foreign Policy,* in which I accused the Johnson Administration of having swallowed "a baited hook"—the calculated escalation strategy of Herman Kahn and his think-tank friends (see his *On Thermonuclear War,* his *Thinking About the Unthinkable,* and in 1965 his *On Escalation*), which one reviewer had titled the game of "Chicken à la Kahn," a strategy that is the mirror image of GRIT, of course. Being in a rush to get it into people's hands, I arranged to have a few thousand copies published privately in the summer of 1965, and I just gave most of them away to individuals and organizations in the government and outside it. It was published a bit later as a small hard-cover volume by Pacific Books in 1966, but it didn't do too well—perhaps because I'd already hit the hard core of potential readers with free copies.

My Three Themes in Parallel
Through the 1970s—and into the 1980s?

I should tell you something else about Dino, my alter ego: He has always had a compulsion toward *balance* in everything he does. I remember how, as a youngster, he used to line up his jellybeans in a segmented row (each segment running from least-liked licorice through indifferent cinnamon to most-liked vanilla) beside the couch, to be eaten systematically while he read about Tarzan or Bomba the Jungle Boy. In eating meals, he always rotated around the potatoes, vegetables, and meats, making sure that he ended up even on the last mouthful. (And he still does!) And now, in the 1970s, he is trying to drive a balanced three-theme wagon into the 1980s—except that each theme seems to want to go its own way. Theme I (psycholinguistics) and Theme II (cross-cultural affective meaning) are usually dominant and competing with each other, but Theme III (survival of the species) occasionally takes over in a flurry of excitement. In 1972, I was elected to the National Academy of Sciences and by the time of this writing, in October 1977, I find myself approaching my sixty-first year and being seven times a grandfather. (After Philip and Gail had each had two children, each a boy and a girl, I told them about the population explosion—for all the good it did!)

THEME I: PSYCHOLINGUISTIC THEORY AND RESEARCH

The Recent Past   We left our middle-aged dinosaur struggling over his APA presidential address and then sitting back to observe the disillusion and divorce in relations between linguists and psychologists in the late 1960s. Needless to say, Dino followed these developments with great interest, and even the casual observer could note the brightening gleam in his eye and the increased vigor with which he flicked his tail. By the mid-1970s, he had discovered a new field of semantic daisies—ones that grew in a wondrous variety of little bands made up of chains of linked blooms, neobehaviorally $[M_1 \longrightarrow (M) \longrightarrow M_2]$'s, where the M's are the componential r_M's of the components of basic cognitions, or linguistically [SNP—VP—ONP]'s, the constituents of simplex clauses. Dino fed upon these semantic daisies with relish while he refurbished and expanded the little shrine for his paradigm. The denouement of the competence/performance distinction had paved the way (some might say, paradoxically) for reconciliation in terms of a new, more balanced, and potentially very productive relation between linguists and psychologists in what Maclay in 1973 called "The Cognitive Period of the 1970s."

The re-engagement has developed along rather different lines than the earlier engagement: Linguists were becoming more concerned with semantics (see the papers by Lakoff, Fillmore, and Bierwisch in the 1971 Steinberg and Jakobovits collection, titled *Semantics: An Interdisciplinary Reader in Philosophy, Linguistics and Psychology* and dedicated to the old dinosaur, incidentally!). In fact, one could say that the thrust of the recent *generative semantics* was to put the semantic horse back in front of the syntactic cart. They were becoming increasingly concerned with *functionalism* and, hence, with the cognitive processes underlying the *presuppositions* of sentences (see the papers by Lakoff, Langendoen, and the Kiparskys in the same volume). They were even becoming concerned with *pragmatics* and, consequently, the role of nonlinguistic, contextual factors in the ordinary conversational use of language.

Psycholinguists, while having become more sophisticated about transformational grammar, were also beginning to shift their focus from the syntax to the semantics of sentencing. They were also beginning to recognize the basic fact that strategies for cognizing sentences have their origins in prelinguistic perceptuo-motor cognizing, a fact that was well illustrated in some papers by Eve and Herb Clark, Samuel Fillenbaum, Charles Perfetti, and a number of others in the early 1970s, to say nothing of the earlier and seminal work of Piaget. These developments had been driven by the disconfirmation of the correspondence hypothesis, by the nonappearance of any alternative psychological paradigm for performance, and by the appearance of a new breed of psycholinguists, who were trained to be about equally competent in both fields, rather than having the alter field "grafted on" (as was the case for dinosaurs of all subspecies).

In the Midwest, this old dinosaur and his companions had also been moving happily into the new relationship. He contributed a paper titled "Where Do Sentences Come From?" to the 1971 Steinberg and Jakobovits collection (Osgood, 1971c): His main point was to demonstrate that there is an intimate interaction between nonlinguistic and linguistic channels in the process of simply describing ordinary events, and hence that these channels must share some deeper cognitive level that cannot, in principle, be characterized by *purely linguis-*

tic constructs and rules. With one of his friends, Meredith Richards, he even invaded the heartland of the linguistic domain by publishing an article in *Language* (Osgood and Richards, 1973b). This article, titled "From Yang and Yin to *And* or *But*," used laws of cognitive congruence and incongruence to predict the discriminative use of these conjunctions in simple conjoined sentences of the form X *is* ADJ_1 ____ ADJ_2 (e.g., *X is sweet* ____ *kind* or *X is cowardly* ____ *honest*)—frames that, linguistically speaking, will accept either *and* or *but*.

In the spring of 1972, Dino had returned from several long trips around the world in connection with the continuing cross-cultural project (which was becoming something like a dinosaur having a bear by the tail!). At that point, what we called our Cog Group at Illinois (including Bill Brewer in psychology, Jerry Morgan in linguistics, and several graduate students in psycholinguistics) began to hold idea-suggesting and idea-critiquing sessions. We were trying to build a fresh conception of "where sentences come from and go to"—or, going back to Watt's notions, it could be said that we were trying to build an Abstract Performance Grammar on psychological as well as linguistic bases. These Cog Group sessions were exciting for the old dinosaur—downright rejuvenating, in fact. A number of doctoral theses and other research papers were generated in these sessions, and they've been good intellectual fun for all—particularly, I guess, when the old fellow tries to put his baby booties back on and intuit how his prelinguistic world was structured cognitively!

The Lively Present   Pondering in his prelinguistic booties has led Dino to the radical notion that what has traditionally been called the indirect object in bitransitive sentences is, in cognitive reality, the underlying direct object—i.e., that what the prelinguistic child *perceives* as the transfer event is [THE BOY / GAVE-A-TOY-TO / THE GIRL]. So Dino pursued the matter, working first with Chris Tanz, ably assisted by linguist Phil Sedlak at Stanford (recommended by fellow dinosaur Joe Greenberg!), and with Quin Schultze in the lab at Illinois. We were able to demonstrate that, both crosslinguistically and in several psycholinguistic experiments, it was indeed the case that the direct object is more tightly bound to the verb than is the indirect object (see Osgood and Tanz, 1977e). More recently, Dino and Annette Zehler have been able to show that the same holds true, and even more so, for three- to five-year-old children (and a paper on this is now in press).

Some other recently completed psycholinguistic papers—all in one way or another exploring my developing theory of cognizing and sentencing—are the following: "Salience and Sentencing: Some Production Principles" (Osgood and Bock, 1977d) reports an experiment demonstrating how inherent semantic vividness can compete with naturalness to produce transformations in word ordering (e.g., for the passive transformation, *Jackie Onássis was sold a painting by the art gallery* preferred over *The art gallery sold a painting to Jackie Onassis*). Another "fun piece," but again very serious, is titled "What Is a Language?" (Osgood, 1979c, in press). In it, I first offer criteria for *anything* being "a language" (e.g., of Octopians from Arcturus whose spaceship lands in my backyard) and then offer criteria defining *humanoid* languages, which leads easily into a review of theories (including my own) of the origin of human languages. And most recently, I have written a paper titled "Things and Words"—appropriately reversing the title of Roger Brown's early 1958 book, since meanings of perceived events clearly precede meanings of sentential events in both species and individual development (Osgood, 1979b, in press).

The Near Future?   Predicting the future in any field is eminently personal, so I leave the doddering dinosaur contentedly weaving his daisy chains and take full credit for my own biases in predicting the future for psycholinguistics. As we move toward the year 2000:

1. There will be a complete shift from emphasis on language competence to emphasis on language performance—and I will try to contribute to this shift by completing my largely outlined *Toward an Abstract Performance Grammar*.

2. As part of this shift, there will be increasing avoidance of dealing with sentences-in-isolation and increasing dependence

on sentences-in-context; thus sentences in discourse, in ordinary conversation, and in nonlinguistic behavioral contexts—in both linguistic and psycholinguistic methodologies.

3. Semantics will be moving into the foreground as syntax, reciprocally, moves into the background. Perhaps better put, syntax itself will become semantically based.

4. Logical, rationalist models of language will be shown to be inappropriate for ordinary language users and will be superseded by more "gutsy," dynamic, psycho–logical models. After all, we *are* a kind of animal, and the basic dynamics of our thinking are not the logics a few of us have managed to achieve but rather the primitive psycho-logics we share with other animals—just take a look around our world today!

5. There will be a shift from ethno-linguo-centrism toward what might appropriately be called anthropo-linguo-centrism; just as Latin dominated the formulation of most traditional grammars, so has American English dominated the formulation of modern generative grammars—even when the linguists, trained in the United States, may be native speakers of other languages. Questions about language universals, at all levels, require *cross-linguistic data matrices* for their answers.

Congruently reflecting this bias, our Center for Comparative Psycholinguistics has recently been shifting from *Atlas* data collections across our matrix of thirty human language/culture communities to cross-linguistic comparative studies on human cognizing and sentencing—e.g., how, in simply describing events on a color-film, languages differentially signal in their surface structures the distinctions that must universally be made in cognizing, how prelinguistically determined naturalness predicts the ease of processing and recalling bitransitive and prepositional single-clause sentences as well as complexly conjoined multiple-clause sentences by both adults and children, and so on. Of course, we are not alone in this bias by any means—witness the work of the Stanford Language Universals Project under linguists Ferguson and Greenberg and the cross-language psycholinguistic research of Dan Slobin and his group at Berkeley.

Will there be a *remarriage* of linguistics and cognitive psychology by the year 2000? I strongly suspect that there will be (see my "How Should a University Be?" 1977b), and it will probably take the form of new departments of, say, *psy-cho*linguistics and *socio*linguistics. These *new* departments will be needed because the "linguos" in psychology and the "psy-chos" in linguistics will be finding that they have more in common with each other than they do with their own de-partmental colleagues. But I see that the old dinosaur—wrapped in a blanket of his own daisy chains—has fallen sound asleep . . . .

THEME II: COMPLETING THE "ATLAS OF AFFECTIVE MEANINGS" AND REPORTING IT TO OTHER SOCIAL SCIENTISTS

The Recent Past During the period from September 1973 through August 1977, *Atlas* data collection was completed for our last eight language-culture groups (Afghan Pashtu, Black English, Brazilian Portuguese, Costa Rican Spanish, Hungar-ian Magyar, Israeli Hebrew, Malaysian Malay, and Rumanian Rumanian). We now have in hand the complete fifty category analyses (CATANS) with data based on all thirty communi-ties. Ten geographically organized ten- to twelve-day group meetings on *Atlas* interpretation have been held, involving colleagues and other informants in nearly all of our commu-nities. So we are now in a position to report this information to other social scientists. But, with an estimated 40–50-page chapter for each of some fifty categories of concepts, the re-porting itself will be a long and arduous task, and we hope to involve a number of young people in the social and behav-ioral sciences in this work.

One reason I have been able to devote so much time to this cross-cultural project is that, in 1965, I was appointed Professor in the Center for Advanced Study at the University of Illinois—an appointment that has freed me from all obli-gations to teach (although I do give my graduate seminar in psycholinguistics once a year) and has allowed ample time for much foreign travel. By the time this volume is in print, I shall also be in the midst of a sabbatical, busily drafting chap-ters reporting our *Atlas* data on the affective dimension of subjective culture to our social science colleagues!

The Lively Present Using our comparable SD instrument, we have obtained a thin, horizontal slice of information about the affective dimension of subjective culture across thirty human societies—in contrast to the thin, vertical slices obtained in most ethnographic studies of particular societies. To use a vivid (even if a bit disturbing) analogy, one may view our *Atlas* concepts as 600$^+$ probes into the "brains" of our thirty cultures—probes inserted in roughly corresponding regions of these cultural "brains." However, each probe yields only three types of signals—the $\pm$E, $\pm$P, and $\pm$A, along with the graded intensities of each—and these only from teenage males in each of the cultures. In our marked CATANS we are looking for cultural *Universals* (e.g., the $^+$E, $^-$P, and $^-$A of domesticated as contrasted with wild animals), *Subuniversals* (e.g., THURSDAY and FRIDAY, as their day of rest and worship, being more $^+$E and $^+$P than SATURDAY and SUNDAY for all of our Moslem communities), and *Uniquenesses* (for example, our Mayan Indian subjects, half of them young married men, giving forth unusually high $^+$P and $^+$A signals for WIFE, MOTHER-IN-LAW, and FATHER-IN-LAW).

We do have in hand two studies that very nicely demonstrate the value of cross-language research in the search for cognitive universals. One (Osgood, 1979d), based on the earlier American English "pilot" by Osgood and Richards (1973b)—"From Yang and Yin to *And* or *But*," shows that exactly the same semantic congruence principles hold for predicting the differential use of *and* versus *but* (in translation, of course) between conjoined adjectives across twelve human language-culture communities, without exception. The other (Osgood, 1977c), using our large Social Psychiatry Category, is titled "Objective Cross-national Indicators of Subjective Culture."

The Near Future? We believe that our comparably measured, quantitative cross-cultural *Atlas* data constitute a rather unusual type of subjective social indicator. It probes into a dimension of subjective culture—how young people feel about a wide variety of aspects of their physical and social environments—which is peculiarly significant because the value, strength, and activity that one attributes to things in his world are important determiners of what he is likely to try to do about them. If subjective indicators of this sort can be related to other, particularly objective, social indicators, then considerable light may be shed on the dynamics of human societies.

THEME III: CHANGES IN MEANING AND THE SURVIVAL
OF THE HUMAN SPECIES

The Recent Past Some very fundamental changes in the meanings people in high places and low have for the crucial social and political symbols of our time will be required if mankind is to reach the year 2000 in anything like his present shape. This theme was developed in my "Conservative Words and Radical Sentences" paper (1971a) for an audience of political scientists. It began with this quotation from Albert Einstein at the dawn of the nuclear age (1945): "The unleashed power of the atom has changed everything except our ways of thinking. Thus we are drifting toward a catastrophe beyond comparison. We shall require a substantially new manner of thinking if mankind is to survive."

With regard to "conservative words," I pointed out, among other things, that the gap between word and thing increases with the remoteness of things from immediate experience, that the words of international politics are typically analogic, that the power of words lies in the way they abstract from reality, sharpening certain features and leveling others, and that we are being led by old men using antiquated semantic maps to guide us through the wonderland of the twentieth century.

With regard to "radical sentences," I noted that the power of sentences lies in the fact that they can be used to assert things about their topics ("Tom is a thief"), that they can "crunch" words together and change their meanings ("He is a Fifth Amendment Communist"), and that they *are* potentially radical, lending themselves to poignant expressions ("She will make someone a nice husband") and novel ways of thinking.

And finally, with regard to "a semantic revolution," I first cautioned my readers that there must be "rules for breaking rules" in sentencing (e.g., to produce apposite metaphors like "Billboards are warts on the face of the countryside" rather than mind-boggling ones like "His brakes shouted at me"), and I warned them to maintain a healthy suspicion of pat phrases (like "mutual nuclear deterrence" and "civil defense"). I then suggested that the most important ingredient in a semantic revolution is using radical sentences to compensate for conservative words—and I took a few such from GRIT-thinking to illustrate my point: "The usual motive behind the threatening behavior of one nation toward another is fear"; "There is no real security in military superiority in a nuclear age"; and "Goodwill among nations is a result of, rather than a prerequisite for, de-escalation of tensions."

On June 26, 1973, I was invited to testify before the Subcommittee on Europe of the Committee on Foreign Affairs of the U.S. House of Representatives, chaired by Congressman Benjamin S. Rosenthal. I used this opportunity to suggest how the GRIT strategy might be applied to a very practical problem Congress was then debating—reducing U.S. armed forces stationed in Europe (which at that time was costing the taxpayers some $18 billion a year, more than half as much as the Vietnam War at its peak). The day of my testimony was a very busy one for the Congress—with a series of important votes on the floor for which the members on this subcommittee had to dash to and from—and I could only outline my testimony, but the whole of it was printed in the record. Subsequently, in 1974, I submitted a revised and updated version of this testimony as a paper to Bruce Russett, editor of the *Journal of Conflict Resolution*. After some heavy critiquing by several reviewers, it was accepted. But, since it would have been coming out soon after the *Mayaguez* affair—which was followed by much breast-beating all through the government, with threats of retaliation of any nation got the idea that we'd gone "soft"—I decided to withdraw it, at least temporarily, because (as my Indian cross-cultural colleagues might say) this would have been a most inauspicious time to make *any* proposal for reducing U.S. forces *anywhere*!

The Lively Present However, this paper, titled "GRIT for MBFR: A Proposal for Unfreezing Force-level Postures in Europe," came in very handy when, in the spring of 1977, I was invited to my first Pugwash Conference to be held in Munich in late August—this again via the intervention of my good friend Jerry Frank.* The full version was distributed to all thirty or so members of my Work Group III (on tension reduction, detente, etc.), and a ten-page summary was made available to all two hundred or more participants. Although I received gratifying comments from many who had read the whole paper or the summary, Work Group III never got around to discussing my proposal—or, for that matter, any psychological or psychiatric aspects of international relations—and I found the whole conference rather depressing. Although several prestigious physical scientists in the plenary sessions complained about the failure of Pugwash to have any significant impact on damping the nuclear arms race and explicitly pointed to psychological and social factors, most of them seemed to feel that "hard" scientists must know more even about such things than the "soft" scientists trained in those fields!

And as part of the very lively present, I must note that just a week and a half from now, as I sit here typing the finale of my autobiography, I will be delivering my presidential address to the Peace Science Society (International).

The Near Future? The title of my address to the PSS(I) will be titled "Mankind 2000 ??" with emphasis on the question marks. The address, as outlined, will be an "essence" of a fairly sizable paperback with the same title that I'm planning to write in the not-too-distant future. In preparation for this, I've been collecting, over the past several years, what now amounts to some ten feet of materials: whole books and articles from sober journals like the *Bulletin of the Atomic Scientists*

---

*For the uninitiated let me note that Pugwash was the name of a little town in Canada where the first meeting of East and West scientists, then mainly nuclear physicists, was held; in recent years Pugwash meetings have been expanding to include behavioral and social scientists as well.

and the AAAS *Science,* from liberal popular magazines like *The Progressive* and the *Saturday Review,* from some radical magazines like *Ramparts* and *Ske₂tic,* and from *The Washington Watch* and *The Washington Spectator,* along with clippings from newspapers and from scholarly papers by people in diverse, peace-related groups. These materials are organized into a wide variety of categories—e.g., MIL/NUC, ENERGY (and ENERGY/NUC), ENVironment, DEVelopment, ECON, MULTINATionals, POLitics, HUNGer, POPulation, SOCiety, and, of course, PSYCHological . . . ending with HOPE??? The emphasis in the planned *Mankind 2000 ??* will be on equally depressing psychological factors—like pollyannaism, psychologic, immediate (concrete) versus remote (symbolic) reinforcement, and Darwinian egoism versus societal altruism—and how these factors (without hardly any awareness of them) are interacting in each of the "substantive" areas, like MIL/NUC, ENERGY, and ENV.

My future plans for both Theme I—writing what will by my magnum opus (!), *Toward an Abstract Performance Grammar*—and Theme II—helping to draft all those chapters reporting our cross-cultural *Atlas* data on subjective culture—both presuppose that there will *be* a Mankind 2000 (people around to read them), and I must confess that, as one who has been keeping his fingers on Mankind's pulse, I am not too sanguine about the prospects. And here I have discovered something interesting about myself: One might think that, as my estimated probabilities for the survival of Mankind in the nuclear age go down (as they have been doing over the past few years), my urge to give highest priority to writing *Mankind 2000 ??* should go up. But just the reverse has been the case. As prospects for Mankind's survival go down, the more I feel driven—like an artist getting ready to "paint his last picture"—to write my last scientific contribution, *Toward an Abstract Performance Grammar,* regardless of whether anyone will be around to read it! It is as if I, too, am subject to a selfish egoism that, under stress, takes precedence over altruism. And even saying this is very egotistical, implying that I might be able to do something about it.

So, I guess I need to show a bit of GRIT myself and do

what I can to help Mankind reach the Year 2000 (even though *I* certainly won't). Now that the old dinosaur—my alter ego from the days of childhood—is dozing off into perhaps his last long sleep, I myself, as ego, should be able to devote myself to altruism. But, then . . . .

1978

Selected Publications by Charles E. Osgood

(with C. N. Allen and H. S. Odbert) The separation of appeal and brand-name in testing spot advertising. *J. appl. Psychol.*, 1939, *23*, 60–75.

Ease of individual judgment-processes in relation to polarization of attitudes in the culture. *J. soc. Psychol.*, 1941a, *14*, 403–418.

(with R. Stagner) Analysis of a prestige frame of reference by a gradient technique. *J. appl. Psychol.*, 1941b, *24*, 275–290.

Meaningful similarity and interference in learning. *J. exp. Psychol.*, 1946, *36*, 277–301.

An investigation into the causes of retroactive interference. *J. exp. Psychol.*, 1948, *38*, 132–154.

The similarity paradox in human learning: A resolution. *Psychol. Rev.*, 1949, *56*, 132–143.

The nature and measurement of meaning. *Psychol. Bull.*, 1952a, *49*, 192–237.

(with A. W. Heyer) A new interpretation of figural after-effects. *Psychol. Rev.*, 1952b, *59*, 98–118.

Method and theory in experimental psychology. New York: Oxford University Press, 1953. (A textbook in experimental psychology for advanced undergraduates and graduate students.)

(with Z. Luria) A blind analysis of a case of multiple personality using the semantic differential. *J. abnorm. soc. Psychol.*, 1954a, *49*, 579–591.

(with T. A. Sebeok [Eds.]) *Psycholinguistics: A survey of theory and research problems.* Part 2. *J. abnorm. soc. Psychol.*, 1954b, *49* (4). (Monograph)

(with G. J. Suci) Factor analysis of meaning. *J. exp. Psychol.*, 1955a, *50*, 325–338.

(with P. Tannenbaum) The principle of congruity in the prediction of attitude change. *Psychol. Rev.*, 1955b, *62*, 42–55.

(with S. Saporta and J. C. Nunnally) Evaluative assertion analysis. *Litera*, 1956, *3*, 47–102.

A behavioristic analysis of perception and meaning as cognitive phenomena. In J. Bruner (Ed.), *Contemporary approaches to cognition*, Cambridge, Mass.: Harvard University Press, 1957a.

Motivational dynamics of language behavior. In M. R. Jones (Ed.), *Symposium on motivation*, Lincoln: University of Nebraska Press, 1957b.

(with G. J. Suci and P. H. Tannenbaum) *The measurement of meaning*. Urbana: University of Illinois Press, 1957c.

Semantic space revisited (a reply to U. Weinrich's review of *The measurement of meaning*). *Word*, 1959a, *15*, 192–200.

Suggestions for winning the real war with Communism. *Conflict Resolution*, 1959b, *3*, 295–325.

A case for graduated unilateral disengagement. *Bull. Atomic Scientists*, 1960a, *16*, 127–131.

Cognitive dynamics in the conduct of human affairs. *Publ. Opin. Quart.*, 1960b, *24*, 341–365.

The cross-cultural generality of visual-verbal synesthetic tendencies. *Behav. Sci.*, 1960c, *5*, 146–169.

An analysis of the cold war mentality. *J. soc. Issues*, 1961a, *17* (3), 12–19.

(with E. E. Ware and C. Morris) Analysis of the connotative meanings of a variety of human values as expressed by American college students. *J. abnorm. soc. Psychol.*, 1961b, *62*, 62–73.

An alternative to war or surrender. Urbana: University of Illinois Press, 1962a.

Graduated unilateral initiatives for peace. In Q. Wright et al. (Eds.), *Preventing World War III, some proposals*. New York: Simon & Schuster, 1962b.

Reciprocated initiative. In J. Roosevelt (Ed.), *The liberal papers*, New York: Doubleday (Anchor Books), 1962c.

Studies on the generality of affective meaning systems. *Amer. Psychologist*, 1962d, *17*, 10–28.

On understanding and creating sentences. *Amer. Psychologist*, 1963a, *18*, 735–751.

The psychologist in international affairs. In N. L. Farberow (Ed.), *Taboo topics*, New York: Atherton Press, 1963b.

Questioning some unquestioned assumptions about national defense. *J. Arms Control*, 1963c, *1*, 2–13.

(with M. S. Miron [Eds.]) *Approaches to the study of aphasia*. Urbana: University of Illinois Press, 1963d.

Semantic differential technique in the comparative study of cultures. *Amer. Anthropologist*, 1964, *66*, 171–200.

Dimensionality of the semantic space for communication via facial expressions. *Scandinavian J. Psychol.*, 1966a, *7*, 1–30.

Meaning cannot be r_m? *J. verb. Learning verb. Behav.*, 1966b, *5*, 402–407.

Perspective in foreign policy. Palo Alto, Calif.: Pacific Books, 1966c.

Testimony before the Senate Committee on Foreign Relations, May 25, 1966d.

On the strategy of cross-national research into subjective culture. *Soc. Sci. Information*, 1967, *6*, 5–37.

On the whys and wherefores of E, P and A. *J. Pers. soc. Psychol.*, 1969, *12*, 194–199.

Interpersonal verbs and interpersonal behavior. In J. Cowan (Ed.), *Studies in thought and language.* Tucson: University of Arizona Press, 1970.

Conservative words and radical sentences in the semantics of international politics. In G. Abcarian and J. W. Soule (Eds.), *Social psychology and political behavior.* Columbus, Ohio: Merrill, 1971a.

Exploration in semantic space: A personal diary. *J. soc. Issues*, 1971b, *27*, 5–64.

Where do sentences come from? In D. D. Steinberg and L. A. Jakobovits (Eds.), *Semantics: An interdisciplinary reader in philosophy, linguistics, and psychology.* Cambridge, Mass.: Cambridge University Press, 1971c.

Testimony before the House Foreign Affairs Committee, June 26, 1973a.

(with M. M. Richards) From Yang and Yin to *and* or *but. Language*, 1973b, *49*, 380–412.

Probing subjective culture. *J. Communication*, 1974, *24*, 21–34, 82–100.

(with W. H. May and M. S. Miron) *Cross-cultural universals of affective meaning.* Urbana: University of Illinois Press, 1975a.

A dinosaur caper: Psycholinguistics past, present and future. *Ann. N.Y. Acad. Sci.*, 1975b, *263*, 16–26.

GRIT for MBFR: A proposal for unfreezing force-level postures in Europe. 27th Pugwash Conference, Munich, West Germany, August 24–29, 1977a.

How should a university be? In D. Lerner and L. M. Nelson (Eds.), *Communication research—a half-century appraisal.* Honolulu: University Press of Hawaii, 1977b.

Objective cross-national indicators of subjective culture. In Y. H. Poortinga (Ed.), *Basic problems in cross-cultural psychology,* Amsterdam: Swets & Zeitlinger, 1977c.

(with J. K. Bock) Salience and sentencing: Some production principles. In S. Rosenberg (Ed.), *Sentence production: Developments in research and theory,* Hillsdale, N.J.: Erlbaum, 1977d.

(with C. Tanz) Will the real direct object in bitransitive sentences please stand up? In A. Juilland (Ed.), *Linguistic studies offered to Joseph Greenberg*, Saratoga, Calif.: Anma Libri, 1977e.

Lectures on language performance. Berlin, Heidelberg, New York: Springer-Verlag, 1979a (in press).

Things and words. In M. R. Key (Ed.), *The relationship of verbal and nonverbal communication*, 1979b (in press).

What is a language? In D. Aaronson and R. W. Rieber (Eds.), *Psycholinguistic research: Past, present, and future.* Hillsdale, N.J.: Erlbaum, 1979c (in press).

From Yang and Yin to *and* or *but* in cross-cultural perspective. *Internat. J. Psychol.*, 1979d, *14*, 1–35.

Other Publications Cited

Bever, T. G. The cognitive basis for linguistic structures. In J. R. Hayes (Ed.), *Cognition and the development of language.* New York: Wiley, 1970.

Blumenthal, A. L. *Language and psychology.* New York: Wiley, 1970.

Brown, R. Is a boulder sweet or sour? *Contemp. Psychol.*, 1958, *3*, 113–115.

Carroll, J. B. *The study of language.* Cambridge: Harvard University Press, 1953.

Carroll, J. B. Review of "The measurement of meaning." *Language*, 1959, *35*, 38–77.

Chomsky, N. *Syntactic structures.* 's-Gravenhage, Holland: Mouton, 1957.

Chomsky, N. Review of B. F. Skinner, 1957, *Verbal behavior. Language*, 1959, *35*, 26–58.

Chomsky, N., and G. A. Miller. Introduction to the formal analysis of natural languages. In R. D. Luce, R. R. Bush, and E. Galanter (Eds.), *Handbook of mathematical psychology.* New York: Wiley, 1963.

Diebold, A. R., Jr. A survey of psycholinguistic research, 1954–1964. In *Psycholinguistics: A survey of theory and research problems* (Reissue). Bloomington: University of Indiana Press, 1965.

Etzioni, A. The Kennedy experiment. *Western polit. Quart.*, 1967, *20*, 361–380.

Fodor, J. A. Could meaning be an r_m? *J. verb. Learning verb. Behav.*, 1965, *4*, 73–81.

Fodor, J. A., and M. Garrett. Some syntactic determinants of sentential complexity. *Perception and Psychophysics*, 1967, *2*, 289–296.

Greenberg, J. H. (Ed.). *Universals of language.* Cambridge, Mass.: M.I.T. Press, 1963.

Gulliksen, H. How to make meaning more meaningful. *Contemp. Psychol.,* 1958, *3,* 115–118.

Hall, E. Nixon and the U.S. are going to become gradually negative for both Russia and China, and simultaneously? (Interview with C. E. Osgood.) *Psychol. Today,* November 1973, pp. 54–60, 64–72.

Hastorf, A. H., C. E. Osgood, and H. Ono. The semantics of facial expressions and the prediction of the meanings of stereoscopically fused facial expressions. *Scandinavian J. Psychol.,* 1966, *7,* 179–188.

Kahn, H. *On thermonuclear war.* Princeton, N.J.: Princeton University Press, 1960.

Kahn, H. *Thinking about the unthinkable.* New York: Horizon Press, 1962.

Kahn, H. *On escalation: Metaphors and scenarios.* New York: Praeger, 1965.

Karwoski, T. F., H. S. Odbert, and C. E. Osgood. Studies in synesthetic thinking: II. The rôle of form in visual responses to music. *J. gen. Psychol.,* 1942, *26,* 199–222.

Kuhn, T. S. *The structure of scientific revolutions.* Chicago: University of Chicago Press, 1962.

Kumata, H., and W. Schramm. A pilot study of cross-cultural methodology. *Publ. Opin. Quart.,* 1956, *20,* 229–238.

Maclay, H. Linguistics and psycholinguistics. In B. Kachru et al. (Eds.), *Issues in linguistics: Papers in honor of Henry and Renée Kahane.* Urbana: University of Illinois Press, 1973.

Miller, G. A., and N. Chomsky. Finitary models of language users. In R. D. Luce, R. R. Bush, and E. Galanter (Eds.), *Handbook of mathematical psychology.* New York: Wiley, 1963.

Miron, M. S., and C. E. Osgood. Language behavior: The multivariate structure of qualification. In R. B. Cattell (Ed.), *Handbook of multivariate experimental psychology.* Chicago: Rand McNally, 1966.

Morris, C. *Paths of life.* New York: George Braziller, 1956. (Originally published, Harper 1942.)

Olmsted, D. L., and O. K. Moore. Language, psychology and linguistics. *Psychol. Rev.,* 1952, *59,* 414–420.

Ono, H., A. H. Hastorf, and C. E. Osgood. Binocular rivalry as a function of incongruity in meaning. *Scandinavian J. Psychol.,* 1966, *7,* 225–233.

Pool, I. D. (Ed.). *Trends in content analysis.* Urbana: University of Illinois Press, 1959.

Saporta, S. (Ed.). *Psycholinguistics: A book of readings.* New York: Holt, Rinehart and Winston, 1961.

Sebeok, T. A. (Ed.). *Style in language.* New York: Wiley, 1960.

Snider, J. G., and C. E. Osgood (Eds.). *Semantic differential technique: A source book.* Chicago: Aldine, 1969. (Includes contemporary bibliography of research related to the semantic differential technique. Compiled by H. Bobren, C. Hill, J. Snider, and C. Osgood.)

Stagner, R., and C. E. Osgood. An experimental analysis of a nationalistic frame of reference. *J. soc. Psychol.*, 1941, *14*, 389–401.

Steinberg, D. D., and L. A. Jakobovits (Eds.). *Semantics: An inter-disciplinary reader in philosophy, linguistics, and psychology.* Cambridge, Mass.: Cambridge University Press, 1971.

Suci, G. J. A comparison of semantic structures in American Southwest culture groups. *J. abnorm. soc. Psychol.*, 1960, *61*, 25–30.

Triandis, H. C., and C. E. Osgood. A comparative factorial analysis of semantic structures in monolingual Greek and American college students. *J. abnorm. soc. Psychol.*, 1958, *57*, 187–196.

Watt, W. C. On two hypotheses concerning psycholinguistics. In J. R. Hayes (Ed.), *Cognition and the development of language.* New York: Wiley, 1970.

Weinreich, U. Travels through semantic space. *Word*, 1958, *14*, 346–366.

Robert R. Sears

Robert R. Sears

I suppose most contemplative people, nearing the end of their active careers, construct retrospective schemas for their lives. Love and work are usually central to them, at least for men. These are the areas that are most prepossessing in youth and through the following decades absorb the most attention and energy. In my schema, the two are intertwined more than for most men because psychology is my work and my wife is a psychologist. The broad structure of the pattern is very simple, having just two time-defined parts—the nineteen years before I simultaneously fell in love and became a psychologist, and all the years since. These latter are separated into geographically defined career segments, since that is my mnemonic device for ordering my past.

The first period is of minor interest in the present context. All it tells is the demographic likelihood that I would become a professor and the unlikelihood, at least from surface appearance, that the professorship would be in psychology.

First the demography. I am a pure enough Californian by birth, but place of birth does not always define the family culture in which a child is reared. In fact, my parents had come from Missouri just two years earlier, and until they had absorbed the new culture, doubtless I might as well have been in Missouri myself.

The Sears family came from England in 1623, settling in Massachusetts. Our branch moved westward, and the family background for several generations was predominantly small-town and solid middle-class. There were a few farmers, but more shopkeepers, clergymen, and teachers, all successful but none notable. My father was born on a farm, the third of eight children, and lived there through his youth. He was probably a good reflection of his forebears. He was a kind man, hard-headed about business matters, exemplary in moral values and conduct, valuing education, and had high achievement motivation toward his professional goals. Evidently the family had always had only modest aspirations for wealth, fame, and power. I infer this from the fact that they did not achieve them, although the family history shows clear evidence of sufficient intellectual competence, and far back is notable for personal stability. What must have determined life outcomes was level of aspiration. Strong nuclear families, with generations of fathers who are satisfied by their own modest successes, do not drive their sons to ride wild horses across new horizons.

With a similar English heritage, my mother's family, the Richardsons, landed in North Carolina in the mid-eighteenth century. They were more professionally oriented than the Sears; doctoring was a common career. The Richardsons moved westward, too, and in the Civil War my maternal grandfather was a surgeon with the Southern forces at Gettysburg while his brother served similarly with the Northern. Both settled into good practices in Cincinnati after the war.

My mother was the youngest of seven children, but unlike my father she did not grow up in a strongly intact family. Both her parents died of tuberculosis before she was four years old. Her father's death, the first, left little scarring—she was too young—but her mother's was traumatic. Through her childhood, she had loving, but multiple, caretakers in different relatives' families. The early feelings of irreparable loss never entirely left her and probably were responsible for her adult

396

emotionalism and love of people. She had a fine strong so-
prano voice, loved being center-stage in any gathering, and had
a dream of being an opera singer.

She and my father taught in rural elementary schools before they were married, but then his impulse toward upward
mobility—away from the rural environment—steered him toward a university education. They decided to go all the way
west, to Stanford, arriving in Palo Alto with $40 six weeks be-
fore the 1906 earthquake. Both had to work to eat, and my
mother delayed enrolling in the university until they could get
a little ahead with money. She clerked in the Education Department library, and my father chipped mortar off the fallen
sandstones to add his share. My mother never did go to college, because I was born on August 31, 1908.

I grew up in Palo Alto, a quiet, single-class university town.
There was a streetcar line running out to the university, but
the whole town was no more than a hundred square blocks;
the population would not have strained fifty of them. I began
reading at age three and found school no challenge when I
started first grade on my sixth birthday. It never did become
more than accustomed routine until I got to college.

Even in those days academics were peripatetic. My father
graduated in 1909, being appointed at once to the Education
faculty with the understanding that he would start work on a
Ph.D. Hence, a little later, we spent a year in New York to that
end. In 1918 we went again, for a quarter, so he could finish
the Ph.D. I had a mastoidectomy almost at once and dropped
out of school, missing fractions, leaving me with an educational deficit I have never overcome. But on a trip to the doctor's office I was caught up in the wild celebration of the false
Armistice, leaving me with an asset, too; I used that adventure
for English themes for years afterward. In 1920 we spent a
year in Minneapolis, where my father made a survey of the
university, and I learned the bitter meaning of minority status;
I was the tallest and skinniest boy in my eighth-grade class and a
foreigner to boot.

Now, as to the improbability of my becoming a psychologist. My early childhood had been warm and secure, and I was
poorly prepared for the birth of a brother just after I started
school. I had thoroughly enjoyed reading before, and now it

became a refuge. As I reached adolescence and high school, this passive fantasy was strongly supplemented by a more active form, the writing of short stories. Along with this came an enthusiastic interest in drama. In high school I won a short-story contest with a pulp-type adventure story, acted in several school plays, became an editor of the school paper, and dreamed always of a life as a writer, an actor, a director, or some other character in the world of make-believe.

Going to Stanford was automatic. Professors' children received free tuition. Going into English was equally automatic. During the preceding summer I had worked at Fallen Leaf Lodge as a waiter in the daytime and a combo piano player in the evenings. John Steinbeck was working there, too. At twenty-three he was vastly older and wiser than I—a significant model. He was clearly dedicated to a writing career, and with his serious talk of literature as the most important profession in the world, my dreaming of such a future hardened perceptibly into planning.

Miss Edith Mirrielees was a Stanford professor of English who specialized in creative writing. She offered a course for freshmen who had some literary experience, people like me who needed discipline in their creative activity. She was a gentle woman, kindly but with high standards; most importantly, she knew how to introduce reality into adolescent career fantasies. Gradually, quite painlessly, she let it become clear to me that, though I could write well enough, I had little to say. Few do at age eighteen; even the wise and experienced Steinbeck produced no real literature until he was thirty. I am sure Miss Mirrielees sensed—correctly—that my creativity was hollow fantasy based on others' fantasies, those of the movies, the theater, and the least esoteric fiction. I began dimly to see that a career in the teaching of literature would be less hazardous than one in the writing of it. The demographics were beginning to tell; my secure, socially protected childhood and the academic background were perfect for a professor, but they had little to contribute to a career of serious artistry.

At that age, however, fantasy and reality are still well mixed. The theater was yet to be explored. A course in Shakespeare from Margery Bailey set me off. She was an accomplished actress herself, playing professionally some summers, and she made Shakespeare come alive. So I dove headlong into both community and university theater. Her doctorate was from Yale; it was a trail worth following. Maybe there would be a chance to work in the new Yale School of Drama, too? Without consulting her, I wrote to the Yale English Department for information about graduate work. To my dismay, they informed me that three ancient languages would be required. That was the end of that, for my interests were in the mystery of people, how and why they thought and felt and acted like they did. My curiosity was inarticulate, but gradually I was getting the sense that the humanities were begging my questions.

At this discouraging point I fell in love. At the beginning of the spring quarter of my junior year, I met Pauline (Pat) Snedden. By June we were engaged. She was going to summer school to make up a couple of missed quarters; I went, too, with the easy excuse that an earlier appendectomy had left me with a missing quarter. She registered for introductory psychology with Professor E. A. Bott, visiting from Toronto; I did, too, having nothing else in mind. The first weeks were not inspiring, but one day, during a particularly tedious discussion of learning theories, the professor casually drew a live white rat from his pocket and put it on the podium, where it sat up peacefully washing its face while he finished the lecture. To me this was a dramatic bit of stage business, and my instant enthusiasm generalized to what the professor was talking about. Maybe it was the white rat, or maybe it was the reinforcing anlage of being in love; whatever it was, that was when and why I became a psychologist.

In the fall, Pat and I took two courses from Paul Farnsworth, an enthusiastic and iconoclastic young behaviorist who had worked with Max Meyer and gotten his degree with A. P. Weiss. To my astonishment I discovered that psychology was a whole science devoted to just the kinds of things I wanted to know. Furthermore, unlike literary study, it had objective ways of finding answers to such questions. I had never known about the experimental method, or exact measurement, or the precise definition of variables. These were very satisfying. I changed my major to psychology, and with encouragement from Farnsworth and one of my TA's, Harry

Harlow, decided to get a Ph.D. Lewis Terman was the department head and an old family friend. He urged me to go to Yale to work with Clark Hull, whose book, *Aptitude Testing*, Terman had just edited and much admired. So I did.

Any psychologist can read between the lines of this developmental sequence. There were the two very different parents: an emotional, insecure mother with artistic longings and a love of people; and a hard-headed, serious, academic father from a stable family background. There was a secure childhood with strong attachment to, and identification with, both parents. But then came the shock of an unprepared-for sibling at age six. Clearly, the more serious deprivation was maternal, and not surprisingly her personality most influenced my initial adolescent interests and fantasy style. The need for a career choice brought into play the reality-oriented, academic hardheadedness of the other parent. Psychology was the best possible melding of the two streams of development. Then, in some curious way, I guess love did the rest.

Graduate Work at Yale

This was 1929. The International Congress of Psychology was being held in New Haven just before school opened. I would go, of course, and get my first glimpse of the great ones I wanted to emulate. But Pat had been at her family's camp in New Hampshire all summer. A telegram reached me in New Haven, an invitation to come to the lake. What to do? Our year-long engagement had been tempestuous, and a fortnight's visit was too tempting to refuse. Pat would be returning to Stanford for her final year, and it was unthinkable not to see her before she left. So I missed the congress and never saw Pavlov. I have had nearly a half-century of summers at the lake, however, for eventually Pat and I did get married.

The Yale psychology department was curiously fragmented. Its central core was tiny and undistinguished—two professors and one assistant professor who taught in Yale College and took responsibility for supervising the graduate program. Somewhere else, in old houses scattered about New Haven, were the great researchers in the Institute of Psychology.

These satellites were what really counted to the outer world—Raymond Dodge, Robert Yerkes, Arnold Gesell—but they were interested only in research. They hired graduate students for research assistants, but other than dissertation direction, did little teaching. Then there was the new man, Clark Hull. He was in the Institute, too, but he proved to be a maverick; he liked graduate students and in that first year offered a seminar each semester. In the autumn it was on hypnosis, because he was "cleaning up the field," and he wanted the second to be on the conditioned reflex, which was his newest enthusiasm. However, President Angell had brought him to Yale to develop aptitude testing; so, reluctantly, Hull gave his spring seminar on that, using it to provide solid training in statistics for our group of eight first-year students.

The graduate program was a curious mix. It included a tough two-year sequence on the history of psychology, taught by R. P. Angier, the department chairman, and anatomist Harold Burr's two years of functional neuroanatomy. There were no other didactic seminars. Mainly we were on our own, with the foreshadow of the distant "comprehensives" to goad us to learn something else in the library. The goad was blunt, however, for even from the first month our own research kept interfering, and neither the faculty nor the older graduate students set a good example; all they talked about was research. (Two years later, as the exams approached, I went to E. S. Robinson with my worries about knowing so little textbook psychology. He was airy: "Oh, you'll pick that up when you get out and start teaching!")

I felt no disposition to change things, for I was enjoying the research atmosphere too much. This objectivity and search for new findings was what had interested me at Stanford. The mechanics of measurement and instrumentation, dealing with phenomena that could be touched and seen, were part of this interest. During that first year, Yale offered two appropriate channels: research on hypnosis for the first-year project, and the discovery of functions for neural pathways. As to the former, there was a certain glamour to hypnosis that Hull ignored, but the idea of attacking a mysterious mentalistic phenomenon with hard psychophysiological measurement was doubly appealing to me. The research challenge I chose from the list of problems that Hull presented was to discover whether the reality of pain could be denied under hypnosis at not only the verbal level but the physiological as well. The answer was to be sought with kymographs, pneumographs, galvanometers—all the trappings of objective behaviorism. I even designed a little gadget to measure facial grimace. This was "muscle-twitch psychology" with a vengeance! There were two questions: Would subjects respond differently to pain under waking and hypnotic conditions? And if so, could they simulate the hypnotic responses by intentional effort? By the end of the year I had answers to both: to the first—yes, in some respects; to the second—no. This work on hypnotic anesthesia provided my first scientific publication (Sears, 1932).

Somewhere along the line, the glamour had gone out of hypnosis. In reading Janet, I had become interested in hysterical symptoms, and now was curious to know whether hysterical anesthesia was similar to its hypnotic parallel. I arranged to spend a few weeks at Bellevue Hospital during the early summer to repeat the study with such patients. Regrettably, all the hysterics in New York must have known that anesthesia was no longer a stylish symptom; I found only one case during six weeks, and the results were equivocal.

My second year at Yale was an extension of the first so far as amount of research was concerned, but the field shifted radically. Conditioned reflexes had already aroused considerable interest. The previous year Ernest R. Hilgard had done his classical study on eye-blink conditioning and I was one of his subjects. Hull was turning to conditioning also, and he replaced the hypnosis seminar with one on conditioned reflexes. Functional neuroanatomy had reached a peak of interest for American psychologists by 1930, and I moved rather briskly into research in both fields. Burr had an assistantship available, but I did not want to work on purely anatomical problems, and recommended that he offer it to Donald Marquis, a close friend of mine at Stanford. Marquis was just finishing his second year of graduate work there but wanted to complete his doctorate elsewhere. To my delight he accepted Burr's invitation. He was well trained in physiology and neuroanatomy; as a roommate, he made an exceptional tutor for me during this second year. Conditioning soon became the rage around our laboratories, and we took delight in conditioning every reflex we could think of. Our most spectacular success was with the abdominal reflex, kymographic recordings of which Hull published in a handbook article.

The first-year combination of neuroanatomy and hypnosis aroused my interest in the unconscious and led me into two quite different research projects. The first involved a patient who had a true hysterical anesthesia of one hand. Using electric shock as an unconditioned stimulus, psychiatrist Louis Cohen and I attempted to establish a conditioned withdrawal reflex to a touch stimulus that she purportedly could not feel. She learned almost at once but, for a time, continued to deny that she could feel the touch.

This peculiar result led me to another query about the unconscious: Could visual stimuli below the absolute threshold be used as conditioned stimuli? Sidney Newhall had built an instrument for measuring visual brightness thresholds. Using suprathreshold stimuli, we established conditioned finger-withdrawal reflexes to shock in normal subjects. Then we tested them with stimuli below their own absolute thresholds. We discovered that a significant proportion of the subliminal stimuli would evoke conditioned finger retraction even when they did not evoke conscious reports of seeing the stimulus. We concluded that finger retraction and verbal reports were somewhat independent response systems to a single mode of stimulation (Newhall and Sears, 1933).

In the meantime, Pat had finished at Stanford, and in 1931 obtained her master's degree in clinical child psychology at Teachers College. With a little engineering, she obtained a research assistantship to William Healy and Augusta Bronner's delinquency project at Yale for the following year.

By this third year, my own interests had turned entirely to the nervous system. K. S. Lashley's work was focusing everyone's attention on the functions of the cortex. A widely discussed question was whether conditioning could occur in the absence of the cortex, and I proposed to Burr a dissertation on the conditionability of decorticate goldfish. He was agreeable and offered me a $600 fellowship for the year, together with a free room in the neurosurgeons' residency dormitory. I spent the summer learning how to use iridectomy scissors to remove the optic cortex of a goldfish without killing it and how to section the brains to make sure that I had gotten all the cortex. By the end of the summer I was ready to start conditioning fish to light stimuli. Not only do goldfish have tiny brains from a surgical standpoint, but they are extraordinarily dim-witted about learning anything. With persistence, however, I found a good method for conditioning them to light stimuli and then was able to get enough postsurgical recoveries to determine the role of the optical cortex in conditioning.

While this rather tedious process was going on, several opportunities were offered for the study of human patients who had suffered cortical damage. Pat had worked extensively with reading disabilities, and when a neurosurgeon provided us with a case of complete occipital lobectomy, we set to work trying to discover the effects on various measurable functions that had been identified in the study of reading disabilities.

The year, the dissertation, the additional researches all gradually came toward an end. This was 1932 and the bottom of the Depression. It was clear that I would get my degree on time, and now, four years after we had first gotten engaged, it was also clear that Pat and I were going to get married. The question was whether we would have anything to eat! April came with no signs of a job in the offing. May came and there was no change. The picture was brighter for Pat; she had two or three nibbles. Finally, in mid-May she was offered a $3,000 clinical position in Hartford. Burr said he would be happy to give me $1,000 as a postdoc for the next year. Pat and I agreed we could live halfway between Hartford and New Haven and both of us do an easy commute. Still, this was not what we really wanted; she wanted to be at a university where she could continue for a Ph.D., and I wanted some headier fragrance than formaldehyde. The Hartford people were pressing for a decision, and finally, in mid-June, I received an offer of an instructorship at the University of Illinois. To my consternation it would involve teaching courses in personality and abnormal psychology, fields about which I knew virtually nothing. I was considered suitable by the Illinois people simply because I had worked on hypnosis and hysteria! But it was a job, it paid $2,400, and we grabbed it quick. The day after I got my diploma, we drove to New York and got married on June 25, 1932.

Illinois

We spent the summer at Stanford; I read vigorously to prepare for teaching, and Pat attended Kurt Lewin's first American course on child psychology. Terman was much impressed with this new action-oriented offshoot of Gestalt psychology. Pat's ten-minute recaps of the early lectures got me sufficiently involved that I joined her in the class. Lewin's was a strange kind of theory, hard for a dyed-in-the-wool conditioned-reflexer to absorb, but it dealt with some interesting problems—e.g., frustration and conflict—that I had not seen treated before in terms of performance alone. G. V. Hamilton's (1925) approach to them had, in fact, included action theory, but I did not realize it because of my prepossession with the learning process.

Going to Urbana was scary. I had never taught a class before, nor even given a speech. The normal teaching load was fourteen class-hours a week; for me that meant ten hours of quiz sections in Psych. 1 and a four-hour lecture course on personality. I was nervous about the sections but decided I could read the text ahead of the students. It was the personality course that floored me—I had no real grasp of what the field comprised, and I wanted a structure for it. Pat suggested that psychoanalytic theory might provide such a framework. She said Goodwin Watson had used it effectively at Teachers College, and there was a new book by Healy, Bronner, and Bowers (1930) that gave a readable and thorough outline of the theory. This proved an excellent solution. I quickly discovered that, for undergraduates, the abstract principles of psychoanalysis needed a lot of substantive examples. I had them—not from living, not from clinical experience—but from Balzac, Homer, Dreiser, Dickens, Shakespeare, Mark Twain, and other writers. Twain in particular served me well. My mother-in-law gave me a complete set for a wedding present, and I loved to browse in *Tom Sawyer* and *Huck Finn*. I went through about half the set that first year of marriage—quite possibly a regressive fantasy much like that of Mark Twain when he was writing the boys' books in the early years of *his* marriage (see my analysis of *him* in Sears et al., 1978). I have never been one to waste any knowledge I might have, and now my discarded literary career stood me in good stead. Indeed, better than I expected, for at the end of that first year the *Daily Illini* awarded me its "Big Shot" teaching accolade.

As soon as the teaching was well under way, Elmer Culler invited me to use his animal laboratory for my research. For some now-forgotten purpose I began conditioning a dog. The dog died. And suddenly so did my interest in neuropsychology. At Yale I had swung to a far extreme from my earlier literary enthusiasms; I had tested the limits, and the findings were clear. The biological part of psychology was not for me. In truth, I lacked all the necessary background in chemistry and physiology and had no interest in acquiring it. So I spent weekends for several months writing up four research papers that had been hanging over from Yale, sent them to press, and cheerfully cast the field to limbo for the rest of my life.

I decided to look further at research on personality and motivation. The only background that I could see as being useful for that field was clinical experience, of which I had no more than I had of chemistry. The opportunity to get some came in the second semester, however, when Herbert Woodrow, the department chairman, offered to cut my teaching load by two hours if I would serve as the Urbana clinical psychologist for the Institute of Juvenile Research traveling clinic. Pat quickly taught me the rudiments of testing, including the Stanford–Binet, and I became *de facto* a clinician. Over the next three years this experience proved valuable for my teaching, though it contributed nothing directly to my research.

Psychoanalytic theory was becoming quite attractive to me, the defense mechanisms especially. I could find a multitude of examples in literature, but more convincingly I could recognize their operation in people I knew—and in myself. There was a nagging doubt about the theory, though. Some aspects seemed very abstract, even farfetched, and my own intuition did not verify them. I knew only what I read of the therapeutic method by which analysts made the observations from which they derived the principles. What I did know, plus what I had learned about hypnosis, made it sound quite susceptible to suggestion. I knew I would feel a lot better if I could verify the concepts by more objective methods. But how? I looked all through the research literature (you could do that in 1933) and found no examples. I read William McDougall and G. V. Hamilton and Harry Hollingworth assiduously, getting lots of ideas one step closer to objectivity, but nowhere could I get a handle on a practical research beginning.

Then one day I was walking home from the office with a friend whom I had previously recognized as a very tight fellow with a penny. With mild outrage, he told me of having gone to dinner with friends, of his wife's having inadvertently left her cigarette case *with one cigarette in it* when they went home, and of his host's having returned the case *empty* the next day. "Can you imagine anyone so cheap and stingy?"

I nearly strangled with suppressed laughter. Here was projection in its purest form. One without insight into his own stinginess levels the finger at another. And here was a method ready for the taking. Within a week I designed rating scales for the triad of anal traits (stinginess, obstinacy, orderliness) and, in three fraternities, had all the members rate themselves and each other. When the data were analyzed, stingy boys without insight (repression) attributed more stinginess to their fellows than either generous boys or stingy boys with insight (nonrepression). Presence or absence of insight was measured by whether a boy's self-rating was equal to or less than the average attributed to him by his fraternity brothers. I had demonstrated the operation of projection. It was my first objective study of a psychoanalytic concept (Sears, 1936a). Two others—one on projection, one on repression—followed a couple of years later. They, too, derived useful methodology from observations of myself and others, a fact worth mentioning because most of my research since has had four similar qualities:

1. It has been on somewhat novel problems not much attacked previously by other psychologists.

2. It has been theory-based but with theories derivative from psychoanalysis or reaction psychology or Lewin.

3. It has used real-life-simulated settings with soundly grounded measurement techniques.

4. The specific hypotheses tested have come more from my direct observation of human behavior than from any prior research literature.

John McGeoch, editor of the *Psychological Bulletin,* heard what I was doing and suggested that I review the data on amnesias and other abnormalities of memory with a view to testing the theories of repression and dissociation. To make repression testable, I reformulated it in terms of Hull's learning concepts, finding particularly useful the notion of conflict between incompatible anticipatory goal responses (Sears, 1936b). Two decades earlier, Watson and Lashley had rejected psychoanalysis vigorously on theoretical grounds. Henceforth, most academic psychologists had ignored it. But a Yale-trained psychologist in the mid-1930s (especially one who had sectioned goldfish brains) was a quite respectable character, and these various studies attracted favorable attention. Freudian theory might still be suspect, but the human problems it comprised could be separated from the theory by being reformulated in more behavioral terms in the context of learning theory. It seemed clear to me that Freud's theory was ready-made for translation.

In the spring of 1935, Robert Yerkes came to Urbana and offered me a research assistant professorship at his Yale laboratory to work on conflict and neurosis in chimpanzees. I was flattered but reluctant. I had left animals behind and did not want to go back to them. So I refused.

A few weeks later our son David was born, and Pat and I at once took him to New Hampshire for the summer. Pat's mother had divided the family camp among her four daughters, and our part became a permanent summer home for us, more permanent than any other. A substantial part of my writing has been done there. Watching David develop during that summer and the following year was a fascinating new experience that strongly reinforced my decision to stay with human behavior. He even served as a subject for an experiment (Sears and Sears, 1940). Our second child, Nancy, would do the same for me three years later—and introduce me to the confounding influences of sex and ordinal position. I had only one discomfort: Illinois met the Yerkes offer with determined calm and without a promotion to an assistant professorship. I was a sitting duck for an offer that came the next spring.

Back to Yale

Hull was disappointed at my refusal of Yerkes' offer; he had liked the amnesia paper and was now getting interested in translating psychoanalytic theory into learning theory himself. Yale was having stirring times that I knew nothing of. The Institute of Human Relations had fallen on evil days. Its original mission was to develop a unified social science. Possibly to strengthen the university as a whole, possibly because nobody knew better, the administration hired several famous stars. The Institute got poor service from all but Hull, for none of them had any interest in collaboration. Each built his own empire. A drastic reorganization was needed.

In 1935, Mark May was appointed director. His first decision was to bring in a corps of youngsters who were known to have collaborative impulses. Some were already there. They came from psychology (Leonard Doob, Carl Hovland, Neal Miller, O. H. Mowrer, Richard Sollenberger, and myself), anthropology (C. S. Ford and G. P. Murdock), and psychoanalysis (Earl Zinn and John Dollard, who was trained as a sociologist). May made it clear that our job was to construct a behavior science to encompass all our various fields and interests. We would get all the support we needed as long as we were going toward that goal—individually and collectively. Hull set the substantive direction of the enterprise by offering his regular Wednesday evening seminar, on the relation of learning theory to psychoanalysis, as a forum for discussion and planning.

We were jubilant but a little awed. We knew enough of the

logic of science to realize that May had placed a tall order. Someone suggested we invite a physicist to our first meeting to tell us how the natural sciences had done it. It was an impressive story, one we wanted to emulate in our own field. So, a few weeks later, we invited the philosopher F. S. C. Northrop to discuss the application of such a logical procedure to the social sciences. He came, armed with a marvelous fluency, but by the end of the evening he had proved there could be no behavioral science until all the problems of physical science were solved. His reductionism was rejected out of hand, and he was never invited again.

We needed a problem. Miller and Dollard suggested a proposition from Freud linking frustration and aggression. There was some protest at the simplicity of their formulation, and when the bald proposal of "Frustration produces aggression" was laid before us about 10:00, I expressed outrage. With a grin, Dollard suggested that the simplicity of the idea was frustrating to me (which it was) and that I was providing a fine demonstration of their proposition! He needed argue no further. Our skepticism was abandoned in the face of the proposition's obvious susceptibility to systematic analysis and its very evident broad social implications. Several of us turned a substantial part of our time to constructing the theory and testing hypotheses derived from it. Most of the research papers had multiple authorship. For two years we seemed to live and breathe frustration and aggression. We lectured on it in classes, argued fine theoretical points at Saturday night parties, and interpreted our own and everybody else's behavior in our increasingly precise systematic terms. Finally, we wrote *Frustration and Aggression* (Dollard et al., 1939), a process involving a lot of both for the eight authors, as Mark May testified in his foreword to the volume!

A note about Northrop must be added. Three years after the reductionistic disaster—our zeal expended and our wisdom *re* the construction of a new science considerably expanded—we arranged a monthly seminar with him. We had proved our point with *Frustration and Aggression* and now were just a little anxious about where we stood vis-à-vis the logic of science. Perhaps Northrop had been a little chastened, too;

our side came out pretty well in the deliciously hot intellectual discussion during the next two years.

My initial appointment was for research in the Institute; the department just bought a little of my time. The first year my teaching was limited to an undergraduate course on abnormal psychology. Then, by a shocking accident, I became a full-time member of the department. E. S. Robinson was struck and killed by a bicyclist on campus. I succeeded him, inheriting his full-year course on Advanced General Psychology for senior majors. His prophecy—that I would learn "the rest of psychology" when I had to teach it—came true.

There was further reorganization. Angier retired, and Marquis succeeded him as chairman. He, Doob, Hovland, and I became the full-time core of the undergraduate department. For years, so it was reported to us, the senior class had voted psychology the worst department in the college. Excited over the success of the Institute research program, we resolved to change that reputation. Each of us designed a full-year beginning course, agreeing to include sufficient elementary psychology to permit a student to go on to advanced courses. Mine, focusing on personality and developmental psychology, rested heavily on the theories and interpretations we were developing in the Institute. These were coming to include not only the kind of motivation and action theory on which our aggression work was based, but Miller and Dollard's elaborated learning theory, which they presented later in *Social Learning and Imitation* (1941). After a satisfactory year with the new undergraduate program, the faculty (now mainly our group of assistant professors) reorganized the graduate program as well. My contribution was abnormal psychology in the first-year proseminar and a seminar on personality. In the latter, I found Lewin's work increasingly useful, not his theory but his variables and problems.

I must go back a step. Pat was anxious to continue with her Ph.D. in clinical psychology, but Illinois was not a suitable place. When we arrived in New Haven, Catherine Cox Miles offered her a clinical assistantship in the psychiatry department. This was to provide a clinical supplement to the regular, not-very-demanding curriculum in psychology, which was much the same as it had been in 1929. But whereas I had spent the remainder of my time on brain-behavior and conditioned-reflex research, Pat spent half-time as a clinician, with excellent supervision. She chose a dissertation problem not from the Institute matrix of ideas but from Lewin's work on level of aspiration. With what I still consider commendable efficiency, she finished running her last subject at 5:00 the night before our second child, Nancy, was born. The following year was infused in part with Lewin, because Pat, analyzing her data, found it possible to convert Lewinian theory to our Institute brand. Hovland and I had already done the same kind of thinking with Lewin's work on motor conflict; Neal Miller had done an even more satisfactory job with rat conflicts. Now, with a graduate seminar and with potential dissertation students available, my interest returned to the method I had used for studying repression, artificially induced feelings of success and failure. I had seen, and felt, a lot of both these feelings in recent years, and what had impressed me more than anything else was the depressive effect of failure. My study of motility (1942) was less a testing of hypotheses (though it did have some) than a search for outcomes. I discovered what I thought was a new defense mechanism, decontextualization; this was exemplified by a subject's systematic avoidance of all stimuli connected with a failure experience. I soon realized the phenomenon had been observed before, but I still think it never has been demonstrated so elegantly.

Pat got her degree in psychology in 1939. She was appointed a clinical assistant professor of psychology in the psychiatry department and added several part-time clinical positions to it, in Bridgeport, Stamford, and Darien. With her additional income we had a full-time, live-in housekeeper who cared for our two children. Four mornings a week I drove Pat to the railroad station and four evenings a week I met her and brought her home. The twenty-minute drive was always stimulating because she would give me one or two case capsules of youngsters she had seen during the day. By the end of three years, I had gotten an enormously rich education.

After my four isolated years in Urbana, with no colleagues to work with on the problems that interested me, the first four years at Yale were pure joy. By 1940, however, I was feeling a little sated with collaborative research, with teaching, and with the intensive interpersonal psychologizing of the Institute. It was a great relief when a Social Science Research Council committee invited me to do a review of the empirical data relevant to psychoanalysis; this would be solitary library work. The committee was after an answer to the same question that I had asked seven years before: How much of psychoanalytic theory can be substantiated by reference to nonanalytic data? I accepted with pleasure and spent a year at the job. The resulting monograph (Sears, 1943) provided an informational and theoretical base from which a substantial amount of others' research would arise during the next dozen years. It also satisfied my own questioning and put an end to my direct investigation of psychoanalytic concepts per se. Pat's clinical cases, my reading of many others', my personal observations of people (including my own children and those of my New Hampshire neighbors), and my theoretical convictions led me to believe that a wholly new approach to human development and motivation must be taken. The what and how of this were not yet clear. Obviously the family provided a learning situation for its children. With an increasingly sophisticated learning theory, we should be able to predict what kinds of child rearing would produce what kinds of children. The problems of how to define both the antecedent and consequent variables of this equation were much in my mind when I taught at Stanford during the summer of 1941, and in the late afternoons sat under a fig tree drinking a martini and watching fighter planes from Moffett Field practice their deadly maneuvers over the bay.

Europe's World War II had started while we were at Stanford for APA meetings in 1939. I stood on the quad with Lewin, listening to the radio news, shaken by his grief and anger. He was at Berkeley that summer, and we had had several excellent seminars, battling with great joy over whether *regression* in his terms was the same as *aggression* in the Yale system. Fundamentally, he was a rationalist, I believe, for he equated the latter with the former. To him, aggression *was* regression to some "more primitive" level of behavior. As I listened to the invasion of Poland that September afternoon, I could almost agree.

Then suddenly we born Americans were in it, too. On a Sunday afternoon in early December 1941, several of our Yale group were returning to New Haven from a meeting of the Psychological Round Table at New Britain. As we drove up to my house, Pat came running out with the horrifying news of the bombing of Pearl Harbor. Someone said "Jesus Christ!" softly. I went into the house and Pat and I listened to the radio. We didn't know it was signaling the end of the Institute, but the fact soon became apparent. First Hovland and then Doob slipped off to Washington, D.C., "for the duration." Then Miller joined the air force and the anthropologists disappeared into the navy. Don Marquis and I were holding the fort, teaching-wise, but it was lonesome. There were interim jobs to do—I gave speeches to the Connecticut police about how to handle panics, and in the spring I created a rehabilitation clinic. With the help of some graduate students, I tested more than a hundred handicapped people, reported their special abilities to a new state office of manpower procurement, and had the satisfaction of seeing a number of them hired in war industries.

One day in the spring I received a letter from George Stoddard. He was leaving Iowa and wanted to appoint a successor as Director of the Iowa Child Welfare Research Station. Two months earlier I had received tenure at Yale, an associate professorship, salary $4,500. Pat was secure in her clinical positions, was developing a good private practice in addition, but was only reasonably comfortable with her full-time home–work relationship. Iowa offered me a full professorship, $6,000 salary, and an administrative position that I was assured would not be arduous but would guarantee that I could keep my own research funded. Iowa had antinepotism rules, but Pat could have a nonsalaried title of research associate and do as much or as little research as she wanted. With our children aged four and seven, she preferred this flexibility to the demands of full-time employment. It looked like an almost ideal arrangement, and after the appropriate visitations, I accepted.

Iowa Child Welfare Research Station

My becoming a child psychologist was essentially by fiat—it was a titular matter. Within a few months the label was legitimized by the publication of my psychoanalytic monograph, the first half of which dealt with sexual development. But except for the personality area, child development was largely *terra incognita* for me. It was the Illinois situation all over again—hired for a field I knew almost nothing about. However, child development was only a few years old, and a good textbook taught me the rudiments. My colleagues soon taught me more.

One rather delicate problem faced me as director. Stoddard and Terman had been at loggerheads for years about the influence of environment on IQ. Terman was a nativist and argued strongly for the relative immutability of this measure of intelligence. The Iowa research had found it definitely mutable. I was—at considerable distance in time—a Terman student. I had taken pains to become fully informed about the Iowans' research, however, and I felt they had made a strong case. I said so, making clear my intention of providing whatever continued support Professor Beth Wellman's work might require.

There could have been another problem, too. Lewin was now at Iowa; he and Hull had been in public dispute about theory, and I was a Hullian. But Lewin and I were good friends, Pat promptly accepted his invitation to collaborate on an important level of aspiration paper, and we kept our theory disputes at a stimulating intellectual level while, as an administrator, I supported his work with vigor.

Administration was a whole new ballgame for me. I had not the remotest kind of experience to prepare me for the role change from Young Turk to Responsible Authority. Furthermore, I was the youngest person on the staff. There was no great problem within the Station, for the faculty were all deeply involved in their own research and teaching. It was simply like becoming a department head, and was doubtless easier in a new group than it might have been with well-known peers. What required more serious and more difficult role learning was becoming a public figure responsible for a large external program of parent education. Being host to hundreds at conferences, meeting with groups of strangers across the state, consulting formally with state boards on welfare matters—all reactivated the normal diffidence of childhood. But this diffidence had to be overcome, and it was. At a high cost. By the end of the first year my outer shell was at ease, but my gastrointestinal system was in a state of persistent turbulence. After my sixty-five-year-old father had a coronary occlusion, I began interpreting my psychosomatic symptoms as "incipient heart trouble." The consequent anxiety persisted in a nagging way until it was put to rest, a decade later, by brief psychotherapy. This bit of history is relevant here only because the therapy was as intellectually interesting as it was therapeutically beneficial and, as will be seen, had an important outcome for my career.

In terms of time and effort, administrative activities at Iowa approximately replaced the undergraduate teaching I had done at Yale. The Station was a graduate department only. My first student was George R. Bach. He wanted to find a way of studying young children's aggression. Just before I had left New Haven, E. R. Hilgard had visited us and described some very interesting work on doll-play therapy that he had seen in Chicago at the Psychoanalytic Institute. Bach decided to try that method. We designed an open-topped dollhouse simulating a nursery school room, made some rag dolls representing a teacher and young children, constructed a time-sampling method for recording the play, and Bach began running four-year-old subjects. He found the boys showed more aggression than the girls, and a lot of it was directed toward "rest period," a daily twenty-minute lie-down for all the children. Ruth Updegraff, director of the preschool, suggested an experimental deletion of rest period for some of the children; their aggression disappeared. It seemed to me that Bach had demonstrated a sensitive and objective method for measuring young children's motivation. During the next couple of years I explored doll play more intensively, with other students and assistants, and finally, after several methodological studies, developed a standardized procedure that seemed ready for use on a substantive problem.

Bach had used a preschool setting, but for the later studies I constructed a dollhouse like a home and used dolls that represented a family (father, mother, boy, girl, baby). This permitted us to measure not only the various motives expressed but also the roles adopted by a child in his fantasy. Gender role had interested me especially, because it seemed to represent the outcome of a sex-typing process for which differential child-rearing practices with boys and girls might be responsible. The wartime situation provided an excellent opportunity to test one hypothesis at least: that absence of a father in the home would decrease the aggression of boys. We designed a study comparing children from father-present and father-absent homes. Margaret Pintler collected the data in various Iowa and Illinois communities, Pat analyzed them, and we published a report on the aggression findings (Sears et al., 1946). Boys from father-absent homes did indeed show much less aggression than boys from father-present homes. A more detailed report on role choices did not come until several years later (Sears, 1951), but with the first promising analysis complete, we were ready to start on a broader study of the effects of many different aspects of child rearing on aggression and dependency in young children.

The what and how that had been troubling me in the summer of 1941 were at last becoming clear. What we needed were measures of the reinforcing and punishing behavior of parents as independent variables, and high-low measures of their children's aggression and dependency as dependent variables. As simple as that. Doll play and behavior observations would take care of the latter—and couldn't we just *ask* mothers about their child-rearing practices?

All this sounds consecutive, but I had a parallel life in war research that kept my direct participation in the doll-play studies at the necessary minimum. By 1944, the war was reaching a turning point, and American forces were engaged in a vigorous offensive in the Pacific. The air force was beginning to receive B-29 bombers. These promised to be very effective as offensive weapons, but their defensive gunnery system was a new one involving a prototype computer to replace the visual judgments and estimations of the gunners. Unfortunately, the sighting mechanism had been designed for easy engineer-

417

ing, not for effective human use, and the best-trained gunners were highly inaccurate. I undertook to do the necessary research for designing a new training procedure that would take account of the physical characteristics of the sighting system. I worked at the B-29 headquarters base in Salina, Kansas, from December 1944 to July 1945, commuting between Salina and Iowa City. Three associates and I finally solved the problem. First, we constructed a quick, economical, and accurate method of scoring gun-camera test films. As an assessment of its acceptability, we brought twenty air force sergeants to Iowa City for a month and had them use our method with bushels of gun-camera film, validating it against measures made by millimeter rulers; the latter was the standard method for air force assessment but was very expensive in time. Then we devised a training method based on constant informational feedback. On a scorching day in July, I lay on the roof of a 50-foot-high shed on a Salina prairie and signaled a Piper Cub back and forth, while our student gunners inside the mock-up shed took the critical test, using a B-29 sighting system with gun-cameras to record performance. *Question*: Had their hits increased? *Answer*: Yes! Their previous four weeks of regular training had brought them up to *0.3%* hits; our new ten-day program brought them up to *33%*. It was a grueling year, but worthwhile. I went off to New Hampshire, slept for three days to recover—waking up just in time to hear the news of the bomb at Hiroshima. Our training method was never used or needed.

Most of psychology's contribution to World War II was made by my age-mates. The major growth spurt in psychology Ph.D.'s came well after World War I, which itself created something of a hiatus in doctoral training of psychologists. Therefore, the generation just older than mine was thin. The next older group, mainly trained before World War I, were also few in number and no longer at the peak of productivity under the stressful conditions of World War II. Now, after the war, our generation was in its late thirties and early forties, a natural time to begin to assume responsibilities on a national scale for the profession itself and for other enterprises in government, business, and universities that engaged the efforts of psychologists. Historically, there is a gradual transition in such changes, with people of one generation giving way, one by one, to those of the next. After World War II, however, the change was more abrupt than I think one would normally expect.

In 1945, I was elected an APA representative to the National Research Council and became chairman of the Committee on Child Development. Shortly thereafter, I was elected a representative to the Social Science Research Council. Then came various APA committee chairmanships and appointments to consult with government agencies. The commuting to Salina turned into commuting to New York and Washington, D.C. The most demanding job came when the Veterans Administration asked APA to accredit graduate schools for clinical training. My Committee on Graduate Training was assigned the task, and as chairman I did all the paperwork; no one thought of hiring an administrative aide. The time and energy required were about equivalent to those for the B-29 job and had a more useful outcome. These were exciting years, perhaps in part because building a new APA and getting the profession reorganized was in the hands of a highly congenial age group. This was the Young Turks all over again, a peer group whose members enjoyed their hard work and felt at ease with one another.

The time had come for a more active research operation, however, and I was anxious to bring together a group of theoretically oriented people who would undertake the studies on the effects of child rearing on children's personalities. Shortly, Carl Hovland came to see me. He was doing part-time staff work for the Rockefeller Foundation and suggested that now would be a good time to start my project. In late 1946, with a $25,000 grant in the offing, I persuaded Vincent Nowlis to join me; the following spring I enticed my former Yale anthropological colleague John Whiting to come, too. Our first design was a straight correlational study of aggression and dependency. We planned to interview mothers about their practices and attitudes, and compare their reported behavior with their children's aggression and dependency, both of which we had been learning how to measure during the war years, first in doll play and then, with considerable precision, by behavior observations either in the free-play setting of the preschool or in contrived and standardized assessment situations.

The research started in the fall of 1947. We interviewed forty mothers about their child rearing, coding their responses on scales relating to various theoretically relevant aspects of the child-rearing process. The basic theory was that of the Institute of Human Relations; the specifics owed much to Whiting and Child's previous scale construction for analyzing ethnographic reports. The forty children of these mothers were in our preschool, and we measured their behavior in three ways. J. L. Gewirtz did behavior observations; E. K. Beller obtained teacher ratings; Eleanor Hollenberg (Chasdi) and Pat did doll play. It was a fairly massive piece of research, with a dozen collaborators, and was the first parent–child correlational study designed to test a series of hypotheses stemming from a well-defined theory. In the end, interestingly enough, the most provocative finding (of a seemingly greater influence of maternal punishment on girls than on boys) required an interpretation in terms of Freud's theory of identification rather than in behavior-theory terms (Sears et al., 1953). This discovery led to another "translation" job—a learning-theory interpretation of identification (Sears, 1957a) that directed much of the research in our later laboratories at Harvard and Stanford.

Meanwhile, at Harvard, President Conant was planning to reorganize the Graduate School of Education, placing more emphasis on education as applied social science. He wanted a social scientist with broadly educational interests as dean. Would I be interested? It was the wrong time. I was happily buried in research again and was getting very tired of administration. So, in the spring of 1948, the answer was "No."

Conant then chose a brilliant young administrator for the position, Francis Keppel, and the next spring the latter asked whether I would come to Harvard and set up a Laboratory of Human Development and be a senior social scientist on the Education faculty. Our data collection was now done; this seemingly nonadministrative position looked more interesting. Keppel went to see Pat and offered her an attractive half-time research appointment with only one course to teach. She was much pleased and was agreeable to going. The Harvard departments of psychology and social relations made friendly overtures, and we accepted. John Whiting agreed to go with us to continue our psychology–anthropology collaboration. To add to the exciting prospect of change, I was elected president of the APA that summer of 1949.

Harvard and Palfrey House

Keppel assigned us an old residence for our laboratory, Palfrey House. I taught summer school, wrote a review article on personality for the first volume of *Annual Review of Psychology*, and supervised the construction of lab rooms with superb one-way mirrors. We had brought three research assistants with us from Iowa, added a couple more in Cambridge, and later in the year Eleanor Maccoby, Harry Levin, and Edgar Lowell joined us. By the fall of 1950 we were in business and ready, with a USPHS research grant, to start the next step on child-rearing research. The Iowa study had directed our attention to identification, so we designed another correlational study, with a far more sophisticated mother interview designed by Eleanor Maccoby, to test several hypotheses concerning the antecedents of identification. The latter was to be measured through children's role choices in doll play. Designing the interview, pretesting it, and training interviewers and doll-play testers required nearly a year. In the fall of 1951 we began arranging cooperation with the Newton and Watertown schools, especially with their PTA's. By June, we were able to get two-hour interviews from 379 mothers and three doll-play sessions with their kindergarten children. During the summer, Maccoby supervised eight interview coders, so that in the fall of 1952 our data were ready for analysis. The collection of the data had been a big job, involving more than a score of people; the data analysis was equally big, for it rested on the efforts of the senior staff.

In the meantime we had begun planning for a number of other studies. Several of our research assistants were anthropology graduate students whose dissertations Whiting was directing. It was our conviction that a combination of laboratory and field studies, and a marrying of anthropology and psychology, would best provide the kinds of findings that would build a science around child rearing. We had a kitchenette in Palfrey House, so we hired a cook for lunches. Daily for two years these lunches provided a setting for staff meetings, a constant batting of ideas back and forth, a continuous planning for the new researches. Mainly these were anthropological. Our first (and too grandiose) scheme was to repeat something like the Iowa study on each of 100 cultures. By 1953 this goal was reduced to six. The Ford Foundation agreed to finance it, and Palfrey House's second major project was under way.

At Stanford, Hilgard had become graduate dean and needed a replacement as psychology department head. In late 1951 he asked me to consider it. I was greatly tempted, of course, but at that time I had been at Harvard only two years and it did not seem responsible to leave in the midst of such an expensive development as my appointment had represented. He offered the position to one of my colleagues, who, fortunately for me, sat on the offer for the better part of a year before refusing it.

Outside Palfrey House, Harvard was becoming less enchanting. Each professor had his own fiefdom; departments were jealous aggregates of these. A temporary calm had been brought to the conflict between hard and soft psychology by the construction of the Department of Social Relations, which served to separate personality, social, and clinical from experimental psychology. But by 1952 the waters were becoming ruffled again, for no good reason that I could see other than the irritability and jealousy of several potentates. As a neutral, in the School of Education, I found myself more and more frequently serving as an ameliorator. Furthermore, even Palfrey House had its problems from my standpoint. It had grown quickly to a formidable size, and the administrative responsibility was almost as great as that at Iowa. I guess it was a matter of "When in Rome . . . ." I had become a potentate, too.

The Stanford possibility was still open in late 1952 and

created a serious conflict. Several years earlier I had served as consultant to a gerontological research project. The interview protocols with retired people made a telling argument for retiring where one had lived, among friends and in a familiar community. When we went to Harvard, Pat and I were both sure this would be our last move and this would be where we would retire. It was near the lake in New Hampshire, for the summers, and Harvard was a stimulating place. So we remodeled an 1810 house near Harvard Square and began putting down personal roots. But *Stanford?* It would be so satisfying to go back.

From a realistic standpoint, Palfrey House had now reached a point at which my departure would not be seriously damaging, for the next steps had to be anthropological anyway. The School of Education at Stanford needed a new appointment in child development and offered the position to Pat; with our children starting high school and college, she was eager to return to a full-time career. So we accepted the Stanford offer.

Then came a shock. On a routine examination, my electrocardiogram showed some divergence from normal. The nagging anxieties about my heart suddenly flared into near-panic. A host of additional tests—all entirely negative—did not allay it. The anxiety had been too long detached from any original causes to respond to reality, and some therapy was clearly in order. An analyst friend arranged for me to see a San Francisco analyst as soon as I arrived on the West Coast, and somehow I survived the remaining three months in Cambridge.

Stanford Again

For all the monster it was, my anxiety responded quickly to skillful therapy. If it did not precisely keel over and die, it was at least so weakened that my zest returned, and within a few months I was hard at work with the department faculty on plans for the future. I had always identified strongly— perhaps a little blindly—with institutions, especially the Yale

Institute and department, the Iowa Station, the APA, Palfrey House and Harvard generally. Somewhere along the line, probably as a by-product of administrative responsibility, I had also become intensely competitive for *my* outfit to be the best. Harvard had only one real game—achieving status. I learned to play it well. On behalf of Stanford, with all the added enthusiasm that attaches to one's undergraduate school, I could practice the game without fatigue, without boredom, without conflict.

The first opportunity came even before I left Harvard. I was invited to serve on the board of trustees of the to-be-established Center for Advanced Study in the Behavioral Sciences. Established where? We looked in the Northeast, of course; that was where most of the scholars were. But all the good sites were too far from a library or too close to a city. Rather diffidently—because it seemed such obvious chauvinism—I urged consideration of the San Francisco Bay Area. Clark Kerr, then chancellor at Berkeley, supported me and, to my surprise, so did Harvard provost Paul Buck, who was quite frank in saying that dispersal of resources across America would benefit all of higher education, that there was already a high concentration in the Northeast. So in early 1954 we looked at the Bay Area; Kerr brought along architect William Wurster to help us. There were no suitable existing buildings, and we ended a discouraging weekend by sitting in Kerr's living room and wondering if there would be time to *build* a center for the scheduled opening in the autumn. I insisted it could be done—on a beautiful hill behind the Stanford campus. Bill Wurster got down on the floor with newspapers and his omnipresent architect's crayon and, in twenty minutes, sketched the plans for a new center. CASBS was built exactly as he designed it that afternoon. It opened on schedule.

At Stanford itself, my first concern was the department. It was high in faculty quality but terribly small in numbers. The graduate students were as good as any I had seen, but there were twice as many as the faculty could handle; we were at the peak of the postwar flood. We needed more senior faculty. President J. E. Wallace Sterling agreed and let us appoint

Leon Festinger at once. We asked Lois Stolz to shift from a part-time to a full-time professorial appointment, and I took on a full teaching load. After another year, I persuaded Hilgard to come back full-time to the department; he had been teaching heavily along with his deaning, but we needed his talents for running a research laboratory and for directing dissertations. Both the School of Education and the Graduate School of Business began to expand, and we made joint appointments with them. Several large research grants—to Patrick Suppes, to Wilbur Schramm, and to Hilgard and me—permitted more expansion by shared appointments. By 1961 we had approximately tripled the size of the department, reduced the number of graduate students by one third, and obtained presidential agreement that planning for a new building should get under way. Some of the new faculty had come in at tenured levels (A. Bavelas, W. Estes, L. Festinger, A. Hastorf, E. Maccoby) and some as assistant professors (R. Atkinson, A. Bandura, G. Bower, L. Horowitz). We lost some good people, too, but on balance the status battle was won, and we had the kind of quality the faculty wanted.

When Pat and I arrived in 1953, the Harvard research was very much on our minds. Pat completed a preliminary analysis of the doll-play role-choice data during the summer and reported it at the APA meetings in September. Eleanor Maccoby, Harry Levin, and I had agreed to write a book describing the extensive normative data on child rearing. John Whiting was engaged in planning the new Six Cultures project. But Pat had a demanding task for her first two years at Stanford—supervision of the elementary teacher training program—and when that was finished, she had already begun a heavy research program of her own in education and no longer could work on the doll-play data. (They still have not been analyzed fully.) Analysis of the normative data took longer than we expected; collaboration across 3,000 miles was hard. We finally published *Patterns of Child Rearing* in 1957 (Sears et al., 1957).

I started no new research during these four years, but the department badly needed funds for student support through research assistantships, so obviously it was time to get back to work. Hilgard associated me with one five-year grant and Wilbur Schramm with another. We took over two old houses near the quad for our laboratories. Schramm and the Sears had one, naming it Owen House after its former long-time occupant; Whiting called it Palfrey House West, with some reason, for my resumption of research was collaborative with Palfrey House East.

It had been six years since the *Patterns* data were collected. In 1958 the children would be in the sixth grade, the last year they would be easily available in groups. By correspondence, Maccoby and I planned a follow-up: my part would concern aggression, self-concept, and gender role; hers would concern dependency and adult role. In the spring of 1958 she collected data on 160 of the children and forwarded my data to me at Stanford.

Meantime, Schramm and I badly needed staff for our research on communication of child-rearing information. Both the Maccobys had sabbaticals for 1958–1959, and they agreed to come help us start. This was a sly trick on our part, because of course we did not let them go back again. Nathan stayed at Stanford as Schramm's associate in the new Institute of Communication Research, and Eleanor as a developmentalist in psychology. Schramm soon moved to new quarters, and for a dozen years Owen House was the child-development center for the campus.

In addition to constructing the follow-up instruments during 1957, I worked with Lucy Rau and Richard Alpert, planning what we hoped would be a more decisive test of the identification theory. This research was performed in the Stanford nursery school during the summer of 1958. It involved an intensive study of forty families. Parallel interviews were conducted with the fathers and mothers, and, for the children, there were doll play, teacher ratings, a large number of standardized assessment situations for measuring adult role, gender role, resistance to temptation, and guilt, and most importantly, many hours of time-sample behavior observations in the free play of the nursery school. By 1961 the basic data analysis was complete, but a book was yet to be written.

Back to the therapy situation. In spite of my long interest

in psychoanalysis and my familiarity with its theoretical part, I had had no personal experience with the method. I had experienced analytically oriented therapy, however, and it reactivated my desire for full analytic experience. The San Francisco Psychoanalytic Institute accepted me as a research candidate, and much of the time between 1955 and 1961, I drove to San Francisco four times a week, first for my personal analysis and then for seminars. The last year I did some supervised psychotherapy in the Stanford psychiatric clinic. By the fall of 1961, I was ready to start doing an analysis myself under appropriate control.

This should have been the high point of my training, but in truth I was reluctant. It would mean two or three more years of rigidly scheduled work, and I wanted a change of pace in quite the opposite direction. Pat and I decided to take our overdue sabbatical in the autumn of 1961, going to Europe for ten weeks just to freshen our eyes and for me to unwind from what had become a too-intensive lifestyle. What I have said about Stanford so far has had that year as a termination date. With good reason. The week before we left for Europe, the president asked me to become dean of the School of Humanities and Sciences on my return. This would mean an end to teaching and research for a while and to psychoanalytic training forever. The prospect was more relief than anything else. Except for a seminar on Mark Twain, I had lost the taste for teaching; the identification research had left me with more questions than answers, and I wanted a little distancing. My personal analysis had given me an unbelievably useful education—both as a person and as a psychologist—but the *ipse dixit* seminars had contributed little. A control analysis might add to what I had already gained in sensitivity to unconscious motivation and to the complexities of causality in human behavior, but I judged the possible cost–benefit ratio as too marginal. So I accepted the president's invitation, and Hastorf succeeded to the department chairmanship.

There was a very positive side to this career change, too. Stanford had undergone a radical development during the 1950s. The psychology department's growth was paralleled in many other areas, and I saw the opportunity to extend my entrepreneurial activity into a much wider arena. The time was ripe for this. President Sterling and his provost, Lewis Terman's son Frederick, the six professional school deans, and I were all out of the same mold. So was the largely reconstituted board of trustees. We were determined to have high status and to have it on honest terms. *Growth in quality* was the name of the game for Stanford. Between 1955 and 1970 it became a truly great university. It had abundant help. The Center for Advanced Study brought fifty Fellows a year to the neighborhood. This made the Easterners enticeable, since they discovered there were no grizzly bears about. For our high-caliber professors, the new 707 jet airplane made easy a continuing contact with the power centers of the world. The Ford Foundation gave a vote of confidence with a $25 million matching grant for a capital campaign. But most important was the spirit inside, a cooperative spirit that did not breed potentates but did breed a conviction that the only thing that mattered was excellence.

My nine years as dean are of little importance to the history of psychology. The new building was approved and built, and I helped design the Bing Nursery School; each year I taught a senior colloquium on Mark Twain (a case-history approach), and on weekends wrote the book describing our 1958 research project, *Identification and Child Rearing* (Sears et al., 1965). Psychology was important to my deaning, however. Anna Freud visited us once shortly after I became dean. I apologized for having stopped my analytic work short of the goal. She looked very thoughtful and said, "If I understand what an American dean's duties are, I do not think you will find your analytic experience wasted!" How right she was! Involuntary psychotherapy, by whatever name it is called, is half the job of a dean.

By 1970, I had come a long way from the time, nearly thirty years before at Iowa, when I had been the youngest member of the staff. I was three years from retirement. I'm not sure when I first realized I was no longer, in Thorndike's wry phrase, "a promising young man." But I knew it now with a vengeance. It was clearly time to get back to being a psychologist. Some choices had to be made. Psychology had boomed in the 1960s. Socialization, personality, and child rearing had been replaced by cognition in the developmental wing of the science. I had to update myself and select a research enterprise that would give me scope in the quieter years ahead. Pat had accepted a fellowship at the Center for Advanced Study for 1968–1969, so I resigned as dean, Hastorf succeeded me—again—and I too went to the Center. I did lots of reading, wrote up some old data for publication, and most importantly for my future self-regard, learned computer programming. I was ready to go back to undergraduate teaching for the remaining three years.

Developmental psychology's shift from socialization to cognition was partly a response to the exceeding complexities of the relation of child rearing to personality, as I have described in my history of child development and child psychology (Sears, 1975). Single variables predicted a very small amount of variance. This seemed much less true for the individual than for the group, however, and I thought that causal sequences within an individual were discoverable, even though they were difficult to discern in grouped data. I decided to try my hand at a life-cycle analysis of one case.

Mark Twain had been with me always. His life and his personality enchanted me, and what I could see of them through his writings had been leading me for years to treat his writing as the kind of fantasy a psychologist uses for diagnosis. He had several advantages as a subject. He had written an enormous amount of fiction, and even what was unpublished had been preserved. Further, the dates of composition for much of the material were known; hence any analysis of it could be matched to other events in his life. He had been a voluminous letter writer, and vast numbers of his letters were available for analysis. My task would be to interpret the fiction and letters and his recorded behavior in the light of his child rearing and the concurrent events of his adult life in order to present a psychological biography of the man. There are technical problems for such a program, but so far at least two of the most difficult have been surmounted. One was the breaking of continuous narrative into psychologically equivalent units for content analysis (Sears and Lapidus, 1973). A second was the design of appropriate content categories for measuring major psychological dimensions such as love, separation anxiety, aggression, etc. (Sears et al., 1978). As usual, I have chosen a research field not much plowed by others. Eventually, I may close, at least to my own satisfaction, the circle that circumscribes a diameter polarized by literature and psychology.

A larger and more conventional enterprise must also concern me. Terman's death in 1956 left me as scientific executor of his gifted-children study. Lee Cronbach joined me in that responsibility when he came to Stanford. In 1972 it was time for another follow-up, which he and I prepared. Like me, Pat was retiring in 1973, and she agreed to analyze the women subjects' data and to present a paper at the Terman Centennial Symposium at Johns Hopkins (P. Sears and Barbee, 1977). I analyzed the men's reports, and presented them in a paper responding to an APA Distinguished Scientific Contribution Award the following year (Sears, 1976b). This fifty-year-old longitudinal research program will continue to serve us well. I myself am a member of the research group, and the most interesting problems are now gerontological; I am approximately the median age of the group, and once again I will be in a position to rely on my own feelings and experience for research ideas.

Returning to psychology from the limbo of administration is like returning from Siberia. All the neighbors know you are home and want to put you to work. In 1970, I accepted the editorship of *SRCD Monographs* because I knew it would help me get back into the intellectual swing of psychology. I reviewed more than 300 manuscripts in the following five years and got a thorough, if sometimes painful, education. In 1973, I was elected president of the Society for Research in Child Development and was thrown once more into the national brouhaha of science policy. Then, in the same year, I agreed to serve as acting director of our new Boys Town Center for Youth Development until a permanent director could be appointed. To everyone's vast delight and amusement, Hastorf was selected as my administrative successor for a third time. On my birthday in 1975, I finally retired from administration for good.

I spoke in the beginning of the demographic ordering of my life, of the inevitability of my becoming a professor. Perhaps I made it appear that the centuries of family history had been focused on me alone. But their influence is continuous; no one generation gets special attention. Pat and I both had professorial fathers, and we both became professors. Now my son David is a professor and my daughter Nancy is a teacher married to a professor, who is himself the son of a distinguished pair of research child psychologists. I note with interest that one of our twelve-year-old granddaughters has memorized the names and functions of all the 246 bones in the human body. Demographic forces are very patient and persistent indeed.

1977

Selected Publications by Robert R. Sears

An experimental study of hypnotic anesthesia. *J. exp. Psychol.*, 1932, *15*, 1–22.

Experimental studies of projection: I. Attribution of traits. *J. soc. Psychol.*, 1936a, *7*, 151–163.

Functional abnormalities of memory with special reference to amnesia. *Psychol. Bull.*, 1936b, *33*, 229–274.

(with P. S. Sears) Minor studies of aggression: V. Strength of frustration reaction as a function of strength of drive. *J. Psychol.*, 1940, *9*, 297–300.

Success and failure: A study of motility. In Q. McNemar and M. M. James (Eds.), *Studies in personality.* New York: McGraw-Hill, 1942, 235–258.

Survey of objective studies of psychoanalytic concepts, Bulletin No. 51. New York: Social Science Research Council, 1943.

(with M. H. Pintler and P. S. Sears) Effect of father separation on preschool children's doll play aggression. *Child Devel.*, 1946, *17*, 219–243.

(with J. W. M. Whiting, V. Nowlis, and P. S. Sears) Some child-rearing antecedents of aggression and dependency in young children. *Genet. Psychol. Monogr.*, 1953, *47*, 135–234.

Identification as a form of behavioral development. In D. B. Harris (Ed.) *The concept of development.* Minneapolis, Minn.: University of Minnesota Press, 1957a, 149–161.

(with E. E. Maccoby and H. Levin) *Patterns of child rearing.* Evanston, Ill.: Row-Peterson, 1957b (Reprinted by Stanford University Press, 1976).

(with L. Rau and R. Alpert) *Identification and child rearing.* Stanford, Calif.: Stanford University Press, 1965.

(with D. Lapidus) Episodic analysis of novels. *J. Psychol.*, 1973, *85*, 267–276.

Your ancients revisited: A history of child development. Chicago: University of Chicago Press, 1975.

Bibliography. *Amer. Psychol.*, 1976a, *31*, 62–65.

Sources of life satisfactions of the Terman gifted men. *Amer. Psychol.*, 1976b, *32*, 119–128.

(with D. Lapidus and C. Cozzens) Content analysis of Mark Twain's novels and letters as a biographical method. *Poetics,* 1978, *7*, 155–175.

Other Publications Cited

Dollard, J., L. W. Doob, N. E. Miller, O. H. Mowrer, and R. R. Sears. *Frustration and aggression.* New Haven: Yale University Press, 1939.

Hamilton, G. V. *Objective psychopathology.* St. Louis: Mosby, 1925.

Healy, W., A. F. Bronner, and A. Bowers. *The structure and meaning of psychoanalysis.* New York: Knopf, 1930.

Miller, N. E., and J. Dollard. *Social learning and imitation.* New Haven: Yale University Press, 1941.

Newhall, S. M., and R. R. Sears. Conditioning finger retraction to visual stimuli near the absolute threshold. *Comp. Psychol. Monogr.,* 1933, *9,* (3, Serial No. 43), 1–25.

Sears, P. S. Doll play aggression in normal young children: Influence of sex, age, sibling status, father's absence. *Psychol. Monogr.* 1951, *65,* (6, Serial No. 323), 1–42.

Sears, P. S., and A. H. Barbee. Career and life satisfactions among Terman's gifted women. In J. Stanley et al. (Eds.), *The gifted and the creative: A fifty year perspective.* Baltimore, Md.: Johns Hopkins University Press, 1977.

Herbert A. Simon

Herbert A. Simon

A layman who had never been exposed to Sigmund Freud might write his autobiography believing that he could reveal honestly and accurately the springs and sources of his behavior. A professional psychologist can have no such belief. The case is even more desperate if the autobiographer's special research interest is human decisionmaking and the theory of scientific discovery, for he will be tempted to see his life as an instantiation of his theories. In the face of these difficulties, this account perhaps should be titled: "The Theory of My Life."

This is an account of my professional life. My wife, children, and friends will not find themselves mentioned often. If I ever write the other half of the story, they will learn what important roles they played, even during periods when research and administration were capturing a hundred hours of my week.

The course of my life up to the present (my sixty-first year) takes the form of a triptych, the three panels being of nearly equal size. The first panel ends on June 15, 1937, my twenty-first birthday; the third begins on December 15, 1955, the day on which Al Newell and I discovered how to program a computer to simulate human thinking. In my account here, I will give a good deal more attention to the first two panels than to the third. I do not mean to imply by this that the last twenty years of my life have been dull. It is rather that the shape of these last twenty was largely determined by the events of the first forty, and these events give a fairly full explanation of the whole.

The First Panel

The first panel is divided into scenes from Wisconsin and scenes from Chicago. Milwaukee was my home through my seventeenth year, and the University of Chicago campus for the next six—that is, beyond the first panel into the second.

WISCONSIN

Answers to a few passport questions will introduce the boy and his family:

Born June 15, 1916; Milwaukee, Wisconsin, in a modest frame house owned by his parents in a middle-class neighborhood of the West (i.e., German) Side.

Father Arthur Simon, born May 21, 1881, in Ebersheim, Germany (a half-day's wagon trip south from Mainz), of Joseph Simon and Rosalie Herf; the seventh generation of a line of vintners and wine merchants; Jews, but by some dispensation, landowners (or landholders) a century before Napoleon overran the Rheinland. Arthur graduated in electrical engineering from the Technische Hochschule of Darmstadt and emigrated to Milwaukee in 1903. Employed as an engineer by Cutler–Hammer Manufacturing Company, and later also engaged in private practice as a patent attorney. Active in professional and civic affairs; awarded honorary doctorate in 1934 by Marquette University.

Mother   Edna Merkel, born January 20, 1888, in St. Louis, Missouri, a third-generation descendant of German '48er immigrants from Prague (Goldsmith, Jewish), and Cologne (Merkel, Lutheran). Her grandfather Alexander Goldsmith was a Civil War veteran, wounded at Chickamagua, afterwards a whiskey salesman. Her grandfather Merkel was a piano builder, and his son Charles, after the family business failed, a piano tuner. Edna attended Milwaukee public schools and the Academy of Music. Piano teacher until marriage in 1910, then housewife. Active in local musical clubs.

Other Close Relatives   Brother Clarence, five years older, who graduated in law from the University of Wisconsin and practiced law in that state. Grandma Ida Merkel and Grandpa Charles, who lived at first two blocks away and then in the boy's home—grandfather until his death about 1927, grandmother through a long life to the end of World War II. Great-grandmother Anna Goldsmith, died 1920, who played checkers, dominoes, and Old Mill with the small boy for hours on end. Uncle Harold Merkel, Edna's younger brother, who died in his early thirties, in 1921. Graduated with distinction from the University of Wisconsin in law. A student of the economist John R. Commons, and a La Follette Progressive; subsequently with the National Industrial Conference Board. The copies of *The Federalist Papers* and William James' *Psychology** on the bookshelves at home had been Uncle Harold's.

At school, the boy soon learned that he was smarter than his comrades, and that became important to him. Although conscientious in his studies, he never had to work hard at them or neglect friends or sports for schoolwork. I have two sets of recollections of him that are hard to assemble into a single, consistent piece.

There was the introverted boy, who had no difficulty in amusing himself with books or toys or collections of stamps or (later) beetles. I see him sitting in the living room on a fall Saturday afternoon—all his friends are at the movies—with a chess board and a chess book in front of him, feeling rather

---

*It was *Psychology: The Briefer Course,* nicknamed "Jimmy."

437

lonely. He spent many hours in that way. With a five-year age gap between him and his brother, he was nearly an only child.

Although the boy was affectionate, he did not share his thoughts much with the adults. He preferred to ask questions of them and listen to them. Suppertime was a time for conversation. His father enjoyed serious table talk, and the rules permitted vociferous argument. Politics was often the topic, or scientific subjects.

I can see the boy also with his father at the basement workbench, "helping" but mostly watching while his father constructed a radio, the first in the neighborhood, or a model sailing sloop. Perhaps the father was impatient, or perhaps the boy was lazy, for he never acquired any great skills in such crafts, although he liked to watch.

I see him curled up on the leather couch in his father's den, at perhaps the age of ten, proving to himself that he could understand *The Comedy of Errors*. The eleventh edition of the *Britannica* was there for him, too.

He kept his education entirely in his own hands, seldom asking for advice. The encyclopedia had an index, and the public library, a card catalog. In books left by his uncle or his brother, he studied economics, psychology, ancient history, some analytic geometry and calculus, and physics. Summers were spent mainly in Milwaukee, except for a two-week family vacation, often in the North Woods. Since many of his friends were away during the summer, he was even more solitary than usual then. One summer, when he was about fifteen, he set himself the task of reading Dante's *Inferno* (with the haunting Doré illustrations), Milton's *Paradise Lost,* and a textbook on ethics; and he translated into wretched English doggerel Schiller's *Das Lied von Der Glocke.* Many other solitary summer hours were spent collecting and identifying insects.

In these activities there are few examples of what could properly be called "creativity." One summer he wrote some adolescent essays on "infinity" and "the existence of God," but there was only one very brief period of poetry writing, no attempt to compose music, no stab at the great American novel. He did not draw or paint.

The boy did not often take clocks apart, much less put

them together again. By the time he finished high school, his chess game was moderately strong, but bookish. He was a student, who prided himself on being able to master anything, independently, and who was often able to make good his (private) boast.

If he had a claim to creativity, it lay in the realm of politics. In about the fourth grade, he drew up a school constitution (students' rights!) and presented it, with the greatest trepidation, to stern Miss Walsh, the principal. Rather to his surprise, he was praised rather than punished for his attempt at insurrection. After that, he was a great reviser of club constitutions and bylaws.

The boy knew that his father made inventions and held many patents. He did not once ask, "Papa, how do you make inventions?" Perhaps he thought it would be "cheating" to ask, that it would be no fun to invent if you had been told how. Being told how was different from reading in books; in the books, you had to dig it out for yourself.

He did often dream of discovery—or perhaps it was only the glory he dreamed of, and not the discovering. Such dreams captured much of his thought as he walked the half-mile to and from grammar school and the later mile to high school. For a long time, Napoleon was his greatest hero. And he resented Columbus for foreclosing the discovery of the New World. His first ambition, to go to West Point, died only when he learned that color-blind candidates couldn't be appointed there.

That gives some picture of the introspective, bookish, and sometimes lonely boy who was proud of his independence in learning. But it says nothing of the sociable boy who appeared at other times—fond of games and sports with his friends, a great joiner and organizational politician. During grammar school years, the time after school was for sandlot baseball and football during good weather, and for indoor games or sometimes skating during the cold and dark of the Wisconsin winter. He was not much of an athlete. Because he had been "skipped" at school, most of his friends were several years his senior, and besides, he was more left-handed than right-handed and, as he often said by way of apology, "ambiundextrous." When the teams were chosen up for baseball, he was among the last to be called by one of the captains, usually to inhabit right field. He often felt embarrassed to be chosen last, but that did not keep him away from the field. His sociability did not usually extend to fistfights. Since he was both small and rather timorous, he seized upon a saying attributed to the Revolutionary War guerilla, Marion: "He who fights and runs away will live to fight another day."

During high school, the sociable boy expended his energy in two directions. He was an active and enthusiastic Boy Scout, with a special love for camping and all manner of outdoor activities, summer and winter. The student clubs at his high school provided his second social arena. He was active in a debating society, a science club, the Christian Endeavor (while insisting on his agnosticism), the Latin club, and the student council, serving as president of most of them at one time or another. He took no part in team sports. He was attracted to girls, but too shy to get on a dance floor with them and, usually, to date them. Besides, he was two years younger than most of his classmates, so that the girls tended to treat him as a younger brother.

How was he viewed, this sociable boy, by his friends and classmates? First, he was a "brain," but evidently modest enough about it so as not to offend. Besides, it counted for him that he was not a "grind." But he had a very sharp tongue, and an appetite for verbal swordsmanship. It was unpredictable whether you would get a compliment or a jab from him. He grew a reasonably thick skin, to take the blows, verbal and physical, that were offered in return, but he became unsure inside about others' feelings toward him and shy about opening himself to them. For a time, he took as his hero Coriolanus, the Roman too proud to court the "mob."

In many respects, his youth was an asset. He could be forgiven many things in his younger brother role that he could not have been forgiven otherwise. Throughout life, he retained a special affinity for working with men a little older than himself—Sidney Kalmbach, Milton Chernin, Don Smithburg, Victor Thompson, Lee Bach. The second-in-command role (he preferred to think of it as the "power-behind-the-throne role," or the "idea-man role") was usually comfortable. In adult life, as he began to work with younger associates, the younger brother became an older brother.

I have said that the boy was a good listener. He was often sought out as a confidant, even by adults and even when he was quite young. When family feuds occurred—and his grandmother had some talents in this direction—he often heard both sides of the story from the principals. Before he was twelve, he had learned that quite reasonable and truthful people could perceive the same set of events in remarkably different ways. Sometimes he found himself the mediator, interpreting for each protagonist the viewpoint of the other. Whatever view was presented to him, he could see merits in the opposing view, and often took it up.

In high school debates, the boy enjoyed taking the unpopular, underdog position—free trade, unilateral disarmament, the Single Tax—usually with conviction. His opponents could seldom match his logic or his careful preparation of evidence. From that he learned another important practical truth: You do not change people's opinions by defeating them with logic. People do not feel obliged to agree when they cannot reply on the moment. The boy later used that insight many times in his own defense. He never felt obliged to assent to doctrines—whether Platonist, Thomist, or Marxist—just because the arguments advanced for them seemed, at the moment, unanswerable. He learned to mistrust human real-time logic.

The debates contributed to his education in another way. They led him to read widely and quite deeply in economics and the other social sciences—Henry George (*Progress and Poverty*), Richard T. Ely (*Outline of Economics*), Norman Angell (*The Great Illusion.*). He didn't understand all of it, but he learned to read critically, using one book to argue with another.

Even when the social activist held ascendancy over the loner, the boy saw himself as different from his friends. I have mentioned his left-handedness and his brightness, both of which set him a little apart. But there were two other things. When he was only five or six, while the family was on holiday in early summer, he went with some friends to hunt strawberries. While the others filled their buckets in minutes, he peered closely at the plants to find the berries among the matching leaves. That is how he learned that he was red–green color-blind.

Finally, the boy was conscious of being a Jew—not a religious Jew, for he had not been inside a synagogue and he attended Congregational Sunday school through his grammar and high school years—but a Jew nonetheless. Sometimes he wished he weren't, although he hardly admitted that to himself, but mostly he felt proud of it and was always careful that it should be known to others around him. He didn't want to "pass." If there was any disadvantage or penalty in being a Jew, he would accept that penalty rather than deny his Jewishness.

Coming from a minority culture, he could not be ethnocentric. Since his red and green were not the red and green of other people, he knew that the real world out there is not identical with the world perceived. Hence both ethical and epistemological relativism came easily to him.

His feeling of being different did not translate itself into rebellion against authority. Although corporal punishment had not been abolished in either his home or his school, he did not experience it often in the former or at all in the latter, and his memories of it are not vivid. It could usually be avoided by staying out of serious mischief. Being a good student gave you a large credit balance that could be traded against minor misdemeanors. It also gave you freedom to use your time as you pleased, even in school.

On a few occasions he felt his principles challenged. During the years he attended the Congregational church, communion services were held monthly. The minister would ask, "Will all members of this church please rise?" Two thirds of those present would get to their feet. Then the minister would ask, "Will all Christians please rise?" Only the boy remained seated. It was very difficult, but he would have felt ashamed if he had falsified his beliefs publicly.

His high school graduating class voted that the boys should wear white flannels at the graduation ceremony. He decided (it was at the very bottom of the Depression) that this was unfair to the boys from poorer families. He persuaded many students to sign an agreement to wear their regular suits. On graduation night, he and two classmates appeared in their dark suits; all the others, somehow, had found means to buy the white flannels. He felt a little betrayed, but proud that he had not yielded.

He had a number of camping and backpacking adventures in Wisconsin with his friend Sid Kalmbach and others, and during several of his high school and college summers, he was involved in an unusual farming venture on a large, wild tract of Wisconsin marshland. These were deeply felt experiences, important to his growing up, but since they had no direct bearing on his later professional pursuits, I shall omit them here.

He graduated from high school in 1933 at age seventeen. It had been, on the whole, a happy boyhood and adolescence. He had had to make almost no decisions, except to take what the world offered him, and the world had been generous. His picture of the future was vague. The answer to "What do you want to be?" had gone from "soldier" through "forest ranger" and "lawyer" to "scientist." His private answer was "intellectual." He calculated that if someone would endow him with $50,000, he could live quite comfortably for the rest of his life doing what he did best—learning. Perhaps the most unusual feature of his boyhood, as it influenced his future career, was his exposure, thanks to the books and the example left behind by his long-dead uncle, to the idea that human behavior could be studied scientifically. He saw, if dimly, the challenge of bringing to social science or biology the mathematical thinking that had been so powerful in physics.

The choice of a college was also not much of a decision. Chicago's New Plan for general education appealed to the generalized intellectual in him; his high school had a fine record of success in the Chicago competitive scholarship exams; he took the exams—in physics, math, and English—and won a scholarship. The world spared him a choice by providing him with a fine opportunity.

Although I have tried to describe the boy in terms of concrete events in his life, generalizations and interpretations have crept into the account. I have an excuse for this. The boy himself was incorrigibly introspective. The generalizations and interpretations I have set down are almost all the boy's own generalizations, quite self-conscious and explicit, and arrived at during the time when these things were happening to him.

When I arrived at the University of Chicago campus in September of 1933, the university was beginning the third year of the Chicago Plan—most requirements for the bachelor's degree could be satisfied by taking comprehensive examinations; all students were required to pass exams covering the major fields of knowledge: humanities, social sciences, physical sciences, and biological sciences; and class attendance was not required. This was exactly to my taste.

I attended very few classes. Since my excellent high school training had nearly prepared me for the examinations of the first two years. I was soon auditing upper division and graduate courses. Ralph Gerard taught, Socratically, a stimulating freshman biology course. Although I was still deeply interested in biology, my color blindness and awkwardness in the laboratory made me decide against following up that interest professionally.

On the other hand, Henry Simons, on price theory, teetering on two legs of his chair, gave me a glimpse of the applications of rigor and mathematics to economics. I resolved to major in economics, until I learned that this would require me to take an accounting course; then I switched to political science, which had no such requirement. (A strange beginning for someone who was later to be a founding father of a business school, and later yet a Nobel Laureate in economics.)

Early in my second year, I terminated my formal education in mathematics when a calculus professor insisted I attend class. From then on, almost all of my mathematics was self-taught, some of it while I was at the university, but continuing fairly intensively until the early 1950s. Self-instruction gave me the courage and skills to master new areas of mathematics whenever I needed them for my research.

During those three years as an undergraduate, I lived as an intellectual. From 6:00 in the morning, when I rose, until 10:00 at night, when I went to bed, seven days a week, I was immersed in books and talk of books. That included mealtimes and most of my socializing hours. The survey courses provided a conversational common denominator, so that there was always shoptalk at the refectory table.

On most Saturday evenings, a half dozen of us got together to drink cheap muscatel wine and read plays or argue philosophy. We were a varied crew. Milton Wolford, coming from a wealthy family in southern Illinois, was pushed and pulled by existential concerns to philosophy. He died, while yet an undergraduate, ostensibly of heart failure but really of *Weltschmerz*. Leo Shields, a lively, attractive Catholic boy from Salt Lake City, was brought to Chicago by the Thomism of Hutchins and Adler. Commissioned an infantry lieutenant in World War II, he died on D-Day, on a beach in Normandy. The rest of us have been more fortunate. Manley Thompson, who divided his loyalties between Aristotle and Peirce, went on to a distinguished career in the University of Chicago philosophy department. Ellis Kohs, who began in sociology because "you couldn't earn a living in music," soon switched his major and became a composer of note and a professor of music. Winston Ashley arrived from Oklahoma, carrying a draft of his novel. The university brought him to Aristotle, St. Thomas Aquinas, and the Catholic church, thence to a priesthood in the Dominican order and a life of service, teaching, and administration in the church. Harold Guetzkow, a Milwaukeean whom I met on the train when we embarked for the university, studied psychology and education to prepare himself for secondary school teaching, but returned to graduate school and a university career in psychology and international relations. There were others, but these will give the flavor of the group.

The University of Chicago community offered a number of philosophical and political options that were religious in their intensity. There was Aristotelianism and Thomism, either in its secular or in its Catholic version. There was Marxism, either Stalinist or Trotskyist. There was even an Aristotelian–Catholic–Trotskyist movement. The latter was the sect to which I was most strongly exposed, for Winston Ashley, Leo Shields, and others of my good friends were adherents.

Alas, I had not the qualities of a true believer. I arrived on the campus a socialist. Milwaukee had a strong German socialist tradition and a socialist mayor, Dan Hoan. "Socialism" meant to me good city government and comfortable living for all. Soon after my arrival in Chicago, a friend took me to a Communist meeting. We found some middle-aged men in a shabby room above a store—denouncing Stalin! It was incomprehensible; I had not until that moment heard of Trotsky.

While I was intrigued by the arguments of my Trotskyist, Stalinist, Thomist, and Aristotelian friends, my distrust of logical inference kept me from belief. So I went out not far from where I came in but I learned enormously about these important social movements and their philosophical bases.

As I finished the College requirements, and began to move into my major studies, these quasi-religious issues gave way to more technical ones. I found several faculty members from whom I could learn much about how to apply mathematics to empirical matters. The mathematical biophysicist Nicholas Rashevsky had a marvelous talent for building simple assumptions into models of biological systems. Henry Schultz provided me with a deep and thorough view of the uses of mathematics in economics and of modern statistical theory. From L. L. Thurstone, I learned factor analysis. And I attended several of Rudolf Carnap's courses on logic and philosophy of science. These men communicated to me in their lectures something of how science—at least science involving the applications of mathematics—was done.

My career was determined for me in a very casual way. Other people in my environment presented me with opportunities. When the opportunities were attractive, I took them. Two or three such choices (hardly decisions, for I did not search for alternatives) set me on a definite path. For a term paper in a course on municipal government, I wrote a description of the city government of my native Milwaukee. My professor, Jerome Kerwin, was then studying the relation between city governments and school boards. Liking my paper and recalling that the administration of recreation in Milwaukee involved cooperation between city government and school district, he suggested that I write a paper on that arrangement.

The paper on recreational administration was also well received. Kerwin wondered, however, why I had limited myself to describing the organization and had not evaluated it. Because I had not the least idea how to do that, I enrolled in Clarence Ridley's course on Measuring Municipal Governments. Since my economics training suggested that the evaluation problem could be formulated as one of utility maximization subject to a budget constraint, I wrote a paper in that vein That led to an invitation to serve as research assistant to Ridley on a larger project he was undertaking.

By that unproblematic route, I found myself, in September of 1936, in possession of a bachelor's degree and supporting myself as a graduate assistant at a salary of $62.50 per month, which freed me from further financial dependence on my parents. About midyear, I received a check for $83.33. Alarmed that this might be a clerical mistake, and that months later I might be asked to repay money I had already spent, I carried the check to the department secretary. She assured me that I had been promoted from half-time to two-thirds-time assistant and that the money was rightfully mine.

My new job virtually ended my formal work as a graduate student. I continued to attend a few classes, but my heart was in the research—the results of which later emerged as the monograph *Measuring Municipal Activities,* coauthored with Ridley. By February 1937, I had my first publication, for we initially put our work out serially in *Public Management.*

Turning out a paper each month on the measurement problems of a different city department kept me busy, especially since I had had virtually no first-hand acquaintance with government when I started, beyond the two term papers I had written. That did not daunt Ridley, who shipped me out to Wichita, Kansas, just as the wheat was sprouting in the spring of 1937, to ride in police squad cars and study police records systems in the department there run by Chief O. W. Wilson.

That brings me to June 15, 1937, my twenty-first birthday, and the day on which the first panel of the triptych ends and the second begins. The political science department secretary (and graduate student) who had reassured me about my raise, was a lovely, red-haired* girl named Dorothea Pye. A friend

---

*"How did you know it was red?" a perceptive reader may ask. Well, I had early been told there were no green-haired people, nor any red lawns. Ergo . . . .

arranged a double date with her and another girl on the evening of June 14. My salary permitted dinner and a play—the Federal Writers' Project production of *Abe Lincoln in Illinois.* We began to date regularly, and on Christmas day of the same year we were married.

But there was even more to the birthday than that. On the morning after our date, I caught a plane at Chicago's Midway airport, a DC-3 that took me on a three-stop flight to New York and gave me a beautiful aerial view, my first, of Niagara Falls. Ridley had arranged that I should represent the project at professional meetings in New York and Washington, D.C. The trip was full of exciting, inconsequential adventures. An indigent actor in Manhattan conned me out of $5 to pay his overdue hotel bill. I stayed up all night on Broadway and played chess, at 25 cents for each game I lost, with an unemployed chessmaster. In Washington, I was taken to lunch at the Cosmos Club, then at its original location on Lafayette Square. *Tobacco Road* was playing at the old Belasco Theater off Pennsylvania Avenue, but I had to miss the last act to catch the B&O train back to Chicago. It was a heady experience for a young man just turned twenty-one.

The Second Panel

The scenes of the second panel of the triptych have a more varied geography than those of the first. Dorothea and I remained in Chicago until the autumn of 1939, then spent three years in Berkeley. In 1942, we returned (with newborn Katherine) to Chicago for another seven years, then left, in 1949, for Pittsburgh (accompanied this time by all our three children, Kathy, Pete, and Barbara). All of these moves, and the pauses between them, had a certain inevitability about them. One, at most involved a genuine decision. During the period covered by the second panel, I searched no more and planned no more than I had done earlier.

CLARENCE RIDLEY

My research assistantship soon transformed itself into a full-time job. When our research monograph on municipal mea-

surement was finished, I began to devote my time to tasks for
Clarence Ridley's organization, the International City Managers' Association, becoming a staff member in 1938. My
duties were partly editorial (serving as assistant editor to the
monthly journal, *Public Management,* and the annual *Municipal
Year Book*), partly statistical (I gradually assumed responsibility
for the statistical sections of the yearbook), and partly auctorial
(writing numerous chapters for the training manuals for city
executives that the association was then preparing). It occurred to me to try to mechanize the statistical job, so I mastered the technology of IBM punched card, tabulator, and
plugboard equipment, and enjoyed my first, prehistoric, experience with computers.

Clarence Ridley was and is a remarkable man. Educated as
a civil engineer, he had served as city engineer and city manager in several communities before returning to graduate
school at Syracuse for his Ph.D., and then coming to Chicago
as director of ICMA. He saw this organization as pivotally located for raising the effectiveness of local government administration, and he exhibited masterly leadership and administrative skill in exploiting the opportunity. For Ridley, the
grass was always greenest on his own side of the fence. He was
never tempted to leave his position at ICMA for others that
were more glamorous. Watching him, I came to understand
that an organization can be a human instrument, and need not
be a human yoke.

My job in ICMA was a marvelous school in administration,
where I could learn both by doing and by observing Ridley. At
age twenty-two, I was writing a major part of a volume, *The
Technique of Municipal Administration,* which was supposed to
inform experienced city managers about how to run a city
administration. Since I had had no administrative experience
and had hardly even observed organizations, except for my
brief excursions to Milwaukee and Wichita and my position in
ICMA itself, it was not immediately obvious to me how I was
supposed to know what to write. Of course, my task was not to
invent a new theory, but to assemble a textbook out of the
existing knowledge and literature.

It was while I was engaged in this work that I first encountered Chester Barnard's newly published *The Functions of the
Executive,* which seemed to me wholly superior to the other

administrative literature of that day and fully compatible with my preference for looking at management in decisionmaking terms. Aided by the theoretical insights gained from Barnard, I soon realized that a little administrative experience goes a long way. Life in organizations did not appear so very different from life elsewhere. Most of the writing on administration, including Barnard's, was based on everyday observation and not on esoteric experimental or observational techniques. Organizations, it appeared, could be understood by applying to them what you knew of human behavior generally.

Still, this state of affairs in administrative theory did not seem very acceptable to me. Systematic observation and experimentation were badly needed if this field was ever to become even moderately scientific. But until there existed a satisfactory theoretical framework, it would not be clear what kinds of empirical investigations were called for. Here were planted the first seeds of *Administrative Behavior.* I decided that I would write a theoretical doctoral thesis on decisionmaking in administration. The process of writing it would raise many empirical questions that could be explored subsequently in my research. This decision set the central strategy for my research in organizations over the next twenty years.

BERKELEY

Again, opportunities presented themselves that required no real choice. If I had any long-run plans while I worked at ICMA, they were to continue with my job, moonlight as a graduate student, and ultimately earn my doctorate. The atmosphere of the Depression put the possession of a job rather in the center of one's thinking.

Ridley and I had become nationally visible authorities on measuring public services, a topic of considerable interest because of the difficult financial plight of the cities—then as now! Samuel May, director of the Bureau of Public Administration at the University of California in Berkeley, looked for Rockefeller Foundation support to continue some statistical studies of local government that had been begun in the bureau with support from federal work relief (WPA) funds. With foundation support, I was asked to come to Berkeley for the summer of 1938 to plan such a study and write a proposal for the foundation. Milton Chernin and I toiled through the summer to produce a document outlining a three-year study that would cost the foundation the munificent sum of $30,000 in all and would support three researchers, a statistical assistant, and a secretary for that period. When the grant was made in 1939, I was invited to come to Berkeley to direct the study. The decision to accept the invitation took no more than ten minutes to make.

My three years at Berkeley as Director of Administrative Measurement Studies proved as exciting and illuminating as the previous three years had been. I learned to manage an organization of considerable size (not only my own staff of five, but about fifty WPA workers who were attached to our project and, during the period of a study we conducted in the State Relief Administration, a considerable group of people in that organization as well). Somehow, I was able—most of the time—to overcome my shyness. I even learned how to fire an unsatisfactory employee. Chernin, a member of the bureau staff and fully twenty-nine years of age, with his Ph.D. behind him, was the older brother who made it all possible and who served as front man when the demands for extroversion were too much for me. The bureau was our social as well as our professional home—an exuberant young group of political scientists who both worked together and partied together.

In the course of the three years, we completed three major studies and produced from them three monographs (Simon et al., 1941; Simon et al., 1943; Simon, 1943). The field experiment we carried out in the State Relief Administration was something I would never have dared had I been experienced enough to understand what it entailed. It was, I think, the largest experiment that had ever been carried out in an organization up to that time—comparable in scope to the Hawthorne studies and more systematically designed. Bill Divine and I have told much of the story of it elsewhere (Simon and Divine, 1941).

While we were at Berkeley, I completed my Chicago doctorate. By prearrangement, I took a three-month leave of absence in 1940 to prepare for my preliminary examinations, which I was permitted to write *in absentia* in Berkeley. With those out of the way, I devoted evenings and those weekends that I could spare to drafting the thesis that became *Administrative Behavior*. The thesis was approved, and I took my final oral examination in Chicago in the spring of 1942.

During the years in Chicago and Berkeley, we were not unmindful of the *Götterdämmerung* that was being prepared and enacted in Europe. The Spanish Civil War, the rape of Austria and Czechoslavakia, the Hitler–Stalin pact, the invasion of Poland, the phony war, the fall of France, the bombing of Britain—all of these evoke vivid memories of anger and frustration. In the terrible summer of 1940, I often sat on the Berkeley hillside overlooking the bay and the Golden Gate, my study interrupted by gloomy thoughts of the destruction of Europe, and perhaps the free world. Dot and I had been active in liberal politics in Chicago—fellow travelers, I guess, whose suspicions of the religion of Communism were confirmed by the Hitler–Stalin pact. Hitler had touched my life directly, too. My father's sister and niece and the niece's husband escaped from Germany; Uncle Julius died during the flight on foot over the Pyrenees.

In the summer of 1941, we joined the Arnons, Dan and Lucille, in a pack trip on the Muir Trail in the high Sierra. Returning to civilization after two weeks, we wondered whether our country was at war or at peace. It was at peace, but the war came, of course, soon after. Since I had been an ardent interventionist, I felt I should enlist promptly. My attempts to enter officer training programs were uniformly thwarted by my color blindness, and I came to realize that if I joined the armed forces, I would be assigned to a desk job for the duration. On those terms, I preferred to stay out until called. My "greetings," postponed because of my family responsibilities, finally arrived the week before Hiroshima, but were canceled again when Japan surrendered and the rules about dependents were changed.

CHICAGO AGAIN

When it became increasingly probable, in the spring of 1942, that I was not immediately going to become a soldier, and when my degree was in hand, I began to think about how I was to support myself and my family when the project ended. Again, I had no real decision to make. Victor Jones, whom I had known first as a graduate student at Chicago, then as a colleague at Berkeley, and who was now returning to Berkeley from the Illinois Institute of Technology in Chicago, arranged for me to take over his position there. I was pleased at the prospect, for it seemed to me that an engineering school was more likely to provide a congenial environment for a mathematical political scientist than most other universities. I was right and have subsequently spent my entire teaching career in institutes of technology—at least until Carnegie Tech decided to change its name and become a university.

Teaching loads at Illinois Tech during World War II ranged from fifteen to eighteen hours a week, summers included. The long teaching hours left little opportunity or energy for empirical research. To supplement a modest academic salary, I took up part-time work with ICMA, editing, writing, and participating in the training activities. A good deal of time went, also, into becoming a skillful academic politician—even to playing bridge nearly every noon to widen my acquaintanceship among the faculty. As a result, I was elected to a postwar planning committee, whose activity greatly increased my understanding of university administration and finance.

But most important, I continued my mathematics and science education by studying textbooks and working the exercises. Occasionally, I sat in on the course of a colleague—Eli Sternberg in theoretical mechanics, and Karl Menger on topology. The three of us engendered some activities in the philosophy of science on the campus, and my association with them stimulated my first writing in that subject, specifically my paper on the axioms of Newtonian mechanics (Simon, 1947).

During the time I was at Illinois Tech, my family and I lived close to the campus of the University of Chicago and had many friends there. Toward the end of the war, I began to participate in the seminars of the Cowles Commission for Research in Economics, a group that then included Jacob Marschak, Tjalling Koopmans, Oskar Lange, Kenneth Arrow, Leo Hurwicz, and a number of others. One of the discussion topics was Samuelson's famous essay on comparative statics and dynamics, which proposed a promising new systematic approach to the prediction of shifts in the equilibria of dynamic systems. Another topic was the estimation of supply and demand elasticities—the root of what came to be known as the "identification problem." I wrote a theoretical piece on the economics of urban migration, suggested by an American history course I was then teaching, and was co-opted by Marshak into the Cowles Commission study of *Economic Aspects of Atomic Power.* (I wrote Chapters 13 and 14, on the macroeconomic aspects of atomic power.)

The association with the Cowles Commission did not diminish my preoccupation with human decisionmaking, but turned part of my activity on that topic into new directions and brought me into the thick of the dramatic intellectual developments that took place in the social sciences just after World War II. The excitement of the time can be conveyed—or re-evoked for those of us who lived through it—by listing the labels for the constellations of ideas that were born then: operations research and management science, the theory of games, information theory, feedback theory, servomechanisms, control theory (these and others collected under the banner of cybernetics), statistical decision theory, and the stored-program digital computer.

The ideas were all closely intertwined, with decisionmaking at their core, and they quickly generated a scientific culture—an interlocking network of scientists with a real sense of community, which was almost independent of the special area in which each worked, and which ignored the diversity of their backgrounds and training. They came from physics, statistics, economics, biology, mathematics, engineering, philosophy, and even a few from psychology and political science*.

My dual participation in the engineering culture of Illinois Tech and in the econometric culture of the Cowles Commission gave me early access to this world. I learned of the theory of games before the von Neumann–Morgenstern book was published, spent most of the 1944 Christmas vacation—days

---

*For another account of the *Zeitgeist* of this period and of this culture, see Newell and Simon, 1972, pp. 878–882.

and some nights—reading it when it appeared, and wrote what I think was the very first review that it received. When the wartime security wraps were removed from computers, my earlier experiences at ICMA and in California with IBM plugboards made it easy to see their immense potential. Statistical decision theory had already formed part of my graduate training, and I had published a paper in the field during the Berkeley period. The operations research techniques formed a natural continuity with my administrative measurement research. Through Gerhard von Bonin, who lived in our apartment building, I met Warren McCulloch, and through the Cowles Commission, John von Neumann.

Shortly before my father died, in 1948, I made a discovery that moved me deeply. It had never occurred to either my brother or me to follow his profession of engineering. The reasons are obscure. Had we been immunized against this inheritance by his own abandonment of the Rheinland vineyard? I don't know. What gradually dawned on me in those postwar years was that I was returning to the paternal calling. As a designer of control gear, my father had been a major contributor to the development of feedback devices. In one of the last letters he wrote to me before his death, he sent me some references I had requested on servomechanisms. Twenty years later, I took great pleasure in printing in *The Sciences of the Artificial* a drawing of a servomechanism he had patented in 1919, just three years after my birth.

During those Chicago years, I revised my thesis, circulated it for comment, revised it again, found an editor willing to risk it (Cecil Scott at Macmillan), and published it in 1947. It was built around two interrelated ideas that have formed the core of my whole intellectual activity: that human beings are able to achieve only a very bounded rationality; and that, as one consequence of their cognitive limitations, they are prone to identifying with subgoals. I would not object to having my whole scientific output described as largely a gloss—a rather elaborate gloss, to be sure—on the pages of *Administrative Behavior* where these ideas are first set forth.*

---

*See especially pp. 39–41, 204–212, and 240–244.

After five years without administrative chores, in 1947 I accepted the chairmanship of the Department of Political and Social Science at Illinois Tech, the beginning of about twenty-five years of departmental and deanly administrative duties. Don Smithburg and Victor Thompson joined me there, and together we laid the plans for our textbook, *Public Administration*, which appeared in 1950. While we did not have time to get off the ground a program of empirical research in organizations, I was privileged, in 1948, to witness and participate in the birth of the Economic Cooperation Administration, the agency created to administer the Marshall Plan. My experiences there as consultant and temporary director of the Management Engineering Branch of the agency are recounted in Chapter 16 of the third edition of *Administrative Behavior*.

A MATTER OF SECURITY

One of my experiences is not recounted there, however. By 1948, Communists and supposed Communists were being discovered under every rug—beginning with Remington and followed soon after by Hiss. A graduate of the University of Chicago was guaranteed a full field investigation before he could obtain a security clearance. The ECA Security Office found me a highly questionable character, who had not only attended that dubious university, but had actually subscribed to the Midwest edition of the *Daily Worker*. When questioned about it, I replied haughtily that a political scientist read a good many things. Only my temporary employment status and the courage of Howard Bruce, deputy administrator of the agency, kept me from being blacklisted at that point. I spent many angry and bitter hours pacing the streets of Washington during those weeks. In the apartment I shared with the Thompsons, we lowered our voices and wondered which of the walls were bugged (probably none). Although *I* knew that I was not and had not been a Communist, I saw clearly how difficult it would be to prove that to anyone else who wished to doubt it. And I saw how corrosive it was to freedom in a society for the burden of proof on that question to be shifted to the suspect.

For the next fifteen years—the last occasion was in 1963 —the question of my "security" erupted periodically in connection with my consulting for the RAND Corporation, but never quite as sharply as in 1948.

The Carnegie Institute of Technology received in 1949 a gift of $5 million of endowment and funds for a building to house a new Graduate School of Industrial Administration that would provide business education for students with degrees in science and engineering. Bill Cooper, a friend since undergraduate days (it was he who arranged my first date with Dorothea Pye, and he also who first introduced me to the Cowles Commission seminars), had joined the Carnegie Tech economics faculty a year or two earlier. At his suggestion, I was asked to come to Carnegie to discuss the new school with Elliott Dunlap Smith, the provost, and Lee Bach, chairman of the economics department. An invitation to join the faculty as Professor of Administration followed. I was not eager to leave Illinois Tech, but I was finally persuaded that the resources of GSIA would permit me to launch the program of empirical research in organization that seemed to me the logical sequence to *Administrative Behavior.*

Life during the early 1950s was literally a three-ring circus. Lee Bach, who quickly became dean of the new school, Bill Cooper, and I played lead roles in developing its faculty and curriculum. Within the school, we developed two major areas of extensive research activity: organizational behavior and management science (or econometrics). I assumed leadership in the former, in collaboration with Harold Guetzkow, who joined us a year or two later. Cooper took the principal initiative in the quantitative area, but I also participated heavily in it, heading up one of the research teams. So during this period I was at once organization theorist, management scientist, and business school administrator.

Almost none of the founding fathers of GSIA had extensive backgrounds in management or business education. We were social scientists who had discovered, in one way or another, that organizational and business environments provided a fertile source of basic research ideas and who therefore did not regard "basic" and "applied" as antithetical terms. Accurately or not, we perceived business education as a wasteland of vocationalism that needed to be transformed into science-based professionalism, as medicine and engineering had been transformed a generation or two earlier. We were most fortunate that we took on this task at the particular moment in history that we did. The postwar flowering of management science and of the behavioral approach to organization theory provided the substance of the applied science we needed. The quantitative undergraduate training of our students made it possible to put that science into the curriculum.

GSIA quickly gained national visibility as the New Model for a business school. European universities, moving cautiously into business education for the first time, generally found the scientism of GSIA a more comfortable model for themselves than the unfamiliar case method of the Harvard Business School. Two national studies of business education (whose directors came from liberal arts backgrounds and were extremely skeptical of business education in general) picked GSIA as the example they thought other business schools might well imitate. The Ford Foundation, selecting the improvement of business education as a major objective, used its golden carrots to start other business schools on the road that GSIA had pioneered.

Keeping the balance of the scientific and the professional, of the economic and the behavioral was an arduous job. Only the complete dedication and superb leadership of Lee Bach held the venture on course. I have written elsewhere that "organizing a professional school . . . is very much like mixing oil with water: . . . And the task is not finished when the goal has been achieved. Left to themselves, the oil and water will separate again. So also will the disciplines and the professions."* By hard work, we managed to keep GSIA pretty well emulsified.

---

*Simon, 1976, p. 356. Chapter 17, from which this quotation is drawn, sums up the administrative lessons I learned from my GSIA experience.

In my management science and econometric research, I retained my consulting ties and close contacts with the Cowles Commission and, through it, with the RAND Corporation. RAND (an acronym for Research and National Development), located in Santa Monica, California, was the original Think Tank, then enjoying tremendous success and visibility as a new way of enlisting research talent to help advance applied goals. Beginning in 1952, I made frequent trips to Santa Monica and spent a number of my summers and one full year (1960–1961) there during the following decade.

My mathematical and econometric work at this time had a number of themes, both substantive and methodological. A good overview of it can be found in *Models of Man* (1957), a collection of some of the papers that I wrote in my first five years at Carnegie. Part I contains papers on causality, deriving from my work on the identification problem; Part II undertakes to show the utility of making mathematical translations of sociological theories of social interaction (Homans, Festinger); Part III proposes several models that explicate the relation between organization theory, as found in my writings and in Barnard's book, and the economic theory of the firm; Part IV formalizes and explores the concept of bounded rationality.

Chapter 14, "A Behavioral Model of Rational Choice," mostly written in 1952, during my first RAND summer, represents my first major step toward developing and formalizing the psychological theory of bounded rationality. It represents, also, the first step toward the computer simulation of human behavior, a topic that occupies most of the third panel of the triptych. The manuscript of the paper contained an appendix, never published except as a technical report, outlining how a chess-playing program for a computer could overcome its bounded rationality by using selective search guided by heuristics (see footnote 4 of the published paper).

THE LOGIC THEORIST

To explain how my love affair with computers came about, I must return to the other, organization theory, part of my life.

Harold Guetzkow and I had initiated a substantial program of research on organizations within GSIA. Our first major venture (with George Kozmetsky, Harold Guetzkow, and Gordon Tyndall) was a study of how accounting organization and cost studies influenced management decisions. That whetted our appetites for detailed studies of executive decisionmaking, and we began to seek out business organizations and executives who would permit themselves to be put under this microscope. As it became clear to us that organizational decisionmaking was inseparable from human problem solving, the minutes of our research meetings from 1950 to 1952 begin to contain more and more references to the theory of problem solving. Harold Guetzkow's psychological training, and the fact that his doctoral dissertation was on the subject of problem solving, probably played no small part in this gradual transformation.

At this very same time (but in the Santa Monica part of the forest), four people—John Kennedy, William Beale, Robert Chapman, and Allen Newell—conceived the grand (or grandiose) design of studying in the laboratory the behavior of an air-defense organization. The laboratory (christened "SRL"— the Systems Research Laboratory) would simulate an entire air-defense unit, staffed with perhaps fifty men. The U.S. Air Force was to supply the budget and the subjects for this simulation.

When, in the planning stages of this imaginative project, the group came to me for advice—because of my previous experience in conducting organizational experiments—I became a consultant and, on my first visit to RAND early in 1952, met Allen Newell. In our first five minutes of conversation, we discovered our ideological affinity. We launched at once into an animated discussion, recognizing that, though our vocabularies were different, we both viewed man's mind as a symbol-manipulating or information-processing system. I think the phrase "symbol manipulating" was mine, and "information processing" was Al's.

The SRL experiments provided the most microscopic data one could want on how radar operators and air controllers made their decisions. Yet Al and I suffered from continuing frustration in trying to write formal descriptions of the process. Somehow, we lacked the language and the technology that were needed to describe thinking man as information processor.

I had continued my interest in computers, reading everything I could find on them and making optimistic speeches to managers (as early as 1950) on their prospective application to business. At SRL, I became fascinated by the method that Al had devised for using a Card Programmed Calculator to produce the simulated radar maps needed for the air-defense simulation. What was remarkable about this application was that the computer was being used not to generate numbers, but locations—points—on a two-dimensional map. Computers, then, were not merely number crunchers; they were general symbol manipulators, capable of processing symbols of any kind—numerical or not! This insight, which dawned only gradually, led Al and me even more gradually to the idea that the computer could provide the formalism we were seeking— that we could use the computer to simulate all sorts of information processes and use computer languages as formal descriptions of those processes.

In the summer of 1954, I taught myself to program the 701, IBM's first stored-program computer, and computers were much on my mind. Driving together to March Air Force Base, near San Bernadino, to observe some air exercises, Al and I began to discuss the possibility of simulating human thinking. We made no specific plans at that moment, but before the year ended, Al took up the task of programming a computer to learn to play chess. A third member was soon added to the team—Cliff Shaw, a highly talented programmer at RAND who had been concerned with the programming systems on JOHNNIAC.

Al had come to RAND about 1950, before taking his Ph.D. He wanted, sooner or later, to acquire this union card, but he didn't want to interrupt the exciting research in which he was engaged. Without great difficulty, I convinced my colleagues at GSIA that it was entirely appropriate for a business school to award a doctorate for a thesis in what we would now call "artificial intelligence." (We were ultimately to award about a dozen such degrees before computer science became a sepa-

rate discipline at Carnegie.) Al and his family were soon instal-
led in Pittsburgh, and the work got under way.

On the basis of their previous programming experience,
Cliff and Al knew that it would be difficult to write programs
for complex processes directly in the language of the computer. What was needed was a higher-level language, more
congenial to the human programmer, which would handle automatically much of the "housekeeping" in the computer and
which would be translated automatically by the computer itself
into machine language. Although all three of us participated
in its design, Al and Cliff took primary responsibility for constructing such an "information-processing" or "list-processing
language." This task was a major preoccupation during 1955
and into the spring of 1956.

Meanwhile, Al and I were considering what task should be
selected for a first effort. Since chess seemed a bit complicated,
we decided that it would be well to gain experience by first
tackling something simpler. We spent some time introspecting
about our own mental processes while solving problems in different domains. By the summer of 1955, discovering proofs
for theorems, either in geometry or in symbolic logic, appeared to be a likely candidate. (The accident that I had the
volumes of *Principia Mathematica* on my bookshelves led us to
the latter task.)

By October, we were beginning to have a feel for the
problem-solving heuristics used in tackling these problems,
and we settled definitely on symbolic logic. Al was then working on the programming language and taking his preliminary
examinations. He and I discussed almost daily our progress
toward specifying the theorem-proving program. My method
of working was to take theorems in the *Principia* and work out
proofs while trying to dissect as minutely as possible, not only
the proof steps, but the cues that led me to each one. Then we
tried to incorporate what I had learned in a flow diagram. We
repeated this day after day, with the flow diagram steadily approaching a description that could be programmed on the
machine. On December 15, 1955, I simulated by hand a proof
of Theorem 2.15 of *Principia* in such detail that we agreed the
scheme was programmable. I have always celebrated that date

as the birthday of heuristic problem solving by computer, although it was not until the following August (1956) that the LOGIC THEORIST, programmed on JOHNNIAC, produced its first complete proof of a theorem.*

The Third Panel

The mountain pass over which Al and Cliff and I crossed with the realization of the Logic Theorist opened up vast views. We saw before us the whole domain of artificial intelligence (though we marked it with a different name on our maps) and the domain of human cognition. On the third triptych are mainly painted the records of our explorations of those domains. The explorations have been exciting enough, but it would be wearisome to enumerate them all. I will simply mention a few of the most important and then turn to the part of my life that was not occupied by my research.

EXPLORING THE PLAIN

The Logic Theorist was soon followed by the General Problem Solver, developed by Al, Cliff, and myself, and later elaborated by Al and by George Ernst. GPS explicated means–ends analysis as a basic psychological process. Another early program was EPAM (Elementary Perceiver and Memorizer), developed collaboratively by Edward Feigenbaum and myself, which provided a theory and simulation of human rote verbal learning. Later, EPAM was combined with some mechanisms for simulating eye movements to produce MAPP (with Gilmartin and Chase), which gave us a theory of the mind's eye of the chess player and of some of the sources of expertness in chess.

Kenneth Kotovsky and I tackled pattern-discovery processes with a simulation of subjects' behavior on the Thurstone Letter Series Completion Test, and Lee Gregg and I showed

---

*The first published report of our success was "The Logic Theory Machine," 1956.

how concept attainment tasks could be analyzed in information-processing terms. Ross Quillian's thesis, describing long-term memory as a semantic net, set off across the country a whole volley of work on memory schemes of that sort.

There were many other explorations over the terrain of psychology, but these will give the flavor of them. In 1972 Al and I put together the whole body of work we had done on problem solving in our book *Human Problem Solving*. Some of my essays and the work of several students on problems of language and semantics were published that same year in the volume *Representation and Meaning*, edited with Siklóssy.

During the first decade after 1955, the work tended to focus on problem solving in rather abstract and puzzlelike domains. We learned more than most people want to know about Missionaries and Cannibals, cryptarithmetic problems, chess, and the Tower of Hanoi. When we felt we had gained a fairly good understanding of human thinking in these well-structured domains, the research began to move in new directions and somewhat centrifugally. An understanding of natural language, and its interactions with other ways of representing meanings, became more and more important to our endeavors. We became interested in the problem-understanding processes that have to precede the problem-solving processes. At present, we are becoming more courageous in tackling problem domains that are ill structured—architectural design would be an extreme example. And we are exploring semantically rich domains—i.e., problem areas where the solver must draw on a substantial body of semantic knowledge and specialized methods.

The "we" in these paragraphs was, at first, Cliff Shaw, Al Newell, and myself. Soon, we were joined by a number of graduate students in GSIA—Edward Feigenbaum, Julian Feldman, Robert Lindsay, Fred Tonge, and Geoffrey Clarkson were in the first generation of them. Then the infection began to spread to the psychology department at Carnegie Tech, largely through the growing interest of Lee Gregg and through Bert Green's membership in the department for about five years after 1960. We acquired an IBM 650 some time before 1960 and, at about the same time, acquired Alan Perlis, who, with Al and myself, was to take the lead in building up what ultimately became a computer science department.

How do you describe the process of gradually settling and cultivating an immense plain that stretches off in all directions? If I undertook such a description, it probably would be far more orderly, and imply far more foresight and planning, than the actual process. During these twenty years, there has never been a lack of problems on the research agenda, and it really didn't seem to matter very much which one was tackled next. (See Simon, 1979, for many examples.)

MISSIONARY EFFORTS

I wish that I could say that the discipline of psychology was eager to embrace the new information-processing paradigm. I am afraid, however, that would be an exaggeration. There was too big a leap from Hullian S-R psychology (not to mention Skinnerian behaviorism) to computer simulation. The use of thinking-aloud protocols as data was sometimes misunderstood as an attempt to revive introspection as a data source. Even the work of Hebb, which had prepared psychology for a more cognitive approach to its concerns, helped only a little, for Hebb gave physiological interpretations to the processes he postulated inside the head and left little room for a separate information-processing level of explanation.

Since I had only marginal status as a psychologist (through my work on social and organizational psychology), and since Al had none at all, it was of the greatest importance that two prominent psychologists, George A. Miller and Carl Hovland, were early attracted to an information-processing viewpoint—arrived at it, in fact, from information theory and wartime human-factors research, just as Broadbent had in England. We joined forces with the former two in organizing a workshop for the summer of 1958 at RAND, where some twenty first-rate experimental psychologists were exposed to simulation, list-processing languages, GPS, and EPAM. Some of them were infected in the process; others were immunized.

Also of great importance in legitimating the new paradigm was the book *Plans and the Structure of Behavior,* which George Miller wrote with Eugene Galanter and Karl Pribram shortly after Miller's exposure at the RAND workshop to the Logic Theorist, GPS, and EPAM.

So psychology generally assumed an attitude of cautious interest toward the information-processing approach, rather than rejecting it out of hand. The cause was aided by the parallel development of research on short-term memory and chronometric studies of perception, which also gradually adopted the information-processing label. (The names of Broadbent, Sternberg, Sperling, Shepard, and Posner will convey the flavor of this work.) The two interrelated varieties of information-processing research—the one concerned mainly with complex cognitive tasks, the other mainly with underlying basic processes—continued to gain adherents, until today the information-processing label has become, regrettably, positively faddish. In addition to our publications, the main proselytizing effort of our group was poured into a number of summer workshops, several at RAND in the early 1960s and several at Carnegie–Mellon University in the early 1970s, based generally on the model of the successful 1958 RAND Workshop.* Actual hands-on experience with computer simulation seems essential to enable psychologists to begin work within the new paradigm.

POLITICS ON THE CAMPUS

Throughout my professional career, I devoted a good deal of time to the politics of science, both inside my university and at the national level. I have mentioned my service on a postwar planning committee at Illinois Tech and my tenure as a department head there and at Carnegie Tech.

I think I can sum up my goals in campus politics and administration by two terms: excellence and innovation. Al-

---

*Some additional history of the period from 1955 to 1958 will be found in Newell and Simon, 1972, pp. 884–888.

though there is a strong correlation between the salaries that universities pay and the quality of their faculties, the correlation is far from perfect. The mere insistence on excellence— on the university's getting what it pays for, and more if possible—at the time of critical personnel decisions (hiring, reappointment, promotion, tenure) will make the difference between a mediocre faculty and a first-rate one. Being an instrument of that insistence is a difficult and not always pleasant task, for it means making decisions about the careers of other human beings. I have always felt it to be a heavy responsibility.

Nothing has given me deeper satisfactions in my university career than the opportunities it has provided to participate in major educational innovations, innovations that were tested on our campus, but that have had impact nationally or even internationally. The first of these was the founding of GSIA. The second was the opportunity, from 1955 to the present, to help introduce computers on the Carnegie Tech campus and to help build at Carnegie–Mellon University (as it had become by 1970) one of the world's earliest and leading computer science departments. The third was the building of a group, within the psychology department, that has played a leading national and international role in the development and diffusion of computer simulation and information-processing psychology. A fourth, still in an early stage of development, is participation in an effort to reconstruct design as a scientific activity and to reintroduce design as a major component in the engineering curriculum.

THE POLITICS OF SCIENCE

A number of opportunities have presented themselves, also, for engaging in politics in a larger context. The earliest of these came, in the 1950s, from invitations to membership on committees of the Social Science Research Council and the committee advising the Ford Foundation on the design of the Center for Advanced Study in the Behavioral Sciences. These committee experiences were invaluable to me in giving me a national acquaintance among social scientists, which came in handy both in campus recruiting activities and in calibrating my standards of academic excellence.

For most of the decade of the 1960s, I served on the Problems and Policies Committee of the Social Science Research Council, and for five years as chairman of its board of directors. Looking back, I do not see that I accomplished much in that role toward my major goals of encouraging "hard-science tendencies" within the social sciences—which meant encouraging the growth of skills and techniques of experimentation, in both laboratory and field, and the applications of mathematics and quantitative techniques.

The social and behavioral sciences had never had a real place in the councils of the natural sciences. Physiological psychology had found a small niche in the National Academy of Sciences, along with anthropology (a "soft" science that somehow retained a reputation of being scientific). The National Research Council was correspondingly narrow. A few members of these organizations began to work to change this unsatisfactory state of affairs. Among the leaders of the insurrection were the psychologists Neal Miller and Carl Pfaffman and the anthropologist George Peter Murdock. Because of my predilictions for mathematics, and then computers, they took me into the fold as a social scientist who could communicate with natural scientists.

Two directions of movement were possible: integration of the social with the natural sciences, or separate but equal status for the former. Many social scientists preferred the second alternative, talked of an independent national academy of the social sciences, and supported legislation proposed in the Senate for a separate research foundation for the social sciences. Others of us preferred integration, on three grounds. First, we believed that the social sciences were politically too vulnerable to stand alone. Second, we observed that the natural sciences were being asked to advise the federal government on many issues of public policy that had large social, psychological, and economic components. Without extensive social science participation in the Academy and the Research Council, those components would either be ignored or handled by amateurs. Third, the "hard" end of the social science spectrum would necessarily be stronger in organizations that included the natural sciences than in a separate social science organization.

Over the decade from the early 1960s to the early 1970s, the integration policy achieved complete success. First, the National Research Council broadened its Division of Behavioral Sciences to cover the whole spectrum of these fields. I served as the division's chairman for two years shortly after its reorganization. Next, the National Academy of Sciences was correspondingly broadened in a series of gradual moves. The constitutional law and politics of academy elections is too Byzantine in its complexity to be described here, but, in any event, I was elected to the academy by a slightly circuitous route in 1967. Finally, the last citadel of the natural sciences (this one mainly garrisoned by the Old Guard, the physicists) was breached when President Johnson appointed me, in 1968, to the President's Science Advisory Committee (PSAC). I have never been able to explain to myself why the revolution was successful or what brought it about at that time. That it had occurred, for whatever reason, was a source of great satisfaction to me.

My main job on PSAC was to chair a Panel on Environmental Quality, a topic to which PSAC had earlier made an important contribution through the so-called Tukey Report. My panel exercised perhaps its greatest influence during a brief period in 1969 when it was drafting the agendas for President Nixon's short-lived Cabinet Committee on the Environment. Gradually it, like other units in the Executive Office, was isolated from the White House by the palace guard and became less and less effective.

I was glad to chair the environmental panel, both because it gave me an opportunity to make a small contribution to a very important national problem and because it allowed me to operate as a "regular" PSAC member, rather than its token social scientist.

Subsequent to my PSAC term, I have had two other interesting Washington assignments under academy auspices. One was to chair a committee whose task was to coordinate the recommendations to the Senate of a bevy of subcommittees of engineers, doctors, atmospheric scientists, economists, and assorted experts who were to advise Senator Muskie's committee on auto emission controls. The other was to chair a committee that reviewed the programs of the National Science Foundation in the social and behavioral sciences.

In one model of the community of science, scientists, when they reach a certain age, are supposed to retire gradually and gracefully from their research and to become elder statesmen, available wherever wisdom is required. My career seems to have run somewhat backwards. I started out with major administrative responsibilities in my early twenties and have gradually been withdrawing from administration throughout my fifties. My greatest pleasures and satisfactions still derive from the world of ideas and not from the world of power—although it cannot be said that I have been indifferent to power during my career.

Early on I said that I have made few choices in life, that I mainly accepted opportunities that were offered to me. As far as the balance between administration and research is concerned, that is only a half-truth. At several points, I had to consider whether I wanted to go one route or the other. The research always triumphed.

A long time ago, an introverted boy, who wanted to be an intellectual and an extroverted boy, who had some hankerings for the world of affairs, started out together in the same skin from Milwaukee. Each has had fair opportunity to use his talents and enjoy his special pleasure, and each has had to make concessions to the other. On the few occasions where they would have chosen radically different paths, the introverted one usually prevailed. I expect that they will always work out that sort of bargain between them for as long as they can continue working.

1977

Selected Publications by Herbert A. Simon

(with C. E. Ridley) Measurement standards in city administration: Technique of appraising standards. *Pub. Mgmt,* 1937, *19,* 46–49.

(with C. E. Ridley) *Measuring municipal activities.* Chicago: International City Managers' Association, 1938.

(with W. R. Divine) Human factors in an administrative experiment. *Pub. Admin. Rev.* 1941, *1,* 485–492.

(with W. R. Divine, W. W. Cooper, and M. Chernin) *Determining work loads for professional staff in a public welfare agency.* Berkeley: Bureau of Public Administration, University of California, 1941.

Fiscal aspects of metropolitan consolidation. Berkeley: Bureau of Public Administration, University of California, 1943a.

Symmetric tests of the hypothesis that the mean of one normal population exceeds that of another. *Annals of Mathematical Statistics,* 1943b, *14,* 149–154.

(with R. W. Shephard, and F. W. Sharp) *Fire losses and fire risks.* Berkeley: Bureau of Public Administration, University of California, 1943.

Administrative behavior. New York: Macmillan, 1947. 3rd ed., 1976.

The axioms of Newtonian mechanics. *Philos. Magazine,* 1947, *38,* 888–905.

Technique of municipal administration (3rd ed.). Chicago: International City Managers' Association, 1947.

(with D. W. Smithburg and V. A. Thompson) *Public administration.* New York: Knopf, 1950.

A behavioral model of rational choice. *Quart. J. Econ.,* 1955, *69,* 99–118.

(with G. Kozmetsky, H. Guetzkow, and G. Tyndall) Organizing for controllership: Centralization and decentralization. *The Controller,* 1955, *33,* 11–13.

(with A. Newell) The logic theory machine. *IRE Transactions on Information Theory,* 1956, Vol. IT-2, No. 3.

Models of man. New York: Wiley, 1957.

(with A. Newell, and J. C. Shaw) Report on a general problem solving program. *Proc. Int. Conf. Information Processing,* June 15–20, 1959, Paris.

(with E. A. Feigenbaum) Comment: The distinctiveness of stimuli. *Psychol. Rev.,* 1961, *68,* 285–288.

(with K. Kotovsky) Human acquisition of concepts for sequential patterns. *Psychol. Rev.,* 1963, *70,* 534–546.

(with L. W. Gregg) Process models and stochastic theories of simple concept formation. *J. math. Psychol.,* 1967, *4,* 246–276.

The sciences of the artificial. Cambridge: MIT Press, 1969.

(with L. Siklossy, Eds.) *Representation and meaning: Experiments with information processing systems.* Englewood Cliffs, N.J.: Prentice-Hall, 1972.

(with A. Newell) *Human problem solving.* Englewood Cliffs, N.J.: Prentice-Hall, 1972.

Models of thought. New Haven: Yale University Press, 1979.

Other Publications Cited

Angell, N. *The great illusion.* Philadelphia: Quaker City Books, 1913.

Barnard, C. *The functions of the executive.* Cambridge: Harvard University Press, 1938.

Ely, R. T. *Outlines of economics* (5th rev. ed.). New York: Macmillan, 1930.

George, H. *Progress and poverty.* New York: Robert Schalkenbach Foundation, 1929.

Gordon, R. A., and J. E. Howell. *Higher education for business.* New York: Columbia University, 1959.

James, W. *Psychology: The briefer course.* New York: Holt, 1910.

Miller, G., E. Galanter, and K. Pribram. *Plans and the structure of behavior.* New York: Holt, Rinehart and Winston, 1960.

Pierson, F. C. *The education of American businessmen.* New York: McGraw-Hill, 1959.

Quillian, R. Semantic memory. In M. Minsky (Ed.), *Semantic information processing.* Cambridge: MIT Press, 1968.

Quillian, R. Semantic theory. Ph.D. dissertation, Carnegie Institute of Technology, 1966.

Schurr, S. H., and J. Marschak (Eds.). *Economic aspects of atomic power.* Princeton, N.J.: Princeton University Press, 1950.

Von Neumann, J., and O. Morgenstern. *The theory of games and economic behavior* (3rd ed.). New York: Wiley, 1964.

Whitehead, A. N., and B. Russell. *Principia mathematica* (2nd ed.). Cambridge: Cambridge University Press, 1925.